C000217648

Who Counts?

The Mathematics of Death and Life after Genocide

Diane M. Nelson

Duke University Press   Durham and London   2015

© 2015 Duke University Press
All rights reserved

Designed by Natalie F. Smith
Typeset in Quadraat Pro by
Westchester Publishing Services

Library of Congress Cataloging-in-Publication Data
Nelson, Diane M., [date] author.
Who counts? : the mathematics of death and life
after genocide / Diane Nelson.
pages cm
Includes bibliographical references and index.
ISBN 978-0-8223-5973-9 (hardcover : alk. paper)
ISBN 978-0-8223-6005-6 (pbk. : alk. paper)
ISBN 978-0-8223-7507-4 (e-book)
1. Guatemala—History—1985– 2. Guatemala—
Politics and government—1985–
3. Genocide—Guatemala—History—20th century.
4. Mathematics—Social aspects. I. Title.
F1466.7.N46 2015
972.8105'2—dc23   2015019168

Cover art: Isabel Ruiz (b.1945) performs *Matemática sustractiva*
(Subtractive math), Antigua, Guatemala, 2008. She tallied
45,000 white chalk marks, one for each of the estimated
disappeared, as someone followed behind erasing them, then
Ruiz began tallying again. The performance was dedicated
to Guatemalan writer Luis de Lión, who was disappeared by the
Guatemalan state in 1984. Photo by Francisco Morales Santos.
Used by kind permission of Isabel Ruiz.

For Anastasia, Santos, Maudilia, and Lochlann

And for Chelsea / Bradley, Edward, and Jake

In the beginning the white men
tried to finish with us using
guns, whips and diseases.
Now they use numbers.

—Kulussi Suyâ

Numbers weave patterns
which people inhabit and
which inhabit people.

—Helen Verran

People need numbers very, very
badly. And they don't give a shit
where they come from.

—Patrick Ball, in Rosenberg 2012, 5

If a steamship weighed ten thousand tons and sailed five thousand miles,
With a cargo large of overshoes and carving knives and files,
If the mates were almost six feet high and the bos'n near the same,
Would you subtract or multiply to find the captain's name?

CHORUS

oh oh oh oh oh oh oh oh oh oh oh oh oh oh oh
Put down six and carry two,
Gee! but this is hard to do;
You can think and think and think till your brains are numb,
I don't care what teacher says, I can't do the sum

CHORUS

If Clarence took fair Gwendolyn out for an auto ride,
And if at sixty miles an hour a kiss to capture tried,
And quite forgot the steering gear on her honeyed lips to sup,
How soon could twenty men with brooms sweep Clare and Gwennie up?
From *Babes in Toyland* (Herbert and MacDonough 1903)

Contents

Preface

Geoff Ryman, in his desperate and beautiful science fiction novel *The Unconquered Country*, describes Third, a peasant girl in a place like Cambodia.

> Numbers were portents too. They were used as oracles. This was a practical thing. Rice shoots were counted; yields were predicted, seed was stored. Numbers spread out in fanlike shapes, into the future. Third could read them. She saw yarrow in her mind, ghost yarrow she sometimes called them, and they would scurry ahead of the real stalks. They moved too fast for her to follow, flashing, weaving. They leapt to correct answers. If anyone asked Third how much rice was in a bowl, she . . . could have answered, "Six hundred to seven hundred grains." The yarrow stalks in her mind would click, telling her how much space ten grains took—as represented by so many lengths cut into a stalk—and how much space there was in a bowl. The ghost yarrow opened and closed, like a series of waving fans, beautiful, orderly, true. . . . She could not follow the waving fans, but she could feel her mind driving them. It was a pleasurable sensation, this slight sense of forcing something ahead. She could make them go faster if she wanted to. It was how she saw the world; it was as if the world were a forest of yarrow, moving all around her, as if numbers were leaves, rustling in the wind.

When a teacher from the rebel movement comes to the village to help the children prepare for the new world they are building, she forces Third to count each yarrow stalk as singular.

"Sit there," the teacher said, and pushed Third back. "Now. One. Two. Three." She laid the stalks down but far apart, in parallel lines that Third knew could never meet. Third. Three stalks together made three parts of a whole. These did not. Third understood, and she did not want to. As if tearing through flesh, the teacher was rending the numbers apart. She was making them alone. Third turned and tried to run. . . . Something terrible had happened to the numbers. They wouldn't work. Third tried to drive the yarrow in her mind, but as soon as they touched on any one of the new numbers, they were snagged by something. They stopped, and had to start again, grew confused or were left naked, hanging, and Third realized she had never really understood how they danced their way to answers. They were going away, like friends. (1987, 5–12)

THIS IS A BOOK ABOUT NUMBERS
It will tell you interesting facts about many simple, ordinary things like counting, money, bones, equivalence, vitamins, pyramids, mines, conjuring, and light. ###

-1 Chapter Minus One

Politics, logic and mathematics are inseparable.
—Helen Verran

In the ornate, brightly lit women's bathroom of the luxury Camino Real hotel in Guatemala City, Santos, a Maya-K'iche' woman, was surrounded. The mostly nonindigenous women crowded around were practically fawning, laughing, asking advice, touching her arm, sharing stories. "Tell us about your trip. What was it like? Is the boat as wonderful as they say?" "How do you do it? How did you win two cars?" It was hard for her to even use the facilities. A woman asked if I were part of Santos's *Red*, or network, then sighed, "¡Dichosa! You are so lucky! She is a wonderful sponsor! So generous!"

Santos had left Joyabaj, El Quiché, at 3 AM in a rented minibus with eleven members of her *Red* to get to the Camino Real in time for the first day of the Omnilife Basic Course. "Usually the managers at an elegant place like this wouldn't accept people like us," she said as we walked in, gesturing to her *traje*, distinctive clothing identifying her as indigenous. "But Omnilife treats everyone the same." The basic course meets one weekend a month for five months and aims at self-improvement through exploring gender and other "*creencias*" (beliefs) via Oprah Winfrey–like discussions and audience participation. Omnilife is a Mexico-based direct-sales vitamin business, and Santos was popular in the restroom because of her personal charisma and generous nature and also because she had mastered the enterprise's multiple scales of counting and associated conversion techniques so skillfully that she had won two cars and several overseas trips, including a Mediterranean cruise. They helped make a poor rural woman "like her" feel "accepted"—like she counted—at a "place like this."

Returning to the glittering ballroom where over 1,000 women were gathered (with a similar number of men next door), we went to work under the gentle but insistent guidance of the course's psychologist-leader. Most women were concerned with home life, unfaithful husbands, wayward children, difficulties making ends meet. But one day, during the fifth month, a member of Santos's *Red* went on stage. Sebastiana is also Maya-K'iche', from Joyabaj's neighboring town of Zacualpa, and, like Santos, involved in Mayan revitalization projects. Addressing the weekend's theme of "lack and abundance," she recounted how the army had tortured and murdered her father in the early 1980s. They burned her house, sending her, a little girl, fleeing with her mother and the younger children into the mountains, where they starved for months. The course leader took it in stride, but everyone around me was crying by the time she finished (see chapter 4).

Guatemalans used to guesstimate the toll of thirty-six years of military state counterinsurgency and revolutionary mobilization by saying every extended family had lost at least one person—so everyone is minus one. Some families, like that of young Eva Morales, whom I met on my first trip to Guatemala in 1985, lost at least fourteen (America's Watch 1985). And in some areas of the indigenous highlands, entire families, indeed entire villages, were almost completely wiped out. In 1999 the United Nations Commission for Historical Clarification (CEH), using interview-based tallies, archival sources, and statistical projections, officially put the number of war dead at 200,000 and found the state responsible for 93% of the human rights violations. In her 2008 performance *Matemática sustractiva*, Isabel Ruiz tallied 45,000 white chalk marks on a red wall, one for each of the estimated disappeared, as someone followed behind, erasing them. Striving to re-present, to make present again, both the aggregate and the particular of each minus one. During the war years, and now in their after-math, people negotiate multiple scales of counting, including death tolls, vitamin profits, statistical estimates, increasingly faint memories of missing family and friends, and what sort of gain might balance out such enormous loss. What sort of account-ability?

Now, thirty years after the violence that surfaced so incongruously yet so matter-of-factly, in that ballroom, 200,000 is a "fact," reiterated in almost every discussion of Guatemala. That aggregate quantity has also been assigned a quality, as genocide against the Maya people. First by the UN, based in four cases, including Zacualpa (but not neighboring Joyabaj); and then by a Guatemalan court in May 2013, when it found General Ríos Montt, de facto head of state from 1982 to 1983, guilty of genocide against the Maya-Ixil.[1] Yet people like Sebastiana and Eva (who received political asylum in the United States) are still working through their singular relations to that plurality of minus ones, of minus 45,000, of minus 200,000.

This book focuses on number and counting in hopes of illuminating the persistence of those minuses as they interlace with additions, conversion techniques, and even geometric gains where a Mayan woman feels adequate to enter the Camino Real (and a cruise ship!). And with ongoing attempts to erase them, to dis-count, as Ruiz displayed. Santos, Sebastiana, and others you'll meet, live simultaneously in worlds of loss and more hopeful calculations, if not abundance.

To explore such worlds we need to start from zero. Not only the ground zero of genocide, but zero as a source of enormous pride for postgenocide Mayan revitalization because their ancestors "discovered" it long before the Europeans. (Only two peoples have autochthonously developed the concept, the Maya and the Babylonians.) This matters because we all live in a world where number is the "modern fact," closely linked to raced and gendered power inequalities, themselves connected to the assemblage that stabilized the "modern zero" of double-entry bookkeeping (which may not be the "same" zero as the Mayas'). The glittery bathroom and the death toll are both effects of an ethnomathematics—mathematics practiced by an identifiable cultural group, in this case early modern Europeans. In fact, the very mathematics that informed the "everyday practices of colonial administration in the Americas, [that] rode in on the back of a new political arithmetic that gave coherence and authority to the Spanish colonial adventure." A mathematics that, Gary Urton argues, affected non-Western cultures at the "ontological level" (Urton 1997, 196–97). But those signs, values, and their manipulation now also count human rights violations, calculate their ethnic proportions and adequate reparations, reveal disproportionate suffering, and provide tools to resistance movements confronting racist exclusion and ecological destruction.

"Mathematics is the only true universal language" is a line from a movie (*Contact*, 1997), but it expresses common sense understanding about numbers and their cosmic truthfulness. The word *mathematics*, however, is both singular and plural. While the authority of colonial adventure relied on a particular formation of numeracy and tried to insist everyone else rely on it, too, number, counting, and math remain more pluri- than uni-versal. That "common sense" was a centuries-long (and quite bloody) achievement. Yet nonetheless, many people live simultaneously, if allochronically, in worlds with several maths. We may need to get as comfortable with binumeracy as we should be with bilingualism. But this would also be an achievement, the effect of struggles to be equi-valued.

And even "Western" number isn't just about truth, sober accounting, and rational cost benefit analyses. It doesn't just "ride in" to settle things after the frenzied violence of those Maya apocalypses of the Spanish invasion or the 1980s mass murder, any more than the manic "irrational exuberance" of derivatives calculations are divisible from the wild functioning of capital itself. Numbers, of various kinds, are part and parcel of those selfsame world-making projects. Horrible, necessary, fun, crazy, and multiple, melding the banal everyday with the most existential leaps of faith and most terrifying falls. Numbers connect "ontological levels" with the mundane embodied experiences of counting money, counting chickens, checking the time, checking to make sure all your kids are there. Mathematics is and are inseparable from politics.

Numbers transverse and transect all terrains of life. They offer powerful tools of generalization and equivalence, but they are also deployed in particular instances, through situated and singular practices, and create complex relations between one and many, past and future. This book engages Guatemalans' experiences via number but also strives to unsettle readers' relations to counting itself. So I invite you to follow number through different temporalities, including twenty-first-century Guatemala, not as a judicial procedure (to determine if it is good or bad) but as a power-infused companion, abstract and embodied at once (a friend, even), in struggles to count.

Part I

When You Count You Begin with 1, 2, 3

0 Bookkeeping

[With double-entry bookkeeping Luca Pacioli] laid the foundation of the modern conception of profit, not as some vague increase in possession, as in antiquity, but as something hard, even crystalline, mathematical and open to empirical test at any time whatever through an interlocking system of books.
—James Buchan

Fortune

Doing number is doing the relation one-to-many.
—Helen Verran

This is a book about counting. Counting the dead after genocide—and those who survive. Counting losses and damages. Negotiating what will count as adequate compensation. Calculating resources and investment opportunities. Figuring input to output. Computing interest rates vis-à-vis current collateral and hoped-for future earnings. Trying to engage with the market forces that are transforming (what's left of) subsistence agriculture. And counting one's blessings.

"¡Dichosa!" Manuel said, laughing, over his beer. "Lucky!" We were crowded around the only table in a small neighborhood sundries store on a late rainy August afternoon. Manuel and Francisco were utterly exhausted. They'd just finished many days of running the Dance of the Conquest for the Virgen de Tránsito, patron of Joyabaj, El Quiché. Francisco, with Manuel as his second, had taken on the yearlong responsibility/burden/sacrifice/honor. This entailed rising at 4 AM, performing brilliantly in the most demanding athletic roles of Tekum Uman and Pedro Alvarado (sometimes twice if the alternate didn't show), encouraging the other dancers, providing food and drink for everyone, and ensuring the expensive rented costumes were all right. Plus paying for it all. And they weren't done yet; there were still the debts incurred. Francisco said he would probably have to cut cane on the south coast.

With Marvin Cohodas, their ethnographer, we'd been discussing my next-day plans to visit friends on my way back to Guatemala City. Fidelia, an antimining activist; Adelita, whom I've known since she was seven, now interning at the Santa Cruz hospital hematology lab; and in Tecpán, Chimaltenango, Don Cristobal, an *ajq'ij*, or daykeeper, whom I'd met a few weeks before at a workshop for Maya people on how to read Maya glyphs. I'd been thinking the day was going to be kind of arduous but it made Manuel exclaim "*!Dichosa!*" meaning fortunate, prosperous, happy.

His comment focuses me on scale, a reminder that something I barely registered was a privilege. This chapter is called "Bookkeeping," meaning to take care or heed in keeping (financial) records—for which the fundamental goal, called the "golden rule," is the zero balance between debts and credits. Yet here was an imbalance to which I'd been heedless. To have the time and money to hop on and off the bus. To have friends and acquaintances scattered across the countryside. To come and go as I please. He didn't seem envious or angry, but "*dichosa*" marks a nonequivalence that pushes me to take care with those historical networks and devices that distribute "luck" and fortune (which are not the same as value) unequally across time and space. The fact that I can travel (and legally, not risking the perils of undocumented border crossings) to marvel at the effort and memory condensed into the dance or sit for months on end to "keep" all that knowledge by writing this book, is no accident. It's not a one-to-one credit-debit relationship, either, given the many layers of the imperial pyramid that link us. Yet my privileges are connected to their difficulties. Both are produced by a post-1492 planetary system that learned to conceive profit as something hard and mathematical.

The bookkeeping here, concerning equivalences and inequalities, quantification and its qualifications, emerges from that space of jokes and sharing and disparity between a Mayan person and a gringa anthropologist in a world deeply structured by—yet always entangled in various—mathematical systems and conceptualizations. Our disparities in luck are somewhat measurable by comparing GNPs, Gini coefficients, poverty indexes, debt payments, and the like. But the subtle pathways and violently inserted funnels that extract prosperity from "subprime" places like Guatemala and accumulate it in "centres of calculation" like the United States can be hard to trace with any accuracy (Latour 1987). That doesn't mean people don't know they're there. "!Dichosa!"

Like Santos and Sebastiana, the people I'll tell you about—much like you and me—are trying to hedge their bets in a world of risk and uncertainty.[1] We are trying to figure our ways through different and simultaneous regimes of counting, measurement, and logic. These regimes include insurance, fault, actuarial accounting, free trade, derivative, and even that odd nongovernmental organization reasoning in which they just *give* things away. Such regimes entangle us in various horologies (timekeeping) as well as the logics that led Francisco, Manuel, and their families to expend so much time, energy, money, and enthusiasm on the dance—which even some fellow community members see as a waste. This is also a book about counting Maya (how many are there?) and making them count: through voting, protesting, revitalizing Mayan math, selling vitamins, coming to matter. "Who counts?" can mean literally who knows how to count or how to do math but also, more existentially, whose lives "count"—whose lives are meaningful and valuable?

Some of this counting is arithmetical, basic adding and subtracting (where changes differ by a constant amount), while some is geometric (differing by a constant ratio: 2, 6, 18, 54), with exponential growth in, say, profits from a gold mine, a sugarcane plantation, or privatizing the national electricity grid. Or exponential loss, as a parent's murder in 1981 sets back generations in terms of schooling, nutrition, life expectancy, and even the ability to feel enthusiasm for one's own life.[2] Yet over the three books I've written about Guatemala—what I've come to think of as the Genocide Trilogy—there is something that feels incalculable. The degree zero, the darkest time, the years 1980 to 1983 of both frenzied and systematic mass murder of mostly—but not only—indigenous people. It continues to reverberate through the years, bursting forth in the most unexpected times and places (like Sebastiana's testimonial). The number of war dead keeps growing, along with the backlog in unexhumed mass graves. And new corpses are added from a different war, the tolls taken by unemployed armed men, poverty, drug trafficking, kidnapping, armed robbery, femicide, gang initiations, and political assassinations. Guatemala's murder rate is now equal to the worst years of the war.

This grinding, continuous, "everyday" war affects everyone I speak to and work with in Guatemala.[3] The home invasion where friends were tied up while the place was divested of everything of value, including their Mayan clothing; the terrifying anonymous calls to a Mayan publishing house from people surveilling their comings and goings to try to extort protection money; the carjackings; the man who didn't show up for our meeting because his brother had been kidnapped for ransom and they were negotiating for his life; the woman whose teenage daughter has had seven friends kidnapped and two killed even though the families paid the ransom; the time the proprietor of a parking lot was killed and my friend stood outside for hours, afraid the police would steal her car; muggings in broad daylight, the men also copping a feel; the neighborhood playground suddenly transformed into a no-child's land by gang territory disputes; the terror of riding the buses because over nine hundred drivers have been murdered by extortionists but not having the money for a cab. These are the everyday calculations of a world in which the military state's relation to territory, borders, and the profits to be made off various circulations were part of the infrastructure by the late 1960s and by the ease with which narco-money can buy elections, mocking the divisions between the state and organized crime (González 2014; McAllister and Nelson 2013; Tilly 1985).

But these simultaneous slow and paroxysmal violences seem like epiphenomena of that deeper, wider, older, heavier assemblage that makes me "*dichosa*": the planetary regimes of adding and subtracting, of extractive accumulation that, thanks to Occupy, are less embarrassing to call by their names: capitalism, colonialism, the military-industrial cybernetic debt complex. These are the relations of production that set Guatemala up to sell cheap by exporting dessert (sugar, bananas, coffee) and buy dear by importing almost everything else. They are upheld by transnational debt regimes, tariff agreements, and armed interventions—two centuries of military dictatorships, the 1954 CIA-backed coup, and US counterinsurgency support throughout the thirty-six-year civil war. We need something like the logarithmic measures of the Richter scale, where an increase by one in the measure indicates a tenfold increase in effects (as Ron Eglash reminds me, damage to buildings is minor in a level 5 earthquake; entire cities collapse in level 7) to attempt to measure how the energy these structures release from small villages in highland Guatemala, via the wiry, generationally underfed bodies of people like Manuel, Francisco, and their families, are amplified through all the underdeveloped folds and byways of the globe to produce the world system and my good fortune.

The colonial record is replete with stories that if such people could count better (not "waste" their time and money in unproductive ritual activities) they'd do better.[4] For example, in 1964 Antonio Goubaud Carrera described Guatemala's indigenous people as "limited by technologies that date to thousands of years before" and "tormented by beliefs that a graph would eliminate" (in Vrana 2013, 124). But my raced, nationed, and classed privileges are certainly not based on my superior calculating abilities, and the disparities that hover between us are no accident. By this I mean that this history was *made*. It is not a logical or moral unfolding of a preordained future.

Accident

Yet accidents, when you look at them, are pretty weird, as revealed in efforts to make them amenable to counting—and thereby to hedging and protecting against them. If it's *you* whose daily commute is suddenly shattered by the car crash or *you* whose quotidian labors are disrupted by the mine cave-in, it's a seismic shock, a violent flinging into emergency time, a cosmic unmooring from the mundane. Yet statistics (meaning "of the state") originated in noticing that mining disasters, apparently such random cracks in the world, were actually foretellable, calculable (and insurable). That's in the aggregate, of course. For the particular—will you yourself, with your anxieties, hopes, and plans, memories of birthday parties and high school crushes, unfinished business, coffee cup in hand, be squashed, maimed, torn to pieces, shot, burned alive, disemboweled, or subjected to any number of apparently random unpleasantnesses? Well, these immensely powerful statistical tools aren't so interested in that.[5] Although someone somewhere might note your demise and add you to the quantum of mortality. Maybe a Mayan diviner could help, if you really want to know.

Jane Gleeson-White (for Italy) and Mary Poovey (for England) tell us how these two forms of knowing—what's now called magic or superstition as opposed to facts, statistics, or "science"—diverged. They show

how number and accounting, especially double-entry bookkeeping, were central to this transformation, and describe centuries of struggle to make number true, factual, trustworthy. It's no accident. Poovey says "That so many of us still imagine . . . that numbers . . . guarantee value-free description . . . speaks to the success of the long campaign to sever the connection between description and interpretation" (1998, xxv). "Severing" is etymologically related to science (and to scissors and score, the action of cutting a mark to keep count, from which we get 20, as in "four score and seven years ago"), and we'll stay mindful of such cuts. Poovey reminds us: "in the late sixteenth century . . . number still carried the pejorative connotations associated with necromancy.[6] . . . Instead of gaining prestige from numbers, double-entry bookkeeping helped confer cultural authority on numbers . . . by means of the balance . . . conjur[ing] up both the scales of justice and the symmetry of God's world" (Poovey 54).

I'd like to spend a little time here with the development of accounting and how number and quantification were made into hard-to-question facts, because it helps us understand what has been both lost and gained in these processes and to follow number as an actant traversing different terrains of life. And rather than a simple "number is good because it's true" versus "number is bad because it's dehumanizing," it's more generative to explore the epistemological (how do we know?) and institutional (how are we organized?) infrastructures that undergird pondering itself. As Helen Verran says, "politics, logic, and mathematics are inseparable" (2000b, 289).

I also strive to "keep" the alluring pull of abstraction grounded in what Jane Guyer calls "the kinetics of counting" (2004, 56) and Jean Lave "cognition in practice" (1988)—its material and embodied experience. This means attending to the flesh-and-bone finger or digit indexed by "digital" and the bodily harm and "real world" damage such activities unleash—as well as the opportunities they engender. I follow these connections through the thread of "adequation," or how to align a real, sensuous thing in the world with an object of knowledge, and through struggles over adequate conditions of existence. The ongoing debates about quantitative versus qualitative methods hinge on whether numbers or words (both abstractions, remember) better capture "the real." Stakes are high. Adequate representation may determine if a human rights violation is punished, if a chemical exposure is deadly, if a state will pay reparations, and if this book manages to make my interlocutors count.

Accounting

> An aura has come to surround numbers and despite the caveats of professional
> auditors, it is those unfamiliar with financial auditing who tend to sanctify them.
> —Marilyn Strathern (2000, 8)

Bookkeeping practices infiltrated Europe via the Italian manual *Particularis de computis et scripturis* (Particulars of Reckonings and Writings), published in 1494 by Luca Pacioli, just two years after Columbus's first voyage and the fall of Granada and three years before Vasco da Gama "found" a sea route to India. Double-entry bookkeeping brought with it from points east the new concept (for Europe) of zero.[7] These practices both supported the networks and techniques that would produce the capitalist race-based world system, and took on legitimacy and increasing power from that emerging system. But the centuries-long project of abstraction that would produce universals, generalizations, and aggregates was also connected to changes in the quite everyday practices of translating household (*oikos*) managing (*nemein*)—that is, economy—into records. At the risk of being "dull and tedious and stuffy and boring and desperately dull," as the Monty Python accountant describes his job (hoping to escape through lion taming), please bear with me because without this brief excursus through accounting we may be too easily taken in by number's "dazzling single purity" (Verran 2001, 109).

Jane Guyer reminds us that quantity (number) and quality (kind) are both scales, unanchored in any foundational invariant. They do, however, share linkage points, or thresholds (tropes), that connect them to each other (and to other scales like nominal, ordinal, interval, and ratio). Significant performances and institutions, like those sketched below, can "settle" those linkages, transforming one into the anchor of the others (2004, 12, 49–60).[8] Over time this happened with and to number, making it seem like a foundational invariant, so that when you count you begin with 1, 2, 3, but zero seems to have always been there—as the unspoken base from which you begin, and as the "golden rule" that you return to when the books are balanced. It is not numbers' fault. But could these performances and institutions have also helped make possible the "modern" ground zero of genocide, the destruction in whole or in part of a people? As well as the human rights imperative to count them and make those losses count? If so, how?

Pacioli's how-to guide describes a series of four books through which everyday transactions are successively disentangled through abbreviations and translations (of, say, the value of jewels into a single currency) until in the final account only credits and debits appear, each appears twice, and as the accountant rectifies—or balances—the sums "on each set of facing pages . . . virtue was made visible" (Poovey 1998, 43).

The first book, the inventory, in which women and young people were allowed to write, was full of homely details. It included a range of scales, a heterogeneous miscellany of documents and precious things, bills of sale, IOUs, family heirlooms, commonplace sayings, prayers, names, money, stock, jewels, goods, lands, bargaining, labor, and risk—even mentioning unsafe vessels and pirates. Pacioli's sample inventory lists a fantastic array of riches, including papal florins, cash in various forms, cases of ginger, fox and chamois skins, a house, and bank accounts, even the names of clerks (Gleeson-White 2011, 98).

The second book, the memorial, in which each day's transactions were recorded, remained prolix, noting names of parties, terms of payment, and the details of merchandise like money, weight, and number. Also called the "waste-book," it was temporary, sometimes updated hour by hour. Once a week, the man of the house should transcribe such goings-on in even more abbreviated form in the journal, where all moneys were transformed into a single currency and every entry is either from or to someone.

In the last book, the ledger, each transaction was entered—now by men alone—as only a credit or a debit, calculated in a common money, written as a series of numbers, and arranged by kinds (not date) as cash, jewels, and the like. This made even time an externality, treated as if the "future has already arrived" (Poovey 62). This, in turn, erases the uncertainty inherent in every aspect of trade, allowing profit and loss to appear "at a glance" (Gleeson-White 100). Pacioli has been compared to Copernicus because of the momentousness of this move: "through its encouragement of regular record keeping, mathematical order, and the reduction of events to numbers abstracted from time and place, double entry fostered a new view of the world as being subject to quantification . . . the heart of the scientific revolution" (Spengler, in Gleeson-White 167).

It was not a scheming patriarchal cabal that transformed major determinants of gain and loss, like haggling, labor, and uncertainty, into excess, trivial details. But it was also no accident that these became associated with women and youth, who were gradually effaced. Parallel transformations in architecture separated the (upper-class) bedroom from the study, severing reproduction from production (Poovey 34–35). The weary policeman's line,

"Just the facts, ma'am, just the facts," suggests how deep this gendered sep-
aration goes today, where the "ma'am" stands for everything excessive. The
idea that numbers (expressing profit) are "hard, even crystalline, mathematical and . . . empirical (Buchan, in Gleeson-White 2011, 161) and that such attributes "count" has associated them with the left-hand side in the post-1492
proposition: white male rich straight Anglo-Saxon Protestant > everyone else.[9]

But numbers don't really stand alone: tropic links between disjunctured
scales allow for what Guyer calls "marginal gains," "profit" of various kinds
drawn from and across those edges. For example, number and morality would
seem to belong to totally different scales (how can a number be "good"?),
yet Poovey says "virtue" came into play in the ledger, the last book, because
the system created writing positions that subordinated personality to rules.
Credit and debit are comparable and checkable via arithmetic, following
those formal, disinterested rules, thereby constituting a system in relation to which one could judge right from wrong. The identity of two numbers could be easily verified, first by simply comparing them and second
by checking the addition that produced them. "To the extent that numbers
were considered disinterested because transparent to their object, so too
were those who produced numerical knowledge" (Poovey 1998, 71).[10]

As powerful as this system has become—so much so that Bill Maurer can
say "accounting theory is the culture" (2002, 6)—it was and remains contested,
especially around that aura-emanating concept of balance and its crystalline destabilizer: profit. In 1623 Gerald de Malynes ridiculed the balance, so
central to double entry, as useless for understanding justice or commerce.
Lacking a referent or a center, "all a balance can do is tell whether one has
lost or gained (not what value is)" (Poovey 76). This is why monarchs and
deities so often appear on money, as the external agent ensuring value in a
centerless system.

Obscured by the zero of the double-entry balance is, of course, the whole
point of trade: profit. When the accountant enters the pertinent information about each transaction twice, once as a credit and once again as a debit,
he is not simply adding and subtracting because expenditures and receipts
almost never actually equal each other, and he elides the variable of time,
as profits are realized in the future, not at the time of investment. From
early on, Poovey says, producing the balance required something in addition
to arithmetic: numbers lacking a referent in the company's business (43, 54).
And thus, the Europeans began to make a world of constant checking and
audit and credit ratings and accounting that (by accident?) also made possible

tulip and South Sea bubbles, 1929, Enron, 2008, and increasingly larger and more terrifying global crashes based on "virtuous, truthful" numbers lacking a referent in the sensual world.

Meanwhile, a similar apparently contradictory set of understandings of the human was coming into being. Mirrors, chairs (instead of benches), portraiture, and autobiography were beginning to produce (albeit differently for different classes) a generalizable individuality (Stone 1996).[11] This sense of being "one" or singular, particular, cardinal, developed alongside aggregation through massifying production and consumption, the rise of collective identifications you "had to have," like a nation or a gender, and the rejiggered sense of self as ordinal (i.e., first, second) or one among many in the urban throng or that emerging collective, the proletariat. Different and simultaneous regimes of morality also emerged: that you personally might be sacrificed if it's for the "good of the many," while social Darwinism justified you doing better than others because you're fitter (not because you can justify the exploitation of their labor).

Long-running debates in Western philosophy began to settle (although never completely) into what Carolyn Merchant calls the "mechanical model," which sees (and makes) the world as dividable and rearrangeable (because composed of particles), based in a natural order from which knowledge and information are abstractable (i.e., context independent) and in which problems can be analyzed into parts that can be manipulated by mathematics (1992, 49).

Production practices and liberal property theories based in an individual's labor transformed what had been dense interactions of human and nonhuman actants—lively engagements of land, soil, plants, rivers, animals, minerals, bacteria, fungi, wind, rain, lightning, temperature, altitude, fire—into extractable and ownable "natural resources." Racial formations merged with imperial labor extraction to overtly enslave millions of people and indenture millions more. Thus humans (some more than others) also came to function as ownable and exploitable "resources."

Money, as a general equivalent, increasingly mixed with wage labor to produce a couple of effects. First, as Marx pointed out, humans (especially those who work for nothing) became "superadequate" in that we produce more than we are paid for. Second, double-entry bookkeeping made money as profit (not just "some vague increase in possession") visible, thereby calculable, slowly transforming commerce from a morally questionable project of gain based in the clever management of money into a process "naturally" bent on acquisition, "an unending, systematic pursuit of profit" (Gleeson-White 167). Third, human value became calculable in time and coin.

On the one hand this latter effect helped co-constitute a transformation in punishment from publicly taking "a pound of flesh" to taking its "equivalent" of time and money via incarceration and fines. Shas, an elder day-keeper in Nebaj, Guatemala, interviewed in the 1960s, remembers: "There was no fine payment, money wasn't taken from people as is done now. Now we can get out of it with money, but then the fine was the whip" (Colby and Colby 1981, 32; also Foucault 1979). On the other hand, this made it possible to imagine something otherwise deeply strange. How did it come to be that a sum of money could count for a person, say, in the form of reparations?[12]

Forgive this quick and dirty run-through of centuries of struggle over practices and understandings of the human in and of the world via counting, equivalence, and adequacy—which remain far from settled. But I wanted to contextualize the European milieu in which number, slowly and stutteringly, become the modern fact and to genealogize the "new wave of values that lay behind the conception of numbers" that Spanish colonial administrators embedded into everyday practice in the Americas. So that Kulussi Suyâ, an indigenous man from the Xingu reserve in the Brazilian Amazon, could say "the white men tried to finish with us using guns. . . . Now they use numbers" (Leal Ferreira 1997, 134).[13]

Number and After-Math

Counting is like taking aspirin—it numbs the sense and protects the counter from reality. Counting makes even hideous events bearable as simply more of the same—the counting of wedding rings, spectacles, teeth, and bodies disassociates them from their context—to make the ultimate obscene blasphemy of bureaucratic insensitivity. Engage the mind with numbing recitation to make it empty of reaction.
—Peter Greenaway

Number as somehow able to "finish" a people resonates with a (thankfully out of date) joke told about the Bush White House: US Presidential adviser Karl Rove goes into the Oval Office and says, "Mr. President, I've got some bad news. We lost three Brazilian soldiers in Iraq today." Bush says, "Oh no! That's terrible! I can't believe it! But wait a minute, how many zeros are in a brazillion?" Confusing a person (Brazilian) with a number (brazillion; not really a number at all!) plays on popular perceptions of the former president as stupid but also evokes the power of number to dehumanize. It's harder for him to imagine a small set of singularities (three Brazilians) than some unthinkably huge aggregate (how many zeros?). Told about a regime defined by war and torture, whose casualties remain uncounted (Ross 2005), it also suggests some people (Latin Americans in this case) count less.

"I am not a number!" the protagonist of TV's *The Prisoner* cries, affirming the human as irreducible to quantification. Yet colonizers assumed that indigenous people didn't count (as human) precisely because they couldn't count, didn't have math, were incapable of abstract thinking (i.e., the joke's proof of Bush's stupidity). "Lack" of numeracy still indexes infantile, primitive, or even animalistic levels of intellectual complexity. Helen Verran, working with Australian Aborigines, quotes Noam Chomsky: "having no elaborated number system, [they] must be considered biologically less than truly human" (2000b, 292).[14]

This tension between the de- and the humanizing effects of number might be simply explained as racism justifying accumulation by dispossession. But it might be worth another quick loop through a history of number in the "rise of civilization" to more adequately understand what it means for number to anchor relations of scale. And why, when I evoke the Bush regime's "uncounted casualties," I am suggesting they need to be counted to be valued.[15]

Histories of number often rehearse the difficulties of producing singularity out of plurality, of keeping track of lots of people or things—like, say, how many went out in the flock or army and how many came back (Ifrah 1985; McLeish 1991)? Human ingenuity figured out how to track each and every one through abstraction, as early epidemiologists piled stones to count each soldier as armies went off to battle then unpiled them upon their return. The stones left signaled the humans lost. Pebbles were later laid on counting tables that then developed columns to represent units, a similar organization to the abacus. (*Calces*, Latin for small stones, gave us "calculation.") Notches in wood or lipstick cases and marks in clay and later on papyrus took the place of those piles of stones, then "Arabic" numbers (actually from what's now India) replaced tallies and unwieldy Roman numerals. English "remembers" this through the term "algebra," from *al-jabr*—meaning reunion of broken parts or bonesetter—which comes from an 820 treatise by Muhammed ibn Musa al-Khwarizmi (hence, somewhat mangled, our word "algorithm") and refers to reduction and balancing, the cancellation of like terms on opposite sides of the equation. Fibonacci (Leonardo da Pisa, ca. 1170–1240), Italian but raised in what's now Algeria, was a bridge between these numeric worlds. He deployed these "new numbers" in both practical and enchanting ways—as with fractals and the Fibonacci sequence, in which each number is the sum of the first two. To the fascination of many, the sequence (and the golden mean and spiral derived from it) appears to "bring a concept into accord with reality," in this case replicating the growth patterns of many living things: shells, flowers, bunny populations, and even the locations of our belly buttons and the arms of galaxies (Gleeson-White 2011, 19–20; Eglash 1999).[16] These numbers slowly spread via double-entry bookkeeping from Venice, seedbed of imperial capitalism, through Europe and across oceans. All these borrowings and developments aided the "leap" from the abacus to abstract calculations, finally freeing accountants from their counting tables. By apparently superseding the incarnated relation to calculation (moving the digits, sliding the beads), they also imbued me with the shame I feel when caught counting on my fingers.[17]

In this process, the modern number, a bit like the liberal subject, came to stand alone. In order to count, "one" must be singular. During (and even after) the war in Guatemala it was as individuals that the Guatemalan state and paramilitaries killed most of their nonindigenous adversaries—because they had made specific choices to question the status quo, because they had specific roles as labor organizers, teachers, priests, guerrillas. Based in a counterinsurgency fantasy that 100% of indigenous people supported the guerrillas, it was as a collective—entire families and villages at a time—that they killed many indigenous people. It is as a jumbled mass of bones in a mass grave that many remain. Counting *these* dead remains a struggle for truth, justice, and virtue to this day.

But what counts as counting? Precisely because of number's power, colonized people, and the anthropologists and educators who work with them, have devoted enormous energy to proving that native "elaborated number systems" exist. Mariana Kawall Leal Ferreira taught math on the Xingu indigenous reserve in the Brazilian Amazon and confronted derisive outsiders claiming that "Indians can't count." Describing the mestizo Antonio, a government agent who supplements his salary by trading in jungle artisanry and who can't figure out why one day arrows have one price and the next day one quite different, she shows that the reserve's residents know very well how to count but what is being calculated is differently embedded in both human interactions and time. For the Juruna, Kayabi, and Suyá peoples, the "price" of an arrow is not based on a singular transaction but tallies a long-term set of relations with the government representative, who is deeply in arrears for a number of goods and services. The arrow exchange is simply a moment in a longer-term reckoning. Leal Ferreira also finds herself disconcerted when a student calculates the following problem. He caught 10 fish and gave 3 to his brother. How many are left? Rather than the expected 7, the student said 13. It takes her a while to realize that for these children giving is not subtractive (1997, 141). Similarly, Ron Eglash shows how African fractal geometries express lived relations to space, other humans, companion species, and understandings of generation and temporality (1999), and Helen Verran explains the Yolngu Aboriginal Australians' understandings of *gurrutu* as a domain of logic and a matrix of kin relations marking relative location in the material world, embodied relations to land- and dreamscape, and patterns of reciprocity and ratio (2000b).

Yet far more often, colonized people are compelled to learn the "master's tools" of so-called Western numeracy and accounting as self-defense. Leal Ferreira is constrained by the demand to prove that even if the Amazonians count differently, they still count—putting the lie, as Eva Csipak pointed out to me, to her provocative title "When $1 + 1 \neq 2$." In Geoff Ryman's *Unconquered Country*, the teacher who wrenches Third away from her organic numeracy is doing it in hopes of liberation (see the preface). When US high school teacher Jaime Escalante struggles to teach math to poor Latino/a students in East Los Angeles, it is to improve their life chances *and* to prove to a disbelieving education system that such kids could actually *learn* math (*Stand and Deliver*, 1988). Certain numbers still isomorphize with modernity, progress, and power *and* with particular phenotypes. But in the movie, Escalante tells the teens that their "ancestors, the Maya" had zero before the Europeans. "Math is in your blood, *vatos!*"

The Maya are curiously positioned in the caliper grip of these tribunals of reason. The preinvasion Maya famously "discovered" zero and developed exquisitely precise systems of temporal and astronomical calculations. *Winaq*, the Maya-K'iche' term for 20, means human being, and the remarkable Classic-era glyphs in which elaborate portrait heads and entire anthropomorphic figures represent number—"singular in their beauty . . . unrivaled in any other script" (Closs 2001, 214)—suggest understandings rather different from the colonizers' numbers. *Those* numbers, however, had armies and priests that, in one of the greatest epistemic losses of all time, systematically extirpated the living indigenous knowledges of Mesoamerica by massive death and dislocation (some unintended, via microbes), severing children from their villages for counterinsurgency reeducation and ferreting out and destroying almost every record of these calculations, almanacs, and astronomical tables. We are left with only three codices in all the world, and some stelae and murals saved by jungle fecundity.

Now their descendants struggle to survive their current-day poverty, illiteracy rates, and malnutrition levels, which led many to join the popular revolutionary war in the late 1970s, some as nonviolent activists, others as combatants. As in Xingu Park, many understood this commitment to change as one in a long temporality of transactions undertaken in hopes of rectifying decades, even centuries, of unequal exchange. And as in Xingu Park, many people did not necessarily see their own possible death in these struggles as subtractive.

In the after-math of genocide (in Guatemala and elsewhere), indigenous peoples (and their anthropologists) work extremely hard to show that they may be different (subtraction and addition may mean different things) but they are really the same (they *do* count). But in transactions with settler states, relation to number—especially vis-à-vis singularity and aggregate— remains fraught. Like subalterns more generally, they are seen to function as tribes or gangs, more as collectives than individuals, where, similar to the joke, a particular set of three Brazilians is dispersed into an undifferentiated and vast number. Maya-K'iche' activist Domingo Hernandez Ixcoy told me, "They still see indigenous people as a mass. They look at some people who have gone to work in the state, Rigoberta Menchú, Rosalina Tuyuc, Rigoberto Quemé, and then suddenly they say every Maya is sold out. Or if they catch people with drugs they become narco-Mayas. You never see headlines about narco-ladinos! We participate as individuals but we are seen as a collective." But Lolita Chavez, a younger Maya-K'iche' activist in Santa Cruz del Quiché, laughed at this stereotype as she told me about a protest there over RENAP, the National Registry of Persons, when about 15,000 people took over the government installations. "You really felt the force of the indigenous in the town that day," Lolita said. "The police said, 'Here comes the F.B.I., the *fuerza bruta india* [ignorant, animal-like Indians], and charged us with all sorts of crimes but we shouted, 'Si meten a uno, meten a 15,000 / If you arrest one, arrest all 15,000! You'll need a new prison!' They didn't touch us, we were too strong."

Guyer says "number as an exact scale seems to have stood *within* the repertoire of scalar values and not at its point of culmination (or reduction).

0.1 2012. Dan Piraro. Used with kind permission.

At each end of the repertoire are enduring propositions: the nature of 'things' . . . and the nature of power. In between, each scale acquired its own elaborated logic in which history and experience played a contingent and changeable constitutive role." And numbers retain their "potential referents across the registers, to words, things, bodily kinetic and spiritual powers" (66). I'm arguing that even numbers with armies are constantly being made to count within different historical and experiential scales (aggregated as "narco-Maya" is insulting but as "F.B.I" makes Maya pretty powerful). Current struggles to count using both "Western" numbers and "Mayan math" are activating the potentials across registers and across time.[18] For example, the lost art of glyph reading is returning today, as I explore, and day counting, against the odds, has endured and is growing as a practice.[19]

In fact, it's this counting that has inspired a global fascination with Mayan numeracy and the 2012 "prophecies of apocalypse," generating hundreds of websites, Hollywood movies, editorial cartoons (a Sarah Palin presidency "would prove the Maya right"), museum exhibits, a tourism boom as every hotel room near a Mayan site was booked, and even a NASA website debunking the many ways the world will NOT end.

Numbers and Confusion

But I'll tell you more about day counting and apocalypse later. Here, to wrap up my attempts to account for a world that made me so lucky—though I'm not particularly good at math!—I'd like to tarry for a moment longer with some peculiarities of number.

0.2 "What is wrong with these numbers?" David Rees. Used with kind permission.

Theodore Porter suggests that "trust in numbers" is related to their properties: uniform, rigorous, universal, freestanding, and self-possessed (1995). Yet numbers are also wily, manipulable, untrustworthy. In a basic sense, numbers are "quick . . . as soon as I add you up, you turn into a new sum!" (Rees 2004, unpaged). Or as the creepy saying goes, numbers are like prisoners, if you torture them enough you can make them say anything. Numbers form the invisible infrastructure for many aspects of bureaucratic modern life, like the zeros and ones behind our computer interface. Yet they also seem active, unruly, agents of a nonhuman kind. David Rees captures some of this ambivalence in his office-life cartoon: "What the fuck is wrong with these numbers in my mind???" When you stop to think about it, numbers seem so clearly differentiated—$1 \neq 2$—yet manipulating them through addition, multiplication, or geometric calculations transforms them completely. With that action 1 becomes 2, or any other number, including 0.[20]

Likewise, Poovey insists that the numeric fact remains "epistemologically peculiar" (1998, xxv): "both essential and insufficient" (xi), it seems to simply describe but also requires a leap of faith (27). This peculiarity will be a burr in this book, a constant irritant, forcing me to think through number and counting as essential *and* insufficient, dehumanizing *and* reparative, necessary *and* complicated!

I was brought into being in the fact-filled world Poovey describes, so it's hard not to think of counting as neutral or even moral. In contradistinction to those who believe Saddam Hussein had weapons of mass destruction or that climate change is hooey or that helping rich people get richer will improve my situation, I prefer to live in "the reality based community" (Suskind 2004) that relies on strong data and hard numbers. But then why the injunction "don't count your chickens before they've hatched"? Why, in the Judeo-Christian tradition, was Moses warned that without a ransom for each person it was dangerous to count them (Exodus 30:11)? Or unheeding this advice, why was King David punished with 70,000 plague deaths simply for holding a census (2 Samuel 24:1; Chronicles 21)?

Perhaps they feared that abstraction is only adequate for nongrowing things, paralleling how Gary Urton and Primitivo Nina Llanos describe Quechua understandings. Because numbers "separate things," it is prohibited to count what is considered inseparable, particularly reproductive groups like animals and harvested produce, and the colors of the rainbow (1997, 52–53, 102). "The potential for reproduction is, in all cases, considered to be based on unity and interdependence." Assigning numbers, creating or emphasizing individualism, represents a force of alienation and threatens the reproductive capacity and unity of the group (1997, 103).[21] In other examples of numbers' ambivalence, Michael Closs says the Crow "do not count above a thousand, as they say honest people have no use for higher numbers" (1986a, 16).[22] Guatemalan journalist David Dubón said that in 1968, after the first terrible wave of counterinsurgency violence, the government held a census but his activist friends joked it was not to determine "*cuántos somos sino cuántos quedamos*" (not how many there are but how many are left). Today censuses seem more fraught by struggles to *be* counted,[23] but there is still a whiff of necromancy about this apparently prosaic act.

In 1812 Robert Southey denounced Adam Smith for estimating man's importance solely "by the gain which can be extracted from him, the *quantum of lucration* of which he can be made the instrument" (Poovey 294–95). And perhaps the fact that collecting data about mortality was an early application of statistics led to the suspicions W. H. Auden evokes, that numbers divide "the tender who value from the tough who measure" (2007, 426). Alan Bishop says for "imperialist powers . . . mathematics, with its clear rationalism, and cold logic, its precision, its so-called 'objective' facts (seemingly culture and value free), its lack of human frailty, its power to predict and control, its encouragement to challenge and to question, and its thrust towards yet more secure knowledge, was a most powerful weapon indeed" (1990, 59). (Yet note the ambivalence: cold power *and* encouragement to question.)

David Graeber is a recent and eloquent practitioner of the misarithrope (i.e., number hater) form, connecting mathematics directly to war, slavery, debt, and empire, a primary engine of forcing people out of their context, cutting them off from human ties, and making them exchangeable. He says: "debt, unlike any other form of obligation, can be precisely quantified. This allows debts to become simple, cold, impersonal . . . [and] transferable. If one owes a favor to another human being—it is owed to that person specifically. But if one owes forty thousand dollars at 12% interest, it doesn't really matter who the creditor is . . . or what the other party needs, wants, is capable of. . . . If you end up having to abandon your home . . . if your daughter ends up in a mining camp working as a prostitute, well, that's unfortunate, but incidental to the creditor. Money is money and a deal is a deal. . . . The crucial factor is . . . money's capacity to turn morality into a matter of impersonal arithmetic . . . to justify things that would otherwise seem outrageous or obscene. . . . The violence and the quantification are intimately linked. . . . violence . . . turns human relations into mathematics" (2011, 13–14).

In one of her infrequent allusions to colonialism, Poovey says Englishman William Petty, a major figure in making the modern fact and in breaking Ireland, posited a world in which the Irish would be forbidden to keep the kind of numerical accounts on which Petty had staked his claim to impartiality and expertise: "'It may be offensive to make Estimates of the Number of Men slain in Ireland for the last 516 years. . . . Of the Charge of the last Warr begun Anno 1641; the Value of the Wasting and Dispeopling of the Contrey'" (in Poovey 1998, 137). She sees no *necessary* connection between the method he developed to produce abstractions like the value of people, national wealth, and population and the kind of brutality expressed in his solution to the Irish problem but admits abstractions tend to emphasize the well-being of the aggregate over individuals and to define "well-being" solely in economic terms (137).

We will see just such effects throughout this book. Yet, here's the peculiarity. Mr. Petty seems well aware that number would *also* be a potent weapon for the Irish. Frantz Fanon puts it elegantly: "The settler-native relationship is a mass relationship. The settler pits brute force against the weight of numbers . . . during the phase of insurrection, each settler reasons on a basis of simple arithmetic . . . when in laying down precise methods the settler asks each member of the oppressing minority to shoot down 30 or 100 or 200 natives. . . . This chain of reasoning which presumes very arithmetically the disappearance of the colonized people does not leave the native overcome with moral indignation. He . . . has practically stated the problem of his liberation in identical terms: 'we must form ourselves into groups of two hundred or five hundred, and each group must deal with a settler' " (1968, 53, 84–85).

And, even as Thomas Malthus was denounced as the demonic spokesman for numbers as the amoral vehicle of indifferent facts, he was bringing into being a new collective subject, the poor, as precursor to the very idea— and mobilizing potential—of the 99%. The number 6 million took over a decade to make into a fact, but it has been transformative. Can the positive effects of "1 in 10" be overstated for a lonely gay boy in Nebraska or the legitimation of queer politics more globally? Or, more horribly, "1 in 5 women" for a survivor of rape, believing herself to be alone and possibly complicit in the crime against her? And in Guatemala the number 200,000—the war dead counted by the United Nations—is an incredibly important (if not completely precise) figure in ongoing struggles for justice. In part because of these powers, numeracy and matheracy have been actively withheld from oppressed peoples and in turn become a liberation demand. Vinicio Lopez, an antimining activist in Guatemala, put it this way: "Why aren't there any schools in the villages? Schools that teach math and history? Because to harvest coffee you don't need to study, you are just *mano de obra* (hands that work) and it's better if *mano de obra* doesn't know their rights, because then they might make demands."

Numbers make visible abstractions that without them couldn't be seen: the market, poverty, the Maya, and fictitious personifications like Stock, Money, Profit, and Loss. Poovey also reminds those of us of more qualitative bent that our critical methods for "seeing through" numbers actually depend on them and on the logics of double entry. "The epistemological conundrum of numerical precision" comes from number as "an object of sense, because we can count," but numbers are also "used to generate mathematical formulas which, though rule bound or precise, might not accurately reflect observable reality at all" (Herschel [1830], in Poovey 1998, 320). The solution devised was to factor "the limits of epistemological certainty into the method of science itself" (320). Engaging with the difficulties of adequation that will accompany us through the book, by the nineteenth century science (hard and soft) was based on "both constant scrutiny of the fit between the data one collected and the actual world, and a ruthlessly honest acknowledgment of the limits of the data themselves" (321).

Yet I think there's more to that "conundrum" of numbers as both object of sense *and* the product of elaboration, emerging new and transformed via calculation. One expression of it might be found in the *enchantments* of aggregation, so beautifully evoked in those "ornate and punning" words that mark pluralities or groups of beings—an unkindness of ravens, a pride of lions, an exultation of larks, a romp of otters, an ostentation of peacocks, a parliament of owls (Gronland 2011, 7). Singles melt into a plurality that in turn merges into an uncanny singularity—sums greater than their parts, outcomes to formulas that are not quite containable by calculating procedures.[24] Like Guyer's links between scales, Gronland suggests the metaphoric linking done by the "x of y" formulation is less description than "invocation" (2011, 7, 11).

An algorithm is a procedure or formula for solving a problem. Sometimes very complicated ones can do quite magical things, like create trillions of dollars out of, quite literally, nothing (at least nothing available to the senses). And similar to aggregates like a murder of crows, a necromantic algorithm can merge quantity (1.5 million Armenians, 6 million Jews, 200,000 Guatemalans, 800,000 Tutsi and Hutu sympathizers) into a quality via that twentieth-century invocation: genocide. Yet is anything—a number or a word—*adequate* to the space/time of a state, quite literally, seeking to create a nothing? A Genocide of Maya.

Perhaps this is Kant's "mathematical sublime": what we feel when we are "confronted with something that is so large that it overwhelms imagination's capacity to comprehend it . . . 'the very inadequacy of our faculty for estimating the magnitude of the things in the sensible world.'" While he understands this as oscillating with the dynamic sublime (a "supersensible faculty in us" that can, through reason, think of infinity as a whole),

The Money Issue

The New York Times Magazine

JUNE 8, 2008 SECTION 6

$$\sigma^2(\hat{R}_{it}|R_{mt}) = \int_{R_{it}} [R_{it} - E(\hat{R}_{it}|R_{mt})]^2 f(R_{it}|R_{mt})dR_{it}$$

[Too-Good-to-Last?]

The Strange Inner Workings of the Hedge-Fund Machine By Joseph Nocera

0.3 Derivatives mangle: an algorithm transforms one dollar into one hundred.

these encounters create a displeasure, a "'negative liking'" (Ginsborg 2013; internal quotes are Kant, *Critique of Judgment*). Even as we affix a word and create museums and write books to encompass its totality, our labors to reason with something like genocide seem always at risk of being undone by what Eric Gans calls "a negative moment between two forms of order, that of the understanding and that of reason" (2002).

Which brings me back to the incalculable, perhaps the crux of the human sciences in general. What counts? Who counts? How do we know? How can we construct or discover an adequate way to grasp the overwhelming messiness of enworlded life, at least enough to lessen the risk of losing it all?

Calculate the Curve, Complete the Figure

Counting, listing, and other quantitative measures inherently conjure up a larger collectivity. Percentages are clear examples of this. Every percentage, of necessity, evokes a whole of which it is a part: a nation, an ethnic group, a language, or a risk group.

—Jaqueline Urla

By designating this Chapter Zero I sought to "keep" zero in view: that invisible but necessary starting point for counting, the anchor that makes numbers seem invariant. Like a sort of "negative moment," it's a number, as Brian Rotman shows, haunted (for Europeans) by *horror vacui*: its relation to nothing, to annihilation, to "ground zero": nuclear blast, earthquake, epidemic, extinction.

Yet it's also haunted by hope: of zero hunger (*hambre cero*), zero waste, or zero death. And perhaps something more. Rotman says zero contains a "trace of subjectivity, pointed to but absent." By representing "the starting point of a process it indicates the virtual presence of the *counting subject* at the place where that subject begins the whole activity of traversing what will become a sequence of counted positions" (1987, 13). It's a beginning.

The U.S. abolitionist Theodore Parker said, "I do not pretend to understand the moral universe, the arc is a long one. . . . I cannot calculate the curve and complete the figure by the experience of sight. . . . But from what I see I am sure it bends towards justice."[25] I don't know how the numbers and words in this book will compute in such equations. Despite so much struggle and sacrifice to influence that bend, it often feels like an asymptotic curve, never reaching its goal.

I situate these questions and bendings in a world of abiding unfairness that is often "externalized" from what counts. I suggest how numbers are deeply entangled in *both* violence and amazement, oppression *and* emancipation. As Donald McKenzie (2006) says, numbers are an engine, not a camera. This world is made, if sometimes accidentally. Whether it bends to violence or wonder is a question of politics, logic, *and* mathematics, which includes, of course, counting my blessings. So here I acknowledge the people who have woven the patterns. Because how I wrote this book is indivisible from the people who made it possible, what follows is both method and thanks giving.

When I first went to Guatemala in 1985, I met some of the people who still explain things and help me see connections—especially as I can spend only a few months there each year: Paula Worby, Luis Solano, Marcie Mersky, Beatriz Manz, Clara Arenas, Liz Oglesby, Domingo Hernández Ixcoy, Ricardo Falla, and Myrna Mack Chang—whose work, twenty-five years after her assassination, still inspires me. Fieldwork always begins with a visit to Myrna's legacies, the offices of AVANCSO and the Myrna Mack Foundation in Guatemala City, and with checking in among friends like Concha Deras, Matt Creelman, Gladis Pappa, Tomás and Pilar, Irmalicia Velásquez Nimatuj, Daniel Hernández-Salazar, Oscar Maldonado, Demetrio Cojtí, Ulmil Mejia, Enrique Recinos, Dorotea Gómez, Adela Delgado, Julia González, Francisca Gómez, Matilde González, Jenny Casolo, Peter Machetti, Josue Chavajay, Pepe García Noval, Carlos Fredy Ochoa, Claudia Samayoa, David Dubón, Rachel Sieder, Mary Jo McConahay, Manuela Camus, and Santiago Bastos (with special thanks for taking me to the Choatalum hearings). Rolando López and Pepe Lara have passed on but enabled so much of my thinking. In 1998 I began to visit Joyabaj, El Quiché, with Liz Oglesby and Simone Remijnse and met Anastasia Mejia, who has become a cherished friend, and I pause here to commemorate precious lost Quetzalí. I also met Santos Ventura that year and later Manuel Lorenzo and their family and, as it developed, their Red/network, including her fictive kin, Sebastiana Gutiérrez Ruiz, Micaela Grave Lorenzo, and Francisca Mutzutz and her partner Nery. I regret that Francisca won't see this book. That's also when I met Felipe Natareno, Tomasa and Miguel Batz, and Micaela Riquici, her daughter Aurora, and her grandchildren Adelita, Dayan, Jorge, and Esperanza, who are my Xoye family. And in Patzulá, José Lorenzo, Encarnación, her son Juan, and her daughters Isabela and María and now grandchildren, and their gracious and welcoming neighbors. Recoiling from the snakes in the baile de la culebra, I made friends with Guillermo and Irma. With all these folks it's an annual ritual to eat, catch up, gossip, lament, analyze, take walks, tell stories, and share our work, whether writing, weaving, planting, basketball, or beekeeping. I am so very dichosa for all they have taught me and for all their forebearance as I return then disappear year after year.

These sharings aren't really interviews, though I may pull out my notebook to keep track of a particularly convoluted story, a beautiful turn of phrase, or to make sure I get the numbers right. Usually I take notes in diary form in the evenings (if I can keep my eyes open) or the next morning or when I get stood up and have several empty hours in an office foyer or café or on the next long bus ride. Like most anthropologists, I find observing much more of a burden than participating. When I meet new people, often through introductions from those who think they can teach me something, it may be more like a formal interview where I do take notes. When I met Saturnino Jiguán on the stalled bus, I pulled out my notebook when he began listing the pillars of the community (a trick Ricardo Falla taught me in 1985!), and although it was pitch dark (and back at my hotel I realized I'd written over other notes), I caught a lot of his words, then filled in the rest from memory. Julio Cochoy, who worked on the Santa Lucia Utatlán DIY truth report, insisted I take notes when we talked at Doña Luisa's. Old habits die hard in a country where clandestinity was a survival strategy for decades, so I rarely tape even the most formal interviews (although Aurora did let me record her ghost stories). As you read, keep in mind the quotes are not exact, but they are good estimations. Whenever someone is quoted without a citation the words come from an author interview. In almost every case people have let me use their given (or chosen) names.

I think that many of the people of a certain generation I write about here were involved in radical (getting at the root) politics in the 1970s and 1980s, but if they don't tell me, I don't ask. Given the terrible dearth of weapons the Left had access to, I doubt many were actually armed. The 1980s counterinsurgency equation of challenging the state (even nonviolently) = death remains powerful in the after-math. Which is to say that Left, and progressive, politics are everywhere in this book, although what counts as progress is kind of complicated.

Many of the stories I tell here emerged through what Bronislaw Malinowski calls gathering and serendipity. For example, Chapters 4 and 5 unfolded through years of accompanying friends in Joyabaj. I met Aura Elena Farfán, who I'd admired from afar, by accident when Pat Goudvis brought me along on an errand. Bumping in to Maury Hutcheson on the Antigua square led to his extremely kind invitation to Rabinal, where he introduced me to members of the San Pedro and San Pablo cofrades and the Xococ patron of the musicians while patiently explaining dances, music, and history. Likewise, discovering Marvin Cohodas sharing our Joyabaj hotel, he let me accompany him with the baile de la conquista, introducing me to Francisco and Manuel and explaining and clarifying many things for me, which he continues to do most graciously. My still limited understandings of "Mayan math" grew from hanging out with people I knew from earlier work on the Mayan movement. They introduced me to people interested in numbers, who in turn hooked me up with the glyph-reading classes and the astounding folks who keep them going. I thank Raxché, who introduced me to Pakal and

Ixchel, and Judie Maxwell, who introduced me to people like Ajpuj, Andres Cholotío, and members of OKMA. Judie has been an exceptionally patient and gracious explainer. Learning with first Federico Fahsen and then Nikolai Grube and my classmates over several years in glyph classes has been a challenge (¡quiere ganas!) and a boon. I especially want to thank Nikolai, Iyaxel Cojtí, Lolmay, Romelia Mó, Alejandro Garay, Don Cristóbal, and all my tablemates through the years, as well as Daniel Law, Stephen Houston, and Barbara MacLeod. There are many interpretations of the Classic materials but I base my descriptions on the workshops I attended because they are the ones circulating among Mayan Organizing 2.0.

As I began to follow the circuitous routes of calculating the dead, accounting for losses, and counting Maya in various ways, I did a bit more hunting, tracking down folks in the forensic anthropology team, the national reparations projects, and the NGOs working on mining, who in turn networked me to new connections. Of course, one still needs introductions, and much depends on the workings of chance and the intensive kindness of strangers. Along these routes I have indeed been fortunate to meet Manuel Mayorga, Alberto Fuentes, and Ruth del Valle. Entering the world of antimining activism started with Luis Solano, who told me to go to San Miguel Ixtahuacán for a protest, and Greg Grandin and Federico Velasquez, who went with me. I would know almost nothing about mining if it weren't for Pancho Guindon, who explained so much at that first demo and who, a few weeks later, drove me back up to San Miguel and dropped me off at Hermana Maudilia's house, telling me she would take care of me when she got back. And how she has! From that first evening, when she didn't blink an eye at finding a gringa literally on her doorstep and put me to work tending a bonfire while we shared stories and jokes, through several years of visits as she braved death threats, wrote her master's thesis, and keeps me in touch via e-mail, I am so fortunate to know her! She introduced me to Padre Eric and catechists Simón, Leonel, and Humberto, who over the years I keep encountering in the larger skeins of struggles for planetary survival. Maudilia also introduced me to Carlos Loarca, the lawyer who helped win the IAHRC case, and to people at ADISMI, including Javier de León, Aniseto Lopez, and Carmen Mejia, and at CPO and to community members in Sipakapa, Agel, and San José Ixcaniché. I am grateful to her and to all of them.

Luis Solano also vouched for me with Vinicio Lopez, at COPAE in San Marcos, who, after our first long interview, introduced me to Johanna van Strien, and Teresa Fuentes, who that very evening took me under their wings, feeding and orienting me, as they continue to do. They have connected me to people at other organizing nodes, like CATAPA and Madre Selva, where Pepe Cruz, and, at La Cuerda, Ana Cofiño, have connected me to ways of understanding Guatemala's past and present and to nodes (as in La Puya and the Zona Reyna) for creating a sustainable and feminist future. I am also indebted to the research and activism of NISGUA, the Guatemalan Human Rights Commission, and International Rivers.

When I dropped by his office in Chimaltenango on a trip back from San Marcos, Domingo Hernández Ixcoy said if I was interested in the consultas, I had to talk to Lolita Chavez. I thank him (for this and so much more) and Lolita for all her time and storytelling and for in turn introducing me to the woman I call Fidelia, without whom I would be even more in the dark regarding the magical powers of El Millionario. I also want to thank the by now thousands of people who have shared a word with me and contributed to this book. They count, even if not by name.

Claude Lévi-Strauss suggests there's a mutilation inherent in our anthropological vocation, in the difficult spanning of our double worlds, caught between field and home, embodied knowledge gathering and the violent abstraction of transforming it into text. It's a responsibility/burden/sacrifice/honor. Yet both endeavors depend on relations of one to many, bigger than the sum of their parts, perhaps a "Kindness of Interlocutors." Bill Maurer started this particular derive by handing me Poovey's book, and S. Lochlann Jain and Jake Kosek created Oxidate, without which, quite literally, this book would never have been written. Thanks to them and Jackie Orr, Joe Masco, Joe Dumit, Michelle Murphy, Cori Hayden, Miriam Ticktin, Liz Roberts, and Jonathan Metzl. Ron Eglash has been a seriously committed tour guide through the politics of math. Jane Guyer, Naveeda Khan, and Juan Obarrio organized the workshop on Number as Inventive Frontier that encouraged this then barely formulated project. Robin Kirk has helped me think about Number and Human Rights, including introducing me to Patrick Ball, who I had also admired from afar. I have also been fortunate to receive feedback, encouragement, and countless gifts from Wahneema Lubiano, Randy Martin, Carlota McAllister, Deborah Levenson, Arturo Escobar, Paul Kobrak, Brynton Lykes, Peter Cahn, Stefan Helmreich, Heather Paxson, Peter Redfield, Katherine Fultz, Sara Martínez Juan, Donald Moore, Lisa Davis, Tim Smith, Pat Goudvis, John Jackson, Deborah Thomas, Elyse Crystal, Karen Booth, Jenny Reardon, Rebecca Herzig, Marcelo Fernández Osco, Marcial Godoy-Anatívia, Anne-Maria Makhulu, Alison Crosby, Ranji

Khanna, Scott Mobley, Jon Hunt, Priscilla Wald, Neta Bar, Stephanie Friede, Megan Ybarra, Ajantha Subramanian, Silvia Tomaskova, Nora England, Emilio del Valle Escalante, Orin Starn, Brad Weiss, Howie Machtinger, Trude Bennett, Michal Osterwald, Warwick Anderson, Helen Verran, Sonya Solano, Emily Adams, Ann Ragland, Rachel Seidman, and Kathryn Williams. Paul and Sommer Sobin made the endurance sitting possible and the graciousness of the world tangible. Along the way I have been profoundly inspired by the Occupies (especially OCHC), Moral Mondays and the profound courage of Claudia Paz y Paz, Yassmin Barrios Aguilar, Bradley/Chelsea Manning, and Edward Snowden.

I also thank Srinivas Aravamudan for, among other things, the Brazilian joke, Arianne Dorval for The Prisoner, Ann Ragland for the Andaman Islanders, Laura Robinson for The Onion, Marcial Godoy for Lagos, Lochlann Jain for Cabinet, Joe Dumit for exponentials, Brian Dinkeldine for The Secret Agent, Netta van Vliet for visits to the West Bank and decades of thinking/ sharing, Brian Smithson, Christina Tekie, and Louis Yako for research assistance, Attiya Ahmad for explorations of conversion, and Mark Driscoll for tarot lessons and other philosophical, philological, and ecological support. Bookapalooza with Cori Hayden, Joe Dumit, and Donald Moore got this closer to adequate. Thanks, too, to Jackie Orr, Michelle Murphy, Rachel Lee, Rob Latham, China Mieville, Marcial Godoy-Anativía and the Hemispheric Institute, Harris Solomon, Tomas Matza, Tal Nitsan, Todd Little-Siebold, Tom Offit, and the Guatemala Scholars Network for opportunities to think via conferences and publications. Thanks to students in Durham and Bogotá who took "The Anthropology of Numbers" and to panel and audience members at several anthropology and science studies meetings, as well as my hosts and interlocutors at UC-Berkeley, University of Chicago, Brown, Rutgers, University of British Columbia, UT-Austin, University of Toronto, and the University of Bergen.

Although I was not a fellow, I enjoyed and greatly benefited from the intellectual infrastructure of the Institute for Advanced Studies, with special thanks to Nicola Di Cosmo, Didier Fassin, Joan Scott, Heinrich von Staden, and members David Eng, Chen Peng Yeang, Yannis Hamilakis, and Jens Meierhenrich.

Although the golden rule of bookkeeping is to get to the zero balance, I know this book will never be adequate to all I've received. I also regret I couldn't elaborate on the many routes suggested by readers and listeners, especially Ted Fischer and Gaston Gordillo (who I also thank for asking about 22). All translations and errors are mine.

Fieldwork was funded by Mellon Title VI funds through Duke University Latin American and Caribbean Studies, thanks to Natalie Hartman, and Duke University research funds, thanks to Tracy Carhart, Pamala Terterian, and Pat Bodager for logistical (and other!) support.

Ken Wissoker, again, has been both gentle and formidable as my editor, and Carol Hendrickson and Larry Grossberg made rigorous, suggestive, and inspirational investments in this book. Thanks to Jade Brooks and the Duke Press publication team, especially Sara Leone for extraordinary grace under pressure and Natalie F. Smith, and to the wonderful artists who have lent me their work: Geoffrey Ryman, Tim Stallman and Liz Mason-Dees, Dan Piraro, David Rees, Stephanie McMillan, Daniel Hernández-Salazar, James Rodríguez, Mark van Stone, Pat Goudvis, Allan Lissner, Isabel Ruíz, and Matthew Looper.

Finally, I want to thank my family, Nelson, Vergara, Townsend, Driscoll (especially Quinn), and Solano Worby; to welcome the newest members, Ben and Lucas; and to bid farewell to Gene. And finally (and firstly) thank the one who counted most, Mark Driscoll. 谢谢 for 10,000 things—being *cien por ciento*, you complete the figure.

1 Before and After-Math

The pretense that numbers are not the humble creation of man, but are the exacting language of the Universe and therefore possess the secret of all things is comforting, terrifying, and mesmerizing. . . . Counting is the most simple and primitive of narratives—12345678910—a tale with a beginning, a middle, and an end and a sense of progression—arriving at a finish of two digits—a goal attained, a denouement reached.

—Peter Greenaway

It's Very Complicated

"It's very complicated. All the numbers!" Encarnación and I were sitting in the kitchen by her improved wood-burning stove, the sunlight slanting in through the board walls, catching in the smoky air. Our kitchen talks are always full of laughter and a lot of hand waving since her Spanish is not very strong and my K'iche' is pretty nonexistent. But these words were very clear. We were talking about a small packet of powder sitting on the table. An Omnilife dietary supplement, she was taking it like a medicine to help recover from a recent operation, but she also hoped to sell packets like it to her neighbors. "All the numbers," referred to the ones Santos had mastered, the multiple accounting systems through which one (hopefully) made some money but also collected points to win prizes and kept track of the networks of fellow buyers and sellers. Encarnación's son, Juan, was in the United

States somewhere (she wasn't quite sure), so she was also keeping track of his remittances, the cell phone minutes left for their monthly calls, the accruing interest on the loan they'd taken to get him across the border, and their attempts to save money for a new kitchen. It was just Encarnación, Juan, and her two daughters, because her husband was a war victim, murdered in the early 1980s.

The Guatemalan civil war officially ended almost twenty years ago with the 1996 peace treaty, but the UN CEH report was not issued until 1999, and UN peacekeepers did not withdraw until 2005. People get on with their lives but the war lingers. Encarnación lives in a tiny hamlet of the municipality of Joyabaj, which did not "count" in the UN report because people were too afraid to sign their names. The report did qualify the quantities of dead and disappeared as genocide based in four cases, including Zacualpa, Joyabaj's neighbor.[1] Encarnación has struggled to have her personal loss count, as an active member in CONAVIGUA, the Mayan widows' group. They have exerted decades of pressure to make the state acknowledge its role and pay reparations, and when they succeeded, Encarnación petitioned the national program. She had not, at the time of my visit, received any money.

"Who counts?" is both a mundane and a cosmopolitical query. Mundane because apparently so basic. 1, 2, 3, as easy as ABC, as simple as do re mi. Elementary, the building blocks of semiotic systems. Yet in a world organized around the Kantian universal subject of rationality and abstraction, the sense that women, natives, and "Third World" peoples more generally can't count has contributed to their historic exclusion and dehumanization. Via the processes I limned in chapter 0, math—as stand-in for science, calculation, development, even modernity itself—becomes a raced, classed, gendered, and postcolonial attribute, "belonging" properly only to some people. Cosmopolitically, quantification—the ability to abstract a number from the mess of reality—undergirds the workings of the "general equivalent," or money, rooting, some might say, all evil in its ability to transform human labor into a commodity.

Second, "Who counts?" asks who is doing the counting? And for what? The state counts votes, gross national product, epidemiological populations, and people in order to transform them into taxpayers, soldiers, and beneficiaries, as well as citizens and "aliens." The market counts, constantly calculating risk, benefit, value—and profit. Human rights activists count the dead, environmentalists count toxin loads to show the "external costs" of a gold mine, feminists, antiracists and LGBTQI activists use counting to illuminate systemic inequalities and disproportionate burdens, and workers and their advocates count to reveal hidden profits and costs in search of "accountability" (exactly what Englishman William Petty sought to deny the Irish). In these ways "to count" means to calculate, but it also means to have value, to matter.

In the aftermath of civil war (1960–96), genocide (1980–83), the postwar development boom (peaking around 2005), and the recent, ongoing economic crash (2008–now), "counting" in Guatemala entails complex calculations encompassing war losses, migration, investment, debt, traditional culture, and understandings of progress, as people quantify, qualify, and measure possibilities for the future. The revolutionary movement came close but did not succeed in dislodging the small, white, violent elite and redistributing its land and wealth. And inequality is intensifying, through accumulation processes variously dubbed neoliberalism, financialization, the great vampire squid, and the new class war. As international trade agreements transform the unseen but deeply felt landscapes of subsidies and prices, the money spent and money earned from cultivating the land get increasingly out of whack. Semisubsistence farming gets harder and harder to sustain, even as people work just as hard or harder. With little in the way of formal waged work, the struggle to earn a living—to achieve adequate nutrition, schooling, health care—follows any path people can conjure. Selling what you can, maybe getting a kid to the States, learning to entice an NGO to favor your project (though they are prone to flight), pinning hopes on a development opportunity, even if it means mortgaging your house for the down payment or losing an entire mountain to a gold mine. People engage in constant calculation, struggling to understand potentials, rumors, a "crash," a "meltdown," what it means to have other people's crises wash up on your hinterland shore, dislocating all sorts of best-laid plans. Out of sight yet affecting every pathway of human connectivity, the mysterious workings of the derivatives' algorithms sum up minute extractions made from subprime loans and liquidating calculations. The familiar surplus mining of workers paid less for a day than minimum wage for an hour in the United States conjoins in the (semi)consensual hallucinations of the stock market in crisis times to (sometimes) make gold worth up to $2000 an ounce. Investments in ruinous resource extraction, megaprojects, and ecocidal monocropped biofuels become thinkable, then "inevitable." The struggles for reparations and accountability, the deployment of and contestations over number and counting and profit, are all attempts to process and calculate and balance out somehow. These calculations encompass the quotidian carnal demands for sustenance and the existential engagement with the night of the world. They are after-math.

"It's very complicated. All the numbers."

Numbers Themselves

> If human rights groups want to up their credibility, they MUST begin to ground their analyses in the realities of the situation, particularly numbers. . . . What they present now is like academic theory which attempts to impose itself on data.
> —Thomas Marks, US special forces counterinsurgency expert

Numbers—and counting, math, money, finance, and accounting—are, in Helen Verran's terms, "inhabiting and inhabited by" people in Guatemala in this hard-to-name period after the "postwar." To "ground" my analysis "in the realities of the situation" (Marks, in Tate 2007, 15) here are five:

200,000—war dead and disappeared

93%—war violence attributed to the state

83%—indigenous victims to all war dead

3.8%—total income earned by the poorest 20% of the population (PNUD 2011)

40–75%—estimated Mayan population (Tzian 2009)

Troubling the usual argument about the dehumanizing effect of numbers, the first three (from the 1999 UN "truth commission" CEH report) suggest their oppositional leveraging in struggles for representational hegemony, giving quantifiable weight to the loss of human life (and its ethnic qualities) and political response-ability for those crimes. Activist statisticians Herbert Spirer and William Seltzer say, "'How many?' is often the first question asked when dealing with evidence of genocide, crimes against humanity, or war crimes," and they show how counting can prove there was an "intent to destroy, in whole or in part" or "widespread and systematic attack," as required by international law (2008, 200). Similarly, the poverty indexed by 3.8% of income earned by 20% reveals a situation deeply inadequate to the survival needs of a fifth of Guatemala's population. This links to the unclear percentage of Maya, in that five hundred years of racist exclusion both made genocide possible and is internalized, making many unwilling to identify as indigenous because it is poor and "backward," unacceptable at the Camino Real hotel.

In war's after-math activists and scientists struggle with and for these numbers. Some by insisting the state pay them back, through "development," and through reparations (although the "monetization" of justice makes many uneasy). Others by encouraging Mayan pride and the desire to survive *as* Maya, so more will count in the next census—with the corollary that if more are counted, they'll count more—in political representation, government attention, and the like. Mayan math—the fact that their ancestors *did* count, often more precisely than "modern people"—has been an important tool in these endeavors.

I share Mr. Marks's faith in numbers' credibility, but I'd like to tarry for a moment with the census and some complications of number. First, quantification is usually more complex than simply tallying, and the war has made it more so. The ladino mayor of Joyabaj complained that "the National Statistics Institute (INE) comes here to do a poll but their workers have no *conciencia* (understanding), and don't have a *forma de pedir* (don't know how to ask). Joyabaj was heavily affected in the armed conflict. Those feelings are still alive here. If you give your name to an outsider people are afraid they will come back later and kill you. 'Why are you making lists?' they wonder. This means there is no clear information. Our population numbers are too low, so they don't send us enough money. There's an imbalance between the real population and the statistics of the INE. They say 6,600 but I know there are over 10,000." Then he added, "There are also many thieves, so people don't want to talk, they don't want anyone to know what they have."[2]

Quantifying qualities gets even stickier (Hayden 2007). It is standard to say Guatemala is a majority indigenous country with nonindigenous people (often called ladinos or mestizos) about 40% (or 70% or 25%). There are twenty-two Mayan ethnolinguistic groups and several non-Mayan indigenous populations. Within each group, local identity can be quite strong. The use of the word "Maya" to reference a pan-indigenous identification is relatively recent and an effect of the postgenocide revitalization efforts I'm calling Mayan Organizing 1.0 (which builds off but is different from organized indigenous resistance dating from the Spanish arrival in the 1520s). So "indigenous" or "Maya" as a "population" is already an aggregate of complex categorizations.

40 to 75%? Even a brief stay in Guatemala is enough to astound the visitor with the distinctive colorful traje (clothing), different languages,

and—many believe—phenotypic markings that identify indigenous people (and many visit precisely because of this alluring difference). It would seem simple to just count them, divide that amount by the total population, and multiply by 100 to get an accurate percentage—as opposed to this deeply imprecise thirty-five-point spread. Counting, of course (as an engine, not a camera), is not quite so simple, especially for something as complexly qualitative as identification within a raciologized colonial order (nor is accuracy; see Mackenzie 1993). Mayan economist Leopoldo Tzian insists that it is precisely "WHO is counting" (and how) that produces such different numbers for the "same thing." He says that to get "real numbers" that would be more truthful than the "official statistics" (2009, 17) entails attending to all the ways the Maya are actively "invisibilized"; that is, how national integration favors "ladinization" (59), how census takers may feel they do people "a favor" by counting them as ladino (57), how being educated, speaking Spanish, using Western clothes, or having a Spanish surname makes one "count" as ladino, regardless of self-identification, and how being objects of "oppression, discrimination, and exclusion" causes disidentification as indigenous, especially when asked by a ladino (49). Demetrio Cojtí Cuxil calls the constantly decreasing official numbers "statistical genocide" (1991), and Tzian emphasizes the politics of counting: "Unequal relations between Peoples becoming more equal will aid in a better register of cultural diversity in national population censuses" (72).

But that "better register" still confronts the question of what is being counted and where to draw the line. "Counting is hungry for categories" (Hacking, in Muellman 2012, 345), but those categories may exist only once the counting is achieved and may in turn produce both equivalence and violent exclusions. Censuses have the peculiar power to turn previously neighborly folks into opposing, even murderous, "ethnicities."[3]

Returning to 22, as in the number of Mayan ethnolinguistic groups casually referenced above, suggests that even when Maya count Maya, it's still fraught. Twenty-two isn't a tally, it's an achievement—in two senses. First, that so many languages are still "alive" (in part due to fierce commitment but also to limited schooling, especially of girls). And because it's a number people fought to "get." Until 2000 there were only 21. I use Joe Dumit's (2012) term for staking a claim to illnesses that lack a clear etiology to mark the labors of taking something so continuous or rhizomatic (Muellman 2012) as vocabulary, grammatical expression, or verb conjugation over swathes of territory, via women from one place raising children patrilocally in another, and through war, mixing, and multilingualism and transforming it into something discrete enough to count. Jacqueline Urla says for Euskara (Basque), "counting implies the divisibility of populations into discrete categories and creates the sense of equivalency of entities within a category" (2012, 114). In the wake of the peace accords, the Guatemalan Mayan Language Academy (ALMG) prepared a formalized script for Awakateko, spoken in Aguacatán, Huehuetenango. Suddenly, people who inhabit the same territory but consider themselves Chalchitekos realized they were not discrete or equivalent. Classified as a dialect rather than a language, they didn't count. So they counted themselves, claiming to number 25,000 against the 10,000 Awakatekos, and counted their grievances, including exclusion from decision making, development funding, and "the name" (of the town and the language)—despite being the majority—and began to agitate for linguistic recognition and local power (Fink 2003, 190–92). In the process they became a "political affinity group" in addition to "a linguistic community" (Urla 2012, xi) mimicking, at a different scale, the Mayan aggregate seeking equality within the larger national collectivity. Dis-counted as "one," they did some division and came to count as the twenty-second. Urla says, "quantification does double duty." It provides incontrovertible evidence of the legacy of repression (here, of one indigenous group against another) and brings into being the linguistic community as a population that is knowable, trackable, and in need (2012, 125).

To make equivalent is a political goal and a mathematical operation (how do you make $3 = 5$? Add 2). To make every human life ontologically equivalent, subject to equal protection and enjoying equal rights, has been the forceful demand of several centuries of human, feminist, and civil rights struggles. Yet most activists do not want equal to mean the same. Chalchiteko $\neq$ Awakateko. Maya $\neq$ Ladino. Woman $\neq$ Man.

Throughout this book we'll encounter similar tensions in many of our engagements with number and its operations—with equivalence and the connected concept of "adequacy" particularly unsettling. Is $3,200 an adequate equivalent to a murdered person? Is $780,000? Are 4,000 quetzales adequate for a piece of land if that's above "market price"?[4] Is a 15% interest rate compounded monthly adequate recompense for the risk of loaning money? Can a book be adequate with a world that's so "complicated!"?

To adequately understand Guatemala after genocide, I emphasize ethnicity as an organizing principle and racism as a central axis of national life

(Casaus Arzu 1992; CEH 1999; Hale 2006). But as Tzian suggests with the difficulties of counting Maya, it's not always so easy to distinguish indigenous from ladino. Plus, treating each as a homogeneous aggregate denies how they disaggregate not only through linguistic but also gender and class inequalities, colorism, political engagements, and rural, urban, and transnational identifications. Without a US-style "one drop rule," "ladinization" may occur by decree or by "choice." When the CEH qualified the vast quantities of war dead as genocide, it made a decisive intervention because international law denies amnesty to such crimes against humanity. The genocide ruling also countered a long-standing national assumption that just as indigenous labor didn't need to be paid, indigenous deaths wouldn't count (Vela 2013). In some cases, however, the ruling has had the unintended consequence of dichotomizing: Maya as victims, non-Maya as perpetrators (Oglesby and Ross 2009; Nelson 2009). This fits nicely with transnational assumptions about romantic noble savages and Euro-American tendencies (in anthropology as much as tourism and new age spiritualism) to self-constitute as noble by taking the (exotic) victim's side (Gonzalez Ponciano 2013).

My own work, beginning in 1985, grows from and participates in these postcolonial savoirs as self-making and as modes of unawareness and sanctioned ignorance. In previous writing I addressed military counterinsurgency, human rights, revolutionary struggles and their shared sacrifices, the Guatemalan state and ongoing imperialism, ladino subject formation as well as indigenous and Mayan (not always the same thing), and the perturbing valences of gender and sexuality within and between them, all from my situatedness as a gringa (a white, middle-class US citizen in relation to Latin America). Tracing complex articulations of identifications and politics, I've tried to represent Guatemala as an analog assemblage, not a digital divide. Trying to think various scales together, however, I have forfeited local intensity, including learning a Mayan language. Trying not to "miss the revolution" (Starn 1991; Manz 1988) while bedazzled with ethnostalgic fascinations which I, along with many ladino and indigenous cadre, feared were apolitical, I have not developed adequate skills in reading rituals and glyphs or counting days. But lately my friends have pulled me along to focus on numbers, which I'm learning are both traditional *and* political. I've come to realize numbers and counting may help us see an emerging form of the Guatemala to come, a symptom and a dream of planetary processes.

To Count, Figure Up

reckoning *vt* [OE *recenian* akin to count < IE base **reg-*, to direct, when RIGHT L. *regere*, to rule] 1). the act of one who reckons (to count, figure up) 2). a measuring of possibilities for the future; 3). *a)* a bill, account *b)* the settlement of rewards or penalties for any action.

—*Webster's New World Dictionary, Second College Edition*

I thought my last book was about the war-wrought subjectivity effects of clandestinity, state terror, and duplicity in Guatemala but finally realized it was about reckoning—in the cosmopolitical sense of settling rewards and penalties for genocide and its relation to numbers and the acts of one (and many) who count. *Who Counts?* is my attempt to do justice to number and the many ways people are calculating, qualifying, and measuring possibilities for the future. I am thoroughly convinced of numbers' power. Yet I chose "I Can't Do the Sum" (Herbert and MacDonough 1903) as my epigraph partly because I identify as math-challenged, ending my formal training in high school and still counting on my fingers—or "digital computer," as I joke when I get caught.[5] Yet in the process I have learned, from Guatemalan friends and from mathematicians and anthropologists, to take the math seriously and try to understand the magic it can do while not fetishizing the quantitative.

Number plays an important role in "adequation," as Bill Maurer suggests, from the Latin phrase *adequatio intellectus et res*, meaning "the action of bringing one's concepts into accord with reality" (2005, xiii) or "the bringing-into-relation of words and things" (11). Number promises unbiased objectivity—why Mr. Marks, the counterinsurgency expert, trusts them—yet numbers also have the peculiar power to make "the invisible visible" (Devlin 2000). Patrick Ball, a mathematician who worked for the UN truth commission said that for many places (like Joyabaj), "because of the situation, we couldn't get anyone to thumbprint [thumb because so many people are illiterate] the figures so we couldn't use those testimonials. We put our fingers to the wind to get the rest—about 18,000." By "fingers to the wind" he meant the work that mathematics can do in the absence of "hard" numbers. "The statistical estimate [can] go beyond the known. People who are missing have a right to existence. . . . They are not phantoms. They were there and those traces in the social memory can be captured in statistics." One of the etymological roots of the word "mathematics" is *mendh-*, meaning "to learn, to pay attention to, be alert, whence Av. *mazda*, memory."

So I'll resist the idea that numbers (and the apotheosis of their abstraction into money) are simply cold, hard, and depersonalizing and suggest instead they are more like Heidegger's "unconcealment" (*aletheia*), or becoming. In the right hands—like this statistician's—they become almost magical, like Lyra's aletheiometer, or golden compass, in Philip Pullman's Dark Materials books (Pullman 1995). In pondering the idea that "knowledge of truth comes from the *adequation* of thought to world," Maurer echoes the *Babes in Toyland* song: "Value, substance, and standardization involve a series of abstractions from a supposedly prior, messy reality, and abstraction begs the question of money's *adequacy* to that reality" (2005, xiii; emphasis added). Yet he also insists on "the pleasure and terror of wonder itself—the excitement of an encounter with the uncanny, and the thrill that comes from the manner in which the "truth" is revealed. . . . In a world dominated by strikingly uniform globalization slogans that proclaim there are no alternatives to neoliberalism, financial integration, or capital mobility, it is important to insist on the experiential metaphysics of this thrill of wonder . . . especially . . . in light of the scholarship on money and commodification that readily accepts quantification's desacralizing and homogenizing claims and looks elsewhere, but never at the mathematics, to find hope" (2005, 120). He cites Peter Winch on the danger that "concepts settle for us the form of the experience we have of the world," yet Maurer finds profoundly *unsettling* cases when he looks at efforts to produce alternative financial forms (11; emphasis in original). "The other side of the sublime is slime—the messiness of desublimation necessary to create the seemingly pure forms of monetary equivalence and the seemingly pure distinctions between gift and commodity, sacred and profane, that animate whole monetary, mathematical, and market worlds" (120).[6] Ron Eglash (2009) champions a similar "oppositional technophilia" and says, "Just as Derrida says text is not inherently alienating, or only valuable in the occasional case that it has instrumental roles, but rather is tapping into what it means to be human at some fundamental level, so too mathematics. We think this of text because we are taught that text is creative, and we don't think it of math because we are taught that there is only one right answer. But that is an artifact of pedagogy, not ontology" (personal communication, 2014).

In the name of "alternate pedagogies" I here turn to the *baile de la culebra*, or dance of the serpent, a "traditional" dance performed by Maya-K'iche' men in Joyabaj, usually alongside the dance of the conquest (discussed earlier). It enacts, among other things, the yearly rituals of being contracted to work in the lowland sugarcane harvest. The man playing a labor contractor and moneylender bends a dancer over to use his back as a table so he can mark names in a ledger book and how much the men owe (actions I've witnessed thanks to Liz Oglesby, who writes about debt, labor migration, and sugar and who first took me to Joyabaj). As the dance progresses the contractor gets his comeuppance in various ways: the names the men give him are false, jokes that cleverly hide insults and sexualized double entendres; his wife (played by a man in drag) is shown dallying with the "shaman" who works for him; and the workers (*mozos*) finally revolt. As the master sleeps they insert a (live and poisonous) snake under his clothes, and after much struggle (and hilarity in the audience) he dies and the workers rejoice. Their joy is short lived, however, as the shaman brings him back to life and the cycle continues. In the dance, unlike real life, the revolt is not followed by a massacre.

The dance contemplates abstraction. In that moment of the book balanced on the back, as the dancers mimic real life, they enact the move from the body into a sign, from lived experience into neat columns of numbers. Illness, hunger, the desire to get drunk, the need for fertilizer for a too small patch of corn, for medicine for a sick child, strong young men's hopes for a nest egg and to prove themselves (especially those who can't afford to go north), even accumulating the money needed for the dance itself to occur, all are translated into quantities of borrowed money, duly annotated. Then weeks or months of sweat, effort, exhaustion, heat, endurance, the rawness of machete-worn hands, the materiality of cutting cane on a mosquito-infested coast, the risk of kidney failure from dehydration and chemical exposure, even the satisfaction of passing quota, are transformed. Some becomes coin or paper money but much of it stays virtual, bypassing the workers' hands and going directly from the plantations to the contractors or paying off debts accumulated while working. Yet all of it is recorded and balanced in the ledger book (in real life now fully computerized), whose language is number (Oglesby 2013).

The dance enacts the simultaneously everyday relations between workers and owners *and* their deadly antagonism and magical excess. Serpents and necromancy accompany the two faces of capitalist accumulation, both the rule-bound transactions between capitalist and laborer that organize factories and agricultural estates and the rapacious and brutal "accumulation by dispossession" between capitalist and noncapitalist modes of production mediated via colonial policy, the international loan system, and war

1.1 Three young male cane cutters in front of a burned sugarcane field. Daniel Hernández-Salazar, 2000. Used with kind permission.

(Luxemburg 1951). Further on we'll hear several more stories about snakes, those nonhuman actants, in relation to money, temporality, struggles with the sacred, death, and life. The ledger is also a nonhuman actant embedded in and enlivening similar relations, a technology that connects indigenous people to translocal power and to systems with a global and transhistoric sweep. While the *baile de la culebra* is also a fertility ritual, with whole segments going on behind closed doors, and carries a mix of preinvasion and Christian resurrection motifs, it also explicitly enacts the "modern" world of market relations, wage labor, credit and debit, and contract.

This is the world in which indigenous men and women (and poor ladinos, too) are, as Gayatri Spivak suggests, subjects predicated as "super-adequation in labor-power (defined by its capacity to produce more than itself)" (1987, 157). "Super-adequation" means that what defines them, at least to the contractor and his bosses and their investors, to those who hedge and disburse and skim commissions off these investments, and to those who in turn profit from the financial forms derived therefrom—this entire pyramid of extraction balancing on the boy cutting cane and the woman making tortillas to feed him—is their ability to produce a surplus that can be abstracted and extracted.

This book explores that quotidian world and its "revolting" aspects, including the aftermath of civil war, through the fraught relation between number and people—as embodied and abstracted, as singular and as aggregates (workers, indigenous, women, men), as simultaneously inadequate and superadequate, and as counting (or not). Guided by the ledger book I contemplate the *work* of number and, following Geoffrey Ryman's *Third* (see the preface), the *pleasures* of number as well. Number and the zero balance in double-entry bookkeeping may stand for truth (uninterested, empirical, neutral) but also for justice, virtue, and transparency. "To count" means "to calculate," "to name numbers or add up items in order" *and* "to be taken into account; have importance, value." Number, the very "thing" that doubles over the dancers, is also essential to struggles for justice and survival.

This is not a revolutionary moment in Guatemala. Indigenous people were massively mobilized in the 1970s as part of a broad social movement, some of it armed, aimed at transforming landholding, labor relations and racialized oppression of the indigenous majority. To return to the numbers, the mass murder and dislocation carried out by the state—calculated by the CEH at 200,000 dead, over 400 villages erased, 626 massacres, with 93% of the abuses carried out by a succession of military governments—brutally smashed these utopian hopes. My first involvement with Guatemala was helping document these violations, and then I followed the early 1990s rise of the Mayan movement for cultural revitalization (see also Bastos and Camus 1993, 1995, 2003; Bastos and Cumes 2007; Cojtí Cuxil 1994, 1995). This was also the period of a return to nominally civilian rule, leading to negotiations to end the war and the beginning of postwar "peace processing."

The Mayan movement (1.0) struggled on many terrains, including language (standardizing orthography across languages and making "Maya" the politically correct term to use); education (curricular changes to acknowledge indigenous people as well as state support for bilingual teaching); increased representation in state institutions and state funding for Maya-controlled projects; gains in human and civil rights, including postwar reparations and acknowledgment that the violence of the early 1980s *was* genocide; the creation of antidiscrimination policies, often through high-profile lawsuits;

and the more subtle labors of encouraging Mayan pride and the desire to survive *as* Maya. This book explores the aftermath of those efforts through Mayan Organizing 2.0.[7] Via what formations, understandings of self, and engagement with emerging global structures are people identifying, collectivizing, and politicking now?

Understanding

qualification (*quails*, of what kind (akin to *qui* who) + *facere* to make; see FACT) 1. Being qualified 2. A modification or restriction; limiting condition 3. Any quality, skill, knowledge, experience, etc. that fits a person for a position, office, profession; requisite 4. A condition that must be met in order to exercise certain rights 5. Moderation or softening (to qualify a punishment) 6. to describe by giving the qualities or characteristics of.

It was late afternoon in August 2010, and the repurposed Bluebird school bus had been flying around the hairpin turns of the two-lane highway from San Marcos to Quetzaltenango, sending the riders sliding against each other, half sharing little smiles at the forced intimacy. Then it pulled to a sudden stop. The line of cars and trucks in front of us looked ominous. Was it an accident? No, word passed along the aisle, a rainy season landslide, the machinery was on its way. . . . As twilight fell and everyone settled in to wait, I struck up a conversation with the man beside me. I'd chosen the seat because he had a shoulder bag from a conference sponsored by the Mayan Languages Academy (ALMG—central actors in Mayan Organizing 1.0), but the bus's grinding gears and my own exhaustion had kept me from starting a chat. In the darkening quiet, though, we talked about his work as a teacher and (what are the odds?!) his passionate autodidactic work with Mayan numbers.

Saturnino is Maya-Mam and grew up in Comitancillo, in the far western department of San Marcos, where in the 1970s a Catholic priest had set up a rigorous school for indigenous kids. ("He was so conservative! So right wing!" said my friend Maudilia, a nun also from Comitancillo. "But it was a very good school.") Saturnino had also worked, as had many of the founders of the ALMG, with the evangelical Wycliffe Bible translators, learning some basic linguistics, and he said that's when he became interested in Mayan math. "I didn't know anything about it and neither did our teachers, so I began asking some of the *guías espirituales*, trying to find people who knew the calendar." Given his connections to mainline Catholicism and conservative Protestant Christianity, this was a difficult, even dangerous project, as horologists and spiritual guides were much denigrated as henchmen of the devil.[8] Catholic Action, the Church's modernizing wing, had been energized in the 1950s as priests ejected from Mao's China flooded Latin America to purge it of pagan atavisms. In Guatemala this movement swerved through Liberation Theology to become the backbone of the popular movement, but the early divide between "pure" Catholics and *costumbristas* remained mostly unbridged during the war. While the army murdered thousands of Mayan traditionalists, understanding them to be pillars of community solidarity, many of them—having experienced Catholic Action as an existential threat—also collaborated in counterinsurgency massacres and policing their neighbors. The "difficult complementarity" that now stunts collaborations between Mayan culture revitalists and the politicized Maya who survived the genocide is rooted in these assemblages (Bastos and Camus 2013; McAllister 2013).

Saturnino got a scholarship to study in the capital while working full time in the state's bilingual education department and also writing for a regional newspaper on indigenous issues. "No one seemed interested in Mayan numbers, and we never got any money to study or publish our findings. So on my own I began to study, trying to learn the fundamentals. I began to realize that numbers are connected to daily life, to the human body, twenty fingers and toes, twenty days in the calendar, *winquan*." He later said, "It's a unity, the twenty. It's very hard, calculating, *me cuesta*. It's not marked because it's not two, it's one." By this he meant that calculating in base 20 (like the Classic Maya) is a challenge for those raised in a base-10 system. Arabic numbers have ten digits (0–9) and you need two digits for 10, three for 100 (10 × 10), etc. Mayan numbers have three digits, a dot for 1, a bar for 5, and a variable symbol for 0. Six would be a bar with a dot next to it, 19 is three bars and four dots. Higher numbers use positional base-20 notation, so in markings for addition, 20 would be "one" unit (not two as in base 10). Like Saturnino, this totally stumped me in the glyph-reading class when we calculated the cycles of Venus from the Dresden codex. Similarly, for us, base-10 time (decades, centuries, millennia) is important (even when it's not accurate—didn't "the '60s" really start in 1967?), while in the Maya ritual calendar, periods of 20 days and 13 months, the k'atun (about 20 years, or 7,200 days) and the b'aqtun (20 k'atuns, or 144,000 days) matter.

Saturnino went on, "I learned how they are connected, integrated. I talked to my father, my *abuelos*, the *ancianos*. I did research, in between all my other work. It wasn't till much later that I realized it was all part of a larger project, what my father said are *pilares de la cultura*, cultural foundations. Numbers are a part of this but also the seeking itself; it opened me to these ways of being, of understanding." By now it was quite dark and the bus was quiet; a few people murmuring here and there, interrupted by updates on the progress of the earthmoving machines.

Barbara Tedlock, an anthropologist who initiated as an *ajq'ij* (daykeeper) in the nearby K'iche' town of Momostenango in the mid-1970s, describes how she came to grasp the concept of understanding, or *cho'bonik*. Counting the days is never "just" a count. It is done for a reason: to understand a petitioner's question, to make meaning of misfortune, to find an auspicious time for an event, to determine the appropriate actions in a certain situation. It attends to the personality of each day and of its numbers (e.g., Don Cristobal, the *ajq'ij* from Tecpán, told me, "Odd numbers are *rebelde*")[9] *and* the day's embedding in the interlocked cycles of years: the *tzolk'in*, or sacred round, the 260-day year of 13 day numbers and 20 day names, and the 365-day calendar known as the Vague Year (made up of 18 named months of 20 days each with a residual 5 days, the *Uayeb*, when the world is "out of whack," as special precautions must be taken and special pleasures may be indulged). Each year is also inflected with the personality of the *Mam*, or the year bearer, and each period by the identity of the day that begins each new 52-year cycle (Tedlock 1992, 89–131).[10] In addition to all these accreted meanings, the *ajq'ij* acknowledges the day and date of the petitioner's birth, which brings added layers to any question. For example, my birthday is *aqabal*, which signifies "night house" or temporal liminality, like dawn and dusk. Other day names signify animals (*k'an* is "snake," *tzikin*, "dog") or a phenomenon like wind (*ik'*). A trained *ajq'ij* also has access to his or her own bodily understandings, called "blood lightning"—movements deep inside the flesh that respond to the question and the count. Tedlock's lengthy initiation emphasized the embodi/meant and *practice*—the kinetics—of counting the days rather than just mindful understanding of them.

Saturnino repeated: "What I was trying to understand—the numbers—was connected to how I had to work to understand them. That's why my father said I was getting at the foundations of our culture." He held up his hand in the near dark to enumerate: "these are

First, Vision—where do you want to go and what will you do?

Second, Listen to the elders—have respect, that is how you become successful.

Third, Discern—accept counsel but you have to decide yourself.

Fourth—know how to work with wisdom.

You see, numbers are also about understanding the world around you, the question of the stars, for example. How they move, the phases of the moon. The songs of the animals. Numbers are symbols, part of what is sacred. The calendar, time, how it moves. We need to find people who are well identified with this, who understand the reasons, the philosophy, that this is from the whole culture of the people, not just a thing to learn. Now I take every opportunity I get, on the bus, in the street, everywhere and anywhere to talk about these issues. When I work with teachers, giving talks, in the new *diplomados* (short courses) we've developed, I have to explain the philosophy, the *razón* of numbers. They say "we have a calculator, we have computers to do the sums, why do we need Mayan numbers?" We tell them, it's because we need to develop our own system of number, not to just rescue it, but to revalue our rights. It is part of learning our languages, getting our *traje* back, even having a Mayan queen in the festivals. This is all part of the same struggle.

We saw that other Mayan groups, the K'iche', the Kaqchikel, have their dictionaries and numbers, all very developed, why not us, the Mam? And we learned about understanding zero, how we were the first, and India developed it later. But the Maya did NOT understand it as nothing, but as an end and a beginning. It is something inside us, part of our being [*ser*].

A similar story is told by Lem José Mucía Batz, one of those "more advanced Kaqchikeles," in his book "*Nik*": *Philosophy of the Mayan Number; The Resurgence of the Mayan Culture* (my translation). He says, "I began to study the writings of our ancestors, the codices and monuments. I found figures, of the flower, the seed, the shell, the profiled face with mathematical functions [all glyphs for zero]. The eternal question arose, WHY? Why a flower, a seed, a shell? Why a face with a hand to its jaw? The answer took much longer to arrive than my questions, but the ancestors heard my petition. At the same time I was finding, on my path, the living Mayan People were awakening, asking questions about the ancestors, so I will try to answer those questions. I sought in research and asking the sacred fire and began to find some answers, and I felt the wonder of a child keeping me going, digging for better understanding of the wisdom of the elders. I began to understand that the Mayan People conserve in our genes, the DNA, our ancestors, the seed of understanding is in every woman-man, sleeping, what is needed is to awaken this wisdom from the lethargy of time. I am more sure now that these assertions are correct because many brothers and sisters with Mayan blood are encountering this way and this form of understanding" (Batz 1996, 7).

Saturnino, one of those awakening brothers, emphasized: "Number is not just a point, a thing you add or subtract, it's a logic. It's an issue of a different logic. Subtraction is part of a cultural philosophy, so students can develop their own analysis. We want them to develop their creativity, give them new elements, make this a dynamic culture. And we realize we can't wait for the government to do things—we can do it ourselves."

The active destruction of these Mayan powers and knowledges, from the Spanish invasion to the modern army's systematic murder of ritual specialists and the more subtle destructiveness of internalized racism and the way both Catholicism and Protestantism equate them with evil, can make doing it yourself rather difficult. Discoveries, insights, and that valuable, indiscrete thing itself—"Mayan culture"—circulate in powerfully ambivalent ways among Euro-American explorers and academics, fascinated laypeople who identify as Maya, ladino, and kaxlan (outsider) and via artists, linguists, archaeologists, epigraphers, former guerrillas, students, ajq'ij, and other spiritual guides[11] and through Guatemalan state institutions, NGOs, workshops, and conferences (both elaborate and seat of the pants) and in popular culture. For example, in addition to the "traditional dances," one of the big events of the Joyabaj festival is the parade where officials, children from all the town's schools with bands and floats, representatives of the sponsoring banks, and cowboys on pure-bred, amped-up horses all march down the town's single street. In 2012, while the business school students carried banners with sample family accountancy in double-entry form (based, oddly enough, on both parents having fully waged jobs), kids from another school carried large handmade banners of Mayan glyphs representing the twenty day-signs of the tzolk'in.

Lem's and Saturnino's numbers qualify, in the sense that they are quantities connected to qualities. And in the dictionary sense, they are connected to "skill, knowledge, and experience that fits a person for a position, occupation, exercise of a right," even if it's an unpaid "job" that is deployed

1.2 Joyabaj parade in honor of the Vírgen de Tránsito, with children carrying Mayan calendar day signs, August 2012. Author's photo.

on buses, street corners, wherever he gets a chance. In what follows I build on Saturnino's story to explore the qualification of number, its sometimes empowering yet often fraught relation to people: as embodied and abstracted, as singular and as aggregates, and as counting—or not. Quantity's qualifications remind us that "to count" means "to be taken into account; have importance, value." But it also means the opposite. "To qualify" also means "to modify; restrict; limit; make less positive."

Powers of Enchant/meant

For the Enlightenment, anything which cannot be resolved into numbers, and ultimately one, is illusion; modern positivism consigns it to poetry. Unity remains the watchword from Parmenides to Russell. All gods and qualities must be destroyed.
—Theodor Adorno and Max Horkheimer (2007, 4–5)

The mere act of enumeration that heaps them all together has a power of enchantment all its own.
—Michel Foucault (1973, xvi)

Despite some sympathy for Adorno and Horkheimer's misarathropic anxieties that "cold hard facts" destroy quality and reduce social complexity to a simple number, I'm arguing that counting is also qualitative—deeply connected to experiences of space, time, subjectivity, the body, the sacred, relationality, the collective, memory, justice, exchange, and power. It's embedded in our play, entertainment, and enjoyment (as my nephew Quinn says, "If they taught math using Red Sox statistics I'd be great at it!"), as well as everyday experiences of buying and selling, tending livestock, planting fields, celebrating birthdays, weaving, and healing the sick. Efforts to count the dead after state-ordered genocide, to restore Mayan math and cultural pride, and to engage with the market forces that are transforming everyday lives, all rely on number and the often unspoken logics of accounting and accountability. Double-entry bookkeeping is *also* an "ethnomathematics" but one with an army. In the after-math of civil war, numeracy is a central component of the personal, cultural, and epistemological effects, and enchantments, of fact making.

Understanding in the deep and wide senses that Saturnino tried to explain to me on that bus, in the contemplations that occur around the serpent and conquest dances *and* the actual labor in the cane fields, in reckoning with the war and trying to figure out how to live in a deeply financialized world even if math is in your blood, *vatos*, is, in Encarnación's words, "very complicated. All the numbers." We'll have to account for how numbers are enchanting in destructive ways (like derivatives, algorithms promising riskless profits) because we are all enmeshed with global market processes where number figures prominently as an index of both hope and despair.

This book tells five stories concerning quantities and their qualifications. It explores increasing Mayan and other Guatemalans' insertion in state functioning—and its disbursal of such desirables as justice, security, and money—and in "modern" relations of wage labor and informality, credit and debt, accounting and speculation. In the two chapters of the next section, "Bonesetting," I analyze ongoing efforts to count the war's dead and what might count as adequate reparation for both particular deaths and that deeply troubling aggregate of a Genocide of Maya. I'll also explore both everyday and wild effects of a sum of money standing in for a person. I begin with exhumations of mass graves and clandestine cemeteries (counting the bones)—inaugurating a theme of precious things of great value buried underground—then trace interconnections with the processes of writing reports (counting the dead), the National Reparations Program (counting the beneficiaries and payments), and court cases (counting perpetrators' payback in coin and time). I trace how "financializing" these relationalities becomes a mundane infrastructure while remaining fundamentally weird.

In "Mayan Pyramids," I first address Omnilife, the diet supplements that Santos distributes and that were sitting on Encarnación's table, sales of which allow people to accumulate points as well as profit from people lower down in their "pyramid." I tell Santos's story over the eighteen years I've known her, as she went from being a hamlet school teacher and cultural rights activist, through increasing involvement in transnational networks that were like and unlike the NGO connections pushing education, development and postwar trauma resolution she once worked for, to being "100% Omnilife." Former guerrillas, grassroots organizers, Mayan movement activists, and doctors and other professionals are now financializing their "social capital" by converting their networks of friends and acquaintances into cash and other prizes. As their houses fill with accounting paperwork, sociality and imaginings of political futures are transformed in hard-to-account-for ways.

Chapter 5 tells how in 2008, a mob from Joyabaj tried to kill a man, known as El Millonario, in neighboring Zacualpa. He had fled, so they burned his home, Hummer, and gas station, on which they wrote "People's Property, Sale Prohibited." This was the fallout from a Mayan-only development project that had pulled in thousands of indigenous people across the highlands over the course of almost a decade. They had placed their faith in a man who promised them half a million quetzals. Actually an elaborate Ponzi or pyramid scheme, he bankrupted families across a wide swathe. Operating through Mayan social networks and financial logics, I explore how people calculated their participation and conjured enchantments and are now dealing with the after-math.

In the last section, "YES to Life = NO to Mining," I explore similar predatory market mechanisms with more hopeful Mayan calculations in campaigns against mountaintop-removal gold mining. Throughout the Americas, "development" increasingly means "free trade" and resource extraction via transnational corporations. In Guatemala the 1996 peace accords accompanied new regulations encouraging exploitation of "natural resources," unleashing a rush for the new El Dorado. In 2005 a Canadian company inaugurated an open pit gold mine in the indigenous province of San Marcos (where I met Saturnino). In response local residents held a consulta, or referendum, in which 98% rejected the mine, becoming the epicenter of what is now a national movement to make (mainly) indigenous people "count"—as in "matter"—through the technique of "counting"—adding them up. It has become one of the most important social movements of the postwar.

In the last chapter I weave together these struggles over counting—which encompass repair, territory, land, subsistence, money, resources, and networks—and connect them to historic memory, which increasingly includes Classic Maya numeracy (like bones and gold, a precious thing extracted from the ground). Reenergized by the global fascination with 2012, activists are drawing on the Maya's famous mathematical skills to re-invigorate "Mayan *sabiduria* (savoir or knowledge)" and "*ser Mayab*" (being). The energies surrounding ethnic revitalization run in currents that, like electricity, can experience disruption and blackouts. Chris Jones (2013) traces intensifications in indigenous organizing: the land reform of the early 1950s, the effervescence in the 1970s and the quincentennial; as well as lows: the 1954 coup, the 1980s genocide, and the failure to ratify the indigenous rights planks of the peace accords in 1999 and the subsequent implosion of COP-MAGUA, the Coordination of Mayan People's Organizations (marking an end to Mayan Organizing 1.0; see also Bastos and Camus 2013). These moments interact with the infrastructural divisions I have mentioned between "*populares*" and "culturalists." Guatemalanist ethnography has tended to mirror this, split between anthropologists attending to political economy, war, ethnic/class relations, and gender inequalities and those focused on village studies, ritual, and meaning making. New Mayan rights struggles combining Mayan math, and its relations to space and time via calendrics and sacred areas, with understandings of a broad defense of rights and territory and the radical demand that Maya deserve to live "beyond adequacy"—to enjoy the promises of "modernity" without always being the ones to shoulder its burdens—may be overcoming these divisions, helping create what I'm calling Maya Organizing 2.0.

These efforts are responses to horrific losses of people and cultural infrastructure. They are also attempts at maneuvering in a field of power organized via a history of empiricism and modernity defined through a relation to mathematics that came to be considered the "modern fact," synonymous with the rational, self-contained, and scientific. These efforts are simultaneously personal, political, pedagogic, institutional, and epistemological, working to empower people and particular forms of knowledge as well as transform systems of power/knowledge and profiteering. So is this book.

Coda: Precious Flows, World Transformer

While mining is the subject of chapter 6, I draw attention here to the central role it plays in all the themes of this book: indigenous identity, racialization, gender relations, money, accounting, labor, finance, adequation, and collection and manipulation of state and market data. The sixteenth-century search for gold and silver was the great galvanizer of European colonization of the Americas (the only products of interest to Chinese creditors). These inanimate metallic actors, pulled at such enormous human cost from the earth's entrails through enslaved indigenous and African labor, "freeing" them to circulate the globe, founded a whole new world system. And not only through specie. The "discovery" of the eerie regularity of mining disasters birthed the modern science of statistics, while the semi-industrial production of coca to keep those workers going in the great mine of Cerro Rico, Potosí in today's Bolivia, was an early harbinger of today's military-pharmaceutical-industrial-financial-carceral complex.[12] Imperial mining transformed race and gender relations as surely as bookkeeping did.

And the metals! Birthed in the godforsaken underground ruled by devilish creatures like El Tío, burnished to represent the most heavenly ecstasies so that gold's chemical symbol, Au, comes from the Latin "glow of sunrise," silver's Ag from "shining, lustrous." Like number, both "an object of sense" and "used to generate mathematical formulas," gold and silver coins are, literally and figuratively, two-sided: both mundane and enchanted/ing. Sensuous, heavy with thingness, and *more*. In its particularity and its aggregation with "the social," the coin is magical, as Marx said. "You may turn and toss an ounce of gold in any way you like, and it will never weigh ten ounces. But here in the process of circulation one ounce practically does weigh ten" (1911, 140). Money, Maurer says, "materializes the problem of adequation. . . . Can a coin, as material substance, ever be adequate to its value in exchange? And where does such value reside—in the metallic substance itself or in the ideas . . . impressed in the metal?" (2005, xiii).

In counting, Guatemalans are engaging, in Randy Martin's words, with "the unholy trinity of money as token, medium of exchange and store of value. Money's desultory formal utopia is for the token to stand for the store, which is posited as existing no place in the virtual expansions of credit and debt" (personal communication, 2013). Later I'll suggest that there are "epistemologically peculiar" moments of suspension—through reparations; through redeeming Omnilife points; through the workings of the Ponzi and the *consultas*, and in lightning flashes and various manifestations of hydro-electric and Mayan power—which are, in Martin's words, "distinguished as an unsupportable claim on the store, not a reasonable exception to its normal utopics. Yet the somatization of allure inverts the otherwise dematerialized store and metaphysical equilibrium by which price is legitimated," by which accountability both "works" and yet, vertiginously, makes accumulation itself possible.

"It's very complicated!" Yet "numbers are also about understanding the world around you."

Part II

Bone-Setting

2 The Algebra of Genocide

algebra—from *al-jabr*. Reunion of broken parts; bonesetter; referring to reduction and balancing, the cancellation of like terms on opposite sides of the equation.

¡¡Ni somos diez, ni somos cien, decimos al estado: Cuéntenos bien!! (We aren't ten, we aren't a hundred, we challenge the state to count us right!)
—Chant shouted at demonstrations in Guatemala

Magic Number

In *Guatemala: La historia silenciada* ("silenced history") Carlos Sabino, an Argentine historian, attacks "the magic number 200,000 . . . repeated ad nauseam" to inflate "the macabre counting of the victims" (Sabino 2008, 365). He promises instead a balanced account, realist and objective, and a rigorous analysis of the war and its losses. Reviewing army and guerrilla documents and human rights reports from the early 1980s, which estimate between 35,000 and 50,000 dead, and delving into the math of the Catholic Church's REMHI (1998) and the UN's CEH reports, he finds that a "shadow of doubt hangs over all the material." He says that REMHI counted 22,463 dead based on 5,465 testimonies but only a fraction of those have been identified. They then increased it to 29,016 to get at the indirect deaths, illness, disappearance, suicide. The CEH took 7,338 testimonies to get 42,275 victims, then applied mathematical projections to get 132,174, to which it then added 40,000 disappeared and a few more to cover any omissions to get 201,000.

Sabino interrogates this number on a range of points: contemporary press reports suggest nowhere near this quantity, many names are badly translated, birth and death dates are inconsistent, and the counting was done by both computer and by hand, suggesting there was a great deal of repetition (he explains in detail the equation used to balance omissions with possible overlap). He also says that there was confusion between war dead and those who died in the 1976 earthquake or were killed in intervillage violence, that people counted as disappeared have subsequently shown up (they'd secretly joined the guerrillas or just run off), and that those counting had a political interest in getting as big a number as possible (Sabino 2008, 377–78). He argues that counting "so-called massacres" is problematic, as this is not an exact term and that, more generally, it's not easy to kill so many people. He asks, "Where are all the bodies?" Forensic anthropologists have found barely a few thousand in 530 exhumations, and most "mass graves" have only 5 or 6 bodies, rarely more than 20. If there were 200,000, wouldn't there be bones everywhere? He concludes that 37,000 dead is more realistic (389). It's been something of a best seller in Guatemala and has proponents in the United States and Europe, all in the name of precision and rigorous accuracy.[1]

"On Exactitude in Science"

Another Argentine, Jorge Luis Borges, once wrote about an Empire where the art of Cartography was so perfect that it created a map with the scale of a mile to a mile. The map of the Empire was the size of the Empire, coinciding with it point for point. But later generations, less fond of the study of Cartography, let it decay and fray. "In the Deserts of the West, still today, there are Tattered Ruins, inhabited by Animals and Beggars; and in all the Land there is no other Relic of the Disciplines of Geography" (Borges 1999, 325).

Memory of Bones: Precision and Tattered Ruins

While the work of NGOs is unparalleled in its rooting out and reporting of human rights abuses, it is the technology developed by social scientists, physical scientists, and mathematicians that arm the international human rights com-

munity with better and better tools for proving their assertions and making their cases valid in the eyes of the world.
—Jana Asher (2008, 17–18)

Which "bodies count" and how . . . addresses the ways in which violence is understood as either acts of war, or crimes of war.
—Amy Ross

In July 2011 two companions and I went to La Verbena cemetery in Guatemala City to visit the grave of our friend Pepe Lara.[2] Leaving the hectic traffic of Zone 7, we entered that strange calm of graveyards, enhanced by the austere cliffs falling away into a massive ravine. Despite instructions from an attendant, the grave was hard to find, and as we wandered around we happened upon an exhumation.

In a back corner near the ravine was a corrugated metal structure with a large banner saying "With your DNA sample it is possible to identify your family member disappeared during the Internal Armed Conflict (it is free and confidential) FAFG [Guatemalan Forensic Anthropology Foundation]." Under the banner were about a hundred photocopied images of disappeared people. We knocked and were graciously received by Jessika Osorio and her team. What we found is a bit hard to describe because it was so mundane and matter-of-fact—and also both literally and figuratively a yawning abyss.

Viewers of TV cop shows may be inured to bones sitting on tables (although usually in glamorous hi-tech settings),[3] but it's another thing entirely to see actual human bones arrayed before you or in plastic buckets with dirt and shreds of clothes or in overflowing supersize black plastic garbage bags, piled floor to ceiling, several bags deep. All of this around a perfectly circular pit. Holding on to ropes so as not to fall in, I peered over the edge. It seemed to descend a long way. In the near darkness at the bottom were more bones, masses of them, piles, heaps, hoards. Intrepid young people were carefully bringing up buckets full as others worked to clean and set them together to make a full skeleton or even just a complete skull.

La Verbena is a public cemetery. In most Guatemalan necropoleis the dead are entombed aboveground—often in stacked rows of crypts (like big filing cabinets). When these fill up, older bones are removed and placed in the ossuary—that pit, which is also where the bodies of the "XX," the indigent and unclaimed go. There are three ossuaries at Verbena.

2.1 Exterior of exhumation site, La Verbena cemetery, Guatemala City with photographs of disappeared people, July 2011. The banner urges people to provide DNA samples to help identify missing kin. Author's photo.

The CEH estimates between 45 and 50,000 people, indigenous and ladino, were disappeared during the civil war, mostly by "unknown armed men" assumed to be state agents, and never seen again. Many were dumped in rivers or the ocean, many others buried in or near military installations, many were left by the side of the road far from their homes and quietly buried by those who found them, and—it had long been suspected—many were hiding in the ossuaries. In about 2004, the forensic anthropologists found that between 1980 and 1985, hundreds of people marked XX were deposited at La Verbena. They had been focusing on massacre sites in the highlands, but Fredy Peccerelli, director of the FAFG, says that he and Clyde Snow, a North American who was legendary for deploying forensic archaeology to solve war crimes, were drinking one night and began pondering the ossuary rumors. They got permission to look at Verbena's logbooks and found hundreds of XXs, 889 to be more or less exact, often many in one day, in groups, mostly young men, with notes by the XXs saying that they'd been shot, hands chopped off or no fingerprints, and often with their faces destroyed (Blue 2011, 9; Snow et al. 2008).[4] Jessika, our guide, said they interviewed the night attendants who told them heavily loaded pickup trucks came late at night, their drivers making it clear the attendants

2.2 Forensic anthropologist Selket Callejas is lowered into Ossuary 2 at La Verbena cemetery. James Rodríguez. Used with kind permission.

should look the other way, then leave empty (so those bodies didn't even get an X). It wasn't until 2010 that the *forenses* got through the red tape to begin the exhumation.

Perennially underfunded, they worked for months under tarps until they could put up a roof. Given threats, they requested state security, but police visit only sporadically. Our unscheduled visit came just after five soldiers from the army's elite Kaibil squad were found guilty in the 1982 massacre of over 250 people in Dos Erres, El Petén. Of 626 massacres documented by the CEH, this is only the fourth with convictions (although no higher-ups were charged nor their financial backers). Horror at the excess—not only the quantum of mortality but the qualities of those deaths—led the judge to impose, at least symbolically, a punishment adequate to the crime. The men were sentenced to 30 years imprisonment per death plus an extra 30 for crimes against humanity, or 6,060 years in all. The FAFG exhumations had helped win the convictions, and the team was receiving threats couched in a peculiarly mathematical language: for every year of the soldiers' sentences they would lose two of theirs ($1 = -2$). These threats echoed early 1980s Secret Anti-Communist Army death squad warnings: "For every anti-communist who falls in a cowardly attack, we will kill twenty."

When we showed up, the *forenses* had already exhumed 2,000 skeletons, with a minimum of 4,000 still to go. Once cleaned and set together, they try to parse what the bones say. Most of the remains in the trash bags were from the ossuary's normal functioning, but they had also found almost 800 with the *tiro de gracia*, or shot to the head.

At La Verbena, as at each of their (by then) over 1,500 exhumations, getting clean, dry numbers to replace such quantifiers as "many, lots, masses, piles, heaps, hoards" takes great effort. There's the (often years of) bureaucratic haggling for permission, plus archive searches and interviews. Then come the labors of decrypting, meaning both to unbury and to decode. Victor Blue describes a descent into the pit. "The earth walls rise above, out of your line of sight. The air is wet and thick. . . . The pile of remains . . . rises slowly from the trench around the edge where they stand. The forensic archaeologists, dressed in white Tyvek suits, wear respirators over their faces and climbing harnesses. . . . Scrambl[ing] delicately over the mound, they brush away the dirt, peel back the remaining scraps of [clothing] . . . recognize ribs, and a shoulder blade. A tea colored skull with a wisp of black hair draped over it emerges from the dirt" (2001, 11).

As the FAFG (2011a) website says, the work is stressful, requiring enormous physical endurance and dedication.[5] The ossuary we saw is over forty-five feet deep, and despite reinforcement there's nagging fear the walls will collapse. Many of the bones are saponified, meaning the disintegrating body's fat has made them soapy, releasing a throat-burning, headache-inducing smell that makes handling and analysis more difficult. They are finding a mix of loose and bagged bones, which makes even the MNI (minimum number of individuals) hard to be sure about. So they focus on left femurs. In the pit, for each find they create a file, logging it with an identifying number and marking depth. They take photographs, often showing a measurement tool, and note who did the excavating, plus any artifacts like clothes, newspapers, and coins. Then the bones are hoisted up the shaft to be cleaned and checked for signs of violence.

At the tables, they mark—if they have them—the skull, jawbone, and left femur, reconstruct them enough to determine sex and age, and, if possible, make a dental record. As with Pacioli's first book, the inventory, these logs are rich in detail: "FAFG case # 1200–2776. Recovered from Ossuary 2, La Verbena cemetery. Name unknown, buried as XX. Sex—Male, between 33–57 years of age. Skeleton—semi-complete, displaying multiple traumas, all perimortem—at the time of death. Thorax—three broken ribs on right side of rib cage. Top two left thoracic ribs broken, left scapula fractured, consistent with a crushing of the chest cavity. Left arm—missing beneath the upper quarter of the humerus, wound consistent with a high velocity projectile impact. Right foot—missing, likely amputated, perimortem. Cranium—present, with posterior trauma to the base of the skull. Massive trauma to the orbital ridge, which is missing, along with nearly all of the nasal cavity. Trauma is consistent with high velocity projectile impact, laterally, and likely the cause of death. Recovered with one white dress shirt, and one T-shirt displaying a 'Puma' logo" (Blue 2011, 8). Regular ossuary remains are reinterred, while genetic material is extracted from those who appear to be victims of the state (where possible, that is; there's not always enough left). Teeth or femurs are cut with an autopsy saw, samples extracted and sent to the FAFG lab for analysis and to be entered in the MFIS, the Mass Fatality Identification System of the Gene Codes Forensic Corporation®.[6] Rather like in the fourth accounting book, the ledger, homely details and various scales of value are transformed into a single "currency," now written as a series of numbers.

The *forenses* are working with bodies that are disaggregated in every way: the person from name, kin, identity, history; and often each piece or shard from the rest. Through double-entry-infused record keeping (moving from detailed inventory to number-based ledger) and the mathematical labors of aggregation, the heaps and piles start to become precise: for the first ossuary in La Verbena "depth was 7 meters, 620 bodies were recovered, 1741 parts of bodies, 52 bags of loose bones, 36 artifacts, and the MNI was 2520." By late 2011 at Ossuary 2 they were working at "24 meters and had found 4690 bodies, 5160 partial skeletons, 174 bags of loose bones and 250 artifacts" (FAFG 2011a). This is an algebra—the reunion of broken parts—of human rights.

If number is the modern fact, then counting the victims would seem to be enough—and with such careful precision—but here's the epistemic peculiarity: it takes more to *make them count*. The bones need a setting. And that's where the banner in front comes in, and the posters hung in markets and storefronts across the country—"Mi Nombre No Es XX" and at the FAFG-sponsored booth at the Los Angeles Fiesta Chapín hoping to find exiled or emigrated family members. These are algebraic "bonesetting" labors, to put those numbers back into "relation" (literally with their relatives) by getting survivors to contribute to the National Genetic Bank (emphasizing it's free, confidential, and painless, just a cheek swab not a prick) so the remains can reaggregate with a name and all its connections.

2.3 "My name is not XX. Your DNA can identify me. 45,000 forced disappearances between 1960 and 1996. The saliva sample is free and totally confidential." Guatemalan Forensic Anthropology Foundation (FAFG) poster.

2.4 "Do you have a disappeared family member? . . . After 30 years we found them!" FAFG poster at Guatemala City bus stop. James Rodríguez. Used with kind permission.

But creating awareness of the identification efforts is difficult (and expensive). Some relatives come forward because of long participation in human rights groups, but the war disaggregated and terrorized families, communities, and political organizations. There are dead with no survivors. And there's the daunting obstacle of *temor, odio, y vergüenza*, fear, hatred, and shame. Hatred can mobilize but also paralyze. People want their family back but may recoil at bringing charges or petitioning for reparations, as for both decolonizing Maya and radical ladinos, turning to their abhorrent enemy, the state, is a betrayal of the very reasons they were and are in struggle (Jones 2013, McAllister 2003). And the powerful effects of shame cannot be overstated. Both the triumphant army-state's reiteration that the dead were delinquents and communists, deserving of death, and the evangelical-flavored discourse of sin and heavenly retribution (Garrard-Burnett 2011) in a country that is now almost half Protestant have been introjected, adding to many people's disgrace and horror that they were unable to protect their families or fellow revolutionaries.

Patrick Ball, statistician for the CEH and expert witness in the Ríos Montt trial, said "because of the situation," people wouldn't testify. That "situation" includes the fact that unified indigenous communities are rarely found outside of romantic imaginaries or paranoid fantasies that "100 percent" are enemies of the state. But the strains of violent modernization metastasizing through the very divisionary tactics the judges found to be genocidal in the Ríos Montt trial—that turned neighbor against neighbor and made many victims into perpetrators—means communities, even families, are deeply divided (as I discuss later). Testifying may open old wounds and even unleash negative spiritual powers (Viaene 2010b). All of which makes it more difficult to singularize—to remember each by name, to make each one count.

And while it's arduous work to build the DNA database—both the evidence from the bones and the bank of possible matches—even that's only part of it. The FAFG has the only forensic genetics lab in all of Latin America that is internationally accredited in every step necessary for identification: DNA extraction, quantification by q-PCR (which replicates specific DNA sequences of interest), amplification of STRs (short tandem repeats), and both computer data and statistical analysis.[7] It took over two years to develop and now is at the level of the most elite labs in the world, of which they're extremely proud and rightfully so. "Advanced technology creates confidence," the FAFG website says, encouraging people to come forward to give their samples. "Popularly speaking, it's INCREDIBLE!" (2009; emphasis in original). But it can take up to five months to get data from bones and far longer to make a match. The first identification from La Verbena was not made until February 2013: Joaquin López López, an eighteen-year-old disappeared with his uncle and brother from Escuintla in 1989.

And the hundreds of La Verbena samples aren't the only ones coming in. In addition to the ongoing highland exhumations of clandestine cemeteries (the backlog is rumored to be a decade long) the FAFG had recently begun work at two army bases and an ossuary in Escuintla. When I said "it's not quite like on TV, is it?" Jessika kind of laughed, then said, "No, it's not CSI! It's an incredibly complicated task."

Solve for XX

We love those shows, "Say Esse EE" [CSI], *Ley y Orden*, *Números*! Everyone here watches them! Sometimes we try to schedule a meeting and no one can make it and then we realize it's because the show is on! It's amazing! There they just need one hair and here we have everything, witnesses, bullets, DNA. And years go by with no justice.
—Enrique Recinos, Myrna Mack Foundation

Fact either means evidence or it means anything which exists. The fact, the thing as it is without any relation to anything else, is a matter of no importance or concern whatever: its relation to what it evinces, the fact viewed as evidence, is alone important.
—G. Robertson (1838)

The Greek word *aletheia* means an "unconcealing," "revealing." Heidegger connects it to bringing out the dead and calls it an opening of presence that is necessary for *adequatio*, that "truth" of correspondence between mind and reality. The FAFG is unconcealing, literally, the bare bones, the material undergirding of the body, and via the bones the DNA, the deeper "truth" of the body's identity (whose match probability is "1 in a quintillion [1×10^{18}]"). "The bones don't lie," as Dr. Snow says. This sets up a couple of issues related to number, counting, and adequation that I'll address in this chapter and the next via the exhumations, human rights accounting (including Mayan numbers), and projects of reparation. First, as I've been suggesting, exhumations are intimately bound up with the practices of aggregation, of estimation and precision, and the relations between cardinal (a singularity) and ordinal (one among many). Second are the ways bones and numbers evoke desires for certainty and clarity *and* anxiety about abstraction. Numbers and bones are condensed stand-ins for things and beings that are not fully present (like stones used to count soldiers who didn't come back). Both seem to be unquestionable, facts, the basis on which knowledge and its subsequent effects are grounded—whether it be mathematical systems, death certificates, court cases, or family reunification. Yet—that epistemological peculiarity again—they have to be part of a larger system that, first, makes it possible to count them and, second, makes them count. We might think of this as the vexed relation between the "objective," disinterested, stand-alone image of number and its "social life" (Porter 1995, Urton 1997).

Which returns us to balance, carrying along the assumptions (and promises) of double-entry bookkeeping to mean objective and truthful, as well as justice: that a wrong has been righted, a loss made good, a debt balanced with a payment, an equivalence rendered. Al-jabr refers to "balancing, the cancellation of like terms on opposite sides of the equation." The enormous efforts I've been describing aim to count as one step in producing an equation that can then be balanced: a child or parent returned (at least their remains), a victim redeemed, a perpetrator punished, an indemnification paid. Later I suggest correspondences with other realms where people make the enormous efforts required to count the days or pay back the debts incurred through dances performed for the patron festivals or through other ritual sacrifices, which are also aimed at balancing: in the give and take of relations of reciprocity with the earth, the ancestors, and aspects of the sacred. Urton and Nina Llanos similarly describe "rectification" as a "fundamental notion" for the Quechua: "the desired and proper state of affairs in the world is one in which resources, labor, behavior, and all other objects, relations, and attitudes are in a state of balance, equilibrium, and harmony. . . . Imbalance and disequilibrium must be rectified. The arithmetic operations of addition, subtraction, multiplication, and division represent several of the principal forms of rectification that may be carried out" (Urton 1997, 14).[8] And in "Western ethnomathematics," an algebra of human rights might be thought of as adding value to one side of the equation so that, through the slow production of a global apparatus in which "the human" comes to act as a general equivalent, a dead Maya will count as much as a dead ladino or white; a poor person as a rich one; a woman as a man.

Decrypting

The science of forensics, what makes it suitable to courts of judicature, is about transforming those estimating words for "a lot" into matters of fact.[9] It quantifies the qualities. It is the work of literally "grounding" ("exhume" is from humus, "earth," which also gives us "human"), the "fingers to the wind" that Patrick Ball, the CEH statistician, did to give "people who are missing [the] right to existence." The FAFG says the exhumations "validate the testimonials of witnesses and survivors. . . . Scientifically and legally they give value to testimony, proving and ratifying the facts registered in other investigations like the CEH" (2011b).

But this is harder even than I've let on. At La Verbena all the remains are in one place. Elsewhere just finding the bones is a challenge. The *forenses* were asked to exhume the site of a military outpost in the hamlet of Choatalum, San Martín Jilotepeque, Chimaltenango, and carried out eleven investigations in 2000 and 2001, but where to even start? The military remains hermetically sealed about where they buried people, and in Guatemala there are almost no surviving political prisoners who might know. When it was abandoned in 1992 the soldiers tore down the buildings and burned everything, so with new growth it's hard to tell where things were. The anthropologists opened twenty trenches to find just three pit burials yielding twenty-two complete skeletons and a number of bones that were *tirado*, just scattered about, suggesting removal of evidence. How many? How to know?

The FAFG's tallies of digs around Patzulá (Encarnación's home) and the northern hamlets of Joyabaj suggest similar frustrations, yielding: 0, 24, 2, 1, 0, 1, 1, 1, 9, 1, and 9 over six years (Encarnación's husband was killed on the south coast; his body remains missing). One that found 9 bodies was in Xeabaj, from a massacre carried out by civil patrollers in April 1982. Estimates of those murdered range from 50 to 200. "A river of blood ran down the mountain," a witness told anthropologist Simone Remijnse (2001, 463). But transforming "estimates" and "a river" into the precision of number confronts both cover-ups and the messiness of the event.

Lots of things happened to the bodies of those massacred or disappeared. In some cases the army forced people to dig graves before they began the killing. In the chaotic aftermath of mass murder people (potential witnesses) of course flee and soldiers or patrollers cover the remains or scatter them into rivers, ravines, wells, or latrines. Testimonials speak to the added horror of seeing body parts carried around by dogs or, as people told Ricardo Falla about Finca San Francisco in Nentón Huehuetenango, of the earth "*negreaba de zopilotes*," blackened by so many vultures (Falla 2011). In Totonicapán bodies of unknown people (but wearing *traje* from Sololá) were found together and buried in the cemetery, but no records were made. Soldiers and civil patrollers have identified burial sites, but their memories— to kill is also trauma-inducing—aren't always accurate. Survivors may also have performed quick and dirty mass burials. Finding these graves is not easy thirty-plus years later. The world changes, trees grow and fall, memory falters. An exploratory trench might be dug inches away and still miss the bones. Court cases stutteringly getting under way may send perpetrators back to the scene of the crime so that, like regular archaeologists, the *forenses* arrive to find sites already looted, precious things already gone.

But sometimes nonhuman actants help out. When the army occupied Joyabaj they took over the convent, which backs onto a ravine, where for years they dumped bodies. It was a classic public secret, but the still-present army and the ferocious ladino-led civil patrols meant no one dared ask for an exhumation, just as few were willing to sign their testimonies for the truth commissions. Although probably as many people died there as in neighboring Zacualpa—one of the CEH's four genocide cases—Joyabaj didn't count. In 2000, however, a landslide revealed human remains, and the Catholic Church's exhumation team was called in. Over twenty-five bodies were found but nowhere near as many as people were looking for. Rumor has it there are many more, but without knowing where to dig and with a long to-do list in other areas, the team packed up and left (Remijnse 2002).

Back at La Verbena, we thanked Jessika and her team, paid our respects to Pepe, and returned to bustling Zone 1, where I met Ulmil, a Maya-Kaqchikel friend from Poaquil, Chimaltenango, for lunch. I told him where I'd been, and he told me for the first time about searching for his father. He said his family had endured dozens of exhumations—twenty-one in all—hoping to find him. It is agonizing, hopeful, wrenching, and slow-going. As bones are unconcealed, they show to even the unschooled eye the brutality of the person's demise. It is homely, as more intimate details emerge: a soccer player in full uniform, a dog buried beside its human companion. Or both strange and familiar, as two Mayan *forenses* described finding someone with a traditional bag, empty containers, and a plastic bag with broken pieces of rock who, they later realized, must have been an *ajq'ij* with his ritual bundle. It is devastating when after ten, sixteen, twenty such witnessings, there is still no trace of the one you seek. They finally found Ulmil's father by accident. Renovations of the town's soccer field, where he'd played as a child, revealed bones, and they called in the *forenses*.

> My mother recognized the belt she'd woven for him. She's a good weaver so it lasted, even under ground. And from the wound in his head. When they were taking him away, in front of my mother, they hit him and you could see it in the bones. So she knew. But also from DNA, my sister and I both gave. But it took so long! My mother is really tired. There is so much pain! The people from the *Resarcimiento* (reparations) came and had an exhibit on the war and the exhumations in our town. It lasted

thirteen days and only ten people went the whole time. I asked my mother, "Why didn't you go?" and she said, "Who wants to remember all that pain?" Our family has always done a lot, a lot of ceremonies and we knew for sure about my father because before we found him there were a lot of bad messages, but after the burial the messages were all good. We knew he was resting. That's not true for my uncle. He is not happy. We know where he is—on the banks of the Motagua River [in eastern Guatemala]—but it's so expensive and so far. Mine was one of the important families in all this [organizing] and we lost almost everyone, across an entire generation.

It is hard to write about this. There is so much pain. And it's so fraught, trying to adequately transmit such stories as an outsider and as someone whose family is intact. It's also hard to winnow down the excess of detail, to try to tell a coherent, concise story, without being so exact it takes fifty years to tell. My desk is covered with printouts and handwritten field notebooks, DVDs of exhumations and other people's powerful writings (EAFG 1995; McAllister 2003; Sanford 2003), not to mention the four and twelve volumes of the two truth commission reports on my bookshelf and the vast digital archive lurking behind the screen I'm writing on. I want to tell you stories of exhumations, but which one(s)? There are hundreds and thousands of stories like Ulmil's, like La Verbena. Each one poignant and heroic, particular and abstractable.

Cobán

Like the Cobán, Alta Verapaz, army base. Aura Elena Farfán of FAMDEGUA (Families of the Disappeared) said they first sought permission to dig there in 2000. It wasn't approved until 2012 and even then under strict military control. The usual international accompaniers (human shields) have not been allowed in, and family members hoping to identify skeletons through clothing or other belongings are given only ten minutes to confront what, by July 2012, were over 200 remains. Military spokesmen warned journalists of a "river of blood" if they wrote about it. As the dead were brought out, revealing torture and murder, an army spokesman said the base was built over an abandoned village and these were "traditional Mayan" mortuary practices. By June 2014 FAFG and FAMDEGUA had identified 49 out of 533 remains. That month the bones of 13 men, ranging in age from fifteen to forty-seven when they died, were returned to surviving family in Pambach, Santa Cruz Verapaz.

Dos Erres

Or like the case of Dos Erres, El Petén, massacred in December 1982. In 1994 it was one of the first exhumations, done even before the war ended and way before any of the structures—the ones that "make count," like the FAFG lab and teams of trained anthropologists—were in place. Visiting Argentines carried it out, finding 162 skeletons, including 67 children, although the MNI was difficult given the fragmentation of the bones. It's estimated 251 people were killed there. In 1999 FAMDEGUA got the state to issue capture orders for the perpetrators, but they were never acted on, so they went to the Inter-American Human Rights Court, which ruled against the state in 2009. This finally led to arrests and the trial with the 6,060-year sentences.

In 2010 there was a second exhumation of the reinterred bones to identify the victims (disaggregating back to the particular), both for the court and the survivors, drawing on the more developed techniques. The few survivors, dispersed throughout the country, hadn't known about the first exhumation. Through publicity and CSI-worthy detective work, most have been found, including a child rescued by one of the soldiers and raised as part of his family (because of his blue eyes and light hair—the residents of Dos Erres were ladinos). Growing up, the boy knew nothing of his origins and later emigrated to the United States, where FAMDEGUA tracked him to a suburb of Boston and later reunited him with his birth father (McConahay 2011; Rotella and Arana 2011).

The FAFG says "some family members who gave us their DNA expressed their hopes for economic reparations to which the FAFG could only respond that we are not involved in the processes of that kind of compensation, that the institution works to dignify victims and their families" (2010b).

So many details, horror, and hopes—for dignity and for money. It's hard to keep track, hard to make sense. This, as we know, is a point of state terror: to produce that overwhelming quantitative magnitude that shakes our very faith in understanding. So what a relief, really, to get back to the numbers, the cleaned-up aggregates.

Count Us Right!

> Most people are used to thinking of themselves as kin, as "having relations" as we say in English. But they are probably less familiar with thinking of themselves *as* relation, as embodying . . . juxtaposition.
> —Helen Verran

One rainy night I shared a meal in a brightly lit cafeteria in the town of San Marcos with Hermana Maudilia and Lencho, both Maya, she Mam, he K'iche'. His childhood disrupted by the war, in his early forties Lencho had returned to middle school and was bemoaning how hard math was. Maudilia laughed, "I remember math as the easiest! I had such a hard time with *castellano* (Castilian)![10] I didn't understand anything! It was so hard to try to memorize. Nothing would stick! But numbers felt good. Very safe, very secure. My best grades were always in math and accounting."

Part of what exhumations do is ratify and verify truth commission numbers, make them "safe" and "secure." To get *those* numbers, *Memory of Silence*, the twelve-volume report of the UN's CEH, drew on its own rigorous investigations and its year-older sibling, the Catholic Church's *Never Again*, which in turn drew extensively on the International Center for Human Rights Research (CIIDH) database, itself based on collecting by Paul Yamauchi and Guatemalan human rights groups. These in turn were based on family testimonies of those organized and brave enough to report their losses and on press reports. However, the Guatemalan press has never had good reporting from the rural areas, and from September 1980 through 1981—the height of the urban counterinsurgency campaigns—it did not report *any* incidents of killings. "Seven journalists were killed in the 8 weeks immediately preceding the press blackout" (Snow et al. 2008, 111). When the CEH arrives at a number of 200,000 dead, 45,000 disappeared, it's important to remember that all numbers have histories (AAAS 2013). Now those numbers seem secure and are cited in this book and just about any writing about Guatemala, from journalism, bank reports, and the forensic anthropology website to voluntourists' blogs, activists' posters, and of course, human rights reports.

They were produced through carefully constructed "rituals of verification" (Harper 2000), drawing on people with the internationally recognized "rank to sanction" relevant numbers (23), via the "social process of agreeing and determining the facts in question" (30) and the mundane labors of

2.5 "250,000 heroes and martyrs, 250,000 voices demanding justice. We do not forget, we do not forgive, we will not be reconciled. Justice and punishment for genociders." HIJOS, Guatemala.

"agreeing to count" which make certain "raw" numbers "seem sacred" (51). The CEH opened offices throughout the country and interviewed thousands of people, painstakingly corroborating each story (Ross 2006). The counters for the CEH, REMHI, and CIIDH reports "ground[ed] their analyses in the realities of the situation, particularly numbers" (Marks, in Tate 2007, 15), and even as Carlos Sabino questions them, any auditor can go back and re-sum-up the cross-checked numbers from the interviews (thanks to double-entry bookkeeping procedures). The reports work like an aletheiometer. They unconceal, via stand-alone numbers, *and* they put into relation, via percentages, which "of necessity evoke a whole of which it is a part" (Urla 2012, 113): 93% of violations carried out by the army, 3% by the guerrillas, with 83% of the victims indigenous. It would seem only an in-denial perpetrator would question them.

However, that nice, round, base-10 number of 250,000, counted via an objective activity carried out by a neutral "subject who counts," makes even some of the people who did the commission's math a little nervous. Patrick Ball explained, "An estimate of 132,000 is the only scientifically defensible figure, although that excludes San Martín Jilotepeque and any deaths before 1979.[11] Because of the situation, we couldn't get anyone to thumbprint the figures for San Martín so we couldn't use those testimonials. We did a thumb suck and put our fingers to the wind, to get the rest—about 18,000. But there was a lot of pressure to use the REMHI figures of 50,000 disappeared, and somehow now that's been added twice—to get 200,000 dead and then again to get the 250,000." He is deeply concerned with rigor and precision and the extremely high costs for human rights credibility if perpetrators can prove the numbers are wrong (as in a libel case won by the Sudanese government). The dead need to be accounted for. Yet as every census taker knows, it's impossible to count each and every one. In the most settled and trusting situations some always slip away, fly beneath the radar, transit when they're supposed to be static. How much more difficult to count in the after-math of atrocity?

Which returns us to that epistemic peculiarity, the leap of faith, the burr, when the CEH's consummate number cruncher insists on what the magic number can do. I return to his words: "There are official lists, with names, even remains, but there's also that other piece, the statistical estimate, that goes beyond the known. People who are missing have a right to existence, but you can't always get people to report them. They are not phantoms. They were there and those traces in the social memory can be captured in statistics." Number's unconcealing is a weapon against forgetting, circumventing the murders of witnesses, the clandestine cemeteries and the stifling aftereffects of a terror state's stranglehold. It suggests a fundamental weirdness to number and the stakes of tangling with it: perhaps we *can* subtract and multiply to get (something close to) the victim's name. Rather than dehumanize, it helps reinforce the relation between singularity and plurality, one-to-many, our relations of juxtaposition. Helen Verran (2001) calls this simultaneously inadequate and necessary process "disconcertment."

The CEH numbers, apparently "immune from theory or interpretation" (Poovey 1998, xii), made death and suffering count in ways that all the earlier recountings were not able to, opening the door for efforts at rectification and reparation. While the commission could not name names or prosecute and it took fourteen more years, the successful genocide ruling against Ríos Montt was partly based on its numbers and reasoning. And the value of such statistics was not only in the eyes of the state or international beholders. People in the most remote reaches of the country traveled great distances and swallowed their fear precisely in order to be counted. Given that Bishop Gerardi of REMHI was murdered just days after that report was released, many people who participated in the CEH fully expected to die for it. To be counted seemed to count as much as life itself. "Struggles over the type of 'evidence' provided by the bodies of those killed . . . influence the aftermath of the violence (Ross 2008, 36). The reality of mathematics is brought into accord with the premise of bookkeeping and promise of the word, *mendh*: "paying attention to," "being alert."

During the war people's experiences were fragmented and disaggregated. They might know what happened in their own lives and local surroundings but had no idea what was happening over the next mountain or in the cities—or that it was so systematic—until those unconcealing numbers were generated. While numbers may be mostly produced for (and by) the state, becoming part of such an aggregation was also generative for victims and survivors. Pullman describes reading the aletheiometer, the "golden compass," as "a glimpse of meaning that felt as if a shaft of sunlight had struck through clouds to light up a majestic line of great hills in the distance—something far beyond, and never suspected. And Lyra thrilled at those times" (1995 118), similar to the electricity in the National Theater when the CEH findings were announced, in the courtroom when the verdict against the General was read, as I thrill when statistics rescue people the state tried to turn into "phantoms."

The FAFG (2009) says "the fact that 'more than 45 thousand Guatemalans were disappeared during the internal armed conflict between 1960 and 1996' shows the necessity of generating consciousness of the magnitude of the harm inflicted by the armed conflict. . . . Publicizing this quantity helps break the chains of shame that families feel due to the constant harassment and subjugation they suffered, as many were defamed and could not defend themselves. Knowing that they were not the only ones affected should help them break their silence and give their DNA sample." Kate Doyle of the National Security Archive said the "numbers provided a strong, crisp basis for drawing the conclusions the commission did about violence, in a way you can't get from testimony" (Rosenberg 2012, 2).

As with that historically new entity "the population," it is systematicity that the CEH numbers generate while apparently only unconcealing. To do this, statisticians from California-based Benetech applied "capture-recapture" or "multiple systems estimation" (MSE), a nineteenth-century technique to count wildlife (the CEH was the first use with humans). It's hard to count every fish in a pond, but if you catch some, tag and release them, then fish again and count the overlaps, and if you do this many times, you begin to get a pretty accurate sense of how many there are.[12] That is, MSE reveals patterns. Like "between 1981 and 1983, 8% of the nonindigenous population of the Ixil region was assassinated; in the Rabinal region, the figure was around 2%. In both those regions, though, more than 40% of the Mayan population was assassinated" (Rosenberg 2012, 3). Maggie Koerth-Baker says, "Any individual list of war dead is probably incorrect. Any attempt to take the numbers in an individual list and use them to understand what's going on is likely to be misleading." But putting lists into context with other lists allows patterns to emerge from the data, often showing "that far more people had died than anybody's back of the envelope estimates had supposed. It's not the numbers from one list that mattered" (2013 unpaged). Amy Ross also shows how counting who died and how only "works" through patterns created by human rights instruments that in turn produce the "facts" of "just war" and "innocent civilians." "Body counts" help divide "acts of war" from "crimes of war" (Ross 2008, 35). Which may be why in Iraq the US military refused to do them (Ross 2005).[13] Patrick Ball says "patterns matter more than numbers." Yet the numbers make the patterns possible.

So, disconcertingly, in aggregating they rehumanize. Lencho, who struggled with math, told me that his older brother was disappeared in the 1980s. The family had no idea what happened to him and endured their neighbors' mockery, insinuating he'd been up to no good. Lencho had only recently discovered his brother's name on the columns in front of the national cathedral in Guatemala City listing the findings of the REMHI report. The particularity of their individual names (and those of massacred villages where individuals were not yet known) is made many times more powerful by appearing in the aggregate. He said the effect on his family was amazing. It was a way of getting him back.

Verran says that doing number is "doing the relation one-to-many" and that all numeration systems consist of the combined activities of "disembedding/re-embedding, disentangling/re-entangling, and disembodying/re-embodying" (2000a, 357). Not a "simple" abstraction, doing number is a generalized mode that consists of a repeated making of both singularities and pluralities, one that translates numbers that "have life" in and to different places. Exploring British census taking in Ibadan (now Nigeria), Verran says that counting people means "the repeated making of singularities: a person steps forward, or a name is uttered and a stone is placed. . . . Second a plurality is made as the stones are taken as a collection. Third, this number is rendered a singularity, the population of a compound. Fourth, a further *plurality* is made as numbers from many compounds are collected to become a further *singularity*, the population of Ibadan. And so on. In a series of recursive switches between singularities and pluralities, a child asleep on his mother's back . . . on a particular day in 1921 enters the ledger books of the British Empire" (2000a, 366–67; emphasis in original). This suggests that "counting us right" is less the loss of the rich, personal story to the cold numeric fact or the collective, embodied, and traditional dissolved into the singular, modern, and individual than about constant scalings and repetitions, the two-faced peculiarity of counting as both to calculate and to make meaningful. In this sense quantification is also qualification: "a condition that must be met in order to exercise certain rights." Once again, "politics, logic, and mathematics are inseparable."

So the relief of getting back to the numbers is a constant: we keep going back to them. But it's also momentary within a larger trajectory. And that's because of after-math. By this I mean the "math" I've been discussing, dealing with quantities, magnitudes, and forms and their relationships and attributes by the use of numbers and symbols. Then there's "math" from "mow," as in cutting grass, carrying references to an unpleasant consequence but also to a second crop, with its emplacement in time and its processes. This is number's epistemological peculiarity, seeming to simply describe, but "only when particulars are interpreted *as evidence* [are] they valuable enough to collect," acquiring meaning and even "identity as facts" (Poovey 1998, 9). As Robertson said in 1830, "its relation to what it evinces, the fact viewed as evidence, is alone important" (in Poovey 1998, xxiv). Number is pattern.

For example, number seems transparent, but you've got to know what it refers to for it to make sense: a list? an amount? a distance? a date? (And is 5/10/13 May 10 or October 5? It may depend on where you are.) Or is it something else altogether? In the death squad dossier, an internal military log from the 1980s revealing the fates of 183 disappeared people, the number 300 frequently appears. It took a while for analysts to realize it didn't count anything. It was code: the detainee had been murdered (see Cuevas Molina 2011). Numbers helpfully condense the thousand and one details of testimonies and exhumations and help keep track of the flurry of data, but all those numbers can also get confusing. A CEH statistician told me "REMHI announced that the guerrillas were responsible for 9% of the abuses, which seemed implausible from the CEH data. . . . Looking at their database we saw at one point how they'd switched the number codes for violence with the number of victims. It wasn't malice, just incompetence and bad design." (And here the system, fullfilling bookkeeping's promise of exactitude and balance, worked just as it was supposed to: making it possible to check and rectify the numbers.) In other words, we need to pay close attention to number's relation.

Exhumations verify truth commission numbers *and* they generate evidence. When I visited the FAFG offices in Guatemala City with Mayan anthropologist Francisca Gomez in 2011, what struck me most (after how young the workers were) were the boxes and boxes and boxes of bones stacked in every available place, taking up half the narrow hallways, in corners, under desks, and filling to bursting—floor to ceiling of closely packed shelves—several large storage rooms. Every one was carefully labeled with a date, case number, and massacre site, many of which slingshotted me back to the very first interviews I did, with Paula Worby, in the Ixil region in 1985, where army resettlement camps were slowly replacing the burned-out villages. Acul, Tzalbal, Pulay . . . already disembodied and disaggregated into bones, numbers, and DNA, they will reembody, it is hoped, in a courtroom—as they did in the Ríos Montt trial. Until which time they await their reinterment.

To conclude these musings on "after-math's" "memory of bones"—on reaggregation, on the formidable challenge of "counting us right well," and on the labors of *algebra*, or "the reunion of broken parts"—I'll tell three brief stories of number's qualification (being made to relate), then in the next chapter turn to Mayan (and other indigenous) numbers and from there to the question of "compensation" that confronted the *forenses* when they simply sought DNA samples and "dignification."

The Fact, the Thing as It Is without Any Relation, Is of No Concern Whatever

The statistics of genocide are fuzzy at best and are likely to remain so.
—Mary W. Gray and Sharon Marek

Making Choatalum Count

As in the Dos Erres case, *forenses* testified in the 2009 trial of Felipe Cusanero Coj, head of the civil patrols in Choatalum San Martín Jilotepeque—a town, remember, that didn't count. He was charged with aiding the army in disappearing his neighbors. Women whose husbands and children were killed had first filed the case in 1983, an act of extraordinary courage, but they were not allowed to testify until 2008. Even then his lawyers argued the statute of limitations made it too late to try him, postponing the case a year until the Constitutional Court made the landmark ruling that disappearance is a *continuing* crime. Women described the murders of family members from 1981 to 1984 and being forced to flee and live in the mountains, where children died of exposure and starvation. Returning to the army-controlled village they lived side-by-side with the men responsible for their suffering. One woman broke down: "Why did they kill him? Why? All he wanted was fair pay for his work. All he wanted was to feed his children." *Forenses* and legal experts were on hand to ratify and verify the women's words (shades of the gendering of the accounting books), and Cusanero was found guilty of abetting the murder of five men and one woman. He was sentenced to 150 years in prison.

The thing is, the *forenses* found 44 bodies in four different exhumations in Choatalum, but testimonies tell of three army massacres in 1982, with numbers of victims ranging between 92 and 250 (CALDH 2011, 10). The bones and the numbers are necessary but inadequate. After all that time and effort, only six people are "accounted for" in the credit-debit ledger of victim and perpetrator. Also unaddressed is the terrifying imbalance between mass murder and only wanting to feed your kids.

The National Police Archive

When the CEH asked the National Police for their war years' archives, they were told no records existed. But in 2005 an almost miraculous thing happened: one day, stockpiled explosives spontaneously combusted at the police junkyard in Zone 6, Guatemala City. Worried neighbors called the Human Rights Ombuds Office, and a small team found—nestled amid acres of detritus, wrecked cars, crashed planes, trash heaps, and parking lots—several nondescript buildings with odd-looking stuff crammed against dirty windows. A sharp-eyed historian recognized the "stuff" as files. Quite by accident they had stumbled upon the police archives (see AHPN 2011; Weld 2014). They existed only because, when ordered to destroy them, the policewoman in charge had bravely refused. (Telling me this story, Alberto Fuentes laughed, saying it was machismo's blowback. Assignment to the archives was punishment for women refusing sexual advances from superiors.)[14]

What they'd found was a mess.[15] Stacks and piles of moldering papers, some in bundles, some just loose, in room after room after room, heaps reaching the ceiling, chewed on or nested in by animals. The dank, smelly building housed rats, roaches, bats,[16] and according to some, ghosts. Investigators found a walled-off section that had been a clandestine prison known as La Isla, "the island" (see Stelzner 2009). There are eighty million documents, a concentrated site of mundane policing activities and accumulated evil in both the particular and the aggregate. Alberto said emotions run high when they find traces of a relative of someone working there. "But everyone has scientific rigor and *mística* and that helps them get through."

It's overwhelming in similar ways to La Verbena, with data from over a hundred years—literally tons of information. The labors to disembed evidence for the years of coups, counterinsurgency, and war (1954–96) rarely find a smoking gun, despite some photographs of mulilated bodies or reports on voltages used during torture. As Alberto explained, the task is more subtle: you have to learn to tell the story of police *logic*, follow the chain of command through the series of index cards and reports, some extending over decades, to pick out the trace of how the police surveilled some one, perhaps picked them up and released them, kept tabs on their movements and connections, then finally disappeared them. And that's where the math comes in.

Kirsten Weld quotes Jorge Villagrán, the project's technology coordinator: It's easy to imagine someone discrediting the project by saying, "it's just a bunch of Commies working there. . . . But the most beautiful part about the scientific rigor, about the quantitative elements of the investigation, is that that risk doesn't exist" (2014, 76). That's because archivists can show the percentage of documents that contain evidence of human rights abuses or the percentage that passed through the director-general's office so they can prove the high command was kept informed and thus responsible. This will "kneecap common protestations that any violations were simply the isolated result of a few bad eggs within the organization . . . and debunk [Police Chief] Chupina's claims that he didn't know. They can show archival chain of command." The data go through intensive standardization exercises to show the codifier was not slanted, and so any critic can try it themselves. This renders data and any qualitative deductions drawn from them harder to discount. "The science just provides the math, the statistics, the method. But the end result is that you have a scientific process used to draw a political conclusion" (77–78).

This is exactly what Poovey suggests about the power of the system to make the numbers (and what they count) count. For the police, the data manipulation system, put in place by 1960s Cold War US money and expertise, produced everything we might fear about the power of number and statistics to dehumanize and disembody. (Although in one macabre case the body *was* there. Weld says they found the "actual shriveled pieces of desiccated flesh sliced from the fingertips of one unlucky citizen and stapled directly to the file card" [74].)

But the counter counters, also supported by transnational money and expertise, are turning those same systems to the tasks of rehumanizing and reembodying by tracking down the disappeared and producing evidence for court cases—for some of Eva Morales's fourteen family members and for Edgar Fernando García, disappeared in 1984. His wife, Nineth Montenegro, helped found the first human rights group for families of the disappeared (GAM, seedbed for FAMDEGUA and CONAVIGUA). The police archive shows Edgar Fernando was a target starting in 1978, when he was only seventeen. Kate Doyle, who participated in the trial, says Daniel Guzmán, a statistician from Benetech, introduced records from the police archive "with a statistical analysis of the quantity and movement of documents found in the collection. . . . [In] the Fernando García case [they] flowed between entities high in the chain of police command . . . at twice the rate [as] within the estimated 31 million records produced by the National Police between 1960 and 1996. . . . His conclusions helped define the universe of police records . . . and offered supporting evidence of the involvement of senior police and military structures in the planning, design, orders and oversight of the operation that resulted in García's abduction" (Doyle 2010, unpaged).

Two police officers were sentenced to forty years in prison for his death, and the trial ended with the "unprecedented order that the government investigate their superior officers" (Doyle and Willard 2011, unpaged). After Choatalum it was the third conviction in forced disappearance, reinforcing legal precedent. And it was "groundbreaking" in Doyle's words, as a sign that the paralyzing terror formation of *temor, odio, y vergüenza* was beginning to come undone. Witnesses "spoke openly about [Garcia's]—and their own—militancy in the Guatemalan insurgent movement. It was the first time that people willingly exposed their links to the political opposition that was the target for state repression during the country's 36-year internal armed conflict." Ana Lucrecia Molina Theissen told the court she and Edgar were members of the Guatemalan Worker's Party (PGT) and when asked about their objectives said, "The goals of the party were to construct a just, supportive and democratic society, in which all would share in the benefits

2.6 Installation of the angel ("so that all shall know") at the historic police archive in Guatemala City, as part of the art project *The Angel Path*, by Daniel Hernandez-Salazar. Used with kind permission.

of the country" (Doyle 2010). In Kimberly Theidon's words, perhaps they no longer have to be "innocent then to be political now" (2010).[17]

The thing is, they still haven't found Edgar's body. And his was already a "paradigmatic case" of the disappearances of union organizers in the CEH report. He is also related to a woman who turned out to be an extraordinary organizer and is now a powerful congresswoman. Their daughter became a lawyer and argued his case. Few of the thousands whose traces are left in the archive or whose ghosts haunt La Isla can count on such connections.

Alberto also said, "I was talking recently with Claudia Paz y Paz, the Attorney General, and I said, 'with what we're finding here, that number 200,000, I don't know. It was statistics, and well done at that time and yet . . .' and she said, 'Yes, *queda muy corto*, it falls short. Someone should get back to that, but no one has the time.'"

General Ríos Montt, Genocider

Also unprecedented and groundbreaking, after decades of effort and attempts in international courts, on May 10, 2013, General Efraín Ríos Montt was found guilty of genocide by the Guatemalan legal system, a global first.[18] A whole set of relations, connecting the Attorney General Claudia Paz y Paz, the victims' organization Asociación Justicia y Reconciliación, the Center for Human Rights Legal Action (CALDH), three very courageous judges led by Yassmin Barrios Aguilar, the findings of the CEH, and the FAFG's exhumations—along with statisticians and mathematicians and even cultural anthropologists[19]—helped reembed the singularity of genocide back into the plurality of victims, survivors, claimants, and indicted.

"The legal definition of genocide contains no reference to the magnitude of the offense . . . and the Convention says nothing about numbers" (Gray and Marek 2008, 37, 40), but counting matters. While rejecting "atrocity machismo" (whose is bigger?), there's a spirited debate in international human rights circles over the question of a threshold. Is there a *number* of killings which would tip the balance between "normal" violence and genocide? Is there a way number might help fulfill the promise of "never again" in the wake of Guatemala, Rwanda, and the like? Would a cardinal number work? Say 10,000? Or would it need to be thought of in relation (i.e., if there are only 20,000 members of that "genos," this would be 50%, as opposed to 10,000 out of a population of, say, a million)? As with any threshold, would that mean that victim number 10,000 was more important than victim 9,999? These are the complications in that apparently simple move from singular—Jacinto Chel, or 1—to plural: adding Juan Ramirez, 2, Baltazar Juan, 3, and all the rest, up to 1,771, which the prosecuting attorneys enacted when, on the first day of the trial, they spent four hours reading the names of each identified Maya-Ixil victim into the court record. The verdict, in turn, moved from the plural back to the singular: genocide.

Genocide can be quite tricky to prove because legally it's about the *intent* to destroy in whole or in part, while a charge of crimes against humanity is based on acts "committed as part of a widespread or systematic attack directed against any civilian population" (ICC 2002). As with a lot, many, piles, or hoards; "whole," "part," "widespread," and "systematic" *can* be made more precise through the kinds of systems that were inaugurated by double-entry bookkeeping and that in turn produce both truth and virtue. In "The Statistics of Genocide," Gray and Marek (2008) say there are two basic methods to help create the evidentiary base that "qualifies" number: (1) count the number of deaths, (2) determine the "population deficit" or "excess mortality"—figures drawn from demographics to reveal the number of missing who *would have been* if the violence had not occurred. Alert readers are no doubt already aware that neither is anywhere near as straightforward as it appears.

This chapter has enumerated some of the challenges to counting each and every one of the dead, and Chapter 1 explored the lack of reliable demographic information, especially of indigenous people, necessary for the second. Survivors and lawyers arrived at the "secure" numbers of 1,771 deaths of Maya-Ixil people and 29,000 displaced through scorched-earth war (including burning entire villages and destroying uncounted food stores, crops, tools, clothing, and domestic animals, thus depriving entire populations of sustenance) in the charges against Ríos Montt.

Stories told on the stand of watching elders, pregnant women and small children murdered are grounded in the *forenses*' evidence of finding just such bones, helping prove victims were not combatants, and as one exhumed grave after another reveals MNIs like 23, 60, 86, 68, 15, 28, and 37 (FAFG, n.d.), a case is built that widespread and systematic attacks occurred. Fredy Peccerelli, director of FAFG, testified that a third of the remains exhumed in the Ixil region were younger than eighteen when they died and 83% had fatal injuries, a figure consistent with execution-style killings. Other *forenses* said that in Nebaj, on average, 2.3 bones were uncovered per individual, meaning the deaths were due to acts of a massive and violent character. Patrick Ball showed that from April 1982 to July 1983, 5.5% of the Maya-Ixil population was killed, while the proportion for the nonindigenous population was 0.7%.

Useful numbers come from other sources as well, what we might call the military state's "algebra of subversion." "In Operation Sofía, 'it said that 100 percent of the Ixiles collaborated with the subversives,' making them 'an internal enemy,' said Juan Francisco Soto, a lawyer for CALDH. 'By assuming that 100 percent were guerrillas, it is saying that everybody, men, women, children, elderly people are all enemies, and by qualifying them as enemies you are legitimizing attacks on them'" (Malkin 2013, A6).[20] Genocide statistics may be "fuzzy at best" (Gray and Marek 2008, 49), but the numbers are essential. It is in relation, literally to family members and to experts and legal decisions, DNA swabs, percentages, global information systems (Madden and Ross 2009), and bones—through disembeddings and reembeddings—that they come to count. Through the slow accruals of testimonies, numbers, and bones, a disembedded DNA sample inspires confidence, and people step forward to help identify and thereby reembed a person into named, communal life. A child, murdered in its mother's womb, enters the ledger books of the trial proceedings, disentangling a general from the impunity where he can joke about "having a policy of scorched communists" and reentangling him in number: the first head of state found guilty of genocide in the national court system.

The thing is, "between 70 and 90 percent of the Ixil villages were razed. . . . The truth commission documented about 7,000 Ixil deaths and estimated that more than 60% of the Ixil were forced to flee into the mountains, where many more died of cold, hunger and disease, or were killed when the army bombed them from the air" (Malkin 2013, A6). So Ríos Montt was held accountable for fewer than a quarter of the documented deaths in this one area. And then there are the "many more." Unlike Borges's imaginary map, Anita Isaacs says a conviction "can never be commensurate with the brutal massacres described in court. As one widow told me, [Ríos Montt] is 86 years old, he got to live his whole life; my husband was just 18 when they killed him" (2013).

The next chapter takes up these questions of the disproportionate and commensurate, which I've been setting up as a sort of burr, an irritant, between valiant and scientific labors to "make count" and "the thing is. . . ." But maybe we need a break from these profoundly difficult accountings, so before that, we'll grapple a bit more with the "disconcertment" of counting by seeing if these "rights numbers" may be brought into accord with Maya number.

3 Reunion of Broken Parts

The Mayas conserve in their languages mathematical concepts that would astound any expert. . . . Informing actual Maya of this accomplishment, and supporting the increased use of these knowledges constitutes a legitimate right. . . . Such an understanding is necessary to have the inspiration, the energy, and the integrity and self-possession necessary for full development based on our own aspirations.
—Guatemalan Mayan Language Academy (ALMG; 2003, 12, 16)

Mayan Counting

Dropping by to visit my friend Anastasia in Joyabaj, I found her busy, so I sat down at the kitchen table with her daughters Ixchel and Quetzali, immersed in homework. To my surprise and delight they were doing Mayan numbers, adding and subtracting with the elegant bar (5) and dot (1) numeration and puzzling over base 20. Mayan and Hindu-Arabic (base-10) numbers are written in a sequence that presupposes zero, based on powers of ten or twenty (Roman numerals, without zero, don't work this way). I was taught to add, subtract, and multiply by stacking them, carrying ten from right to left, while in base 20 it jumps faster.

Base 10	Base 20
100	400
10	20
I	I

It can be hard to remember that a 0 in the second or third position represents 20 rather than 10; 400 rather than 100.

When Anastasia joined us I asked if this were her doing? As an *ajq'ij*, active in local cultural expressions and political struggles as well as in national-level Mayan organizations, the local school curriculum seemed a site ripe for her intervention. "No," she said, pointing to the next lesson in Roman numerals, "It's in the section on *dead* systems. They don't teach it *because* the kids are Maya. It's part of the past, not something alive."

Mayan activists Raxché and Son Chonay, authors of *Ajilanïk: La numeración kaqchikel* (1995), remind us, however, that Roman numerals *are* still used to mark centuries and book chapters, while Mayan numbers are mainly found in tourism literature and ethnostalgically on quetzals, the Guatemalan currency. The authors highlight the peculiar position of Maya number: "so admired throughout the world and so little known among the actual living Maya" (7).

Being "little known" is deeply rooted in *temor*, *odio*, and *vergüenza*, fear, hatred, and shame, the last embedded in the linear time that leaves Maya numbers in "the past," superseded by today's indisputably universal math (Eglash 2001). (I am reminded of the power of this conceit—that there is no math but the one math—every time I describe this book as influenced by ethnomathematics and people laugh incredulously and say "what's that?!") Gary Urton says, "After, perhaps, the God of Christianity, numbers . . . [for keeping census and tribute records] represented one of the most powerful instruments of colonial rule" (1997, 205). Nora England says, "the system of Maya numeration was the first semantic field that fell into general disuse after the Spanish invasion. In many communities few people know the numbers higher than ten" (1996, 93). But some do (especially if number is thought of expansively, as in measurement) while others—particularly women weavers who perform quite extraordinary calculations counting threads and producing complex geometric designs—know numbers very well (Hendrickson 1995; Judie Maxwell, personal communication). Their vocabularies are important resources for those seeking to reconstruct Mayan numbers and put them into wider use. Alas, this rarely means these women "count" themselves as authors of books or through adequate remuneration for their astonishing creations. And in number's peculiar relation to "the modern," as more Mayan women study and work outside the home, fewer learn to weave and therefore to count.

But time may not be so linear, and number—like bones and other precious things preserved by going underground—is exhumed and put back into relation, disembedded and slowly reembedded. *Winaq*, meaning "twenty" in many Mayan languages and also "the whole person," is the intended audience for the numerous workshops, Saturnino's on-the-bus proselytizing, and the flurry of agendas, wall calendars, posters, and books published since 1994 on Mayan science, technology, and math—like *Let's Learn to Write Mayan Numbers from Zero to 1000: United to Create the Multicultural Nation* (Nojib'sa 2003); *Mayan Science and Technology Maya' No'jb'äl* (ESEDIR 2001); *Reconstitution of Mayan Being* (Uk'u'x B'e 2008); and *Uses and Applications of Mayan Cosmovision* (ASINDI 2009). And *winaq* is the hoped-for future of such efforts. They all emphasize that only two cultures developed zero. "The Maya were using zero 300 years before Christ while in Europe, even just 500 years ago, it was barely known" (Raxché and Son Chonay 1995, 18). "The fact that our ancestors invented a mathematical system that was so perfect and so much earlier than the European should fill us with profound pride in their accomplishments. . . . The system is more than 5000 years old and it is still alive in the hearts and in the daily practices of the Maya today" (Nojib'sa 2003, 17). "Our ancestors . . . are known as the 'Lords of Time' and to be deserving of this inheritance we have the obligation to take back our units of measurement and our own forms of counting" (Raxché and Son Chonay 1995, 19). Many of these publications include encouragements: "¡*Adelante!*" (let's go!), "¡*Buena Suerte!* (good luck), and "*Manos a la obra!*" (let's get to work).

Neither these boosters nor I suggest that five hundred years post invasion there's a fully functioning, untouched authentic system. Mayan numbers may be more like Borges's map: once perfectly accurate and completely covering the countryside with everything accounted for, but now existing mostly as shreds and tatters in out of the way places. And while not all my readers are Maya, perhaps we all have an obligation to understand a bit of the "number system of the prodigious Maya" (ALMG 2003, 12).[1] ¡*Adelante!*

Now, I remember with some shame how I quailed when visiting Japan and asked how to count to ten. Told "it depends on what you're counting," I immediately gave up! This is also true for Mayan numbers, and the numerical understandings expressed through classifications, which distinguish human and nonhuman, animate and inanimate, and even shape (things that are cylindrical, flat, or long) although differently among the twenty-two languages. Number words also gesture toward Guyer's "kinetics of counting," its material and embodied experience. For example, *winaq* is used for twenty days (and humans) while *k'al* is twenty things. Michael Closs links *k'al* to *may*, also 20, and both to bundling—perhaps related to commerce and tribute—and to the round or bundle of 20 days of the *cholq'ij*, or 260-day sacred calendar (1986b, 295). England connects it to the transitive verb *k'al'*, to tie, as in groups of twenty threads in weaving. Judie Maxwell told me, "*may* is interesting, it may count years, but not solar years (365 days), and is used for tobacco, which comes in packets of 20 cigars, often used for ceremonial offerings and also called *may*." Closs says in Kaqchikel the word for 8,000 is "*sack*," apparently connected to the pre-Columbian "custom of packaging cacao beans—an important commodity and also a medium of exchange" (1986b, 293–94). Maxwell says Maya-Chuj has a noun classifier for counting three related things: people, time, and serious diseases, suggesting an underlying categorization distinguishing the superanimate from the less so (this is a field of understanding in which everything is considered animate).

Mayan quantity concepts, as well as importance based in age, social category, and sex, are grammatically marked, as in the way certain nouns get a plural suffix (see also England 1996, 96). The very young, before speech, don't get it, some but not all animals do, and the *kaxlan*, or outsider (Spanish invaders, anthropologists), don't either. It marks those who "understand." Maxwell told me that in Kaqchikel stars as big gaseous balls ("science") don't get the plural form, but in the sense of spiritual beings that influence your life, they do. "Mayan people live in both worlds." To help me understand (as I was clearly struggling), she said, "in English we have nouns for things that come in a mass, that aren't differentiated, like snow, sand, or salt, but we can't talk about 'chair.' It needs something that clarifies how many: 'a' chair, 'the' chair, 'five' chairs. We are forced to notice. If you pay attention you see these are cosmograms, clues to the way people see the world." It can be hard for *kaxlan* to understand a mountain as superanimate so that it takes the plural. Maxwell said, mountains are called "*ajaw*," often translated as "owner," yet linguistically there's more a sense of manifestation, of being a part of, but it's more an inherent possession, the way I have a relation to "my" bones, blood, and veins.

Urton and Nina Llanos suggest a similar sense of possession in Quechua plural numbers. "Westerners" just lay them side by side (23), but for Que-

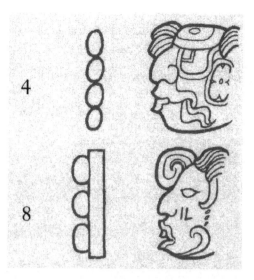

3.1 Mayan numbers 4 and 8 with head variants. Mark Van Stone. Used with kind permission.

chua a number can incorporate or possess another, for example, the complete unit 10 can possess the incomplete 3 to become 13. "These units are both likened to, and can be used as synonyms for the social groups called '*ayllus*'"—a system that connects by possessing territory, labor, ritual, and kinship (Urton 1997, 52). While Quechua understand number to have an "inherent property" of separating things, possession markers "in number names represent cohesive forces counteracting, or counterbalancing" such alienation, maintaining "the unity of collections . . . otherwise known as numbers" (53).

While Westerners (except those of us still mired in a mystical world of "lucky" numbers, lotteries, or retaining a childlike wonder)[2] tend to see numbers as neutral tools, for many Maya they have symbolic or metaphoric significance. Four is related to the sun because it defines the four directions as it travels from east to west, and 8 connects to corn and its germination period. In the head variants of the pre-Columbian number glyphs 4 is the sun god with the k'in glyph for day on his face and his upper incisors filed to a T; 8 is the young maize god, his face smooth and unwrinkled, a maize plant or spiral on his forehead and maize foliage falling over his face (Closs 1986b, 334–43).

Turning to the Quechua for continuing help in "thinking other" (Guyer 170), Urton and Nina Llanos say they count corn (among other things) with the first ear as *mama* and the second as her first offspring, the third as the second child, and so on. This way of counting is less a summing than "identifying and specifying a relation of hierarchy and succession uniting a group of things into an ordered set without regard to the total number of members" (1997, 102). *Mama* is the "origin of numbers and ordinal sequences" and is connected to women because of our capacity for augmentation and pluralization (160). Many Quechua women claim they can't count, but Urton argues that they mean they can't (or won't) count *money*—and not because they don't know numbers but because it's related to the market, where peasants are easily cheated and they don't want sole responsibility. Urton shows how, just as in Guatemala, women count quite expertly as they weave.

The central argument of *The Social Life of Numbers* is that *every system* of arithmetic and mathematics is an "art of rectification," seeking to derive equations displaying harmonic number relations and expressing equilibrium and balance.[3] Quechua arithmetic and mathematics have moral and ethical value because their purpose is to establish and maintain "such states *in the real world* (as in the distribution of resources and human actions)" (1997, 218; emphasis in original). That world is never simple or conflict-free, but it seeks to be.

Nora England (1996) says there are two Mayan ways of counting: first, adding, as in $40 + 1 = 41$, which Closs calls "counting from the lower level"; and second, progressively, or *toward* the next set of twenty, so 41 is "one of the third twenty" (94), which Closs calls "overcounting" (1986a, 31).[4] For example, progressive counting a child's age, she is four for the entire year between her third and fourth birthday as she is heading for, en route to, the next number. My people count what's completed, but this counts what's commencing. Similarly, in Classic Maya horology the twenty-day month was counted consecutively from one to nineteen, with the last day represented by the glyph for "seating" or "installation" of the incoming period; so rather than 20 Yaxkin or "end," it's written as the seating of Mol, the next month, and transcribed as zero (Closs 1986b, 298). This is like the contemporary Maya-Awakateko word for zero: *kyi'k-at*, meaning that which has no value and at the same time gives value (ALMG 2003, 17). Similarly, the Classic Mayan zero was understood as a beginning—not the null and void that so horrified Europeans (Rotman 1987), meaning it may not be the "same" zero—and was represented as a seed, a shell, or women's genitalia.[5] Perhaps a similar logic explains why Quechua *women* are allowed to count

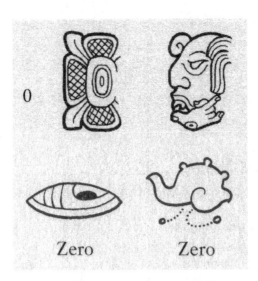

3.2 Mayan glyphs for zero: flower, head, seed and shell. Mark Van Stone. Used with kind permission.

the uncountable. They "are considered to possess most profoundly the capacity for multiplication . . . all potentially *mama*, the origin (and owner?) of numbers" (Urton 1997, 160, 103).

I encountered a somewhat different set of "Mayan numbers" in 2008, at a workshop I attended on how to read Mayan glyphs. Under the direction of the renowned German Mayanist Nikolai Grube, we were working on the Dresden codex, puzzling out glyphs for offerings and deities, and trying to calculate the phases of Venus (complicated in itself and even harder in base 20!). Over lunch one day, Romelia Mó gave a presentation called "Racism in Numbers." She laid out the statistics on indigenous malnutrition and lack of public services like health care and education and then showed the monetary cost of being Maya: a median Q4,260 annual difference (and worse for women). She finished by asking, "Why are you studying Mayan culture?" And answered herself: "To strengthen our ethnic identity so we can change these numbers." "These numbers," both the Classic (the glyphs and calculations we were learning to take pride in) and Current (statistics on inequality) are meant to initiate a process, not close the book. They seek rectification.

In Quechua a number generates or "'pushes ahead of it,' each successively higher number" (Urton 1997, 84). There is a similar binding force that pushes odd numbers toward even, marked linguistically by *ntin*, so that "the motivation for *two* is the 'loneliness' (*ch'ulla*) of *one* . . . it needs a 'partner'" (*ch'ullantin*) (78). Mayan "progressive" counting evokes a similar sense of number yearning. It desires connection, a movement toward. And in that, perhaps it's not so different from "Western" understandings. Peter Greenaway says, "Counting is the most simple and primitive of narratives— 12345678910—a tale with a beginning, a middle, and an end and a sense of progression—arriving at a finish of two digits—a goal attained, a denouement reached" (1996, 28). Brian Rotman says counting is a process, "a whole activity of traversing what will become a sequence of counted positions" (1987, 13). In English we "arrive" at numbers.[6]

Verran suggests numbers are active, giving them a "holographic effect": their "capacity to seamlessly connect a child . . . with the ledger books . . . and at the same time negotiate a scale shift from the minutiae of family life to the macro-social category of British Empire, depends on figuring and a recursive re-figuring," on "repeated activities with hands and words," and on reaccomplishing singularity from a background of plurality (2000a, 367). She says thinking this way means giving up foundation (number as freestanding) to focus instead "on the doing, the enacting." It also involves the recognition that "as objects, numbers and numerations are not (not ever) complete objects; their making as objects is a project that cannot be completed" (366). She suggests the metaphor of a trek—the singularity of steps and the plurality of many steps that in turn make up the singularity of a journey, getting from here to there (369). Privilege (¡*dichosa!*)—when "your" system counts as the universal one, when you know where your dead are— can make it harder to see how all numbers (and people) are traversing and in relation. However, while all counting might work this way, not all counting counts (yet).

That's why the Mayan collective ESEDIR emphasizes that "*Equi-valorar* is giving the same value or status to our science and technology as we do to the 'universal' science and technology developed out of contributions from the whole world" (2001, 94). The yearning, the journey, is to rectify this holographic inequality that devalues numbers and (as?) people at every level, from the minutiae of schoolbooks to the "energy and self-possession" needed for integral development, to the macrosocial category of genocide. The struggle is to relate math to politics, to solve for XX, to balance debit and loss with credit and repair in algebras of Maya and human rights. It is for adequation, equalizing, equi-valuing: what we yearn for.

When Francisca Gomez and I visited the FAFG offices, our young non-Mayan guide spoke of the special relation the Maya have to their dead and why it was so important to exhume, identify, and then reinter the bodies with proper ceremonies. Walking away along the tree-lined street, Francisca snorted, "Does she think Maya are the only ones who want to know where their dead are?! No one wants their family in an unmarked grave." The ALMG says, "Mathematics is a personal intellectual adventure, how we seek to measure and compare all that surrounds us, to understand our place in the universe" (2003, 12). In the spirit of equi-valorar I've led you through some aspects of Maya measure as an "intellectual adventure" in and of itself (and as very much alive). Now I'll explore how it helps us understand the "social life" of all forms of measure.

Off-Balance, Reparation, and the General Equivalent

At no time have the family members of the victims sought to charge a price for the lives of our loved ones because life has no price. However, as it was state agents . . . responsible for the disappearances, for the torture, and for the deaths, and as the state invested in the war, invested in the bombs and also invested in contracting international advisors to design and execute its criminal and often clandestine war operations, this same state has the responsibility to provide individual and collective reparations.
—Rosalina Tuyuc, Former National Reparations Program President

Like counting, the aftermath of the war is often described as a journey. In the map gracing the Alliance against Impunity's textbook on the "road to reconciliation," it passes through "truth," "acceptance of responsibility," and "justice" to "reparations." Taking a plurality of steps brings Guatemala from here to there: a bright day just over the next hill (Alianza 2004, 28).

Reparations are generally understood as the obligation of the wrongdoer to compensate people who have been injured and to amend and redress damage done. In the wake of subtraction and division, addition and multiplication are needed to rectify loss. They are meant, as far as possible, to wipe out the consequences of an illegal act and restore the situation that would, in all probability, have existed if that act had not been committed (Redress 2013). Emerging from a history of states (generally the losers) compensating each other after hostilities, in the twentieth century reparation meshed with emerging human rights accounting (that equi-values violations) to make individuals and substate collectivities conceivable as beneficiaries. This seems to be the origin of military payment of solatia (compensation or grievance payments) for civilian wartime deaths, which the United States began in Korea and Vietnam in the 1950s and 1960s and continued in Afghanistan and Iraq.

A bit like the disconcertment of a brazillion, the (mathematically) sublime hopes and painful qualifications proffered by reparations may be best captured by a macabre joke. In 2007 *The Onion* (a satirical newspaper) reported: "With more American military casualties . . . than any year since the war began, a bipartisan group of House representatives introduced a bill Monday that calls for nearly 4,000 U.S. soldiers who have been killed in Iraq to be brought back to life. 'These brave men and women gave their lives for our country. . . . The least we can do is give them back.' . . . Article III states that everything will go back to the way it was before. . . . John Boehner (R-OH) [says it] is the most effective way to ensure that the growing casualty rate in Iraq is instantly reversed and reduced to zero. . . . 'I assure the American people that the reborn troops will appear just as alive and vital as they did mere moments before they were killed. In no way will they be an unholy abomination of undead flesh,' [Rep.] Braley said" (52).

Victims and their allies in Guatemala, like the rich and expanding literature on reparations as an aspect of transitional and restorative justice (Barkan 2001; Minow 1998; Torpey 2008; de Grieff 2008; Eng 2011), are grappling with the paradox that makes this simultaneously horrible and funny. The very singularity of the person who has been lost makes it impossible to replace them—nothing is the same as them. Yet this very specialness makes them valuable and thus their loss so grievous that it demands some sort of compensation, indemnity (meaning literally "unhurt"), balance $(-1 + 1 = 0)$. And someone must attend to their "dependents," to those social relations through which loss reverberates through time. For several hundred years now, insurance regimes have allowed members of certain classes to "master time and discipline the future" (Ewald 1991, 207) by paying premiums to hedge against such losses.[7] But these logics intertwine with "regimes of fault" that make *perpetrators* responsible—in *The Onion* case, the very state that put soldiers in harm's way. The "least" they can do is give the life back. Or barring that, "pay back" some of what they've taken, even if it only symbolically evens things out.

Indemnity also seems fair for losses even harder to count than a dead body: time lost to imprisonment; security in and enjoyment of one's own corporeality lost to rape and/as torture; the loss of food and desecration of a sacred substance when a cornfield is burned; futures that might have been with the presence, love, disciplining, and earning power of a parent. And that's so even if those particular people aren't exactly missed. After describing the murders of his uncles and father, a Maya-Tzutujil man said, "my father drank a lot and he beat us often. Maybe it's for the best." A Maya-K'iche' war widow and organizer from Quetzaltenango told me that her husband had been very controlling and violent. "I could never have done this work if he were still alive."

Freud reminds us that the ambivalence that turns loved (and feared) family members into ghosts and invests the home with the *unheimlich*, or uncanny, is deeply rooted in the patriarchal structures of the heteronormative family, themselves writ large in Church and State. The ensuing therapeutic logics—developed in the same century as human rights reparations—entail a (re)turn to these sites and actors as a necessary component of repair. The wound is healed only by the sword that smote it. Perhaps this is also true for the deeper, historic losses revealed in Leopoldo Tzian and Romelia Mó's "Mayan numbers." Looming behind each singular loss and even the aggregate of genocide is an older colonial imbalance, so that there can never be a fully adequate repair. Things cannot, not ever, go back to how they were. To try is to get entangled with unholy abominations of undead flesh.

But you also cannot, not ever, give up on something that might be called justice. Rosalina Tuyuc, Maya-Kaqchikel, founder of the widows' organization CONAVIGUA and a savvy activist, says "life has no price" (2007, 22). But this is precisely where number and politics are inseparable. The state, which invested in damage, must pay. The state, as the sword that smote, must heal. Life ≠ $ but at least inadequate is > 0.

In Guatemala demands for reparations began in the long, slow end of the war (extending from the 1984 constitution to the 1996 peace treaty). The peace accords signed by the government and the URNG guerrillas, under enormous pressure from civil society and victims' organizations, agree on the need for *resarcimiento* (compensation, repayment, reparation of damage), and it is one of the major recommendations of the 1999 CEH report (which, by accounting for the war and acknowledging genocide, itself served as an instrument of repair). The failure of the 1999 *Consulta Nacional* (national referendum) to institutionalize the peace accords, with their more holistic provisions for indigenous rights and socioeconomic reforms (including broadening the tax base), left activists struggling to achieve more piecemeal attempts to count and to rectify. These included a wide range of DIY (do-it-yourself) projects—of memorials, reports, and other forms of co-memoration; through collaborating with non- and semistate institutions like FAFG, REMHI, and CEH; by bringing cases in national and international courts, like the OAS Inter-American Human Rights Court in Costa Rica (IAHRC), and insisting on state-supplied *resarcimiento*. I'll give you a taste of some of these vibrant efforts, then focus on the state's response: the National Reparations Program (PNR).

Dis-Member/Meant

> You could say that it is like a beehive that was destroyed: they all go their own way, you cannot bring them together anymore.
> Maya-Q'eqchi' man (Viaene 2010a, 13)

Following widespread dreaming of a white cross emerging from a mountain, which villagers in the Saha'kok region of Cobán, Alta Verapaz interpreted as their relatives requesting proper burial rituals, in 1995 people collected the names of 916 victims from twenty-eight communities and wrote them on just such a cross (Flores 2001; Viaene 2010a). Mayan ceremonies are held there for November first, the Day of the Dead, and for Easter. The list includes people who died of famine, exposure, or *susto* (fear) as well as those directly murdered by soldiers or patrollers. Now monuments grace hundreds of highland towns and Guatemala City.

In the wake of the necessary but incomplete truth commission reports—Simone Remijnse says Joyabaj's priest, after energetic collaboration, said, "My memory of Joyabaj seems to be much bigger than the memory REMHI has of Joyabaj" (2002, 268)—many communities have produced their own. These include (all title translations are mine) *¿Qué fue lo que pasó? ¿Chajari xc'uluri?* (What Was It That Happened?; CECEP 2012); *Oj K'aslik estamos vivos* (We Are Alive; Museo Comunitario Rabinal Achi 2003); *Porque queríamos salir de tanta pobreza* (Why We Wanted to Escape from So Much Poverty; Impunity Watch 2011); *Tejidos que lleva el alma* (Weavings the Soul Carries; ECAP 2009); *Voces que cuentan, memoria nuestra* (Voices That Speak, Our Memory; Grupo Hace 25 Años, 2006); *Memoria de los caídos* (Memory of the Fallen; Fundación Guillermo Toriello 2006); *Rompiendo el silencio* (Breaking the Silence; Consorcio Actoras de Cambio 2006); *Nos salvó la sagrada selva* (The Sacred Forest Saved Us; Huet 2008). And this is just my incomplete collection! I list them to convey the yearning (and *effort* expended) for an accounting, often linked explicitly to processes of repair.

Other actants are also involved in rectification. Lieselotte Viaene (2012b) says that many Maya-Q'eqchi' people understand *q'oq* as "the invisible spiritual force of the pain, tears and sadness that somebody or something feels due to being treated wrongly" with "retributive consequence[s]" for perpetrators (2012b, 297–99). This force is responsible, people say, for the local military commissioner becoming blind and lame and for the dementia suffered by General Lucas García, who as de facto president oversaw the first stage of the 1980s genocide.[8] Viaene says that the value placed in seeking balance and worry that they themselves would invite such consequences if they harmed their victimizers might explain why few of her interlocutors have sought justice or reparations in the human realm. Manuel, Maya-K'iche' from a hamlet of Joyabaj, seemed satisfied after exhuming his father that now the patrol commander was the one living, as he and his mother had, "afraid, afraid, and locked in his house." Nonindigenous activist Aura Elena Farfán, after thirty years seeking her disappeared brother, said that the paralysis suffered by General Mejía Victores (de facto president 1983–86) was "maybe a punishment," and saw something similar with General Héctor Gramajo and his son, who died together of bee stings. "I imagine the pain, the fear, the anguish. He can't breathe and he sees his son the same and he can't help. A parent unable to save his child. For me, that was something."

Yet many do demand more, even as achieving state-supplied *resarcimiento* has been a trek through many byways and doubling backs. One avenue has been the IAHRC, the Inter-American Court. Beginning in 2001, with the "white van death squad" case, the Guatemalan state was forced to acknowledge crimes against citizens, apologize, and pay significant sums to survivors, in this case $519,345 for the death squad's 11 known victims. Since then the IAHRC has decided thirteen cases encompassing 469 victims and granted $60,000 for the kidnapping of Maritza Urrutia, $396,000 for the disappearance of San Martín Jilotepeque community leader Florencio Chitay, $784,000 for the murder of Guatemalan anthropologist Myrna Mack Chang, $498,000 for the disappearance of Maya-Mam guerrilla leader Efraín Bamaca (husband of US attorney Jennifer Harbury), and $9,881,643 for the massacre of 284 people in Plan de Sánchez, Baja Verapaz, with a total of $20.8 million disbursed. Over eighty-five cases are pending (Andrés 2012).

In the Myrna Mack case, family members didn't want money, but they say the court insisted they sum up lost wages and other losses to create a monetary equivalent. Such adding is meant to *make* count. Calculating her worth to make the state literally pay is part of a strategy to increase the costs of human rights violations—inputting different numbers into future cost-benefit calculations.[9] Money is a sign the state can read. By paying, it implicitly accepts responsibility (probably why the US military energetically insists that solatia payments *only* show compassion, not admission of fault).

I have explored the disconcertments of the un-equivalence of such sums (as between stockbrokers and cleaning staff indemnified by the September 11 Victim Compensation Fund) elsewhere (2009). The actuarial and insurantial logics that calculate the monetary "worth" of a life are quite mundane but still strike me as epistemologically peculiar (see chapter 6). Repair via the general equivalent of money puts us off balance again. Existential and banal, life may not have a price, but it's calculated on a daily basis nonetheless (and often in ways that transform adding into division). Natan Sznaider says, "it is not the payments themselves so much as the side-effects of the process that really count. But the money is what made the process possible" (2002, 110).

I'm suggesting that money is itself an actant which, of course, "really counts"—as when the settlements go to feed, house, and educate the next generation or, for Myrna Mack, continue her work by funding her research institute AVANCSO and scholarships for anthropology students. And like number, money also counts in more mysterious, even "sacred" ways. In Guatemala, monetary recompense from the entity that caused the injury is, indeed, a demand: as the FAFG found when family members contributing their DNA "expressed their hopes for economic reparations," hopes the FAFG could not fulfill. As Remijnse says, describing the qualified effects of the REMHI report in Joyabaj, "People thought the report would tell it all . . . they hoped that the perpetrators would be caught, financial compensation would be paid. . . . But nothing changed" (2002, 269).

The Sword That Smote It

Austere and symbolic.
—Former Chilean President Ricardo Lagos describing reparations
for Pinochet's victims

The other two forms of state *resarcimiento* were also only achieved under great duress. In June 2002 thousands of ex-PAC, former members of the civil defense patrols, with support from AVEMILGUA, the army veterans' association, took over the northern department of Petén, demanding compensation for their "service to the state" in militarized duties as guards, trackers, and sometimes killers. With unseemly haste in the eyes of many—given PAC collaboration in war crimes, no large-scale *resarcimiento* for victims, and strong suspicions of vote buying—the Portillo government agreed to three payments of Q5,241 ($660) each over about ten years (Sáenz 2004).

A Guatemalan archaeologist told me the first payment disrupted his dig. "Suddenly half the workers didn't show for a day, then two days, and then almost everyone was gone. That's when I realized it was the money. Everyone was drunk." In Joyabaj, Micaela, a Maya-K'iche' mother of eight, grandmother of seven, and struggling proprietress of a small restaurant, was so hurt and enraged that her husband spent his entire wad on drinking with another woman ("Not a penny for us! Not even for our debts for Joel to go to the States!") that this reverent Catholic finally kicked him out of the house. A nonindigenous man told me, "When they said they'd pay, my father called me and told me to get organized to get the money, but I said that money *llora sangre*: it cries blood. It's not good money. [Perhaps this is why so many drank it away?] And it's only Q5,000. You'd spend that in just paperwork and travel. It's not worth it! I'd rather work instead. Earn my money."

Pilot projects for *resarcimiento* for *victims* began in 2000, but not much happened until 2005, when the PNR was more sturdily established under the leadership of Rosalina Tuyuc and as a line item in the state budget—and then only due to tenacious organizing. The CEH recommendations, social movement agitation, and official documents of the PNR itself all insist that *resarcimiento* must be comprehensive: dignifying the victims; providing cultural, material, and monetary restitution, psychosocial repair, and physical rehabilitation and ensuring access to justice. The four places identified by the CEH as genocide cases were prioritized and received close to the full panoply of remedies, although what would count as "cultural repair" has been an ongoing ethnically coded fracture, further complicated by the government's/military's refusal to accept that genocide—entailing *collective* repair—occurred. Inside the program and out, *resarcimiento* has been a site and stake of struggle, less a thing than a journey, or as Verran might say, a constant accomplishment.

When I visited the PNR's bustling Zone One office in January 2005, the mostly Maya staff were enthusiastic about finally fulfilling people's hopes, opening the first of nineteen regional offices, creating radio and print ads, fine-tuning guidelines for audit regimes, and compiling lists of beneficiaries.

Those who can prove relation to a victim will receive Q24,000 (about $3,200) for their dead relative. Sexual assault and/or torture survivors receive between Q10,000 and Q20,000 ($1,370–$2,750). Beyond the simultaneously banal and existential issues raised by money's relation to the human, basic commensuration is also sticky. No matter how many family members were killed, the PNR will compensate only for two, and the payment for torture, like rape, is one-time, whether you were assaulted once or held for weeks, months, or even years in rape houses or places like La Isla. (Even getting rape to count at all was highly contentious.) Nothing else counts. Loss $> 2 = 0$.

Comparing IAHRC-mandated sums of $396,000 for Florencio Chitay to $784,000 for Myrna Mack Chang and both to $3,200 for a PNR recipient shows how balance (state crime to state payout) constantly tumbles through imbalance, even as each amount is based on careful calculation and energetic efforts at precision. In the name of fairness, in fact, the government of former general, President Pérez Molina, petitioned the IAHRC to devolve all pending cases back to the PNR, so everyone would get the same amount. (Ignoring the fact that the court hears cases only after plaintiffs prove satisfaction is impossible in the national justice system.)

Over time, as testimonies were compiled and beneficiaries listed, PNR staffers were surprised to find something else that didn't count: 70% of their cases did not appear in either the REMHI or CEH reports. Before there was too much fear, Ms. Tuyuc said, people didn't have "the courage or confidence to speak of what had happened. They said 200,000 dead and 40,000 disappeared. But it looks like we'll have to add more."

We (mostly) live in a world in which a human's importance is estimated by the "quantum of lucration of which he can be made the instrument" (Southey, in Poovey 295), so it makes sense that victims demand pecuniary recompense from the state. As time went on, however, individual financial compensation increasingly became the PNR's be-all and end-all (the word *finance* comes from *finer*, "to end," as in to settle accounts). In March 2008, a human rights lawyer said, "Sadly, the search for justice has been monetarized."[10] Aura Elena Farfán, involved in the struggle for reparations from its 1980s beginning, echoed this: "'solo cheque, solo cheque,' is what people say (it's just a check), and it creates divisions in families." And Viaene, monitoring the PNR in Alta Verapaz, says that "individual financial compensation is the 'easiest' to implement of the five measures recommended" (2010a, 9), and victim organizations strongly demanded such compensation (as well as restoration of destroyed possessions and titles to their lands; Viaene 2010b,

297). Gustavo Porras, writing from inside the program, says that people began to view the PNR as an "omnipotent institution, as if by itself it could fulfill all state functions . . . once the distribution of checks began an unstoppable avalanche of demands followed" (2007, 33–34).

Checks are easiest, of course, because of money's magical powers of abstraction. Just as for numbers, with the "leap" to calculations in your head, coin—that handy general equivalent—simplifies market relations, which now speed by like a ray of light thanks to the "imaginary money" of paper and digital signals. You don't have to send a brace of oxen over eBay to pay for that vintage Journey album or schlep actual bills, coins, grinding stones, housing materials, hens, and hoes over bandit-infested and barely passable mountain roads to northern El Quiché or Huehuetenango. You just bring some checks. In the market they'll magically transform into the very material goods people lost. (Of course, handing out checks assumes people's insertion into the infrastructures of the financialization of daily life, like having a bank account or access to some institution that will cash it—for a small fee.)

As many investors know all too well after 2008, the magic can also manifest in spectacular disappearing acts. A Mayan woman who worked with the PNR vividly remembered one day in a village where people had suffered massacres and then had to jump through the reparations hoops. Finally, everyone was gathered and they were ready to hand out checks, when word came down that the private bank holding the state's money had crashed, and the checks had no money behind them.

The reality represented by gold in its circulation is the reality of an electric spark.
—Karl Marx (1911, 150)

There are many ways to interrogate reparations as I ponder the algebraic bonesetting (reducing and balancing) of Mayan and human rights, but I'll focus on some peculiarities and disconcertments in this "easiest to implement" measure. And as with number, rather than assume the warm, qualitative, singular, mysterious, special human is incommensurable with the cold, quantitative, aggregate, transparent, general (i.e., profane) money (human ≠ $; human ≠ #), I'll suggest neither side of the equation is so clear cut and may be in much closer relation than the ≠ would suggest. Because that's what general equivalents do.

Remember Guyer's suggestion that quantity and quality are both scales, unanchored in any foundational invariant until threshold points, performances, and institutions "settle" a link, transforming one into an anchor for the other. Yet seeing them as "cosmograms," symptoms of the "social life" of measurement, is also deeply, excitingly, unsettling. I want to both set up and disconcert money's apparently banal ability to ground value—similar to the way number (neutral, objective, standing alone) promises to get us "just the facts, ma'am," and bones seem to prove exactly how many died. The thing is . . . while money is apparently only a simple intermediary, a means to transact, it is, like Mayan (and maybe all) numeration, influenced by its relations. Some of the ambivalence around *resarcimiento*—entailing both enormous satisfaction and deep anxiety—emanates from the *relation* it constitutes between the state and its "beneficiaries." Getting *money* out of the state, not "just" an apology, shows it is serious in acknowledging responsibility. (Plus, who can deny money's power to get you stuff you need—and want—or that warm glow that comes from having it in your pocket?) But demanding and accepting that particular money has consequences.

First, of course, getting it requires giving testimony to the state, attached to your name, ID number, address, and phone. Part of audit culture's banal rituals of verification, it also gets you into scary uncontrollable databases. And it's costly: in money to acquire proper documents, for translation, and travel; in the psychic toll of testifying; and in time, as Maya survivor Pedrina Alvardo said: "every benefit we've received has cost us years of struggle" (Grave 2012, 26). It can also unsettle community and family relations. Not everyone gets verified, and for a while only deaths caused by direct violence were compensated, plus there have been contentious debates over payments to ex-PAC (who, remember, were almost all the men in the highlands) and former guerrillas.[11] This means that not everyone has received reparation, often causing guilt among those who have, as well as envy and rancor. More troubling for many is the way it can divide families. The sums are small, especially to be disbursed among a constellation of relatives: parents, spouse, siblings, children, grandchildren. People complain that young people take it from their aging mothers or via primogeniture the eldest son takes it all. In New Río Negro, Juan, a Maya-Achi' man, said, "The thing is, the system creates fighting. It sets us against each other and not against the real enemy."

Second, accepting the money can bring a sense of balance, of settling. But it can also unsettle, given the incommensuration between Q24,000 and the loss it's supposed to cover. Not to mention suspicions that the payee is motivated by more than compassion. Once payment is accepted you can't really ask for more. You've let the state off the hook (finance/finish). In the Ríos Montt genocide trial defense lawyers tried to delegitimize victims' testimony because they'd received reparations.

It can also feel like forgiveness of the unforgivable. A friend in the United States, offered compensation for being wiretapped by the FBI, said, "I wouldn't accept it. I didn't want to give them the satisfaction." For those who have organized their lives around the concept of the state as enemy, any negotiation with it is a betrayal of their hard-won ethical consciousness (McAllister 2013). Comments from members of the US military on "compensation" seem to justify such refusals: "'It's hard to digest that the value of a human life is a few thousand dollars,' said Gordon-Bray, the general in Iraq. 'But you know that in their economic situation, it is the equivalent of much more, and *you feel better*.' In 2007, General David Petraeus . . . described the tactical element of condolence payments: 'The quicker you can do it, the more responsive you can seem to be . . . the more valuable it is, and the more helpful it is to your operation'" (Currier 2013; emphasis added). The generals seem to voice David Eng's argument (2011) that reparation is meant to make recipients love the very thing they hate (for Melanie Klein the breast, here the military state), suggesting *resarcimiento* is "war by other means," part of counterinsurgency civic action. And how unfair is it that even the solace is for the perpetrator?

Perhaps less existential but no less disturbing, reparations may form just one of a range of clientelist options states deploy to buy votes, curry dependency, and placate demands before they turn radical. For example, reparations fit nicely with World Bank and USAID microfinance logics and direct cash transfers (Ferguson 2009). Yet in Guatemala as elsewhere, activists invest "years of struggle" to drag the state kicking and screaming to take out its checkbook. *Resarcimiento* and solatia are not fully reducible to winning "hearts and minds" (or profits on microcredit interest payments).

This is in part due to the weird liveliness of money itself; as Sarah Lochlann Jain says, it "can mutate in purpose from compensation to punishment, while so easily mutating again through desire and greed" (2006, 3). While there are those who interact quite pragmatically with reparations payments, I have spoken to many for whom the money itself takes on a moral valence, a personality, a tenacious set of characteristics that can extend through time, the way ex-PAC money "cries blood." Asked why she didn't apply for reparations, a Maya-K'iche' woman said, "that money is no good. You don't prosper with that money. It's like money earned from a *cantina*" (meaning benefiting from others' suffering). After grinding down their mother's reluctance to apply for their father's murder, Maya-Kaqchikel friends in Patzicía said they've just put the money in the bank. "We all feel uneasy about it," said Alberto, "I don't know. I guess we'll use it if there's an emergency or an illness. It was harder than we thought to accept the money. We can't really think about investing it, using it for other objectives." Others say that it comes from death so it will carry death into any investment: land will be fallow, plants wither, animals remain barren. It isn't laundered in its passage through exchange. Something creepy stays attached, even for something as basic as food. A Maya-Q'eqchi' man told Viaene, "*K'ajk'amunk*, paying for violence, we do not like it. . . . It is like for my mother, they are going to pay me for her, I will eat my mother, I will chew my mother" (2010a, 16).

In July 2012 I met Julio Cochoy at an archaeology conference (see Chapter 7). He told me he was involved in a DIY truth commission report in his Maya-K'iche' hometown of Santa Lucía, near Lake Atitlán, and had a different experience of *resarcimiento's* liveliness. "There was a widow, her son was disappeared. She was a midwife, an important woman in the community. Her son was sixteen. Some time in 1981 the army came, breaking down the door, and her thought was that she would open it and talk to them, reason with them. This was her logic. She had hands that had only ever given life. She trusted they would respect her. But . . . they pushed her aside and took her son. When we came to take the testimony she was silent. We had the recorder on, all ready, and she said nothing. Fifteen minutes passed. Half an hour. Finally we left, and only then she came after us, crying. 'It was my fault! My fault! I opened the door.' She had carried that all that time. That it was her fault."

When they started taking testimonials, he said, "*Odio, temor, temor, odio*, there was so much fear and so much hatred. It was POISON. But little by little people opened up." They collected thirty-six testimonials and created a booklet and CD. This was about the same time the reparations program was starting, and they debated applying. "The needs were very great yet we thought, 'But the money, it seems like a way to *comprar conciencia*, to shut us up. . . .' But we created a huge pile of papers, a stack of documents, and we were one of the first, with Rabinal, to receive. There was a big ritual in the Palace . . . and at first I didn't want to go. It seemed like they were using us, putting on a show, but the women, the victims, the widows, they really needed the money, it could make a big difference." (I'm sharply condensing his discussion of these vacillations.)

He said that when the midwife "came back from the palace, something had changed. President Berger himself had handed her the check and said, 'Perdón.' And that was her *saneamiento*, healing. The paper. It symbolized that it was not her fault. It was not money, at that moment. She took it home and put it in a basket with flowers and candles on her altar. She wouldn't cash it. She kept it there in the sacred place. That paper direct from the president's hands. It was so important!

"But then her kids came to me and said, 'Mom is not cashing the check! What do we do? We need the money!' and I said I'd help, so I went to her and told her I'd take a picture of it and she could keep the image there among her things, and she was content. When she was dying she sent her husband to find me and she could barely speak, but she held my hand and kissed it and said, 'I'm going, I'm going but I'm content.'"

Here money and (is?) its chain of imaginary representations (check, photograph) work through dream logics of displacement and condensation, winding down like an umbilicus into the dark and mysterious sites of loss, doubling back overdetermined, sometimes bearing relief. Like the two sides of a coin: one face is mundane, precise, a specific amount, often a number, while the other bears likenesses pointing to the ineffable and overarching, supposed simultaneously to ground value and to emanate from it (on early coins a bee or stag stood in for a nature goddess; later we got gods, royalty, and presidents).[12] Money is never just a simple, "natural" thing. In this case it resembles those special quantifiers meant to capture the "more than the sum" whole of a murder of crows, an exultation of larks, the Quechua "uncountable" of living, reproducing things. Perhaps also the "accomplishment" of a numeric "object," the Genocide of Maya, understood in Verran's sense. "As objects, numbers and numerations are not (not ever) complete objects; their making as objects is a project that can not be completed" (2000a, 366). And perhaps this, in turn, is due to the generativity of these intersecting relations: mother-son-number-president-state-activist-money. Less settled foundation than doing, enacting.

But sometimes reparations money has the exact opposite effect, losing its shiny algebraic promise of bonesetting as healing, indemnity as unhurting, state acknowledgment of wrong as cleansing of shame. It shows its other face of the coin as the dross and filth that accrue to those who touch it, the slime on the other side of the sublime, and perhaps not surprisingly, this emerges from the same seismic split that divided the feminized space of the home and bedroom from the masculinized realm of virtuous book-keeping and profit.

Activists in CONAVIGUA, the National Union of Guatemalan Women (UNAMG), and the Team for Community Studies and Psycho-social Action (ECAP), and historians like Matilde González in *Se cambió el tiempo* (2002) have struggled to make rape count, to prove it was integral to the army's counterinsurgency (like almost all male-organized mass violence) and should be considered an aspect of genocide (ECAP 2009; Crosby, Lykes, and Caxaj 2016). Men and women, Maya and ladino/a were raped, but the CEH found that in 89% of its cases of sexual violence, indigenous women were the victims. It took strenuous effort to make those victims count for the PNR and extraordinary courage for women to come forward and testify. And despite decades of labor to dignify them, *vergüenza* remains strong. In an unprecedented acknowledgement of this, Ixil women testifying in the Ríos Montt trial were allowed to cover their faces. Setting an important international precedent, the judges ruled that mass rapes *were* attempts to destroy a people. Yet while there's always a bit of hoopla when the PNR comes to town—Mayan ceremonies, national and local dignitaries—rape compensation is done discreetly. But somehow neighbors find out, and then the money effects a mutation. State reparations payments are meant to convert a rampaging psychokiller into a meek supplicant, transforming a shameful subversive—whose failure is her crime and her suffering a just punishment—into a victim and then into a dignified recipient of official acknowledgment of wrong. But it can also turn a victim into a whore. What else is a woman who accepts money for sex?

Patterns Which People Inhabit and Which Inhabit People

When the Army came up with the word solatium, it set some very strange magic loose in the world. For me it will always be a reminder . . . of how totally, appallingly, even insanely resolute we remained in believing in our good intentions. Solatium. What's in a word . . . when . . . there's still so little solace for anyone, American or Vietnamese? As an American, still trying to come to terms with what we did there, I hang onto it for two very specific reasons. It won't bring that boy back; and it won't make him go away, either.

—Philip Beidler, former soldier, reflecting on a boy killed in Vietnam

In early 2013 with the US economy staring down a "fiscal cliff," great hilarity was derived from the "absurd" proposal to mint a trillion-dollar coin "emblazoned with 'In God We Trust' and a 1 with 12 zeros behind it" (Lowrey 2013, B2). Republicans warned the amount of platinum needed to mint it would sink the *Titanic* (although the *New York Times* made the "technical point" that the coin wouldn't need to contain a trillion dollars' worth of metal). Even our master of suspicion, political comedian Jon Stewart, mocked the idea. "If you're going to make [*beep*] up then I say go big or go home. Why not a 100 quillion dollar coin . . . with a unicorn felching a centaur?" Nobel laureate economist Paul Krugman tsk-tsked Stewart for forgetting that finance is a fiction and later made a similar point about bitcoins (untraceable online money, mostly used for speculation and illicit transactions), calling them useful lessons "in the ways people misunderstand money—particularly the desire to divorce the value of money from the society it serves." He acknowledged the strangeness of bitcoins, which "derive their value, if any, purely from . . . the belief that other people will accept them as payment" (although he tries to hold on to gold having "real" value because of its nonmonetary uses). It's a philosophical misconception and impossible dream "to long for a pristine monetary standard, untouched by human frailty." Money is a "'social contrivance,' not something that stands outside society. . . . Some people are just bothered by the notion that money is a human thing, and want the benefits of the monetary network without the social part. Sorry, it can't be done" (2013, A19). And it's not only the general public that is bamboozled. Bill Maurer reminds us, "When it comes to money, scholars across the disciplines are continually surprised to discover that money is 'just' meaning, or that finance is a fiction. When faced with the question of money's being adequate to anything at all, people often stop in wonder, and the reflection leaves their practical activity at a momentary impasse" (2005, xiv). Strange magic has long been afoot.

Money may buy solace, but monetary reparation also holds us in a peculiar epistemic space, a certain timelessness of not bringing back but not making go away, of wondering and reflecting on the disconcerting coconstitution of legal tender and human frailty (Beidler 2001). Like a fact, it may mean evidences or "anything which exists"—because that's what it might take to equivalue the enormous deficit produced by the fundamental unfairness of the Cold War counterinsurgency behemoth murderously arrayed against the popular mobilizations of the 1970s, that frail skein of students, peasants, indigenous people, priests, nuns, revolutionaries, and cross-border solidarity. Jacinto, a young PGT member at the police archives, said, upon reading of a fellow student's early 1980s assassination: "To see the documents attesting to how they followed X or Y person. You say to yourself, look at this whole structure, all lined up against one person . . . it wasn't fair, it wasn't one-on-one—it was a structure. Hundreds of people against one. It's frustrating and it makes me so angry" (Weld 2014, 161). Matilde González says the Maya-K'iche' she worked with insist "that the magnitude and the extension of the violence visited upon them by the state—in both the distant and more recent past—was terrifyingly difficult to understand because they were so out of proportion to their demands for justice" (2002, 263). And Rosalina Tuyuc reminds us that "the end of the armed conflict was really just a ceasefire, there was no de-structuring of the political, economic, and military system, which today remains intact, and this makes it very difficult to advance in the search for reconciliation" (2007, 24).

Which returns us to that older, larger exponential deficit, the one that might take everything that exists to balance. When the activist widow at the Choatalum hearing said, "Why did they kill him? All he wanted was to feed his children," she was expressing her disconcertment at that still-structuring "system." As was Fernando García's companion, describing their hopes for a "just, supportive and democratic society, in which all would share."

Historian J. T. Way asks, "what is life like in a world where labor is worth nothing?" (2012, 86). This is the quincentenary imbalance, of unrequited toil and planetary devastation, the one that might demand that "every drop of blood drawn with the lash shall be paid by another drawn with the sword" (Lincoln 1865). The one made possible by the more general crystallization of racism, patriarchy, colonial expropriation, and double-entry bookkeeping's ability to calculate the hard, mathematical conception of profit *and* by the specific, historical forms it has taken in Guatemala. In other words, the conditions of possibility for extracting a quantum of lucration via superadequation: humans' ability to produce a surplus. It is what makes poor Mayas and ladinos seem like the Maya-Awakateko concept of zero—that which has no value and at the same time gives value (ALMG 2003, 17)—rather than *winaq*, 20, whole, complete. It is the exploitation that *grounds* the surprise and wonder at the fiction of finance. It is the inseparability of politics and number.

Way goes on, however, "Try though the corporate system may, it cannot simply relegate people to starve to death with passivity" (177). I've tried to show numbers' role in refusing passivity and how the struggles over reparations—via counting, bone seeking, court cases, Mayan numbers, and resarcimiento—insist on number and money as "human things." Mathematical calculations (determining not only sums but averages, percentages, etc.) put numbers and the people they reference in relation so that at the Ríos Montt trial statistician Patrick Ball can make number show that from 1979 to 1986, the army killed 18.3% of the indigenous population and 3.2% of the nonindigenous population. While numbers cannot speak to intentionality, relating them to acknowledged genocides like Rwanda and Srebrenica (with murder rates of identifiable groups around 20%) shows not only what was gained and lost but also quality—it equi-values.[13] As Bruno Latour argues, in such a chain of connections "the word 'reference' designates the quality of the chain in its entirety, and no longer adequatio rei et intellectus. Truth-value circulates here like electricity through a wire" (Maurer 2005, 15). Drawing on the capacities of number and money to work as general equivalents, activists have made death and injury count in new ways through the simultaneously essential and insufficient labors of quantity and quality, singularity and plurality, cardinal and ordinal, double-entry accounting and accountability. In the midst of the genocidal mathematical sublime these dogged, strenuous, heartbreaking efforts ground us in the political struggle and "intellectual adventure" of seeking "to measure and compare all that surrounds us, to understand our place in the universe."

Part of what is heartbreaking is that people with simplistic understandings of precision struggle to revise the numbers down in the name of number as apolitical. Too, you may turn and toss and circulate an ounce of gold till it practically weighs ten, and turning and tossing and circulating reparations they practically become microfinance, "millennial capitalism," solace for the generals, or reinforcement for the acceleration of the creepy unification of moral and market cosmopolitanisms (Sznaider 2002, 107–9).

Yet turning and tossing and circulating number and monetary reparation, they may practically weigh in other ways as well. Exploring debates over translating the Castilian resarcimiento into Maya-Q'eqchi', Viaene says both k'irtasink (healing) and xiitink (to mend damaged fabric) were considered and xiitink was chosen because repair is impossible but tears can be mended (2010a). The fabric will never be the same, but it is still usable. Eve Sedgwick (2007) also suggests the possibility of assembling or repairing part-objects into something like a whole—though, she emphasizes, not necessarily like any preexisting whole. The map is in tatters. There are too many missing pieces of bone to set them just as they were. But as with progressive counting, people still yearn for completion. Through figuring and a recursive refiguring, through repeated activities with hands and words (Verran 2000a, 367), they reaccomplish new, prosthetic wholes and cobble together different patterns of habitation. Our place in the universe is peculiarly constituted by the money-circuit, 250,000 dead, debt-bondage, tribute-system practices, a Genocide of Maya, strange magic, and military systems that remain intact, making it difficult to advance in the search for reconciliation.

Pondering the hopes for repair laid on *testimonio* in postgenocide Guatemala, Carlota McAllister differentiates the (neoliberal) therapeutic form, for which trauma is the only "true event" and aims simply to restore the integrity of everyday worlds, from testimonies that evoke the passionate purpose of suffering in active pursuit of revolutionary futurity, that make a call to "go on." I am arguing that counting can be just such a testament.

Restoring everyday worlds *and* constituting a futurity—in which, as a member of the Communities of the Population in Resistance said, people are "free in our work, free in our lives, free in our own land. . . . This is why we go on" (McAllister 2013, 97–98)—constitute a journey. Out of the ground zero of neocolonial genocide, the yawning abyss of the ossuary, the unsettlings of finance, the messiness of desublimation, emerges Rotman's counting subject, to "begin the whole activity of traversing what will become a sequence of counted positions" via the struggle to count.

Part III

Mayan Pyramids

4 100% Omnilife

The aspiration to modernity has been an aspiration to rise in the world in economic and political terms; to improve one's way of life, one's standing, one's place-in-the-world. Modernity has thus been a way of talking about global inequality and about material needs and how they might be met. In particular, it has indexed specific aspirations to such primary "modern" goods as improved housing, health care, and education.

—James Ferguson

One's Place-in-the-World

Envy . . . is the topside of the anger, the rage against the unnatural dispositions of wealth that would manage your affective relation to the world while at the same time eating your lunch.

—Wahneema Lubiano

In 2000 I accompanied Liz Oglesby to the Joyabaj hamlet of Patzulá to interview young men who migrate to the south coast to cut sugarcane. We slept in the school and ate with Encarnación. Her son Juan, himself a cane cutter, introduced us to others and guided us along the narrow footpaths winding houses together. Mornings, while the men worked their *milpa* cornfields, Liz and I wrote up field notes in Encarnación's lovely garden. One day a young visitor suddenly said to Liz, "How I wish I looked like you. You're so pretty!" She roughly pinched her own strong upper arm, "Not like us with this darker skin, who wear these clothes [traje]. My nephew is blonde, much lighter, with lighter eyes. My brother married a canche [whiter-skinned person]. Now they have a canche baby."

Liz is blonde and blue eyed, and her presence elicited a number of similar comments. Children showed us a beat-up doll, half its yellow hair gone and only one blue eye left. They stroked it saying "utz [beautiful], like you." Late at night, Juana, who proudly teaches the new Maya-centric curriculum, expressed a similar desire. "I wish my children looked like you, not dark like me."

Human and Maya rights efforts to equi-value all lives (indigenous and non-, "subversive" and "innocent") and thereby make them count are made against the vast raciological backdrop that gives rise to longings "to look like you." They return me to "adequation," how to align a sensuous thing (like the doll) with an object of knowledge. To adequately grasp such yearnings means tracing their emergence from the Redes, or networks of unequal power that are also the conditions of possibility for superadequation, for extracting the surplus produced by those strong brown arms. And it's not just across the threshold of white and brown that excess—pecuniary as well as affective—is generated.

One morning I asked María, Encarnación's daughter, if she would braid my hair with ribbons to look like her. Giggling, she and a friend agreed, then ran and got a guipil (woven blouse). You see, the hairstyle is part of the whole ensemble. Growing up in the United States, where white people's appropriation of indigenous cultural expressions is reviled as the colonial practice it is, I felt uncomfortable and was relieved when it didn't fit. About half an hour later they reappeared, a bit out of breath, with another guipil. They had run to the far side of the hamlet to borrow it from a very fat neighbor. Now I could not really refuse, so laughing some more, they dressed me, adding corte (wraparound skirt), necklace, and two-sizes-too-small plastic sandals. This caused a stir, as people insisted on pictures and indulged in great hilarity. When Liz stood beside me in her traje (boots, jeans, blouse, cap), a woman asked if she were my husband. After the photo shoot everyone insisted I leave the clothes on, so we went about our interviews and that evening accompanied Encarnación and her family to a wake. Liz was ushered to a chair, as we both usually were, and

I was instructed to sit on the floor. When helping hands were needed I was expected to be one, while Liz relaxed with the guys.[1] I had changed gender.

In what follows, I explore different efforts to count than the exhumations and reparations, different relations to the complex singularities and pluralities of a Genocide of Maya. Fear not, we will encounter numbers and calculations, and also counting as mattering, as an aspiration to Ferguson's "modernity," "to improve one's way of life, one's place-in-the-world" (2006, 32). Wanting "to look like you" expresses this desire to count in a world where what counts as beautiful (or male) is always a *relation* to privilege. Sometimes tipping into envy and rage, it recognizes the constitutive exclusions that not only leave you hungry but, as Lubiano suggests, take your most intimate affective terrain as a site and stake of struggle (2014, 2). We'll tarry in its wellspring, the debt-ridden, comic, and mystical world of the market depicted in Joyabaj's *baile de la culebra*, where men play women, and transform into *mozos* (those who work for nothing), doubled over under the debt notebook. It's a world structured by superadequation working through raced and gendered hierarchies that are upheld by sometimes overwhelming violence *and* through the trickier byways of yearning and internalized self-loathing. Yet also through moral purpose emanating from service and self-sacrifice.

Joyabaj and neighboring Zacualpa were both *fincas de mozos*, or "worker plantations." During the liberal reforms of the late nineteenth century indigenous lands were privatized (stolen), and people were "allowed" to keep working their parcels in return for migrating to harvest sugar (Oglesby 2003; Remijnse 2002). The twentieth century laced these relations of production tighter through debt and its accompanying accounting procedures. The Mayan Language Academy (ALMG) seeks "the inspiration, the energy, and the integrity and self-possession necessary for full development based on our own aspirations," and in this chapter and the next I follow these Mayan aspirations via vexed and productive relations between the desultory politics of survival and the magical logics of number and finance. How *do* people "go on" in the wake of a genocide aimed at extinguishing revolutionary hopes and in the midst of still-intact political, economic, and military systems—what I call a "Misery of Mozos"?

Aspiring to Count

The dreams for which so many *compañeros* died are still legitimate.
—Domingo Hernández Ixcoy

Patzulá is beautiful and high. On a clear day you can see all the way to the Pacific coast volcanoes. Without electricity until 2011, the nighttime sky is brilliant. It's known as a hamlet with get-up-and-go, very active in the Catholic Action mobilizations in the 1960s and 1970s and deeply committed to education. In fact, it exists because of the school. Originally a neighborhood of Chorraxaj, parents organized to get their own teachers and then negotiated a new hamlet. Since 1998, when I began visiting regularly, they have "*gestionado fondos*" (petitioned for state and other monies) and organized human labor to extend the road—still pretty impassible in the rainy season—and quadrupled the size of the school.

Joyabaj didn't count in the CEH report, but the war exacted a massive toll. On July 10, 1980, the priest, Faustino Villanueva, was murdered. Army massacres began in the villages in early 1981. "Tightly organized communities like Chorraxaj were the most prominent targets, with the first recorded massacre in January 1981. Nine of the 14 people killed were children" (Remijnse 2002, 117). At first, people in Patzulá sheltered those fleeing, then the army killed both hosts and refugees. Patzulá was abandoned for months as people lived "like animals" in the surrounding hills. Men, women, and children were killed, and families were barred from burying the dead. "They were eaten by dogs . . . until they got fat. . . . If someone tried to [bury them] he would die just like the corpses," a survivor recalled (2002, 117).

Joyabaj was where one of the first civil patrols was introduced, precisely because the army viewed it as subversive. Patzulá's patrol commander, José, was a catechist and remembers that time of horror, when he had to live with "two faces, one turned towards my people, the other to the army." He is now widely acknowledged as a leader for his work on the road and the school.

This is where I met Santos, one of the teachers Liz and I roomed with (she seemed perfectly happy with the color of her children). Her home is in Joyabaj but she lived five days a week at the school, getting herself up the mountain every Monday, often walking several miles when pickups couldn't get through the mud. Her husband, Manuel, is also a schoolteacher in a village closer to Joyabaj. Hooking into postwar development aid, individual sponsors, indigenous-rights funding, and loans, they'd managed, on minimal salaries (about $250/month), to have all seven of their children in school, one even studying medicine at San Carlos University (USAC) in Guatemala City. Overall, Maya constitute a tiny percentage of university students, and only 0.2% have any postsecondary education at all (for nonindigenous it's only 3.2%; PNUD 2012, 88).

As director of the school, Santos seemed indefatigable: teaching, grading, meeting with the parents and village organizations. She also helped network them with local authorities and with the NGOs and international representatives that trickled through Patzulá in the late 1990s. During ten years of "peace processing" close to a billion dollars in foreign aid was apportioned to Guatemala, and its distribution had to look good in embassies', development organizations', and charities' end-of-year reports. Bits of this money made it to Patzulá, some used for Santos's students once they exhausted local offerings.

Santos was completely devoted to Mayan identity and the right to bilingual education,[2] and she always and proudly wears her *traje*. Then and now, all of Patzulá's teachers are indigenous and deeply committed to cultural survival. In 2000 several were studying intercultural education on the weekends in the departmental capital of Santa Cruz. Patzulá, like most of Joyabaj's northern villages, is 100% indigenous, and the school proudly displayed the banner of the ALMG, which had developed the school's Maya-friendly curriculum.

Here is when Santos stood beside me for our portrait, and you will note the huge size difference. She and her family comment on it every time I return with photos, and this startling ratio is what most impacted Marcelo Fernández Osco, an Aymara friend from Bolivia, when he visited Guatemala. He couldn't believe how small the Maya were! I reminded him that Guatemala's land reform, unlike Bolivia's, was cut short in 1954, and he said, "Yes, being there was like looking at pictures of my grandparents." His remark threw into sharp relief the almost Lamarckian effects of several generations of nutritionally acquired robustness: what so many Guatemalans died aspiring to.

Like turning hoards and piles into carefully counted skeletons, Dr. Peter Rohloff more precisely enumerates the "huge size difference." He says in Guatemalan rural communities "[a]ll children are at least six or eight inches shorter than they should be," and 80% are stunted. Many interventions fail for lack of political and financial investment but also because measuring (*aletheia*, unconcealing) is so difficult in the essential first two years of life

4.1 In front of the Patzulá school. Author's photo.

that parents and health care providers don't see the problems (Gowan and Martelli 2010).[3]

But as the CEH emphasizes, the massive organizing in the 1960s and 1970s was based on people measuring—perhaps not with perfect precision but accurately nonetheless—what it would take to end stunting. People in Patzulá, as elsewhere, worked through the church, the Campesino Unity Committee (CUC), and other sites for better wages, credit and production cooperatives, and their own school. They were counting and struggling to count. You might even say they were speculating (Harney and Moten 2013). "All he wanted was to feed his children." Now in war's aftermath, José, Santos, and their neighbors are laboring to exploit what openings exist to create infrastructures for ongoing struggle. Like Rotman's counting subject, they are starting from zero, journeying, as Verran says, out from genocide. They are relearning to work scale (a baby on a back up to the level of empire) and confronting a complicated array of accounting procedures, new financial mechanisms, profit and loss computations, and monetary alchemies, some powerful enough to change gender and race.

Omni — "All, Every, Whole" — Life

On subsequent trips I usually visited Santos in Patzulá, but in 2004 I found she'd begun working for a bilingual education NGO. This let her pursue her passion for Mayan empowerment at a different scale, throughout the villages of Joyabaj. She was also earning more, sleeping in her own bed, and thriving on new challenges. And it was important to be closer to home because her husband and a daughter were suffering mysterious health crises.

On my next visit we didn't find time to meet, but the following year, 2006, we finally caught up. Sitting in the rather bare front room of her house, she slowly unwound a quite amazing tale of her past two years, beginning with a gentleman she met through the NGO suggesting medicine to help her daughter, who was about to drop out of school. Miraculously, it worked, and her daughter (and her twin sister) were nearing graduation. Even better, without completely understanding how, Santos and her husband won a free trip. With mounting excitement she revealed the details: a poor indigenous woman who had rarely even ridden in a car, had been on an airplane! And there were photos! There she was with Manuel, before take-off, in flight, and arriving. In Madrid! And then Barcelona! And then onto a very large boat, a cruise ship!! They visited Nice, Monte Carlo, Florence, and Rome. Then, wonderfully, several days at sea where there was always food. Day and night! Buffets that never stopped! You could eat whenever you wanted!!! Everyone was so wonderful. The hours were filled with fun, meetings, workshops, and treasure hunts. The days flew by, so many happy times, and then, more excitement, getting back on the plane!!

This was all thanks to Omnilife and its products (nutritional supplements and energy maximizers in powder and liquid form). Santos believed it had saved her daughter. I was, of course, amazed, and not quite sure what to make of my friend's exciting experiences. The products she served me were mostly vitamins, some aspartame, and caffeine. Biocrus®, one of the most popular, consists of Vitamins A, C, E, B1, B2, B6, and B12, calcium, zinc, folic acid, chrome, taurine (I had to look this up: an amino acid—meaning it comes from bile!—used in many "energy drinks," it may aid athletic performance, reduce high blood pressure, and have positive cardiovascular effects), phenylalanine (another amino acid), and 60 milligrams of caffeine (comparable to a cup of coffee). It was hard to make these rather everyday ingredients jibe with the miraculous cure.

When I returned the next year, Santos and Manuel had won a car and been on another trip to the Bahamas Atlantis resort. And the photographs! Santos and Manuel in the newspaper with their new ride, Santos and her recovered daughter, resolutely garbed in their Mayan *traje* on the beach under the brilliant blue sky—with a faux Mayan pyramid / water slide in the background. Santos and Manuel at a table loaded with food, with large, nonindigenous people ("he's a doctor from Mexico!").

In 2006 Manuel had told me his illness had worsened. He suffered nervous attacks and was hospitalized for severe depression, but nothing—even the exercise regime and antianxiety drugs—seemed to help. He no longer enjoyed anything: not teaching, not even his children. He had entirely left off his work with the Catholic Church and Mayan organizing. "It's because of the war. We lived *entre miedo* (in fear) and it was so long!! 1979 to 1985," and he began to count on his fingers. Twice through he counted, "79, 80, 81, 82, 83, 84, 85 . . . seven years! All that time we were always afraid! Always! You just don't recover from this! I saw such horrible things, the army, the patrol. I saw people killed. I saw people tortured. And I couldn't do anything. I was afraid, so afraid! And I couldn't do any of the work I love. I couldn't support development. I couldn't help people. Because I didn't know," he paused; "you didn't know if what you were doing might get you killed. The army deceived me. I saw the terrible things they did." Later, out of Manuel's hearing, Santos scoffed a bit at his diagnosis of war trauma. "It's because he's a Mayan man. He has to accept that." I wasn't sure what she meant.

While Manuel knew the gentleman who introduced Santos to Omnilife and was thrilled their daughter was recuperating, he was uninterested in selling it. "I don't know," he said, "I've seen a lot of people who are *engañadores* (con artists) and I thought this might be an *engaño* (a trick), too. We have worked for many years to help our people, to develop our community. Many people trust us. I am afraid to lose that. What if it doesn't work? What if we lose their trust?" However, lured by the adventure of accompanying Santos on the cruise, he signed on as codistributor, then slowly began to sell a bit on his own. In 2007 Santos took the plunge. "I'm *cien por ciento*, 100% Omnilife," she told me, quitting her NGO job to go full-time. Manuel continues to teach and began to study with an *ajq'ij* because one diagnosis of his illness was that it was the call to serve.[4] It's what Santos meant by him being "Mayan." Manuel's earlier identification as an indigenous activist, strongly influenced by the church's horror of encroaching paganism, was more in the "modern Maya" form of seeking rights and representation, while the call to accept the burden of study and service seems to come from a different stratum of Mayaness, perhaps more related to Saturnino's "understanding" (and encouraged by the church's increased flexibility in response to Mayan Organizing 1.0). Now he sees his sacred work as perfectly compatible with serving people by selling them vitamins (and their son, the medical student, OK'd the ingredients). Santos was happy and relieved he seemed more stable and was sharing her work with Omnilife, as part of her *Red*, or network.

As I was leaving she said, "So, what do you think?" I said I was pleased she seemed so happy and had visited such exciting places. (My own *dichosa* ability to travel is a constant topic of conversation in Joyabaj, where people are openly, even insistently, curious about why their family members must risk their lives to visit my country.) "No, what do you think?" Santos said. "Don't you want to be part of it too?" It had not crossed my mind. After all, I already have a house, a car, and go on trips. "OK, but maybe next time?" she said as I made my ungraceful farewell.

Next time was March 2008, when I returned with Liz and we both got the hard sell. What we intended as a social visit was instead formally organized. We were invited into a room in their newly remodeled home, served Omni coffee, and apprised of the schedule. First, we would get a better sense of the products and organization through the company's DVDs, then have a chance to talk about ourselves, and then the opportunity to fill in forms and put our Q230 (about $30) down. Liz, who hadn't seen Santos in several years, was bemused at the change in our friend. The first DVD showed the founder, Jorge Vergara, holding court at an "Extravaganza," a boisterous convention for distributors in Guadalajara, Mexico, the company's home base. He was tall, white, and seemed at ease on the stage talking about expansion into new countries and distributions of bigger and bigger checks. The large crowd was very enthusiastic, waving their signature bottles of Omni water in the air.

After numerous stories about the positive effects of Omnilife on people's health and on their economies, Santos urged us to focus on the testimonies of three indigenous people. Two men and a woman from Oaxaca came onstage in their *traje*. They described stubborn illnesses, with one, Don Nico, adding enormous detail, first of his life as a simple peasant, then every symptom and doctor's visit, till Jorge jokingly asked him to hurry it up. He was in constant pain, dying, but the doctors could do nothing. Then he discovered Omnilife through a teacher, and he listed products to knowing cheers from the crowd. Not long after, miraculously, the teacher gave him a piece of paper. "We didn't know what it was. We were going to throw it away. 'No! No!' the woman said, 'that's not paper! That's a check!' but we didn't know what a check was." The crowd laughed. "'It's money,' she told us. We had no idea!" Here Santos poked me and said, "Just like me!" Then Nico's companion said she had never imagined she might go on an airplane. Again, Santos poked me, "Like me! Thanks to Don Jorge Vergara!!"

Later I would watch Santos show this DVD to other Maya, and their suture also seemed strong onto the Oaxacans, with their familiar clothing and grammatical patterns of Castilian as a second language. Santos subsequently met them in Guadalajara on a factory tour she'd won (which she described with oohs and aahs: "It is huge! State of the art! So modern!"[5]) and has hung out with them at Atlantis. One month the entire Omnilife glossy magazine was devoted to indigenous people, and Santos proudly showed me her testimonial printed near Nico's (putting "ethnic cultural difference to work" [DeHart 2010, 2; also Comaroff and Comaroff 2009]). More recently she joined them in a promotional DVD. (She was a bit embarrassed but also quite enjoyed being flown to Guadalajara, fussed over by the makeup people, and feeling she counts in this rather spectacular way.) She and Manuel have also made artisanal DVDs of their trips for family and Red enjoyment and seem to particularly like one of a long and wildly raucous conga dance, led by the Filipino waitstaff of a cruise ship.

Watching her watch the Oaxacans and herself and watch with the people she's training and collecting into her Red as she watches me watching is enchanting in complex ways. The turning and tossing and circulating of images of a life beyond the simply adequate, of the rambunctious breakdown of the stiff, freighted Maya-nonindigenous divide, it's the reality of the electric spark, even as I wondered at the mystery of those checks (and cars and trips) seeming to appear out of nowhere.

Now back to my induction. The second video Liz and I watched was of a youth conference held in Cancún. Santos's youngest son, Pedro, had qualified to go, all expenses paid, and he eagerly added firsthand accounts. "There were kids from all over Latin America, and even Russia. The best part was the spirit. They had hope, energy, engagement. There! There! See the Venezuelan contingent? They were amazing!! [Definitely the rowdiest among an extremely peppy crowd.] I've never met people with so much energy, so much drive! It was so exciting to be there. It's not like here. Here no one has energy, people don't seem to have any ideas or even dreams, but there, it was different. I came back ready to work, eager to do more. There was just so much energy!! In Guatemala young people are afraid. They are afraid to fail. They are ashamed and think that people look down on them." He was proud that he didn't have to seek people out to tell them about Omnilife. Instead they come to him because they see his energy, his spirit. "'How do you have all this stuff?' they ask me, 'where do you work?' and I tell them 'I don't work, what I'm doing is *pasatiempo*, having fun.'" He was especially proud to be financing his university studies in Santa Cruz without taking money from his parents.

The final DVD was more explicitly about "economy," with Vergara and others repeatedly mentioning the size of their twice-monthly checks ($350,000 for Jorge at that time). "The first check I ever signed was for 50 pesos, about $4," he said, "The last one was for 200,000!"

Then Santos kind of nervously launched into her spiel. She was very happy we were here to learn more about these opportunities in "health and economy," a company motto. She asked us about ourselves, our health, our relationships. "We're glad to share with you. Like the Russian woman said in the video, there are no races, no countries in Omnilife. We're all together, people taking care of people (*gente que cuida a la gente*—another company motto). You both know lots of people, so this will be very easy for you. You can share with your *compadres*, students. You must have some three hundred students, right? Maybe they have problems, you can advise them. The product is good for many things, gastrointestinal problems, constipation, liver issues, kidneys, diabetes, menstrual problems, even cancer! And the product was created by a gringo. Jorge Vergara went to the US to buy the patent."[6] She explained that the Q230 sign-up fee wasn't really a payment because not only did you receive a lavender Omnilife bag (which, Don Nico joked in the video, made him look like a "*maricón*"[7]),a copy of the magazine, and the paperwork to make your first order but also a container of the product, retailing at about Q230.

When she first started it was all *nubes*, clouds, nothing was clear. She didn't understand the sales, the network, the points, the bronze, silver, and other levels, how the first check seemed to just appear and the first trip kind of fell on her. Only later did she begin to understand, so we shouldn't worry. Then she told a more complex story of her own recruitment. It wasn't just a friend suggesting she could get the products more cheaply if she signed up. It also included a formal visit from three people, a ladino doctor and two Maya, who came all the way to Joyabaj. She didn't like it, tried to put them off. Like us, she was skeptical. She had a job, a family, she wasn't interested, but they kept pushing. They were impressed with all the people she knew and asked her to call a meeting of leaders so they could explain things. That's when they enrolled her and a few other people. And this is when Santos enrolled me.

As she has many, many people. Later, trying to calculate in her head how many people were in her *Red*, she wasn't able to count them all (although as a dedicated participant in audit culture she has all this information in her files), much less all the people that they in turn had signed up, making her a "grandmother," "great-grandmother" and "great-great-grandmother" many times over. I will return to the *Red* as a journey from singularity to plurality and back and as a (faux?) Mayan pyramid later, but first I will ponder the body politics and body mathematics of *salud* (health), *economía*, and adequation.

Economy and Health

"Our family has changed," Santos told me. "We pay more attention to our health, to what we eat. I was just in Patzulá to support my *Red* and explained that the product is all-natural. Unlike soda and greasy food, Omnilife is healthy and natural. When children cry, their parents buy them a snack or a Pepsi and don't realize they are becoming addicted. And a woman said to me, 'So this is just like our ancestors' food! This is the way we used to eat.' And that's when I realized that the product is very Maya, it is helping us get back to a more traditional diet, more vegetables and fruit, less meat and *Pollo Campero* [the KFC of Guatemala]." She was also pleased that Jorge Vergara seemed sympathetic to the Maya cosmovision's respect for nature, as the company is going green. The magazine devoted several issues to global warming, and they'd recently switched from paper checks to direct deposit (meaning everyone needed a bank account).

Santos's story of fear and frustration as nothing worked for her daughter, like Don Nico's of being at death's door, resonates with generalized grievances with chemical medicine but also with indigenous people's specific experiences with "modern health care." Catching up during annual visits frequently elicits tales of health crises, cavalier or even abusive treatment by doctors, and the limited efficacy of expensive medicines, understood as racism and/or classism.[8] Anthropologist Pedro Pitarch, working in Chiapas, says, "Each time one returns and asks . . . what has happened during one's absence, what follows is a lengthy list of illnesses . . . right down to the last detail. But it is clear that from the Indian perspective, what could be interpreted as an explanation of a medical nature is also considered to be a social and political profile" (2010, xix).

In Joyabaj Tomasa made exactly this link: "They treated me badly because they think I'm poor and I won't pay, just because I wear *corte*. When I told them off they treated me worse, because now they're afraid of me." Her husband is Miguel Batz, pharmacy owner, labor contractor, moneylender, and elected town official, so they are actually part of the small postwar indigenous elite (perhaps why she felt secure enough to tell off a ladino doctor).

I will explore how Omnilife may be "very Maya"—and a "social and political" profiling device—as well as my (problematic) surprise when Santos said this, but first I want to suggest how it fits and extends the everyday "medical pluralism" that Maya (and most of us) practice—which also connects to dis-counting. In Joyabaj, as throughout Guatemala, a large section of the market is devoted to "traditional" medicines, dried leaves piled high on tarps, newspaper cones full of (to me) mysterious substances. People are advised on their uses by family members, the sellers, or experts sought out in their homes (who can be paid in kind—some eggs, a few ears of corn). Only illnesses that present to "official" doctors become part of the daily statistics sent to the Health Ministry. In what T. S. Harvey (2006) calls "undocumented wellness-seeking," those redressed by this communal self-medication don't count (except in stories recounted to visitors).

Pitarch says it took him a long time to understand the relationship among body, illness, and language for the Maya-Tzeltal, and I also didn't realize till later that when I checked the Omnilife ingredients and felt underwhelmed by their effects, it was because I'd missed a central component. That is the testimonial, which is usually less about any particular product than the miraculous turnaround. And the fact it is shared. Harvey says, "As an interactional or communicative practice, K'iche' Maya *achi'lib'al* (companionship) can be described as . . . language use governed by . . . cultural rules that encourage the coauthoring of sickness narratives across multiple participants." It is "living life accompanied" (2006, 7). (Of course, collective healing is not only Maya.)

And it's not only physical ailments Omnilife addresses. One morning we were sitting in Santos's front room as she attended to members of her *Red*, advising patients on a range of health issues, mostly in Maya-K'iche', and walking her distributors through the forms and paperwork necessary to place orders, keep track of points, or deal with the bank (calls and visits typically begin around 6:30 AM and she's often up till 10 or 11 PM finishing her own paperwork). In a brief lull between visits, she turned to me and said, "Omnilife has cured me of *envidia*, envy [a potentially hazardous affect]. Fermín there, in the corner, he was just made director of his village school. Before Omnilife I would have looked at someone so young with such an important position and have been envious, I would have felt bad he had accomplished something like that. But with Omnilife I am sincerely happy when I hear that other people are doing well."

Another of her greatest satisfactions is that Omnilife is helping war victims like Encarnación. "Not very much yet, but a little bit, she's consuming and selling. She can't read or write, she speaks no Castilian, but she can benefit too!" (Santos also commented on the benefits of enrollment for Mayan women with little or no formal education. "The ones with school have forgotten how to do sums, but they get back in practice, and the others learn.") Encarnación had recently survived a frightening health emergency. Very tough but undernourished for a lifetime, she's a tiny woman, much slighter than Santos.[9] Afflicted with terrible abdominal pain, she visited Santos for product. Manuel told her, "We cannot lie. There are things the product cannot do. You need a doctor." At the local hospital doctors told her she needed an operation on her gall bladder, but her daughter María, also monolingual in K'iche', didn't seem to understand and wouldn't give permission. Santos whipped out her cell phone and frantically called Juan, who was working in Kansas, and got it worked out. But the operation could not be done in Joyabaj, so Santos, Manuel, and Pedro bundled her into the Omnilife prize car and rushed to Santa Cruz. Afterward Encarnación spent a month in Santos's home, recovering and taking a lot of product. It was after this that she joined Santos's *Red*. When I saw her in July 2008 she was still in some pain but working, and was thrilled that Juan had been deported (he did not share her joy). That's when she asked if I were also in Santos's *Red* and then said, "It's very complicated. All the numbers! And the product is so expensive!!!"

"Economy": Wealth and Resources, Household Management

And here's the rub of Santos's exciting and hopeful stories. A single packet or dose of the product might run about Q8 ($1) retail, while a large (but more economical) bottle of vitamin powder was over Q200 ($30). It's considered best to take three to five doses a day, more if fighting an illness. Products are rarely prescribed alone, and it was somewhat de rigueur to consume them with bottled water, so "*salud*" could get pretty pricey pretty quickly.

In Joyabaj there are a lot of people with almost no access to the cash economy. For those with land, most agricultural production is for subsistence or local markets. Harvesting cane earns a pittance and options for waged work are few—tending a store, construction, municipal government (depending on family and political party connections), or the one or two NGOs in town—and wages are very low (after a one year "apprenticeship" working seven days a week from 5:30 AM to 10:00 PM in a sundries store, Silverio earned about $130 a month). A government teaching job is highly coveted yet in a month pays only enough to buy about eight bottles of Omnilife product. Labor contractors (often also moneylenders) and store owners are better off, and as ladinos fled Joyabaj during the violence, more indigenous people filled these positions. In general, women's labor is most criminally undervalued. Hours of shopping and food preparation may garner only one or two quetzals of profit per meal, and the weeks of work and extraordinary skill necessary to weave a *guipil* may net the weaver as little as Q40 ($7). This is the "informal" sector that J. T. Way contends "would be more appropriately called *the economy* itself, since it accounts for some three-quarters of all economic activity . . . relegated to secondary status despite its centrality, [it] is epitomized by and was co-created by women's labor" (7). Guatemala is a society of vendors "who, nearly single-handedly, perform the life-sustaining task of keeping the population provisioned" (2012, 10).

This is the survivalist grind of daily life for many, producing a statistic like 80% of rural children are malnourished, existing alongside the massive economic and social transformations of emigration and dollar remittances (Camus 2007). This is a gray economy, so figures are unsure, but the telltale signs of late-model cars, multistory concrete buildings, satellite dishes, and stores selling luxury tiles are everywhere, as are the banks. Lots and lots of banks.

Every conversation in Joyabaj at some point turns to emigration, till it seems as if everyone has gone, is there, or is planning to go. It costs between $3,000 and $4,000 (dollars, not quetzals) to get to the USA, and most people go to *dueños de dinero* ("owners of money," with "dueño" evoking the relation to the mountains, "owned" in the sense Maxwell explained in chapter 3). There, if you are lucky, interest rates are 10% *a month* (banks offer more reasonable rates but more onerous collateral requirements). The debt grows quickly and can take several years to pay off—*if* the migrants make it and *if* they keep sending money. Felipe Natareno, former mayor of Joyabaj and now a notary public, explained, "Maybe 40% manage numbers well enough to benefit from going to the States, but 60% lose. But everyone, you don't think the same way about the future. It costs 35 to 40,000. Borrowing 5,000 can quickly get to 50,000. Then that's about 70,000 after one year, 76,000."[10] Even before work dried up in the United States and the deportation regime metastasized (de Genova and Peutz 2010), young men and women often started families in the north (sometimes a second or third one), limiting the money sent back. (Juan had a son in the United States but was estranged from his partner even before *la migra* came to his door and whisked him off to jail in his pj's, losing everything). Homes and land have been ceded when families lost the migration gamble, meaning there are also families who are accumulating as lenders or are able to buy those properties with dollars sent home. I have heard of parents taking their children to *ajq'ij* to both bless their trip and curse them if they fail to send money.

For some, heading north is a straight cost-benefit analysis: earnings increased by 7.5 quetzals to the dollar. The glitter of consumption and the allure of adventure draw others. As Oglesby says so poignantly, "international migration is more than just an economic option . . . it's the social project of a postwar generation, one that arguably demands as much ingenuity as joining a revolutionary movement must have required of their parents" (2003, 670). For most it has become a necessity. There just aren't other ways to make money. Several years ago José, the Patzulá leader, was thrown from a pickup on the road he worked so hard to build. He still can barely walk. They decided the only option was to remove a son from school and send him to the United States.

Grayer still, there is narcomoney sloshing around the Joyabaj/Zacualpa area. Whispers circulate: that workers in a restaurant sell cocaine, that a huge SUV belongs to the local dealer, whispers of a mysterious gentleman nicknamed *El Millonario* (the millionaire), who, asked to contribute to the Zacualpa festival, reached into his fanny pack and pulled out Q20,000 in cash ($2,600; just Q4,000 less than a reparation payment).

These emerging postwar structures of inequality layer on to the still unsettling effects on health and economy of the years of crops destroyed, education disrupted, and family members murdered, starved, exiled, disappeared, or barely functioning because of war trauma. Loss and gain, lack and abundance, may be configured differently now than before the war—with some indigenous people sharing a bit more in the bounty—but they are densely intertwined.

So there's simultaneously a lot of money circulating through Joyabaj and large, if shifting, populations with no earthly access to it. People must calculate hard "choices." Do you risk your *milpa* and possibly a child's life in hopes of remittances? Do you stand in line for several days (and perhaps swallow your horror at participating) to get the Q5,200 payments for ex-PAC? Do you position yourself as a victim and petition the PNR? (Encarnación gave her emotionally taxing testimony, turned in the required paperwork, and has waited several years for money to arrive. The last time I asked Juan if they'd received it he said emphatically "¡Nada! *Nada, nada, nada* [nothing]!") Do you agree to move some cocaine in your truck? Do you tackle the numbers and try to sell an expensive product to your equally poor neighbors?

In turn, some of that circulating cash is being spent on Omnilife. Some to counter the effects of migration: anxiety about family members abroad or, for returnees, the physical effects of the journey, the rhythm and physicality of work in the United States (Juan pulled twelve-hour shifts on a slaughterhouse line), and what it takes to return, corporeally and emotionally. Some are probably taking them for similar lingering effects of the war, from which many, like Manuel, find it hard to come back.

"Health": Being Whole, Sound, or Well

> "Vitamin" was coined in 1920 from Latin *vita* "life" referring to organic substances essential for normal metabolism, in other words, required for life. They cannot be synthesized so organisms must obtain them from their diet.
> —Wikipedia http://en.wikipedia.org/wiki/Vitamin

When Jorge Vergara customized Herbalife ingredients for the Mexican market, he was responding to already burgeoning demand, as increasingly impossible claims are made on the organism—what we might call super-duper-adequation—and people scramble to supplement sufficiently to keep up. Try making ends meet on land continuously decreasing in size and productivity or by cutting sugarcane, where men averaged one ton a day in 1980 but are now expected to cut six, while a quarter of them manage NINE—even as wages remain inadequate to subsistence and the harvest season compresses (Oglesby 2013, 150). In *maquila* factories workers are asked to sew 3,500 labels a day, even as studies show the *machines* cannot work that fast. Both individual brain and massive computer power are expended to more smoothly extract this surplus: calculating input to output, the combination of proteins, carbs, vitamins, and sugars that will get a body through a day yet fit within the *oikos*, the family's budget. The body makes its own calculations, in extremis drawing sustenance from its own muscles or shutting down systems trying to keep others online, laboring till it finally fails.

Interviewing Juan and his friends in Patzulá and physiologists, chemists, and accountants on the sugar plantations, Liz Oglesby encountered a potent mix of quantitative and qualitative data crunching on both sides. "Town pharmacies stock a dozen brands of Vitamin B injections, and migrant cane cutters start buying them weeks before the sugar harvest starts, at half a day's wage for one shot." Two brothers told her of working from 6 AM until 7 PM or even later, with truck headlights helping them see. "The only way I can take it is because of the injections. I pay for my own: Nervión, Nerotrópica, Tiamina [all forms of Vitamin B], and Sin Sueño ["no sleepiness"; a stimulant]. You don't feel the sun that way. You don't get tired." His brother said, "People take other things, too, things that make them talk like crazy people, and they walk around like drunks. The ones who cut ten or twelve tons a day, many of them take drugs. Not just vitamins, but real drugs, then you can't work without them" (2013, 163).

Plantation managers and doctors keep careful track of each man's numbers: output, weight, muscle measurement, diet, and the results of time-motion studies (plus marital status, ethnicity, religion, landholding, and off-season occupation), as well as the more elusive category of "psychological disposition"—that is, their attitude: docile or rebellious, eager to push toward quota or lackadaisical. Pep talks and Sylvester Stallone movies stoke machismo as an affect amenable to surplus extraction (Oglesby 2003, 661). But these numbers and accountings *come* to count in particular relations. On February 18, 1980, via the *Red* of CUC, they were converted into a strike encompassing eighty thousand workers at eighty sugar plantations. Today, in genocide's aftermath, the carefully calibrated *vita*-min doses and biopowerful accuracy and precision of the databases put health more in the service of profit than life. The World Health Organization warns that deaths from chronic kidney disease have risen almost 30% since 2005, traced to dehydration, heat stress, and strenuous labor. Along Central America's Pacific coast young men are left to try to balance their vitamin doses and out-of-pocket expenses as they "literally work themselves to death" (Oglesby 2013, 162–63).

"Escape" to the United States, especially to slaughterhouse labor, is also dangerous, from the border crossing itself—close to 500 (under)counted deaths in 2012—to labor's toll, ranging from "cuts, strains, and cumulative trauma [to] . . . fractures, amputations, illnesses caused by exposure to chemicals, blood, and fecal matter," and even death. These costs go largely uncounted—so egregiously that the US General Accounting Office has censured bad record keeping by OSHA, the Occupational Health and Safety Administration (Squier 2012, 110–11).

Conjoining health and economy, sugar (the colonial capitalist pick-me-up), meat (that delicious protein pack), and Omnilife are all simultaneously nourishment, source of gustatory delight (or horror), and commodities on the market, that awe-full collective enterprise that gives life and lets die. In turn, Omnilife—the vitamins and the networks that distribute them—may seem a rather flimsy shield against such necropolitics. But like other tonic remedies, folk pharmacopeia, snake oils, and assorted elixirs, it helps people deal with a bewildering variety of diseases and symptoms. Ernst Bloch included patent medicines in his inventory of "the principle of hope."

What Percent Are You?

My friend, his first check was for Q250, then it went up to 3-something, then it went up to 400 and then half more again, 800, then 1,000, every fifteen days, and I was earning 1,000 a month and only with working a year at the store. So he beat me, because every fifteen days he had 1,000, that's 2,000 a month and I was only at 1,000 a month and working all the time. One month, imagine!
—Silverio, seventeen years old

In the midst of these desperate strivings Silverio watches in amazement as his friend's Omnilife checks grow with incredible speed, I watch in amazement as Santos jets off to another cruise, and her recruits at the weekly support meetings at the Las Vegas hotel in Santa Cruz watch in amazement as Nico, a simple peasant, almost throws away an apparently worthless scrap of paper. What feats of tossing, turning, and circulating make possible these transformations? Perhaps not surprisingly, it's the concatenation of singularity and plurality in the Red of distributors that is the source of the mysterious checks and points one collects to win trips and other aspirational goodies (and supplies Vergara's biweekly $350,000). Omnilife distributors accrue them, as well as cash, in a number of ways.

First, they buy the product from the company and "displace" it. It's adamantly not called "selling," nor do they "recruit" new salespeople. They educate friends and acquaintances about health and economic opportunities. They are never supposed to exhibit the product or sell it in stores. "Displacement" occurs through person-to-person contact, with emphasis placed on showing people you care. Santos explained this was because "Jorge Vergara was thinking of people like us. If Miguel Batz, who owns the pharmacy on the main square, were to sell from so central a place, what would happen to us, so far away from the market? But Jorge wants everyone to have the same opportunities. You don't have to read or write, you don't have to speak Castilian well, you don't have to be rich already."[11] Such transactions require only basic accounting: debit when you buy and income when you sell (time spent and the rigors of affective labor don't count).

Second are the (multi)levels, where it gets more complicated (and amazing). In 2011 I sat by Encarnación's kitchen fire with Micaela, the director of the Patzulá school. Micaela is in Santos's Red and she asked me, "What percentage are you?" At first the question seemed rather existential till I realized it was Omni lingo. I admitted I was probably less than 0% as I didn't buy or sell, and she laughed. "I have trouble selling, too! I'm really just in it to consume." Signing up gets you a discount when you buy, and depending on how much you purchase, for your own consumption or to sell (each product has both a monetary and point value), you can buy at gradually steeper discounts while still selling at retail price (these discounts and other privileges are designated by levels named after precious minerals and jewels like silver and diamonds). Beginners get 20% off and as they consume more can gradually reach the maximum 40% discount. In addition, as people in one's Red sell, a bit of their profit returns to the person who signed them up (for different "generations," depending on the percentages). This is where it gets complicated, and although Santos tried very hard to explain it to me, I rely heavily on Cahn (2011) and my Independent Distributor Manual for what follows.

The percentage you "are" has a big impact on what you accrue. If you can get to a 25% discount and recruit someone who starts at 20% then you get 5% of her total purchases, up to 20% as the difference between your levels increases. Getting to 40% discount makes you a "wholesaler," and if you purchase or sell 1,000 points every two weeks for two months, you reach the "bronze level." (There is no one-to-one equivalence between points and coin. For Mexico Cahn estimates this at about $400, or $1,600 over two months; in Guatemala it is points equivalent to $100 per period based on the exchange rate determined by Omnilife.) Similar to the way monthly compounding interest transforms one's relation to time, here the fortnight becomes saturated with affect, what Cahn calls the "omnipresent imperative to keep up point totals" (2011, 93) as the clock resets every two weeks and points do not carry over. But reaching bronze allows you to claim up to a 4% commission on purchases by wholesalers (people who have reached 40%) in your first through third generation (they don't have to have a lower percentage than you). In other words you and someone in your first line need to "be" 40% for you to "be" bronze. Micaela and I are Santo's first, or front line, and anyone we recruit is our first and her second (thus her interest in my "300 students").

As members of your front line and then of theirs reach wholesaler status, they begin to change status and receive percentages from deeper generations. To "be" silver takes three wholesalers in the front line, each maintaining purchases equivalent to $100 in their Red, plus nine active wholesalers (who must consume 50 points per period either personally or through their Red) in your second line. "Being" silver entitles you to a percentage of up to 4% from four generations of your "downline." Gold requires six wholesalers at $100 in the first line and eighteen with 50 points each in the second line and gives you access to a 4% commission from five generations. Diamond requires nine wholesalers in the first line and a minimum of twenty-seven in the second to receive commissions from the sixth generation as well. Cahn says Luisa, his sponsor, sees "phantom income," what she would have earned if she'd qualified to capture a portion of her fifth and sixth generations, rather than "stagnating" in silver status. These are "escalating numbers [that] demonstrate how the volume of product purchased increases dramatically with each successive generation" (2011, 93). This is what Silverio witnessed with his friend, making him realize he should sign up, too. (Yes, attentive readers are right to suspect nefarious undergirdings, but let's not dismiss too quickly the wonder of seeing someone you know—like you, indigenous, poorly educated, not part of the military hierarchy—get to escalate numbers on the credit side rather than the debit.)

So people can make money from both distributing/selling and the commission checks, and they are also, through a separate but parallel system, accruing the points that will be converted into trips, cars, and other incentives. These are organized through time periods during which distributors must keep up a certain number of points every month to qualify. Santos is often in the midst of such incitement periods when I visit, and she's both anxious and tingling with anticipation, enjoying daydreams of Greek islands, Istanbul, or Jerusalem. Faustino, Santos's brother-in-law, remembers with great chagrin missing out on a trip to France by a mere 100 points and in the penultimate month of the contest. Worst of all, he believes it was due to an accounting error. "I was so close!!" But he soldiered on and later managed to win a motorcycle.

I say "he" soldiered on because in many ways the singularizing and privatizing of the Omnilife (and other direct sales) experience is remarkable. Much is made of being "independent" and like any franchise, distributors are expected to be responsible to Omnilife, but Omnilife has no responsibility to them. They are not employees and have no right to wages, benefits, insurance, retirement, or sick days. But, and this is a big selling point, there is no boss either. (This is simultaneously neo-, pre-, and post-liberal—small-scale peasants with land live this dream, and it's the future desire expressed as "free in our work, free in our own land." In other words, "the dreams for which so many compañeros died.") Each distributor, especially those who are 100% Omnilife, shoulders those risks. The company does supplement people's individual "psychological disposition" with online and radio shows and, for a small fee, DVDs, magazines, rallies, extravaganzas, and courses, but as with any entrepreneurial activity, it's up to you to make it work in a "new, unforgiving discipline of personal behavior" (Cahn 2011), all fully enumeratable.

Such discipline and quantifying is not limited to Omnilife distributors. Oglesby shows how the sugar plantations strive to instill such independent work regimes (also using prizes like T-shirts) and Monica DeHart analyzes similar self-governance for those left behind in Guatemala and tasked with investing remittances, requiring "constant managerial vigilance and precise bookkeeping" (2010, 56). Kevin O'Neill describes analogous processes in Guatemalan call centers, where young people "subject themselves to rigorous self-improvement programs" involving "perpetual training, promotion schemes, and . . . competitions, with winners receiving anything from iPods to buckets of Red Bull" to bonus checks and "connected to an intricate compensation" system where they are docked for every second missed and receive "controlling doses of shame" via emails that track their attendance records (2012, 23, 29, 30). These are, in turn, like Protestant accounting practices in which believers "calculate character" to assess their inner selves and police co-religionists (O'Neill 2009, 60–86), which themselves resemble (while disavowing) the accounting practices of Catholic confession, where sins/debts are listed, then "paid" by reciting the rosary. Omnilife participates in an emerging logic of deepening (if not completely neo-) liberalism and draws on older modes of affect management and quality's quantifications via the colonial-inflected religiosities that for five hundred years have allowed someone else to eat your lunch while you pay out of pocket for vitamin supplements.

All that quantification means Omnilife's got some very powerful computers calculating points and time periods and levels and percentages and human connections in order to spit out checks (now direct deposits) and produce what may amount to dozens of pages of single-spaced printout for each distributor detailing each biweekly commission amount. I'm frankly boggled. Santos said it was all *nubes*, but now she has it down and expertly inputs all the necessary data every day, keeping track of her *Redes* and helping her downlines do the same, involving many hours of work. This new numeric and temporal organization is also spatial, as two rooms of her house are now devoted to Omnilife. One has walls adorned with messages of uplift ("I Think, Therefore I Succeed"), photographs of her travels, lists of products with costs and point values, and quite prominently, a calendar. This is where she receives clients and daily deliveries of product. The second has tables and shelves and cabinets full of paper, where I've also noticed brightly colored pamphlets and workbooks from the SAT (Guatemala's IRS) trying to encourage a "tributary culture" (paying taxes). All of it, as arithmophobes warn us, binding people's very being ever more tightly with "all the numbers!"—avalanches of them. So much so you "become" a percentage.

Did your eyes glaze over reading about the math? Can you picture trying to keep track of all that, with maybe a primary education from a rural, racist school? And I wasn't even encouraging/distracting you with sparkly self-help mantras and insistent promises that if you just maintain the right attitude all your dreams will come true. Cahn says the combination "shift[s] the distributors' attention from trying to look for loopholes toward accepting the alchemy of 'using and sharing'" (2011, 91) but that "to profit from Omnilife's business model, distributors need to pay attention to numbers, exactly what the trainings discourage" (98). This (plus the overlapping scales of numbers) may make it harder to count costs like the outlay for product, phones and minutes, electricity bills, taxes on the prizes, weekly rent on a hotel conference room, travel for upkeep of one's downline, and investments in the motivational products. Cahn says, "promises of wealth limited only by distributors' imaginations do not stand up to mathematical scrutiny." To earn the advertised $100,000 a year would take 29,523 active distributors (2011, 97), reversing the exponential rice on the chessboard to be extracted from the king (see chapter 0). He cites David Owen who—like the Christmas killjoy who each year determines the "true love's" price tag for "twelve drummers drumming" down to "a partridge in a pear tree"—calculated what it would take to follow the advice to recruit one person and double the number each day. It "would surpass the population of the earth in less than five weeks. This is not a business for the fainthearted" (Cahn 2011, 97–98). Mayan intellectual Demetrio Cojtí, not faint of heart, said he was recruited to sell Amway, the world's largest multilevel marketing company, as a young father recently returned from graduate studies in Europe. But he found that everyone he tried to sell to was already selling. "Guatemala was completely saturated!" Motivated by Santos's stunning successes and her generous and down-to-earth demeanor, it can be hard to remember that the sea of recruits (and buyers) is not endless.

That's why multilevel marketing (MLM) or direct sales—like Omnilife, Herbalife, Mary Kay, Tupperware, and Amway—are also called pyramid selling.[12] Those who get in early (i.e., on top) can do amazingly well. Their success fuels the dreams of those below, and some do make it, adding to the success of those above and the desires (and envy) of those below.

I, and many others who analyze MLM as neoliberal individualizing, focus on its singularizing tendencies, but it's the plural where the magic happens (like the very idea that a Red could encompass the planet's population in a month!). When Micaela asked me my percentage, she was "evoking a whole of which it is a part" and asking me my teknonym—a name or identity one achieves through relation. You can't do it alone. The percentage I "am" comes from other people—the very thing disavowed by the emphasis on independence and individual positive thinking. So Omnilife is liberal and modern in its entrepreneurial promise of no boss, no office, no time clock, no safety net, and individual shouldering of risk and, possibly, spectacular gain. But it is also modern in its "organic solidarity," the way we are deeply dependent, not only on others to feed, clothe, and house us materially but on their desires and "likes," their willingness to buy and sell (think of how, through the relations concocted and calculated via the stock market, an investor's value relies on others' actions, loosely if at all connected to anything like use value). These are the mysteries of exchange and of value, both particular and plural. And they are why metaphors from the religious realm, like faith and fetish, are so often deployed.

But testimonies about miraculous cures and giving oneself over 100% to Omnilife are not just *like* religious experiences. They *are* conversion stories, resonating with Christian experiences of "seeing the light," and with revolutionary experiences, as well as with Mayan narratives of being healed, as Manuel was, by training to be an *ajq'ij* (Ahmad 2010, McAllister 2013). They plug in to older hopes and promises of transformation, of escaping inadequacy so as to "look like" someone else. But those mysterious checks and miraculous prizes also emerge from converting in the economic sense, transforming so-called social capital (your friends and family connections) into money, points, and trips to Atlantis—and into financial capital (meaning it grows). Like a rather creepy aletheiometer, Omnilife "reveals" the precise exchange rate for such amorphous goods as people's trust in you. While the extraction seems nowhere near as clear or brutal as plantation or factory labor, somehow enough surplus is being skimmed from subprime places like Patzulá to pay for cruises, *futból* teams, and Vergara's jet. In this, perhaps it's more like the "work" one does for Facebook, which feels like *pasatiempo* but where your friendship networks are publicly traded to the tune of $50 billion from Goldman Sachs in 2011 and $5 billion from the 2012 IPO.

Matt Creelman, a long-term observer of Guatemala with whom I've shared my wonder about Omnilife, told me, laughing, "you love Santos too much to criticize what's going on here." I do love her, but I can also see how *Red* participants may be "bright-sided" by "cruel optimism," unable to accurately calibrate precisely how they are being exploited (Ehrenreich 2009; Berlant 2011). It has been difficult at times to watch Santos caught in the frenzy to maintain volume and points that is the other, defetishizing side of the operation "organized around the steady, mathematical, inexorable growth of income," the world "reduced to a collection of potential dangers, potential tools, and potential merchandise . . . [as] human relations become a matter of cost-benefit calculation" (Graeber 2011, 319).

The nadir of our relationship was when Anastasia's eleven-year-old daughter Quetzali, with whom I'd pondered Mayan numbers among other delights, died of leukemia and Santos seemed to blame the victim, sniffing, "I tried to tell them about the product and how it cures cancer, but she didn't pay me any mind." (For a while Anastasia had dabbled in selling the rival Herbalife.) It's also hard to watch it take a toll on Santos in ways "the product" makes harder to address. On one return visit, sitting with just her family in the house, I asked about an issue she'd mentioned the year before. She said it was fine, but as I was leaving she followed me out to the street and asked me to never mention such things, ever. She didn't want to trouble her family but she also couldn't let members of her *Red* know. Being *gente que cuida a la gente* has qualified Santos for experiences beyond most people's— not just highland Mayas'—dreams, but there are costs to the benefits, even for those lodged higher up in the pyramid. Yet just as converting a holiday counting song into the price of ten lords a-leaping can help reveal such "costs," it doesn't quite measure the pleasures of singing the song together. Too, with Omnilife, something about the relations between singular and plural throws off surplus that can be counted and extracted but is still amazing.

What's Left?

Between Joyabaj and San Martín Jilotepeque there is a school with a colorful mural. It depicts the violence of the Spanish invasion and the more recent horrors of the civil war, culminating in images of healing and cultural revival: kids in school, a mangled tree growing new runners, and the postwar motto of the Campesino Unity Committee (CUC): "they cut our branches, they burned our trunk, but they cannot destroy our roots."

Arriving in San Martín I spot a T-shirt with a similar tree and motto: "Strong Roots, Healthy Tree." I'm cheered. "Because of the situation" San Martín hadn't counted for the CEH, so it was gratifying to see someone publicly supporting the CUC. As he passed me, however, the back of the T-shirt told a different story. He was an Omnilife distributor.

The CUC emerged in the 1970s, out of the difficulties people faced as they aspired to count within a developmentalist paradigm: to enjoy better wages, decent nutrition, safe work, health care, and nonusurious credit (Brett 2007; Konefal 2010). Francisca is a Maya-Kaqchikel woman from a hamlet of San Martín. In the late 1970s her older sister started organizing with CUC. Their father was worried but their mother was enthusiastic as Francisca also joined. But then local military commissioners started making death lists and the army began rounding up men and boys. Francisca served as a guard, warning of army incursions. One day a group of women

4.2 Mural showing events of the civil war and a tree growing again from strong roots, San Martín Jilotepeque. Author's photo.

ventured into town to purchase necessities. Intercepted by the army (walking to her village Francisca showed me the exact spot), soldiers beat the women and children to death, killing at least thirty people. That's when they decided she should join the guerrilla. Her sister was already in the mountains. It was several years after the fact that Francisca learned her mother, brother, and a niece were killed by the army soon after she left. Her sister died in battle. After almost seventeen years in arms, in 1997 she and her husband were demobilized. It was not until the mid-2000s that she was able to exhume her mother's body for a proper burial. It was only then that she could finally sleep without troubling dreams of her mother's unhappy spirit.

I met Francisca through Santos, who told me, laughing, that she was my great-great-great-grandmother in Omnilife. We were introduced in that bright and sparkling clean bathroom of the Camino Real Hotel at the weekend-long inauguration of the Basic Course. Among the *Red* members (all Maya-K'iche') Santos had brought down in the minibus were Micaela, the Patzulá school director, and Sebastiana from Zacualpa, who worked for the Defensoria Maya in Santa Cruz. This was Santos's third Omnilife course, and she was energized by the content and how, as she repeated the courses, it got easier to understand. She also clearly enjoyed the stature she was gaining at the national level, expressed so often in that glittering bathroom by indigenous and ladina distributors alike (see chapter–1). She commented on, and I watched, her pride and growing ease with nonindigenous people, her contentment at being recognized. I began to see her not only cured of envy but also of some of the infamous submissiveness of indigenous people when facing ladinos, experts, and authorities. Now people wanted to look like her.

Santos made it through primary and a few years of middle school. When she was fifteen she went with her father to a plantation where he harvested coffee and she made tortillas, starting at 11 PM and ending around 7 PM, sleeping about four hours. By the end of the first month she was ill from fever and exhaustion. While recovering, she received a telegram about a job for a woman who spoke K'iche'. She hurried back and found it was an NGO called Alianza, the first to work in Joyabaj. Although she did not speak much Castilian, they hired her to do women's community organizing. That's where she met Manuel, and they began their family.

Alianza, an international development organization, began work in Joyabaj after the 1976 earthquake that destroyed 95% of the buildings and killed over six hundred people. Simone Remijnse (2002) says the work of Alianza, which joined progressive ladinos and indigenous people, angered elite ladinos. The 1978 victory of Felipe Natareno, Joyabaj's first indigenous-identified mayor and member of the left-leaning Christian Democrats, increased the anxieties of a long-feared balancing out of debts.[13] The excruciating pain that Manuel expresses, that he was not allowed to "do any of the work I love . . . support development . . . help people," was a result of the counterinsurgency response to these fears. Remijnse says, words like "'social promotion,' 'community organization,' and 'awareness raising' were branded as subversive activities by many authorities. . . . These words were central to Alianza's work. An indigenous woman remembers, [the military] said [Alianza] were bad people. They said that the help of Alianza was bad help . . . that Alianza had planted the guerrilla'" (2002, 104). After Padre Villanueva was murdered and family members of Alianza employees were tortured and killed, the program shut down. I have talked to Manuel several times about this period as we ponder the stubbornness of his depression, but Santos has rarely mentioned it. It was from the stage in the brightly lit convention hall at the luxury hotel, surrounded by hundreds of Guatemalan women, Maya and ladina, all Omnilife distributors, that I heard more.

Fleshing out my description in chapter -1, the Omnilife Basic Course has five modules, and I attended two: the first, Gender Identity, What It Means to be a Woman and What It Means to be a Man (March 2008), and the last (July 2008), continuing the themes of the fourth: Lack and Abundance. I missed Creencias, beliefs—where participants explore unexamined assumptions and the mind's power (imagining slicing a lime and the thought alone makes your mouth water)—and Perdón, Forgiveness. Men and women meet separately. Modules feature short lectures; individual reflection; small group discussions; frequent breaks to stretch, dance, sing, or meditate to music; and film viewings. In public testimonials with the leaders, who are clinical psychologists, volunteers are pushed to understand their own roles in making an unhappy situation and how to use the course tools to change what makes them unhappy. The dynamic is very Oprah Winfrey, with tough love and strong engagement from the audience.

To my surprise the workshop leaders made no mention of Omnilife. They never talked about selling or commerce of any kind. They (like Santos) reiterated that the course was for personal development, nothing more. Having self-righteously assumed I would be watching unsophisticated folks bludgeoned with slick sales talk and low-rent motivational speaking (it cost Q150 to attend), I was taken aback to hear the same analyses of gender as a cultural construction and relation of unequal power (not a biological fact) that I teach in my Women's Studies classes (and used earlier to understand how changing clothes changed my gender).

After the first day we reunited with the cismen of the Joyabaj contingent, who seemed enthused and confused. Under a vast chandelier, we were joined by a ladina woman from Santos's ancestor side who laughed at their befuddlement. "You've just seen the movie, haven't you?" she said. "Don't worry! It's complicated!! It's taken me four or five times to understand it." The men seemed grateful to have their feelings echoed by a native Castilian speaker. What might this mysterious film be!? The next day when we women got to watch, I found to my surprise that it was Fried Green Tomatoes, an arty US film with an explicit antiracist message and not so implicit lesbian heroines, as well as cannibalism and a woman who breaks through walls.[14] Afterward we spent several hours dissecting it, addressing how attendees identified (to my surprise several saw themselves in the abusive husband who ends up on the grill) and what messages they took from the film.

In July, on the first day of the Lack and Abundance workshop, I sat beside Sebastiana as we meditated on loss, focusing on what we felt we lacked, instructed to assign first a color and then an animal to our feelings. Then the therapist made us aware of our body language, slumped over, facing down (and it was true as I sneaked a look around the room of some 600 women—down about a third from March). Then we meditated on images of abundance and everyone perked up. We shared our images one on one, and Sebastiana told me she had been enrolled in Omni for four months but couldn't sell anything, it was only for her own consumption. She said she wanted to talk on stage but was too afraid. The next morning the therapist was winding down a session with a story about a wedding in Cancún being disrupted by rain, but some guests refused to let it be ruined and danced on, not worried about clothes or hairdos. "That is abundance! When you find joy in what others see as loss." Sebastiana raised her hand, and when the therapist didn't notice (Sebastiana is quite small), she stood up. The therapist was welcoming and congratulated her for insisting on being heard. I felt aghast at the distance between what we had just heard about the bourgie beach wedding and what I knew Sebastiana was about to recount.

Sebastiana took the microphone and told the story of losing her father when she was eight years old and fleeing into the mountains, starving, trying to keep the little ones alive, afraid, afraid all the time. She had to grow up without her father's love. Without his support. Trying to help her mother when she was still a child herself. The therapist asked if there were others with similar experiences and several hands went up. She invited them to the stage and to my surprise Santos went up. They stood behind Sebastiana, placing their hands on her back and shoulders. Then the therapist began to work with her: "If your father were here today, what would he say? What would he want for you?" Sebastiana couldn't speak at first, she was crying (like most of us). Finally she said, "He would say he loved me and he wanted the best for me." "So," said the therapist gently, "how can you, in your life today, attain what your father wants for you? He is dead. He is in a better place. You are alive. The past is past. We can't let it hurt us. We can remember it, but we can't let it hurt us."

After pushing Sebastiana pretty rigorously she asked the other women to tell their stories, and Santos began to recount how, during the war, she and Manuel were working to help people, to support their community. But then they heard that this very work, their good work, was bad. It was dangerous. The army had a list of names, and Manuel's was on it. He was on the death list. They didn't know what to do. So Manuel just hid in the house, hiding away, so afraid! They had a little store, and a cousin, who was mentally a bit slow, helped look after it, but one day he was taken by the army. Santos put her baby on her back and went to the convent, where the army was stationed. She was afraid, but she had to get him out; he didn't understand, he was just helping. It was horrible inside. She could hear people screaming, smell things, and the soldiers made fun of her. They said, "Do you want to spend some time here? We'd be happy to have you and your baby stay here too." Here she had to stop and collect herself. The other women on the stage put their hands on her. "I got too afraid then, I had to leave him there. What could we do? Thank God, fifteen days later they let him go. He was starved, tortured, but he was alive."

The emotional intensity of these testimonials was then channeled into a small group exercise of shared massages and meditation, culminating in each woman telling her companions positive phrases, "you are wonderful," "you deserve to be happy," which we repeated back to her as we circled her for several minutes, finishing by laying our hands on her as we fell silent. Most people in our group cried and one fainted. My academic skepticism also trembled in the face of such powerful affect. Finally, we spread out on the floor with sheets of cardboard, scissors, glue, and old magazines to create a dream map, helping visualize futurity and how to get there (an Oprah technique; Grose 2008). All of the women around me, Maya and ladina, pasted images of cars, exotic locales they hoped to visit, and houses. Some had images of children in school. Santos had all of these and an advertising image of a hot white guy energetically exiting a fancy building. I teased her about shopping for a boyfriend, and she said, very seriously, "No, I want my husband to be this happy and this confident again."

Mayan Organizing 2.0?

So is this Mayan Organizing 2.0? Enlisting your friends and relatives and their friends and their friends in complex selling and accounting practices that magically convert a package of vitamins into a trip to the Bahamas or even a private jet—if you got in on top? Is cultural survival now just a monthlong theme for the Omnilife magazine, just after the "green" issue and before "What will the Internet mean?" Wanting someone you love to be happy and confident, wanting your children to "look like" a *canche* who has been well fed for generations but still be proud to be Maya, wanting your school chums to not be afraid, "afraid to fail." Can anyone be faulted for such aspirations? Like counting bones, counting points and accounting for whom one can count on—even as it entails selling overpriced vitamins to undernourished neighbors as the past uncannily surfaces in the Camino Real ballroom—this is after-math. And it is deeply entangled in long histories of number and counting that trouble any digital—either liberatory or pernicious—summing up of Santos's experiences.

For example, in ways both odd and delightful, our conversations increasingly feel like those I have with academic and other middling-class friends in the United States about diet and exercise, relationships, theories about mind and body, and reminiscing about food and experiences in far-off locales, like seeing Michelangelo's work in the original or crossing from Israel into the Occupied West Bank. Describing her cruise on the Nile (someplace I've never been), Santos marveled at how Alexandria made her remember, with surprising intensity, her struggles to memorize the port cities, major exports, and GNP of different countries in her tiny hamlet schoolhouse decades ago. It's through strange byways indeed that a country like Egypt and its people became miniaturized into numbers, a list, and geographical coordinates for extraction, emerging from a very specific and epistemically peculiar moment in planetary history—post–World War II, with the installation of the Bretton Woods financial system—and mobilized so as to lodge in a young Mayan girl's brain to emerge as she, through complexly connected *Redes*, rides on that mythic waterway toward the sea. I learned those figures, too, and am as entangled as Santos is in accounting procedures and subject production rooted in double entry and the ways its race-gender-labor-nutrition-affect quantifications *qualify* people—in part, for the kinds of work and rewards associated with Ferguson's "modernity." The very work and rewards, in turn, that are made harder to achieve, for almost all of us, by corporate globalization.

Indeed, how different is Omnilife from what I'm doing? The same characteristics that drew Alianza and the Omnilife recruiters to Santos are surely part of what make us friends. I also "use" her singularity to access a larger plurality and, in my more earnest moments, do it in the name of "helping people." In hiring and promotion I am also judged on and internalize minute scales of supposedly hard-to-quantify qualities like impact, the tier of the press or journal I publish with, student evaluations, and the like; I depend entirely on others, like students and interlocutors in Guatemala, to "be" who I "am"; and I expend time, energy, and out-of-pocket expenses cultivating my psychological disposition to maintain productivity (yoga, anyone?). Plus, the $200,000-plus my students "choose" to pay to attend Duke University may be no more or less helpful to their health and economy than some vitamin B and aspartame plus testimonials about how it can change their lives.

I'm not outside what I think I'm critiquing, which is too complex to simply say Santos and her Red should know it's standard-issue neoliberalism and refuse its lures and snares. While apparently falling prey to Omnilife's sophisticated manipulation of indigeneity, consumer sparkle, and self-help affirmation, they don't seem any more conned by it than the rest of us caught in late capital's meshes of commodified subjectivization and the boom in affective labor. Santos, Manuel, and Francisca say—and I have seen it in action—they participate in Omnilife because they deeply enjoy helping people. And because it is "Maya." And my surprise when Santos bestowed an ethnic value to the vitamins in their nice clean bottles, packaged in clear doses rather than messy dried leaves, reveals more my own problematic assumptions that Maya "still" aren't "modern" (and maybe shouldn't be?!). It exposes my ignorance of the long-standing roles of testimonials and achi'lib'al (companionship) in the coauthoring of sickness and associated traditions of healing others and thereby healing oneself.

So "displacing" Omnilife products is not resistance in the guise of neoliberalism. It is a capital-formation complexly linked to prosperity-gospel forms. But networking Omnilife to Mayan heritage and postrevolutionary dreams of improvement is not just duping. The Redes formed through the product and its articulations (self-help seminars in luxury hotels, demobilized guerrilla fighters, global warming and localvore cultures, cross-ethnic friendships, Oprah-style public psychotherapy engaging the aftereffects of mass violence) are complex machines linking pre- and postwar forms of organizing and self-making with the folk-medicalizing of a transnational product. It might not have been the form they would have chosen under other circumstances, but when I asked Francisca about how being a guerrilla jibed with her Omnilife work, she sighed. "Jorge Vergara is an empresario, a businessman. We know that. But who else will give me a job? I don't speak Castilian well. I never went to school. I have no résumé. After the war, what could I do?"[15]

The market effects of Omnilife in Joyabaj are unfolding within spaces shaped by the massive—unimaginable, really—violence of the war, of the Genocide of Maya, and by the war's context, a Misery of Mozos. Shutting down nonmarket options, people are left to DIY, do it yourself. I may wish it weren't Omnilife that is providing some of what the state and the Left are not—recognition of indigenous people, spaces where ladinos and Mayas interact, houses, cars, travel, a bit of class mobility, therapy, pleasure, body work, support for aspirations, or a bit of security (for some) within a deeply insecure world. But it also behooves me to remember that, despite oligarch and army paranoia—and leftist hopes—Maya were not organic communists, somehow outside market perils and promises until Omnilife snuck in (Fischer 2002; Goldin 2009; Smith 1990). Because of it, for now, some aren't risking internal or cross-border migration. Or narcotrafficking. They are not living *entre miedo*, constantly in fear. And, as Mayan anthropologist Irmalicia Velazquez Nimatuj reminded me, they don't have to kill anyone—one of the steep costs of revolution.

Too, "seeing through" people's enthusiasms to reveal—via more precise cost-benefit analyses—how they are really being exploited when they think they are helping people may make me feel smart. But it mystifies my own embroilment in a system that sucks its quantum of lucration out of me and simultaneously affords me the very method I use to get such "facts." In other words the system of double-entry bookkeeping, installed through number and from which number draws its amazing powers. Those epistemically peculiar powers also include the *nubes*, which are no more separate from number than dross and sacredness are from money. It's a creepy joke to say an "*indio*" with money becomes a ladino (even if she is spending that money on traditional ceremonies, as Santos and her family become more involved with Mayan spirituality), but it gets at its uncanny transformative power (like clothes gendering me). No more than we, can number or money be separated from the relations that make them count.

So to return to the faux Mayan pyramid at the Atlantis resort, this Mayan pyramid–selling may be less fake than complexly recalibrating into a momentarily singular plurality that is Maya but not like any Mayan whole that existed before. And in this—like the pyramid in the next chapter—it may actually be like an "authentic" Mayan pyramid. By this I mean, early in the first Christian millennium Mayans at Uaxactún and other sites built pyramids that worked like giant clocks. The three small temples on top were built so the winter solstice sunrise hit one, the equinoxes landed square in the center, and the sun finished its yearly sickling on the third temple at the summer solstice. Perhaps "modern" pyramids also help us keep track of our current coordinates in the amazing and terrifying time and space we inhabit.

In this chapter I've followed people's diagnoses of malnutrition and envy (and rage) as explanations of a medical nature that are also social and political profiles. What will it take to transform them into sincere happiness at someone else's success, to grasp the "whole" life promised by the Omni products, perhaps in a world where we can eat lunch together (*cum panis*)? In the next chapter I describe a pyramid rising from exactly this enchanting hope.

5 Mayan Pyramid (Scheme)

We're still working our way through the aftershocks of the orgy of irresponsibility and greed that brought America to this nadir.
—Frank Rich

One day while Santos was attending her Red, she got a call from the United States. She went into the back room for almost an hour, and when she came back she was crying. She said, "Remember I was telling you about Miguel?" He'd recently returned from the United States and signed up, quickly becoming one of her most promising initiates. Ecstatic to be home, he was successful in recruiting and solicitous in *cuidando a la gente*. But one day, without a word, he disappeared, leaving everyone in the lurch. Santos had to take on a bunch of untrained newbies and was doubting herself for trusting him. "Well," she said, "He's back in the US and he wants to kill himself. His mother gave all their money to El Millonario."

Here is another story about the vexed and productive relation between the desultory politics of survival and the magical logics of number and finance in after-math.

The *Delirio*

"My people! My people! How could they have done this??!!" Anastasia was suddenly close to tears. It was July 2008, and we were at her kitchen table discussing the strange case of El Millonario, laughing at its preposterousness. He had four wives up in his hilltop mansion. A Hummer. He'd whip open his fanny pack full of cash and donate to any cause. He was going to help people get *medio millón*, half a million quetzals. Some had already taken home baskets of money. "It's like a *telenovela*," I said. She'd agreed, giggling, "It's impossible!" But moments later she was shaking and grief stricken. "If you were me what would you do? What can we do? People want to believe. They think you can get rich without struggle, without sacrifice."

El Millonario (no one ever used his name, few seemed to know it—or want to admit they did) had pulled off a mind-boggling *estafa*, a swindle that had devastated the economies of a number of towns. He promised *medio millón* to anyone who put in a (at first) small down payment. A local indigenous man from a hamlet of Zacualpa, he had spent time in Mexico—perhaps in a war-related exile—and people noted he couldn't even speak Castilian very well. One man recalled him as a normal person, a *campesino*. "He was an *arenero*, he dug sand for the road building projects." But when he came back he brought a development project.

People remember he had papers, pamphlets, cards with his name and the NGO, all legit. He said international funders wanted to help the neediest people, the victims of the war. Only indigenous people were allowed, as ladinos already had plenty. Don Neto, the indigenous mayor of Zacualpa, said he was asked in maybe 1997 or 1998, when he was working in a different development project, to help get people together. "It was a project to *regalar* money, to give it away. The NGO was called ANECOF, Asociación para las Necesidades con un Solo Corazón y Fé (One Heart and Faith Association for Needs), and they wanted to give the money directly to the people. If it passed through the president, governor, or mayor it would just be stolen." He claims he was too busy to get involved (although many think he was). As time went on, the initial down payment of Q200 began to grow as the funders—apparently convinced by moral hazard arguments—needed proof the beneficiaries were serious, not just waiting for a handout.[1]

Then, some say, the story changed. The funders were from the Middle East and wanted to help victims of American imperialism. Perhaps bin

Laden himself! But George Bush wouldn't let the money through—imposing a sea blockade. A bit more money for taxes, lawyers, travel, and lobbying would be necessary, and they had to store the money, with bodyguards and guns to keep it safe. Inscription rose to some Q1500 (about $200), but you could join only once, so people were signing up their spouses, children, even unborn babies and the deceased, hoping for half a million each (unlike reparations, where everyone shares a single payout for a maximum of two family members, regardless of how many were lost). Some ended up "investing" hundreds of thousands of quetzals. By 2002 or 2003, said Don Neto, it was a "*delirio*. People were drowning in their hopes for salvation, people put all their money in, every little bit to contribute. *Se contagiaron*."

"People were pressuring me, pressuring me to join," said a man who transports people and livestock. "They said, 'What's wrong with you? We're going to have new cars, new trucks, so many animals we'll have to buy land to pasture them all, and you'll be left with your stupid old truck. You'll be sorry then!'" He held out and now has a new vehicle, bought with the proceeds from ferrying believers up the Cerro Kumatz, or Snake Mountain, where El Millonario began to hold nighttime ceremonies. That's because at some point the story changed again. No longer an earthly donor but the *Ajaw* itself, the world spirit, would provide the half million. The *Ajaw* required an undivided heart and unquestioning faith evinced in ritual actions, like crawling over gravel (people spoke of seventeen hours of kneeling in "sacrificial ceremonies"). This is when outsiders like the Catholic priest and local doctors realized something was going on. The hospital was full of patients ill from exposure and with infected knees. The priest found even his best catechists unable to kneel at mass.

An indigenous woman from Zacualpa who claimed she had resisted the *medio millón*'s allure told me her midwife had related some of the odd goings-on. "It was all so strange. There were tons of people up there on the *cerro* as the day got close. They were told they had to show penitence, had to kiss the feet of a huge man, he was fat, gigantic! and had his face covered. There were huge candles everywhere. They were calling on the Seven Powers [carrying traces of *exu* and *loa* from West Africa syncretized with Catholic saints]. If you have gold in your mouth you have to take it out, if they see it, they won't help, it's wealth. So people pulled out their own teeth. Menstruating women weren't allowed either, they said it would want the blood. It was like a horror movie!"

It was not until July 2011 that I finally met someone willing to admit she had been involved. Fidelia told me, "Ay! If we told you the whole thing it would take days, many days!" She explained,

The donors are spirits. They don't walk here on the earth, they walk in the air. They are angels. Apostles, prophets. If you say anything, the angels are listening, listening. They say the angels have names: Rudy Fernández, Rudy Ruben Jr., and Janet Zaragoza. They say they walk in the sky, in the heavens, but now I think they are people. We were *locos*, crazy. They gave us food, meat, soup, but it made us crazy. There was something, who knows what they put in it? *Se descontrola* [you get out of control]. You stop caring about anything, your work, your children. Day and night, night and day, all you can think about is the money, what you will do with it. You can't concentrate. Just the *negocio*, the *negocio* [the business]. It must be some kind of poison. *Me tontea la cabeza* [my head got all foolish]. Diana, you need to be very careful. They might try to give it to you. We had to sing and pray for the project. It was all mixed, a new church, they said, with *costumbre* [Mayan traditions], Catholics, Protestant pastors, even police were there. There were idols, candles, marimba, everyone singing.

Meanwhile El Millonario was cutting a larger-than-life figure. He had a yellow Hummer, maybe two. He had a Norteño band, featuring himself as the lead singer, and imported some of Guatemala's best musicians as backup. Its overwhelming sound system needed several trucks just to transport the amplifiers. He had an album, videos (still on sale in the Joyabaj market), and postcards showing him in full-on narcogangster drag. (There were rumors that this wasn't just a show.)[2] He paid Carmen, a young ladina woman, Q2000 for a few hours of work each month to help him with the Castilian lyrics to the Mexican *corridos* he loved to sing. She claimed he was practically illiterate. But people remember with great satisfaction the blowout party he helped sponsor (with his band performing) to inaugurate the new four-story municipal palace in Zacualpa—quite modern and an object of enormous local pride.

He was also renowned for that fanny pack, the Q20,000! in cash! he donated when asked for a contribution for the fiesta. He sponsored the women's soccer team, providing fancy new uniforms, and silly contests—like seeing who could drink the most soda at one sitting, with handsome cash prizes. "He was very popular for that!" Some say he hired four young women to live at his house and work as his accountants. Others say there were seven women and they were all his "wives." Several were sisters, the rumors went, and he had bought them from their father. How else could the man now have a truck and many animals? These were the stories that made Anastasia and me laugh at the tale's soap-operaish over-the-top-ness but also shiver at the suggestion of human traffic and its uncanny horror-film-like aura.

There *were* doubts. When Felipe Natareno, Joyabaj's indigenous-identified former mayor, returned from internal exile, he ran again for mayor, almost winning several times with strong indigenous backing. But when he raised questions about the *medio millón*, he suddenly found himself to be a rich ladino. "People got mad and said anyone who says it's lies is someone who already has money, who just has *envidia* and is jealous because poor indigenous people want to have some, too!" He said, "I tried to get people to reflect, to inject the idea that we know the government manages so much money, but they are refusing to pay even Q1,500 for the civil patrol reparations. They control everything. They can *make* money, and they won't give it away. How, then, can the *medio millón* give so much??" (In other words, do the math!) Being on the campaign trail, though, he decided to hold his tongue rather than risk losing votes, since so many were involved. And, he admitted, all those people mortgaging their land was good for his business as a notary public.

Manuela, a young woman from Patzulá, visiting from her boarding school in Chichicastenango, said,

People came to our house, catechists from Chorraxaj, to talk to my father. There were committees working for the project. They came and told my dad about the *medio millón* and that he wouldn't have to worry about paying for our school, there would be a lot of money. My brother and I, who are both studying, we thought it didn't sound very true, no projects just give money. We cautioned him against it. But they kept saying it will come, it will come. People were renting pickups, trucks, getting ready to go get all the money. They were going to have land by the road, houses. But there were also strange stories. Our neighbors, they were involved, but when we decided not to they stopped talking to us. It caused a lot of divisions. I heard women only went up to the mountains. They had to wear special *traje*, only black *guipil* and black *corte*, only those. They went up on the Cerro, all night, on their knees, so the next day they couldn't walk. But everything had to be secret. They were very mad at us because we did not participate.

While Manuela and her brother prevailed on their father, in many families it was the young people who pushed to get involved and elders who hung back. Communities *and* families split.

In other cases, entire hamlets got involved, as in Tzajmá, north of Patzulá. The same night Micaela asked me what percent I was, she told me, in hushed tones, that Encarnación, unbeknownst to Juan, had also put money into the project, maybe Q1,000, but as the quotas got higher she couldn't keep paying so had to drop out, losing the money.

In early spring 2007 the Catholic priest began to speak out against the scheme. One particularly impassioned sermon, where he announced that he was receiving death threats for doing so, impacted people strongly and represented a turning point in the saga. But when the priest called El Millonario a liar and a thief from the pulpit, he said, it angered many parishioners. One catechist told him, "Padre, you don't have a wife or kids. You don't need money and so you don't want us to have money." Many saw him betraying their hopes for a better life and stopped coming to mass altogether. By this time, they were deeply invested, having mortgaged whatever they had—often at 10% monthly interest or more. Others had gone into debt *and* had skipped the odious trip to the south coast, secure their investment would pay off by Christmas—leaving them with no money whatsoever.

This doesn't mean that people gave up their peasant hardheadedness. To assuage doubters El Millonario invited people to his well-guarded mansion and showed them rooms full of money, from floor to ceiling. One man said, "He brought leaders, the *sacerdotes mayas*, the Mayan priests, he showed them big bags of money. It was all Maya, only Maya working at every level. *Palparon!* They touched them. They *felt* the money so they believed."[3] Others say he did distribute some *costales* of money, but warned that if the recipients had ever had doubts, the money would disappear on the walk home. While some made it with their cash intact, others found the bills converted into cut-up old newspaper.[4] But as I discuss later, maybe it wasn't just the money, the visions of plenty that made people delirious ("new trucks, so many animals"), or even the delightful millenarian idea of the world upside down in which finally indigenous people count; the *mozos*, not the owner, benefit; the Maya, not the ladinos and *canches*, get the payoff. Perhaps it was also a whiff of the utopian: the sensations and allure of pleasure, hope, enthusiasm, the outpouring of collective vocation at its most feverish and committed, a special joy (Jameson 2005).

In mid–2007 all the turkeys disappeared from the markets, with the few that were left selling at exorbitant prices. El Millonario had said everyone had to supply one for sacrifice, so the money would come.[5] That's also when you couldn't find a costal, the large baskets used to transport merchandise, anywhere, for love or money. The money was coming, and everyone needed to get ready to carry it home. But just as the great distribution was about to occur, someone torched El Millonario's mansion, burning all the money to a cinder. They say inspections found charred newspaper rather than quetzals: the mountains of money were mostly worthless paper, with a few real bills on top.

Whatever was sustaining people's faith collapsed, and in its place an equally secure and widespread intention emerged: get that hijo de la gran puta. Word spread quickly through the villages, and a lynch mob of several thousand people formed in Joyabaj. They went to Zacualpa to hunt down El Millonario, with the crowd growing along the way. They burned his Hummer, his house, and the gasoline station and three-story hotel he was building on the edge of town. On the remains of the buildings they painted Prohibido negociar. Propiedad de la gente—People's property, sale prohibited. Some say they even had a marimba to accompany the festival of destruction.

To everyone's great disappointment, their quarry had fled. They had to make do with several of his associates, including a man I'll call Tito, a young indigenous schoolteacher. At least four of El Millonario's men, maybe more, were hauled up the mountain to a hamlet that was infamous during the war for its brutal civil patrol. Again, stories differ, but all agree the men were held in the school and tortured—beaten, strung up for days (some say over a month), and starved.[6] "Who knows why they let them go and didn't kill them?" said a fellow Mayan schoolteacher. "People were definitely out for blood! But that Tito is a very smooth talker. Somehow he convinced them he was a victim, too, that he really believed, and was only trying to help. He said that only if they let him go was there a chance to get some money back. What's amazing is that he came down the mountain and ran for mayor of Joyabaj! And he almost won!!!"[7]

El Millonario remains missing, reportedly hiding somewhere in Mexico. Thousands of families lost everything. In the village of Tzajmá maybe five

5.1 El *Millonario*'s gas station after it was torched. "People's property, sale prohibited" is spray painted on the building. Author's photo.

or six families still have their land. Everyone else lost theirs to the moneylenders. For a while dozens of families were living down by the river under tarps. People scattered, the women who were mad at Manuela for not joining went begging to relatives in other areas, the family broken apart. Others went to the abhorred south coast to eke out any living they could find. Many families, like Miguel's (Santos's Omnilife recruit), had invested migrants' remittances in the scheme and so lost their future homes rather than their actual ones. While in less debt, they're starting from zero. Micaela said, "People have nowhere to go. They lost everything."

About the *gran estafa*, no police report was ever filed, nor has any formal process been opened against El *Millonario*. The only official coverage of a scam that affected an entire province, bankrupted tens of thousands of people, and "disappeared" close to a million dollars was one piece in a small progressive newspaper (Naveda 2008). Returning to the city from Joyabaj in July 2008, I mentioned the stories about El *Millonario* to an economist friend and he helped me find the article. "When I first read it," he said, "It seemed like a rumor or a myth. Like a dream. It was impossible. What makes people believe this?" Mayan cultural analyst Edgar Esquit said, bemused, "It made me think of García Márquez."

Calculating Winners, Losers, and the Interconnectedness

> Maybe I should start with the world that has made conspiracy theory . . . ever present, unavoidable, pervasive, compulsive, fun, frightening, and fascinating. . . . The burgeoning new world order of starkly divided camps where haves and have-nots have become, more simply and efficiently and finally, winners and losers. . . . The sure knowledge (and experience) that everything is interconnected and merging—a seduction, a dreaming . . . coupled with the . . . moment of terror when something whispers in our ear that the interconnectedness is all controlled by a dark and monolithic Other and we are in it, no exit.
>
> —Kathleen Stewart

Shame at having been tricked seems as endemic as anger at El Millonario—as you can tell by my account, only one person admitted to having fallen for his wiles. Most of what I "know" about it and am sharing with you comes from the unstable circulations of rumor—*post facto* reconstructions, with their accrued fantabulations, and extremely hypothetical projections of the sums of money invested and lost. This is the uncanny, illiberal moment of enchantment, of swooning into a *delirio*, a *locura*, a dream. Yet the harsh reality that it was too good to be true is an agonizing awakening. The psychic and material pain at falling victim to fraud is amplified by the humiliation of knowing that you collaborated in your own undoing. You couldn't count. Only now do you see it doesn't add up.

For those involved, their once sincere beliefs now look impossible, laughable. Numbers, those simple descriptors whose mathematical manipulation is governed by a set of invariable rules, were supposed to turn a few hundred quetzals into *medio millón*. Because these days what kind of fool sticks with addition and subtraction, credit and debit, when all around there are palpable expressions of geometric growth? But now those numbers are shown to be as capable as guns, whips, and diseases at finishing people off. The "neutral counting subjects" who believed in them stand homeless and exposed as *babosos*, fools. Only horror films and magical realism seem adequate to account for it.

Wasn't it obvious? Shouldn't they have known? This is the hackneyed query at the fall of every Ponzi scheme or market bubble, and like many analysts poking about in the postcrash ashes of Wall Street's bonfire of the vanities and the Eurozone, many are happy to blame the victims—subprime borrowers, hedonistic Catholics,[8] credulous Maya. Tomasa's ten-year-old grandson (ladino-identified, although she is indigenous), said, "Only *gente bruto* [brutes, expressing animal-like stupidity] would do such a thing." A ladino man said, "*De los babosos comen los vivos* [smart folks eat / live off the fools]."

Not surprisingly, indigenous people are far less sanguine about the suffering involved and well aware of the ethnic overtones of "*bruto*" and "*baboso.*" Sitting late in Encarnación's kitchen Micaela and I cried. "*Tan triste, tan triste! Que lástima!* What a shame!" she said. "The children are sacrificing, being in the US, sacrificing, working to make something better for their family, to get a house, and then all that work and sacrifice goes for that, it's so unfair! They despair when they find out it was all for nothing." Micaela's grief was palpable, her sense of what it takes to earn that money and the horror of finding it wasted; first for the interest payments to migrate and then for this. Someone else is living extravagantly off your labor and what option do you have but to keep working, keep sacrificing? Or, as Miguel was contemplating, suicide?

In July 2008, when Anastasia expressed despair and grief that "her" Mayan people had been so shatteringly deceived, some was for the economic devastation that the fraud had wrought on families barely getting back on their feet after the human and material losses of the war. (And perhaps a bit for her own pocket, as a businesswoman where no one has any money.) But as an activist she is keenly aware of the racist stereotypes of indigenous people as easily duped[9] and, in Lenin's infamous depiction of peasants, as a "sack of potatoes," an undifferentiated mass, an aggregate. Declassified army documents, like Plan Sofia's "100%," show elites and the military command suffering a pervasive, compulsive, and frightening dismay at Mayan communities' continuing cohesiveness and opaqueness, a central plank in the racism that unfurled into genocide.[10] Some communities, like Francisca's, did the math and did decide en masse that it was better to die fighting than die of malnutrition and disease. The same adroitness at solidarity and clandestinity that kept their cultures somewhat intact through the Spanish, criollo, and ladino occupations and guerrillas safe during the war kept El Millonario's project a secret from all non-Maya for close to a decade. Such strategic silences may contribute to the stereotypes of "stoic Indians," draining them of agency and revolutionary consciousness when they were actually participating in calibrated and collective tactics (McAllister 2013).

The same stereotypes animate the fascination and horror at the numerous lynchings or mass, rapid, and summary violence—often carried out against supposed thieves, murderers, Satanists, and baby snatchers—that villagers collectively tried to mete out to El Millonario (Burrell 2013; Gutiérrez and Kobrak 2001). Lynchings occur in nonindigenous communities, but these images traffic in the sense of indigenous peasants as aggregates—a Mob of Maya—not modern autonomous subjects. A crowd, a horde, a disturbance, a panic: these are the magics plurality can produce out of singularity. Anastasia is committed to undermining such ways of "knowing" her people. Yet here they were, caught up in a ludicrous scheme, hoping, against any possibly rational hope, that they could get money for nothing. How could people who had already suffered so much make such a huge, pathetic mistake?

Sitting at Anastasia's kitchen table, just after the Bear Stearns investment bank collapse, I tried to reassure her: "It's not only highland Maya. People in the US, with years of education, also put all their money into worthless schemes. The stock market, maybe capitalism as a whole, is based on the same thing." I was feeling a bit of lefty smugness that I had it all figured out.[11] It seemed to make Anastasia feel a bit better, too.

Then, of course, the whole shebang crashed. Not just "the American El Millonarios"—Bernard Madoff, Robert Stanford, and all the "mini-Madoffs" (Wayne 2009, B1)—and not just major investment firms and some of the world's largest banks but the organizations that rated and insured them, the accounting firms, and even some governments supposed to regulate them collapsed, devastating the global economy. In a 2009 letter to shareholders a chastened Warren Buffet likened our financial institution's recklessness to venereal disease. Even the innocent were infected because "it's not just whom *you* slept with" but also "whom *they* are sleeping with" (Rich, 2009). Buffet, the palpable embodiment of US capitalism and its geometric promise of getting something for very little, is humbled, now seeing the entire system riddled with a contagious disease (he lost $35 billion in 2008; perhaps I'm bad at math, but I really can't conceive what that number means). The whole planet *se contagió*.

The leap to a language of pathogenic contagion to describe the epistemic peculiarity of the rational market cycling out of control and suddenly (apparently) unamenable to the orderly and transparent functioning of numbers and mathematical logics seems to acknowledge that "other side of the coin" Maurer and others highlight: the unsettling, magical one. When someone like Buffett metaphorizes finance's mysteries via biology, it's usually postcrash, when the magic that made them "winners" has turned against them (although he seems to have recovered nicely). Before that, the rational workings of the invisible hand ("look, Ma, no fetish!") seemed discernible, calculable, and profitably manipulable by captains of industry. At least for a moment that algorithmic mangle that transformed one dollar into a hundred as smoothly as ironing a sheet is now revealed to mangle—in the sense of injuring and maiming (see chapter 0). Like the tales of El Millonario, shot through with the uncanny, contagion—like the slime of the sublime—symptomatizes trouble in the (neo)liberal self: no longer active, independent, and self-possessed but revealed as vulnerable, acted on, made via relation (Wald 2008).

It Takes a Pillage

> Abuse of Power Comes As No Surprise
> Protect Me From What I Want
> —Jenny Holzer, Truisms and Survival

> Utopia serves as the mere lure and bait for ideology (hope being after all also the principle of the cruelest confidence games and of hucksterism as a fine art).
> —Fredric Jameson (2005, 3)

But first, let's remember that there are rational reasons people invest. El Millonario, like Madoff, perpetrated what's called a Ponzi, or pyramid, scheme, paying off early investors with money from those who got in later. In 1920 Charles Ponzi, an Italian immigrant to the United States, offered enticingly high returns based on taking advantage of (aka arbitraging) a price differential involving postal reply coupons issued in war-wrecked European currencies and redeemed at face value in US dollars. Pioneer investors got a 50% return in just ninety days. As they reinvested and their example encouraged others to put new money in, the pot miraculously grew. In a few short months Ponzi made $4.59 million in 2008 currency. People began mortgaging their houses and investing their life savings. By August 1920, however, the scheme collapsed, and Ponzi was tried and jailed. (Seeing certain resemblances, I asked Manuel if the Omnilife *Redes* had been hurt by association with the *medio millón* pyramid collapse. He sighed. "It's true, there are many parallels. But the difference is that we have a product that people want to buy. It's not just promises." A similar rationale has saved many US MLMs from exactly these accusations.)

Similarly, Madoff began with a perfectly legal financial innovation to make money in the interstices of the system, specifically in the OTC (over-the-counter) market by paying clients for every share they traded. Money was made by "pocketing the difference in the 'spread,' or the gap between the offering and selling price for the stocks" (Creswell and Thomas 2009, B8). His firm was also one of the first to computerize trading.[12] It's unclear exactly how legitimate earnings (within capitalist ethics, at least) morphed into the taking-from-Peter-to-pay-Paul-form of the Ponzi, but a *delirio* took hold. Clients (at least on paper) were consistently making far better returns than the market rate, and people begged to hook up with Madoff, even coughing up huge membership fees for country clubs where they *might* meet him and *perhaps* get a chance to invest. Most clients now say they invested reasonably at first, but with handsome payoffs they invested more and more, until rational people, Nobel laureates, sovereign wealth funds, and shapers of our most intimate fantasy lives (like Steven Spielberg and Jeffrey Katzenberg) gave him tens of billions of dollars. Some gave him everything they had (Henriques 2011; LeBor 2010).[13]

Don Neto, Zacualpa's mayor said, "It was not a ladino who lied to us, it was one of the same poor people as we are." Many remembered El Millonario's organization as Maya, all Maya. On that journey to make pluralities into singularities and then back into pluralities, they say he started with the traditional authorities in outlying hamlets, the *sacerdotes mayas*, the *ajq'ij* (perhaps, I was told, because his father was one), and then the catechists and even some evangelicals. As with the catechists who visited Manuela's father in Patzulá, Don Neto said local leaders went door-to-door, drawing on the esteem people had for them. "Maybe some did it for the money," he said, "others just wanted to help." Felipe Natareno says that they organized through the *cofrades*, the "brotherhoods" that care for saints and coordinate the important yearly festivals. "They are organized and credible, and people are used to *aportando*, contributing for the greater good, to sharing money and resources through them. This is our *estilo cooperativo*, you give something and then you get." El Millonario also had "*promotores, enganchadores, contratistas, habilitadores, adelantados* [all ways *mozos* have been organized to work since the nineteenth century]; they helped get to people, it became like a company. Those who were in the war [organized through the URNG], very few of them signed up, but among those who weren't, many *cayeron*, fell prey." (However, CUC leader and Zacualpa native Daniel Pascual said, to his chagrin, that CUC members did help organize for El *Estafador*, the swindler, through their *redes*, "probably with the understanding it was helping people.") Felipe went on: "It's a shame! The *Señor* had a great power of persuasion. He showed people the moon, the stars, everything. 'You won't have room for your cattle, your cars, there will be so much money, so much money!' It was a *locura de riqueza*, an insanity of riches."

Calculated or not, the project drew on already existing substrata of everyday enchantments. People working their fields often turn up enigmatic ancestral stones and charismatic zoomorphic figures that often make their way, like the midwife's reparations check, onto people's home altars to join the phantasmagoria of candles, flowers, lithographs of saints, the Seven Powers, and photographs of deceased family members. The past hugs near. For many, agriculture's risks are hedged by Monsanto products as well as careful rituals around the seeds, sexual abstention, and eating only traditional foods (nothing associated with the Spanish occupiers) before planting. It is very important that domestic life be calm and a man's heart be right, happy and balanced, when he furrows the earth to prepare new crops. Families make offerings of *pagos*—vegetable food or animals buried in the corners of fields—to telluric deities to reciprocate for what they will take with the harvest (López García 2010; Wilson 1995).

In the late 1990s, when El *Millonario* began to collect "the neediest" to his cause, another form of enchantment was becoming everyday via Guatemala's postwar development boom. In even the most out-of-the-way hamlets, strangers were coming out of nowhere and giving things away—chickens, building supplies, tractors, medicine, a workshop on Mayan rights, even free money. The aid bonanza of the peace process created many "Pedro Projectos" (less often Pedrinas)—people adept at *gestionando*, maneuvering through the paperwork. Throughout the highlands, such policies had unsurprising effects. A Mayan accountant hired to audit a rural Mayan organization said he found every paid position was held by members of one family. When he asked about it, they offered to put him on the payroll of a project on Mayan spirituality. "I'm an accountant," he said, laughing. "Not really the most spiritual person!"

The flood of aid energized hopes, employed thousands of people, and, yes, encouraged some corruption. It supported reforms in health care, education, ethnic relations, legal structures, human rights, traditional culture, refugee resettlement, and the environment. For a while, it felt like magic. You just put your hand out with the correctly filled-in forms, and you could start your own Mayan women's organization or turn a struggling coffee plantation into an organic fair trade cooperative. The 1990s didn't roar only in the United States (Stiglitz 2003). Such largesse was certainly rather odd—given such recent violent dispossession—but it didn't seem crazy to try to get on the gravy train. Too, Mayan Organizing 1.0, the postquincentennial global focus on indigenous people, and the CEH genocide ruling all contributed to making Mayans count in ways that made a "Maya, only Maya" project seem perfectly reasonable. Summing up the immense losses from the war—four hundred villages destroyed, 200,000 people killed, and between 10 and 20% of the population displaced—and in a context of agitation for financial reparations, who wouldn't put a hand out? Who hadn't struggled and sacrificed?

In each of these cases an existing and functioning assemblage, legitimate and authorized—an investment system, a stock exchange, development culture, labor markets, a religious or political organization, many undergirded by accounting procedures, warranting reports, and official-looking paper and ledgers—inspires confidence. Most Ponzis (much like Omnilife) also work through preexisting networks of kin, ethnic, religious, or national identities (often beleaguered ones) to produce communities of faith. Ponzi started with fellow Italian immigrants, Madoff worked through Jewish connections. Lutherans, Scientologists, Togolese, Colombians, Romanians, and Albanians (as the USSR broke apart, about half the Albanian population ended up "investing" the equivalent of the nation's entire GNP; Porter 2008) have all been Ponzied. But there's also the *locura*, the dream logic, the cinematic experiences, and traditions of reciprocity, conjoined with newfangled prosperity cults and the financialization of the everyday,[14] that mash up these old and novel forms of social organization, along with complex understandings of human relations with that nonhuman actant: money.

At night, by firelight, people tell each other stories about wondrous worlds that lie under the mountains, overseen by the *dueño*, the earth owner (Lara Figueroa 2002). Some are delightful trickster tales, as Judie Maxwell reminded me, contrasting alluring suggestions of deal making and admirable defilement with the more decent standards of honesty, industry, and respect. But some are also horrifying, of kingdoms full of souls traded for wealth in the mortal world now working off the debt for untold centuries underground. Everyone knows that on *Cerro Kumatz* you can make such deals.

One evening, as we finished our supper by candlelight because a sluicing downpour had cut the lights, Aurora (whose mother is Maya but who identifies as ladina) began to recount ghost stories to me and her kids. One went like this (sadly excised of detail and her delightful performance). There is a mountain north of town where people do ceremonies. They go up there to try to get money, to make a deal with the devil. It's a very strong place. I know a man. I know him. This *señor* went there with a *sajorín* [someone with esoteric knowledge, a "witch"]. They went to request money. They did all the rituals, and the *sajorín* told him a truck would come and he would have to jump on the truck and then all the money inside it would be his. Then the *sajorín* left. As midnight came, sure enough, the man heard exactly the sound of a truck coming up the mountain, although there were no roads. [By this point I had goose bumps and was glad Jorge, her warm little son, had crawled into my lap.] The man was very frightened but waited, and then there appeared a *culebrón*, a *huge* snake with three heads! Three heads and bright fiery eyes! It must have been the devil, don't you think, Diana? That's what it looks like. And hanging on it was all the money, baskets of cash, *costales*! And the man jumped on, but just as he was going to take the money he had second thoughts and fell off. The snake disappeared. When the *sajorín* came back the man was almost dead. The *sajorín* had to come many times to cure him. But he survived. The *sajorín* was very angry he didn't take the money. It is dangerous and hard work to call up the snake. The man had lost his chance to be rich. The man himself told me this story. Himself! That's what happens when you try for too much." She also told me Miguel Batz, the moneylender and pharmacy owner, hid a pig's tail under his pants, acquired when he made just such a deal, and he'd been seen sacrificing drunks— people no one would miss—at midnight in a rural chapel to maintain his good fortune.

Somewhat similar to Santos's amazing (but more individual) experiences with Omnilife, the depth and breadth of what was condensed into El Millonario's project is extraordinary, producing vibrant escape zones into shared temporo-lucrous imaginaries that, looking back, can only be explained by some hallucinatory drug slipped into the food. They concatenate Mayan ethics and the spirits of capital in a postrevolutionary financializing moment. Recapitulating Michael Taussig on devils and commodity fetishism

(1980), they limn the fascination and horror that accompany money's workings, its strange accrual through interest or the exploitation of surplus value by people who don't struggle or sacrifice. Such stories are warnings about the unnaturalness of such doings but also incite a contagious jouissance-streaked hope. Maybe this time it could be me with the *costales* of money, my family who enjoys rather than suffers, my kids who are well nourished, my people who accumulate rather than being constantly exhausted and depleted. Not for them the much hyped but tiny incrementalizing "benefits" of microfinance! They want half a million. Now. And for everyone.

But it wasn't all promises and moonlight with the *medio millón*. There was the philanthropy. And there were also threats. Some were benign: What are you waiting for? You'll be sorry! How can you deny your children? Others a bit less so: If you stop contributing you lose it all. Or even more intimate, if you doubted, you might not be worthy to receive. And then there are the rumbles of something darker, something scarier, hovering around the edges. Discussing his plans as the new mayor of Joyabaj, Don Lencho (a ladino who had barely squeaked into office, with Natareno and Tito, El *Millonario's* minion, close behind) lamented: "This *estafa* has had terrible effects. Many families have nothing anymore. The entire economy is paralyzed. People lost houses, land." When I asked him to explain he suddenly got nervous, although we were alone in his office. "It's better to not talk about this. And I won't say anything more. The leaders are still around and they are armed. I don't want any problems." The teacher who told me about Tito became very distressed when I asked if I might talk to him. "Oh no! Oh no! He would send to kill me if he thought I told you to talk to him!" One day Anastasia pointed out a black SUV on a ride to Zacualpa. "That's a *sicario*, a hit man. El *Millonario* had those people around him, like guards. They ran his errands for him. They were always heavily armed."

Working Our Way through the Aftershocks

It's via tricky byways indeed, through violence *and* the vexed and productive relations between everyday efforts to survive and the magical logics of finance, that people are converted into a sum of money: that through their doing they are undone. As I said to Anastasia, of course not only "gullible Indians" are so converted. The apparent singularities of El *Millonario's* project connect to a plurality of similar rackets, which are in turn rendered into a singularity, the Ponzi scheme. (Just as, with census taking or multilevel marketing, individual people are made into an aggregate, similar to how the forms themselves are modular, usable anywhere—even as they take on startlingly local characteristics like *cofrades* and *contratistas* in Guatemala or country clubs in the United States.) And that's why I think this pyramid, like the Mayan pyramid at Uaxactún, functions like a giant clock, helping us find our place in space and time.

In what follows, with the broad outlines of El Millonario (and the global crash) in hand, I turn back to Fidelia's particular experience and the recursive switches it took for her—like that baby on its mother's back in a compound in Ibadan who, as Verran recounts, was entered into the ledger books of the British Empire—to become just one of the thousands defrauded, perhaps a line in an accountant's book. But I also explore how, working through the aftershocks and their utter devastation, she has begun to use "math," in the ALMG's words, as a "personal intellectual adventure . . . to measure and compare all that surrounds us, to understand our place in the universe." Her very particular life, in all its terrible pathos and struggle, materializes all the concerns of this book and hooks us back in to global relations among "politics, logic, and number."

Fidelia and I met one morning in September 2011 in town because she wasn't sure it was safe for me show up alone in her hamlet. Lolita Chávez, an organizer in Santa Cruz, said I should meet her. "You know, she's the only person who ever put in a *denuncia* [police proceedings] against El Mil-lonario. People there still think the money will come. They say it's her fault they haven't given the money, because she denounced them." Lolita had called from Santa Cruz to set up the meeting and assure her I was OK, but Fidelia's first question was "Are you a good gringa or a bad gringa?"[15] I tried to reassure her as I bought a three-liter jug of soda (a standard visitor's gift, although Santos might remind me it's not Maya nor nutritionally sound) and as we took a minibus to her village. Then I tried to reassure her family, who gathered around as she settled me on the bench on their patio. Her mother, sister, and five children, all sniffling and bundled against the cold, were interested but suspicious and kept a safe distance. Lolita had told me the kids were kicked out of school because Fidelia talked about El Millonario. As we spoke and she slowly brought out documents from her court cases against the local instigators and stacks of letters her brother had written from the United States, it dawned on me that she couldn't read, making homeschooling out of the question. Later, as we negotiated how to be in communication, I realized she didn't know numbers either (in the sense of being able to note down a phone number). As our conversation made clear, however, she knew how to calculate.

We talked for a long time about what I was doing there. Would it help with the case? Should they let me take notes? Finally accepting my good intentions but relative uselessness, they began to tell me the story. "We have been threatened. We are frightened. My brother wouldn't stay. We told him you were coming but he said it was too sad. His heart couldn't bear to think about it, to go back to what has happened to us. He couldn't stand it. *Tanta tristeza, tanta cólera!* He's so sad and so angry! It's unbearable. But my mother wants people to know. It is the same as the armed conflict. We were victims."

Her father had been murdered by the army during the war, and her mother had struggled to raise the children. Her brother had gone to the United States as soon as he was old enough. "He worked day and night, day and night, for fifteen years, and he lost everything, we all lost everything. He can only cry when he remembers how hard he was working and *every* thing he worked for is gone. We had a good house, a car, land, we had fields and forest. The fraud took everything. They are evil people, killers, *demoniado*, demons. Our heads, our hearts, we can't bear it, but thanks to our mother we aren't afraid. No one is a god. There are so many lies, but I am never going to believe in anything again."

Then she told me how it happened. "They came and called people together to say they wanted to celebrate a project. It was Cirilio Pacheco Sacarias. Make sure you write down his name. He lives right down the road. He organized it, with his family. They came to offer, it's a project, a church, and they were our neighbors. You can read about it in the documents we made [to bring charges]." Part of drawing people in included giving them trips, sometimes to the ocean, and big meals. Then she talked about being out of control: *me tontea la cabeza.*

Her family got more involved as her brother began to work in El Millonario's house in the village of Pasajop.

He was taking care of the money and he saw the dollars. It was coming in from the airport everyday. All the guards brought their wives to help, but my brother didn't have a wife so he brought our mother. She saw it, too. Day and night they were bringing in money. It's a lie when they say it was only newspaper. Other countries were sending help. They started to control us more, what we ate. They said salt and chili were prohibited. Then we couldn't wear red underwear or any adornment, no earrings or gold teeth. The donors didn't want that. Es *muuuuccchhoooo!* There's so much to tell! They wouldn't let people wear sweaters. We had to pray, on our knees, do sacrifice. We weren't allowed to eat, only once a day, and we had to do ceremonies all the time, sleeping during the day so we could be up all night. The house was full of guns. There were children there, nursing mothers. I don't know how they fed their babies since they were eating almost nothing! We had to sleep on the floor, outside. We were treated like animals, living like pigs, without sweaters or blankets. We had to sing and pray for the project. We went up to the hills, on the rocks, our bodies were torn to pieces, our knees. We got desperate. We wanted to kill ourselves.

Altogether it was Q400,000 from her brother (some $50,000), plus what she put in, and for her mother, her sister, all the kids. "*Está seria.* We got money from the bank. We sold our land and got about 25,000 for each *cuerda* so about 100,000. We have a right to demand the money. It was our own sweat that earned it, and it is other people's money, too, the borrowed money. The US money is gone, all the money we had is gone, we sold the forest, the land, the water, and we borrowed from every place we could get money, FAFILES, FUNDAP, FONESOL, BANRURAL, Grameen,[16] most at about 3% interest, but also with people, *dueños de dinero,* and they charge 10%, 15%. We have a big debt, a huge debt. What are we going to do? We can't pay for food, for school."

When it fell apart, Fidelia's family organized a few other neighbors, and they got a lawyer who helped them draft their accusations. She showed me copies covered with thumbprints, since most of the accusers are illiterate. Fidelia laughed, "The lawyer said the story gave him a headache. He couldn't understand it." But then she said, "Thinking about it feels like a torture in the brain." They gathered their courage and made their declarations to the public ministry (MP) but were told "'but it's *por gusto,* you wanted to do it, so it's not a crime.' *And* we didn't have any proof. We don't have receipts for the money. Finally, the MP said we had to get more people, we needed to find people willing to denounce them. They asked us, 'why doesn't everyone get together? You are thousands!' At the ceremonies there were people from Chiché, Chinique, San Andrés, Joyabaj, Canillá, Uspantán, we didn't even know where everyone came from, we didn't know them. There weren't just a few people, it was almost all of Guatemala. And they won't investigate!"

At this point Fidelia's mom, who had been silent, said that I needed to be very careful. Just hearing the story might put me in danger with the *malos*. "Bad things have happened to people." "Yes," Fidelia said,

> they die on the south coast, bitten by snakes, there are accidents, or they get sick. One woman killed her husband. My lawyer turned on us. He changed, he was defrauding us, too. My *own* lawyer! Maybe he was bribed, I don't know. But it's another headache. I don't know if I have the strength to endure this. And my husband left me. He got tired that we were so poor and always accusing, of me always being sick. He went with another woman, just a few months ago. It's too painful, my heart is breaking. He never sees the children. Maybe it's the *malos*. But how can you not be sick? All we eat is tortillas with salt. Every week it's time to pay. We weren't like this before. We have photographs, you can see. We were fat, happy. We had what we needed.

"When we were working with the MP my brother *se descontroló*. They had to take him to a psychiatrist." Her mother said again, "You need to be very careful. You might not feel anything, but they can get you." Fidelia said,

> "Yes, we all got *susto*, fright illness. We were close to dying. We had insomnia. We couldn't eat. My brother got all swollen and bloated. He had to go to work but he was so sick. God gave money for all of us, but a few are left with all of it. They are eating. They have cars, motorcycles, clothes, vitamins. All the things they have and we have nothing. We are enduring so many needs, we don't have anything even for medicine, and we are all sick, very sick. My mother has lung cancer and we can't get treatment. El Millonario divided other families, too. *No animan decir*, no one wants to talk about it (and it didn't happen to us, thank God!), but they raped a lot of women, and when their husbands found out they got mad and abandoned them. Many people are suffering."

Fidelia and her family did have allies in late 2007, when they were working with the lawyer. "People started to come to find us, to say we were right, if only they had done that, too. 'You have enthusiasm. You are struggling. But we don't have anything.' Then they would cry. People are too sad to organize, they are also afraid. But many are still saying the money will come. If you don't say anything it might still come. They *gave* us something so we couldn't think anymore and they are still giving it to people. That's why they don't join us in denouncing." Her sister interjected here, "They call us *bruto* but *they* are still waiting!" Fidelia continued, "People don't want to talk. They say we are *pura culebra*, snakes. Because we stick out our tongues [talk too much]. We are *serpientes*. But I told the judge and I told the lawyer, 'it's all true. You can't lie in front of the law, and I'll tell anyone."

> And the *estafadores* threaten us. They say they will come in the night, or when we are on the road, they'll get us. We are so afraid. Don Manuel Pacheco, he was a soldier. He says, "If you speak badly of the army, remember many people died because they were guerrillas." One time there was a meeting at Cirilio's house with the people who are still waiting. Well, we went to try to get our money back and they beat us. Cirilio and his sister and mother (again it was important I write down the names), Lucia Pacheco, Paula Serach, Josefa Sacaria. They sent me to the hospital, the beating was so bad. My God! They grabbed firewood and smacked me on the head. They beat my mother. She was bruised all over.

This finally led to Cirilio's arrest but he spent only one night in jail before paying the fine. "We were happy. But then he fled. No one knows where he is, but his uncle is still *estafando*."

By this time we had been talking several hours, and one of the children went to get the soda. Then Fidelia started to cry. "I'm so sorry, we can't offer you lunch. It's too hard. I'm so sorry. We just don't have anything." It was one of those abyss moments of fieldwork, when the well-fed gringa feels the wash of their humiliation as my presence renders anew their shame and pain. Razor-wired into those dubious equivalents, complexes of reciprocity and inadequate exchanges, trespassing in a zone of *estilo cooperativo*, I tried to reassure them it was fine and how grateful I was they were sharing their story and how I would do what I could, knowing that was completely inadequate. Here I was, wanting to understand the weirdness, the occult economies, the magic and mysticism, all of which she was matter-of-fact about. She in turn wanted practical help for the court case, which I was not able to supply.

On a happier note, they did get Rufino Pacheco, member of the *estafador* family, arrested, and somehow their lawyer got his bail money of Q50,000 turned over to them.[17] But it went directly to the *dueños de dinero*, another threatening force in their lives. "They say if we don't pay they will kill us. We say we're trying. We're not eating. We're giving everything to you. But they say it was our fault. They have no sympathy."

They had also come into some money through the National Reparations Program. "We heard that people were coming to give money, money for the victims of the war. We were very suspicious. It was *more* people promising money, just like El Millonario! But we learned more and I became convinced. Even so, we were divided. My mother felt it wasn't right to take money for our father. But we finally talked her into it. It was easy for us, fortunately. We just needed our IDs and we gave our testimony about what happened, and it came quickly. About three months later we got a call that the check was ready." They received the standard Q24,000, and it went directly to the *dueños*.

Yet the *estafa* is continuing. "The same people, now they're in a political party, offering that for Q150 they will get Q10,000 back if they win. People still believe. And they are looking for international help. They've gotten used to eating off of us. They have our names, ID numbers, and it seems like we support them but they are getting all the money. Thousands of dollars, millions, the cooperation comes, the gringos come and take pictures."

By now it was turning into midafternoon, and Fidelia wanted to make me copies of the court documents, but distrusting anyone in town, we had to go to Santa Cruz. Before we left, her mother insisted on praying for me. We formed a circle, and her mother called on her dead husband and on the church, asking God to keep me safe from the dark powers. We knelt and kissed the ground, and by then we were all crying, except Fidelia's teenage son, who looked quite serious. I felt almost overwhelmed with *tristeza* and *cólera*, looking out at the sky about to rain, the corn planted right up to the house (borrowed from a cousin) to use every centimeter of land, their drawn faces, pondering the awful things that had happened to them and how much the debt weighs on them, the threats, the fear. What would happen to that teenage boy trying to be a man? To those little girls without school? How could Fidelia bear the heartbreak of so much loss? But then we hugged each other and promised to see each other again, and the everyday of good-byes and rushing to catch a bus cast off some of the heaviness.

In Santa Cruz I bought Fidelia lunch and said I wanted to contribute a little money for medicine, so after we'd eaten we grabbed a *tuktuk* and were whisked off to what I assumed would be a discount pharmacy. Instead we stopped at a small private home with an Omnilife sign over the door. I almost fell over. How did she get involved? I asked. Well, she was in the reparations office filling in forms when a young man asked if she knew about the products. She didn't know if he was from Joyabaj or San Martín. (But if it *was* Joyabaj, then no way! She *hates* them! She *hates* Zacualpa!! *ANYONE* from those towns. They were all with El *Millonario*.) He told her a little bit, but she wanted nothing to do with it. It was too much like the *Millonario*, promising trips, prizes. But a few months later they were getting more worried about her brother. He was so sick, he was all swollen. "Who has the money to go to a doctor? It can cost Q1,000 or more and then it doesn't work. I remembered the boy who had asked if we were sick, and I thought, who wouldn't be? But we couldn't stand seeing our brother like that, so I decided to go to the Las Vegas hotel and find out more." When she went, it was Santos's weekly information session, and she almost left when she saw Santos wearing the Joyabaj *guipil*. It was her son, Pedro, trawling the PNR office. But she stayed and learned about Biocrus and Omniplus and paid Q160 for everything. In just fifteen days her brother was completely cured. Now the whole family takes it. "I thought it was like El *Millonario* but then saw that they really do help." We talked about if she might start selling, and she said she didn't have the money and can't do the math.

Much as I love Santos, I think Fidelia may have calculated correctly Omnilife's likeness to El *Millonario* (despite her self-proclaimed innumeracy). But lo and behold, it worked.

Doing the Math

Maybe that's because there's a product, not "just promises." But I remain disconcerted at thousands of savvy Maya, many quite good at math, actively and willingly collaborating and now, tragically, living in tents along the river, sharecropping land that once was theirs, eating only salt and tortillas. When I seek to explain, by revealing corruption and extraeconomic coercion, analyzing the postwar development boom, "traditional" beliefs in mountaintop ceremonies, and how "irrational exuberance" is grounded in actual, palpable money or at least visible increases in an account or portfolio, I still don't quite get at the "epistemic peculiarity."

Tales of both El *Millonario* and the Wall Street meltdown return me to the magics of aggregation, of wholes greater than their parts, like a romp of otters, a murder of crows, a Mayan pyramid. Human superadequation now converted, like dross, into money to be skimmed off. And yet . . . what must it have felt like to be up on that mountain all together, waiting for the invisible donors to be revealed? The money to come? Or rushing down the mountain all together to burn things and punish an evildoer? Perhaps like Augustine's enchanting description of being "scattered in time—scattered, because we are never stable, never in one temporal or bodily place" (Saler 2006). Or Jane Bennett's "mixed bodily state of joy and disturbance, a transitory sensuous condition dense and intense enough to stop you in your tracks and toss you onto new terrain, to move you from the actual world to its virtual possibilities" (2001, unpaged). Or Kaushik Sunder Rajan's "promissory conjuration" of the "future perfect, present tense" (2006, 136). Charlie Piot calls a Ponzi scheme in Togo "a hope machine . . . hope in a new register, promising—and for a while giving—people money they had always desired . . . by an entity they had willed and fantasized into being. In a very real sense, the people were performing and fabulating their own desire" (forthcoming, 7). In the face of enormous injury, and despite doubts, these are moments that express the desire for totality, in which one lives outside the "normal" world of counterinsurgent divide and conquer through class division, civil patrol coercions, gender limits, and racist hierarchies (even as these are also "psychological dispositions" and "affective relations to the world," managed [partially] by people who plan to eat your lunch).

Dispersing El Millonario's enchanting affects into rational choices and calculable risks bludgeons away what made them compulsive, fun, frightening, and fascinating in the first place (Stewart 1999, 13). I penetrate the veil but lose its hallucinatory quality (Conrad, in Taussig 1987). Trying to "save" the Maya by making them nonduped or disenchanted—like us moderns—or just saying we're all enchanted—"we've never been modern"—I am missing the point, dissolving difference into the One, resisting enchantment's wiles, playing at sovereign individuality.

Helen Verran wrestled with this very problem when she went to postindependence Nigeria to teach math and to contest the double delegitimation of "not counting": not knowing math and not mattering. She spent arduous years deciphering Yoruba numeration so that it could be taught legitimately, like bilingualism, in Nigerian schools and so it could be explained to non-Yorubans, allowing them to marvel at how complex and enchanting these different number logics were. To her disconcertment, when she presented this relativist analysis to Yoruba speakers, they laughed. She came to realize that in challenging neocolonial universalism she had reinscribed an "ultimate division" between "us" and "them" that failed to recognize communities of practice as creative and generative of "collective life as a logical going-on in actual times and places" (2001, 28–29). "I might say that in those classrooms we all 'believed' in numbers. Yet to say 'I believe in numbers' seems a quite foolish statement, for numbers do not seem to be something that it is necessary to *believe* in. Numbers are familiars that seem to 'do' us (make us who and what we are) as we 'do' them" (2001, 30).

The inextricability of doing and done is a different mode of thinking things-in-relation than a digital all or nothing or the sense that quantity and quality are completely separate scales. It helps us focus, as Guyer suggests, on the conceptual "hooks" that link "one to the other without reduction to a common denominator" (2004, 49). It refuses to relegate enchantment to an "out there" that differentiates believer from believed—even if, postcrash, it feels like you were drugged or suffering a contagious disease. It thus decomposes the Ponzi-inspired question of "why would they believe such a thing?" (Perhaps akin to the postinsurrectional exhaustion that wonders what made people believe that rising up would change anything?)

Verran also helps me remember that "doing the math" *can* render "reasonable" explanations but that the math itself is (part of) what produces unreason. Number (like money, like development, like Ponzi schemes, like lynch mobs) is a "familiar" doing us as we do it. And "doing number is doing the relation one-to-many" (Verran 2000, 357). We've seen this in the way human rights accounting entails both counting the dead *and* the numbers that save those who have left no bones from becoming phantoms, in the way accounting through Omnilife's *Redes* both extracts surplus and injects hard-to-quantify enthusiasm, plus amazing prizes.

Thinking of numbers this way, as inextricably "familiar," helps rebridge the divide whereby double-entry bookkeeping achieved the accuracy effect by separating the "fact" from haggling, uncertainty, trust, desire, and the multiple forms of value (jewels, various currencies, land, reliquaries, etc.) that had appeared in the inventory (i.e., cutting off the office from the bedroom). It was this divide that "promoted dispassion while naturalizing the mania to trade" (Poovey 1998, 90). My disconcertment at the Mayan pyramid's numbers may be due to my continuing enthrallment to double-entry logics that mystify how dispassion is only accomplished by off-booking mania and its dark twin, superadequation. And how this is the *source* of the very profits it seems to only be counting (remember those strung-out boys wandering the rows of sugarcane, Santos working eighteen hours a day making tortillas). As Graeber says, the middlemen seem "sober, calculating, unimaginative," while "at either end of the debt chain, the whole enterprise seem[s] to turn on the ability to manipulate fantasies and to run a constant peril of slipping into . . . phantasmagorical madness" (2011, 347). The court documents Fidelia showed me also bridge this divide, detailing, first, how the "Band of *estafadores* and extortionists known as El Millonario . . . operated with a well-planned strategy, using actions oriented to the manipulation of people via: psychology, the culture, therapy, and primarily through Spirituality. Key witnesses also say that the gang had high caliber weapons like AK-47s and organized bodyguards in the same communities." And second: "the facts are terrifying . . . official justice, based solely in conventional laws, is not sufficient."

El Millonario, with his AK-47s and the threatening moneylenders, no less than the war machines of empire with their enslavement and indenturing, function through extraeconomic coercion but also through the contracts and accounting notebooks burlesqued in the *baile de la culebra*. And these in turn simultaneously divide and inextricably connect singularities, like a Community of Maya, into and with their pluralities (young, old; *cofrade*, Protestant, catechist, *ajq'ij*; contractor, *mozo*, *dueño de dinero*, bank; CUC member, civil patroller; women with black *guipiles* and those without). Felipe Natareno invokes a Mayan *estilo cooperativo*, the bonds of trust (as well as betrayal) that extend over years and are both remade and sometimes torn through shared ritual projects, reciprocities, *achi'lib'al* (companionship), mobilizations in self-defense (as in Francisca's community), and *redes* of various kinds. Understood as a brutish refusal to produce and consume for the world market, or as "naturally communistic," it takes enclosure, displacement, mass murder, and the shredding of community bonds deployed by occupiers and states to pluralize these apparent singularities (which are not, of course, timeless entities but constantly doing and done). The facts are terrifying, and official accounting is not sufficient.

This is also because, just as it apparently divides labor from the laborer and dispassion from mania (making it hard to see the magic that makes profit possible), official accounting seems to stop time every time it reaches a "conclusion" of zero. But then, so does a Ponzi scheme, only at an earlier point in the transaction. In those long years between the promise of half a million quetzals and delivery, it seems like eddies in time and space were opened and people lived their ordinary lives while also, ecstatically, suspended in that vanishing moment when money takes on its magical powers of facilitating exchange and stops being a simple natural object.

Here I'm drawing on Spivak's weird kitchen metaphor of opening the lid of Money as a seemingly unitary phenomenon to discover a forever-seething chain in the pot (1987, 157). She represents this as Value^{representation} → Money^{transformation} → Capital, and says that "at each step of the dialectic something seems to lead off into the open-endedness of textuality: indifference, inadequation, rupture" (160). Perhaps tarrying in the space/time of Money^{transformation} holds off descent into "Realization," which dissolves the thing and releases the commodity from the circuit of capital production into consumption. It was a giddy elongation of what usually transpires in just a second or two, a dwelling in the midst of the tossing and turning and circulating that can change one pound into ten.

Emerging in the early "postwar period," among people so recently faced with the utterly violent shock and awe so frenziedly deployed to embargo their futurological revolutionary projects, El Millonario's scheme cobbled together and concatenated (even as it direly deformed) fragile, preliminary attempts at reimagining collective wish fulfillment. It provided a pregnant node of self and other that prolepsised past, present, and future by mixing finance capital's scandalous ability to create itself out of the future (Rotman 1987, 96) with a "new church" and vulnerable emerging identifications like all Maya and only Maya. It was a disastrous and devastating fraud. But it also revivified and reembodied some of the sensations and analyses of the stymied revolutionary projects, themselves "modern" enactments of longer-term memory forms kept alive in performative rebellions like the dance of the snake and the forms of social organization it chastises (labor contracting) and that sustain it (*cofrades, costumbre,* Catholicism, and now the banks). It was also an implicit critique of some of the gender and ethnic limits of the 1970s and 1980s revolutionary processes that expressed indigenous demands but had few indigenous or women leaders and often split communities between traditionalists and modernizers. Such articulatory practices also galvanized the lightning-quick recruitment for the lynch mob to get back what was theirs. A grisly end for the El Millonario (or the Wall Streeters who have brought us down) is alluring, although it may not be the most PC utopia. The *means* to it, however—collective action—might be.

In this, El Millonario is like Omnilife and like capitalism (and like churches—in the Durkheimian mode). Like Omnilife, scientists agree that a balanced diet provides all the vitamins the body needs but hundreds of millions of people take a supplement (including 65% of the professional advisers for the American Council of Science and Health; Cahn 2011, 74). And lo and behold. They work. Like capitalism, money is really no different from the mountains of worthless newspaper piled in El Millonario's house. Yet lo and behold! It works! And yet we are still continually surprised to discover that it's "just" meaning, that "finance is fiction."

"Numbers weave patterns which people inhabit and which inhabit people." Geometric numbers with their fantastic promises.[18] "In the red" debt numbers that predicate a subject of "unreasoning responsibility" (Spivak 1999, 102), razor-wired to community networks and tribute systems that keep her paying, shouldering the burden of extracting—impossibly it would seem—so many hundreds of thousands of quetzals, dollars, lek, rupees, yuan, from subprime places and peoples who seem to have nothing to extract. This is the pyramid as clock or, reconfiguring Pitarch (2010), an explanation of a numeric nature that is also a social and political profile. It shows us the contours, in Matt Taibbi's immortal words, of the "great vampire squid wrapped around the face of humanity, relentlessly jamming its blood funnel into anything that smells like money" (2009, 1). This is the terrible antiutopia of capitalism *as* a planetary and intergenerational pyramid scheme of looting, mayhem, and dispossessed "losers."

Making Count

Fidelia and her family are sick all the time, reduced to eating only tortillas with salt as almost every penny goes toward paying their creditors, including their reparations check (and what little's left goes through Santos to Jorge Vergara as they struggle to maintain the bodily ability to bear it). Yet foreclosed almost completely from use-value by their obligations—as everything, everything goes to the *dueños de dinero*—they remain committed to justice. In fact, Lolita hadn't introduced us because of El Millonario but because Fidelia is active in the exploding movement to use *consultas* (referenda) to close Guatemala to foreign mining operations. Alluring images of development, jobs, and wealth through resource extraction have been demystified by Fidelia and her family's terrible experiences. "Mining," Fidelia said. "It's the same as El Millonario. They are coming again to steal from us. Mining brings another sickness, worse than the other."

But her immune system is better developed now, and she is going to national-level meetings, which is how she met Lolita, and connecting to organizations that link indigenous and environmental rights through national and transnational law and through the accounting procedures of the referenda technologies. She has traveled to see mountaintop removal in San Marcos, helped organize a consulta in her town, and campaigned for a political party that opposes mining and has hung a big banner on the main road that says "Sí a la Vida, No a la Mineria!" Yes to life, no to mining![19] She said, "We are evangelicals, and the pastor is with us, too. He says the earth is sacred, it belongs to God. Water, trees, rocks, without water we can't live. What can we do to stop it? We want to make it so people no longer hurt other people." Fidelia is enjoying the organizing work, and as of 2014, over one million people across Guatemala have said no. "It feels good to be connected, part of that larger world."

Part IV

YES
to Life =
NO
to Mining

6 A Life's Worth

Poor people are easy to buy.
—San Miguel Ixtahuacán choir

Our defeat was always implicit in the victory of others. Our wealth has always generated our poverty by nourishing the prosperity of others, the empires and their overseers. In the colonial and neo-colonial alchemy, gold turns into scrap metal and food into poison.
—Eduardo Galeano (1979)

Open Sky

As the women arrived at the San Miguel Ixtahuacán parish compound, in their varied *traje*, they greeted Hermana Maudilia (like them, Maya-Mam) as she tracked down incense and tuned her guitar. After helping set up benches in the cavernous meeting hall, I hung out in the courtyard amid a small curious crowd. "Oh, you want to learn more about the mine? Well, you know someone was killed last week after the demonstration? I heard it on the radio." "The problem with the mine is when there's a child with a rash or a health problem, they pay so people won't say anything." "The mine says, if there are broken houses, they were falling apart before." "I sent my son to the US but there's no work. We borrowed Q12,000 ($1,500) but with interest it became Q60,000. I had to sell my ten *cuerdas* of land." Cutting into the flow of brief stories, each with its hook of pain, Maudilia began to gently urge us into the hall.

There, women had arranged a beautiful mandala-like altar with candles and flowers. They launched into a song in the Mam language and then realized there were too many people, so we laughingly reorganized. Then they switched to Castilian as the two representatives of COPAE, the Catholic Church's Peace and Ecology Commission, had arrived from San Marcos. Like many of the women, they'd gotten up around 5 AM to get there. While they set up their computer, we kept singing.

> Could it have been You who sent the miners?
> They rape the womb of the Mother Earth,
> They take the gold, destroying the mountains;
> A gram of blood is worth more than a thousand kilos of gold.
>
> What is happening with my people?
> And you, my God, where are you hiding?
> Fear has paralyzed us,
> My people have been sold and we don't even realize it.
>
> The water is drying up, it's the same color as hell;
> The air we breathe is already polluted;
> We seek miracles, but it is too late;
> We seek to cure the sick and the mortally wounded.
>
> A poor people are easy to buy,
> Gifts quiet suspicions and doubts;
> Paychecks disappear in the town's cantinas,
> Homes grow dark and my people live divided.
>
> You created a garden and not a desert;
> We want progress but with respect for the environment;
> Hunger for gold consumes more and more of the earth,
> And You, my God, you wonder,
> What are my people doing?

The song (my translation), created collectively by the parish's choir, sets up some of the quantities, qualities, and alchemical equivalencies I examine in this chapter—of blood to gold, of people to commodities that can be bought, of minerals to food and drink, both hungered for—and the disjuncture of progress to respect and to divisions in "my people." The song was set to music by Padre Eric, the Belgian priest who has served San Miguel for almost 30 years. When we finished singing, volunteers led prayers and lit candles, as we all moved to face the four directions. Before 1992, this would have been unthinkable, but Mayan Organizing 1.0 had opened space. While Padre Eric, who is fluent in Mam, and Monseñor Ramazzini, then bishop of San Marcos, are respectful of Mayan lifeways, it was Maudilia who introduced this form of prayer and organized the monthly women's meetings, like this one in July 2009.

Then Maudilia introduced Vinicio and Teresa, and Vinicio began to explain why the church was trying to close the Canadian-owned gold mine that had opened, only a few miles away, in 2005. Vinicio is an experienced organizer and spoke carefully so that women working in their second language could understand. But he did not simplify. He first asked if they had questions and women quickly jumped in: "Is the water affected?" "People are getting sick." "There are lots of conflicts." "Why are they lying?" "They are killing the men." "Can we drink out of our wells?"

Then he said, "Let's talk about our country. It is little and we have had a war. 50,000 people were disappeared, we don't know where they are. 200,000 people are dead. Why? It's a problem with the land. You've worked on fincas, you know how big they are: we say "a saber cuantas cuerdas," but they aren't even measured in cuerdas [20 m²]. They are measured in bigger quantities: manzanas, hectáreas, caballerias,[1] which are 1,000 cuerdas. Ten caballerias is a finca. That's 10,000 cuerdas. How much do your families have? 12, 15? Some have only 3 or 5. This is what is called inequality. But why do they pressure us? Lie to us? Refuse to let us live in peace? Because they're not content, even now. 70% of the population is poor. But you can go to market and buy corn and beans. That's because this is not a poor country. We produce. We are not poor because we are lazy. We are poor because the riches are concentrated in just a few hands. You've harvested coffee. You earn 10 to 15 quetzals a tarea [about $1.50–$2.00 per task], but if you are a woman, you only earn 5 to 10." The women seemed really with him, nodding. "And why aren't there any schools in the villages? Schools that teach math and history? Because to harvest coffee you don't need to study, you are just mano de obra [hands that work] and it's better if mano de obra don't know their rights, because then they might make demands. Guatemala has always exploited its people and resources. You go to the coast to harvest and you leave here strong but when you come back you and your children are sick." The nodding became more emphatic. "In 1996 the war ended. But now there is a

6.1 Goldcorp's Marlin gold mine. Allan Lissner. Used with kind permission.

new exploitation, of what they call natural resources. The same group that decides who will be president is also selling the licenses. Do you remember this mountain?"

With this, the Powerpoint presentation came on, and there was the mine. A wave of agitation coursed through the women. Some startled, drawing back. They whispered and pointed, a few stood up, some had their hands to their mouths. Vinicio was drowned out by voices and the fluster of movement. "The mountain is gone," whispered the woman next to me. For a moment Vinicio tried to continue, but then realized he needed to let the enormity sink in.

The Canadian mining company Goldcorp, through its subsidiary Montana Exploradora of Guatemala, is extracting ore at its Marlin mine (nestled between San Miguel Ixtahuacán and its smaller neighbor, Sipakapa) through mountaintop removal, or *cielo abierto*, open sky. Several hundred meters in altitude are gone, leaving a broad slash of dun earth that looks like nothing so much as a scar.[2] With the unearthly green of the large tailings lagoon, the cyanide-infused water stored in an open air pit, the sight is pretty consternating.

While Vinicio didn't go into the details, perhaps you'd like to know how it works. First, all the trees are cut down and vegetation is scraped away.

Then dynamite and heavy machinery expose the rocks containing the gold until the entire mountain is obliterated, transformed into pits that can be several thousand feet deep and more than a mile wide. Tunnels are blasted even farther down that may extend for miles (often damaging surface structures like adobe houses). The ore is crushed and soaked with a cyanide solution to leach out the gold, which is collected and piped into tanks, where the gold collects onto activated carbon granules. These granules are then filtered out of the cyanide solution, which is returned to the heap, and the gold is removed by a hot, concentrated cyanide and alkali solution, then passed through a tank where an electrical current plates it onto cathodes. When it is finally melted into gold doré, helicopters ferry it out (Van der Maaten, n.d., 37–38). A mountain will generally be depleted within 6 years (although Marlin is going strong at over 10), after which time the company is supposed to restore the area.[3]

By their surprised reactions it seemed that while the women knew about the mine, they hadn't really confronted its thereness. One turned to me and said, "Is it possible these people will leave?"

Vinicio went on: "This is an industry. It is not a development project. It is an industry." He emphasized this because Goldcorp was ramping up its public relations campaign. Outside Guatemala's international airport, at regular intervals along the Pan-American highway, and dotting the road from San Marcos to San Miguel were billboards with variations on the theme of "Lo valioso es el desarrollo" (what matters is development). One reads "We believe in a country that works with effort" (with a picture of a huge earthmoving truck), another "We share with the people of a country that doesn't rest" (with a picture of the brightly lit mining installations shining like a small city). And "A mine with secure technology for human health and the environment, strengthening the integral development of San Miguel, industrial security" (see also Fultz 2009). Another listed how much Montana paid in taxes and royalties—which looks like a lot until you realize it was only 1% of their earnings. The Marlin mine is Goldcorp's third-best-performing investment in a global portfolio, with the lowest production costs in the world (Zarsky and Stanley 2011). It earned $98 million in the first quarter of 2014 (although gold fell to $1,297/oz. from 2013's $1,622; Globe and Mail 2014).

It also prominently displays its "corporate responsibility" through its NGO, Sierra Madre (mother mountain). People debated how much Montana actually invested in schools, roadwork, and the new hospital, but the

6.2 Tailings lagoon with earthmoving vehicles. Allan Lissner. Used with kind permission.

6.3 Goldcorp billboard: "We believe in a country that works with effort." Author's photo.

company certainly claimed them, with big signs and their trademark blue and green squiggle painted on buildings and water pumps. The squiggle did not appear on the new Protestant churches, but Catholics were sure these too were funded. Local radio waves were also inundated, with actors saying, "I sell more in my shop now that Montana is here," and full page newspaper ads contested claims of polluted water and sickened humans. In June 2009 the company staged a peaceful march in San Miguel with iconography borrowed from widely covered protests in the capital against the social democratic–leaning government. About 80 miners and their supporters, dressed all in white and carrying white roses (not native to the area, hence expensive), marched to the church accusing Padre Eric and Hermana Maudilia of threatening their jobs, even twisting classic protest songs like "*No Basta Rezar*" (It's not enough to pray) into pro-corporate anthems. Eric and Maudilia shrugged it off, along with frequent threatening phone calls, but many local activists expressed fear of reprisals.

For example, at the demonstration of July 14, Aniseto López spoke to a crowd of about 1,500 people in the central square of San Miguel. He works for the local grassroots organization ADISMI. He greeted everyone in Mam and thanked the representatives from different areas for their solidarity.

6.4 Goldcorp billboard: "We share with the people of a country that doesn't rest."
Author's photo.

Then he switched to Castilian. "We have problems. We've been hit hard
by the company. Our lives are threatened. We risk death. Eight of our *compa-
ñeras* are being persecuted. They are mothers who are claiming their rights.
It's the state authorities, but behind them is Montana. But *ánimo*, friends.
This is how we defend life. And we are defending it against a gigantic power,
a global economic power. That's why it's not easy what we are doing. Talking against the mine you might end up dead. We've said goodbye to our
families. We are ready to die."

A Gram of Blood, a Thousand Kilos of Gold, Half a Million Say No

> Through a democratic consultation more than half a million people have ener-
> getically rejected the presence of Goldcorp and defended their territory of origin.
> —Arturo Méndez (NISGUA, 2008)

Then Aniseto began to tell the story of the mine. How in 1996 the company
arrived, "offering development to the mayor, saying they would support
infrastructure, production, women, youth, environmental protection. Our
authorities were manipulated. The company said that San Miguel wants us
and began to install themselves. They were going to grow orchids and bring

prosperity. They bought land, plots that were worth Q1,500 a *cuerda* they would pay Q3,000 or Q4,000, and people's hands got hot, they began to sell. In 2002, the problems began. They began to *desnudar la montaña*, to strip the land. People realized they couldn't find firewood anymore. They said they had found minerals and then the beautiful mountain wasn't a mountain anymore. It was a hole. And what's under the mountain?" The people yelled, "Water!"

Aniseto continued,

They penetrated the mountain, going into the aquifers and springs. They use up to 250,000 liters an hour. That's how much a family would use in twenty-two years! Our water is drying up. Even if we go down on our knees and do our ceremonies [referring to Mayan rituals], this water will never return. Without water, what will we do? How will our animals survive? Even though our umbilical cords are buried here, where will we go when there is no water? We may see people driving in their new Hilux [luxury pickup truck] because they work at the mine. They may go around with two or three women. They have money. But our health is in danger. The tailings lagoon, it is open to the sun. We breathe this air and it is changing our bodies. They say there is no pollution but then say "Don't touch the water!" The soil is a filter, the chemicals go into the ground and into our water. It is a problem for all of us. But the company insists it is helping us develop. I went to their meeting in Vancouver and they showed children receiving food in beautiful new schoolrooms.

People in the crowd shouted out, "Those are lies!" Aniseto went on, "They show kids who are fat. They said we no longer have to go to the coast to pick coffee. Is that true?" "*MENTIRA!*" "Lies!" shouted the people.

He concluded:

What is development if our lives are ruined? If we are divided? People need to develop but if we are sick and dying what is development? Now is the time to say, Sir, do not play with my dignity. Do not use my poverty to justify what you are doing. Today they say that the mine has bought me, I am getting thousands. But I say, my life is not worth a million quetzals if I and my people are sick. I can barely buy socks. I can barely buy food. And they say I have a million quetzals. It's ridiculous! They are using every trick to try to divide us. We deserve a good life. We do have needs. But we can't progress on the suffering of our neighbors.

6.5 How much later? Stephanie McMillan. Used with kind permission.

I congratulate those who have done your *consultas*. It's time to decide, it's now or never. They will kill us with the other eight mining licenses. But we are not going to defend ourselves with pistols or machetes. The violent times are over. We need to protect ourselves with ideas, not armies, with dialogue and *consultas*. We want to be free of the Montana Company.

Who Counts?

Beginning in June 2005, the province of San Marcos became the epicenter of what is now a national movement of *consultas*—consultations or referenda. After the "shock doctrine" of genocide (Klein 2008), meant to convince people that resistance was futile, survivors are beginning to input different numbers, working to produce a different after-math. In this chapter I address mining via counting in three modes: first, counting people through the *consultas*, including who counts and how; second, counting that measures toxins and thresholds; and third, ac-counting in the weighing of costs and benefits, prices and values, and possible alchemical transformations. I explore the qualities of such quantities and their qualifications (limits), including the relations between precision and uncertainty.

In some ways a consulta is quite simple. Townspeople are brought together and asked a question like, Do you want mining in this community? Then just add up the number who say yes and the number who say no, and the answer with the biggest number wins. In Sipakapa the counting was done by hamlets. Just as Verran describes the census in Ibadan, there were several moments of making the plurality of inhabitants into a one (in one hamlet 70 said yes, 200 said no, so the No wins), then each hamlet's yeses and no's were added together to get 13 hamlets said no, one said yes, and one abstained, and so all those people and votes translate into "Sipakapa says No!" "Sipakapa is not for sale!" This was then translated into slogans on banners, chants at demonstrations, and the title of a video (Caracol 2005).

Traveling via technologies of perception—tallies, a film, a Powerpoint presentation, maps of mining concessions—Sipakapa's counting is multiplying. Through many people's labors the technique of the consulta has leached out of tiny isolated villages to assemble people (literally) under the banner of Yes to life, No to transnational companies. So that many miles away, over the mountains in Santa Cruz del Quiché, Lolita Chávez says they began to hear rumors. "We kind of heard about what was happening in San Marcos, Sipakapa, but it was far away. In 2007, I think, someone showed the video, but we didn't really relate to it, except to feel sorry for them. Pobrecitos! Their hair is falling out! We never thought it could happen in Santa Cruz! But then, in 2008 or 2009, an economist came to talk to us and he showed us a map. We were mapped! We had no idea, but he showed us, in full color! How much of Quiché had been signed away for exploration. You can't believe the impact that had on us. Now it wasn't about being in solidarity with people over there, but it was right here. We had to defend ourselves!"

But it wasn't easy! In Sipakapa, four years after they held theirs, an elderly man remembered for me while we ate lunch after a COPAE alternative development workshop. "For the consulta, the mayor was GANA (the ruling party). He was under heavy pressure. But we all got together. In my hamlet it was about 300 of us and we all signed. We voted by signing. Only the adults, if not we would have had many more. It was a happy day. We felt good. Only one hamlet voted yes because their auxiliary mayor was with the mine, and he pulled a lot of people. We all came together from all the hamlets to present it to the mayor, and he wouldn't sign off. We pressured and pressured.

6.6 Yes to Life, No to Transnational Companies. In defense of life, Mother Nature, land, and territory, the K'iche' People's Council. Lolita Chávez reads the document ratifying the community consultation. James Rodríguez. Used with kind permission.

We held him there till 2 AM!" he said, laughing. "But finally he did. Then we sent a delegation down to the city to present it to the government."[4]

One stormy night, on a bus full of national and international antimining activists traveling from Sipakapa to San Miguel, two men told me the story of their September 2007 *consulta* in nearby San Ildefonso Ixtahuacán. "It took about a year and a half from when we started. We already have a mine[5] and we couldn't touch that, but there are licenses for three others and we had to stop them. The mine is *cielo abierto*, and the mountain doesn't exist anymore. We can't plant. Nothing grows. So we had everybody, the auxiliary mayors, the development commissions, all the religions are affected, so we worked with the pastors, the teachers, the ex-PAC, we all have to be together." Even in the dark they sensed my reaction to the PAC. He explained,

> We were all in the PAC and there were PAC massacres there. They did bad things. But now it is mostly a progressive group. We have kept that organization. The ex-PAC were great. They have people everywhere, 5,000 men! Representatives in every hamlet. We assigned tasks and they did everything. People talk badly about them but they really helped with

6.7 Maya-Mam women from San Miguel Ixtahuacán showing how a *consulta* is done. James Rodríguez. Used with kind permission.

the *consulta*. It was an election year and all the candidates supported the mine at the national level, and there were just two of us, really, doing everything. But all in one day we had thirty-five centers and 14,000 people came. We had [the NGO] CEIBA, national youth groups and Mayan organizations, they all sent observers. We did it. The people said no.

I haven't participated in a *consulta*, but in accounts and videos the festive air is palpable. The masses of people are impressive, crowded into halls to discuss, waiting in long snaking lines to be counted, kids playing, music, the bonhomie of a gathering and collective purpose. "It was a happy day, we felt good." But while the observers were representing audit culture, they were also present because, as Aniseto said, they are "against a global economic power." Even years after the peace treaty, war hovers close, violence a constant threat.

In 2005 troops opened fire on protesters blocking the Pan-American highway to stop a huge cylinder destined for the San Miguel mine. One man was killed but there have been no prosecutions. Far more macabre, in June 2007, in a hamlet close to the mine, a little girl found the headless body of Pedro Miguel Cinto, a 60-year-old Mayan activist. A few days later the head was found across provincial lines in Huehuetenango and returned by the Montana company, "causing uncertainty and panic among his neighbors" (ADISMI 2007, 32). The circumstances of his death have not been clarified. Then, in May 2010, two unknown men came to the door of Diodora Hernández, a single mother living near the mine. She became an activist when they built part of a school on her land without permission. The men asked for something to eat (standard practice in hamlets without a restaurant), but she had nothing to sell. They insisted, just some coffee? Please? So she agreed but as she was serving them, one pulled out a gun and shot her in the head. Hermana Maudilia told me later: "Her children were screaming and screaming and the neighbors got her down to San Miguel. She was bleeding everywhere! We sent her first to San Marcos and then to the capital. Fortunately Rigoberta Menchú stepped in and helped with the medical side, the money, and the press." Diodora lost her eye and is still recovering, but she walked out of the hospital on her own. No one has been charged. On January 8, 2013, security guards opened fire on mine employees seeking unpaid benefits, wounding at least seven. And still no prosecutions (and this is only a partial list).

So, counting yeses and no's is "simple" addition, but when people band together to be counted, they do some pretty complex calculations of risks, life's worth, and playing the odds.

New Equations, Counting for Life

Yet in the face of death, "98% said no" is now a fact of life, used in the national and international press and by antimining activists. And little by little, as town after town holds a referendum, another fact takes on life, a single number begins to emerge from adding up all the no's, so that in 2008 Aniseto López and Arturo Mendez, representing San Miguel at the Goldcorp shareholder meeting in Vancouver, Canada, could say "half a million people" reject the presence of Goldcorp. By 2014 it was close to a million.

As consultas add up, these quantities make the equation "Yes to Life = No to Mining" count. The people of Concepción Tutuapa San Marcos, a 100% Maya-Mam town, organized a consulta comunitaria in 2007 to decide if they wanted mining in their municipality. As was becoming the custom (this was the 14th), outside observers were asked to attend because, somehow, rural indigenous folks counting themselves, even with the technologies of audit culture—ledgers where names align with identification document numbers and signatures or thumbprints; photographs of every detail—is still not considered reliable *enough*. They don't quite qualify. And for safety, outsiders were stationed in each of the 64 hamlets.

Camilo Salvado was one such observer. A young ladino from the capital, he told me how impressed he was with people's consciousness. They were incredibly *aware*. They knew about conditions in San Miguel, streams drying up and poisoned wells. They understood filtration (explained later), how cyanide and other chemicals leach into aquifers, and that one 18-carat gold ring creates 20 tons of contaminated waste rock. One gentleman said, "Everything we do to the earth gets passed on to the water. That is the sickness they have in San Miguel" (Salvado, n.d., 8). Without electricity and deep in the mountains, most of their information comes from word of mouth and community radio run off car batteries, but several people went to see for themselves (as Fidelia had). Even so, not everyone was against it.

In the hamlet of El Mirador, over 200 people, children and grown-ups, talked in Mam for over three hours. Some thought a mine would bring development, roads, schools, health clinics, jobs. Several men argued that the license was conceded under the Free Trade Agreement (CAFTA), so a *consulta* couldn't stop it. People wondered if technology existed that could remove the gold without harming the rivers. They talked about poverty and the difficulties of surviving. Maybe there was a way to make this work?

What decided it was an elderly man who said, "We want to be peaceful here, we do not want this horror to come here, those foreigners to come here and make holes in our mother earth, that will dry up our trees, that will dry up our water. . . . We don't know how the government decided, we don't know how the government gave them permission to do this, but this land doesn't belong to the government. This land belongs to our ancestors" (Salvado, n.d., 10).

This sealed it, and all 200 residents, children and adults, raised their hands to be counted, 100% against. Leaders insisted the children be there, as it is their future at stake and because their little bodies are more vulnerable to toxins. It's also a civics lesson. But they didn't count for the official tally. Resonating with the missing bodies of war dead, many rural people, especially women, don't have government-issued identification papers so, like children, don't count for the state: an important audience for the sums they are producing. In El Mirador only adults with papers could sign the act, and these qualifications reduced the no votes to 98. In the whole municipality over 20,000 people participated in the assemblies and raised their hands against the mine, but fewer than 10,000 counted "officially."

The national press undercut the count even more dramatically, reporting that only 400 countable people participated. In spreadsheets charting the *consultas*, however, Concepción Tutuapa appears with 11,300 no votes and 0 yes. Of course, such apparent imprecision is not only the domain of stereotypically "innumerate Indians" or due to the sedimented racism in outsider reporting. It's part and parcel of the epistemic peculiarity of counting itself.

The quantification labors of the *consulta* included organizing 20,000 people to show up on a specific date with 64 outside observers willing to walk hours into the mountains. After the count, elders from each hamlet went to town to submit the numbers and to witness the creation of an act that prohibits mining in their area. Those of us who fear the alchemical way numbers' abstraction disqualifies may feel torn here. Getting the count—first 98 and then 11,300 and then each town across the country counting as 1 to get to a national aggregate opposing mining would seem to qualify as a political win. Those people, almost all of them poor, rural, and Maya—the historically discounted—now count. But the quality of those hours of discussion, the creative ground-level alternatives, are lost. And the vote is qualified, in the sense of "restricted," as so many people didn't count in the ways that matter to the state. Perhaps this is why organizers insist that numbers are only part of a *consulta*. It also informs, organizes, and gets people together to *do* something. Salvado contrasts the living democracy he experienced in the community assembly with the *democracia muerta* of national politics, where top-down decision making by elites is backed up by the remilitarization of the countryside under the guise of drug interdiction and where private property and the "letter of the law" are more important than life itself. "The legitimacy of the *consulta* goes beyond any numeric question" (Salvado, n.d., 10). As Sznaider suggested about reparations, it may be "the side-effects of the process that really count," but the *number* is what makes the process possible.

In turn, a *consulta* is not simply counting yeses or no's. For it to "count" it needs legal infrastructure. The numbers, like any fact, are only meaningful within particular systems. Not unlike the Mayan prayer in the Catholic Church, such a frame has emerged from work and struggle: some of it global, via the International Labor Organization's Convention 169; some national, as in changing the constitution and municipal codes to create the very form of the *consulta*.

And these labors have constituted a new terrain that Goldcorp has to play on. While publicly scoffing that *consultas* don't count, mining companies fight them legally and extrajudicially, violently, and deploying "Mayan culture." In the eastern highlands a transnational nickel company and the Guatemalan Ministry of Energy and Mines hired a respected *ajq'ij* to perform a ceremony asking permission of the *Tzuultaq'a* (earth owners) to begin operations. Apparently they said yes (González 2005). In Sipakapa Goldcorp got a court injunction and sued the municipality for unconstitutionality before the *consulta* was even officially approved. Sipakapa prevailed in both cases, and so just beforehand the company blanketed the hamlets with disinformation, saying the *consulta* had been postponed. Also to no avail. Goldcorp then fought it all the way to the Supreme Court, where after two years, caught between the constitution, with its vestiges of democratic guarantees, and the 1996 neoliberal laws, the Court ruled that the *consulta* was legal but not binding!

The community and its lawyer, Carlos Loarca, then took the case to the IAHRC (Inter American Human Rights Court) where after a two-year wait, they won a major victory in May 2010. Mine activity was ordered suspended to prevent irreparable harm to the life, physical integrity, and environment of indigenous communities.

Practicing Counting

Before turning to some of the numbers and qualifications that led the IAHRC to back the equation that Yes to Life = No to Mining, I'll tell one more story of a *consulta* and the vexed and productive relations between plurality and singularity.

El Pueblo Manda, The People Are in Charge

A Guatemalan hamlet is a pretty face-to-face place. Generations of families have lived in the same house next to the same neighbors. Always age- and gender-stratified, communities have been stressed by divisions introduced by the plantation system (*promotores*, *enganchadores*, etc., used to organize a Misery of *Mozos*), the national government (auxiliary mayors, military commissioners, the civil patrol), and postcolonial religion; by histories of forced labor and internal and transnational migration; and of course, by war. People live in frictioned intimacies. Working close by in small fields, selling each other foodstuffs and thread for weaving, boys and men playing *futból* together, meeting to discuss roads or schools, grieving each other's dead, stopping by to share peaches and gossip, intermarrying, having a common language and *traje*: these are the conditions of possibility for the 100% no votes coming out of many hamlets. *Consultas* are held in municipalities, composed of a town and all the surrounding hamlets. A town can be more of a challenge: larger, usually more ethnically diverse, with more hardened class divisions. What hadn't been tried until 2010 was organizing a *cabecera*, a provincial capital.

It took a call from Domingo Hernández Ixcoy, a well-respected activist, assuring her I was "a *gringa buena*," to get an interview with Lolita Chávez, the woman who took up this challenge. She was suspicious of outsiders and *la cooperación* (NGOs, foreign aid) for dividing organizations and indigenous people. "They are subtle enemies. They side with the ones who want to be the *Maya bueno* and make us look like the *indios bochincheros*, rioting Indians." But she agreed to meet.

In the midst of various struggles, she said, they began to hear rumors about the *consultas*. Lolita began to see the map of mining concessions at meetings and at the 2008 Social Forum of the Americas in Guatemala City. "I got to understand it more. But how to do a *consulta*? We are 87 hamlets and 6 zones in the city. We had to organize all of them. And doing it in a *cabecera*?! No one had done that. We got help from the people in Huehuetenango (ADH), the Consejo de Pueblos del Occidente (CPO), COPAE, and ideas from the south, from Bolivia. Something about 'passing our voices,' *auto-convocatoria*, self-convening, and it helped us think. But the process was *laaaaaaarrrrrrgggggggiiiisimooooo*—so, so long! So many meetings! But we finally decided to do it."

Just outside Santa Cruz lie the pre-Columbian ruins of Gumarkaaj, ancient capital of the K'iche', whose warrior Tekum Umam defended his people against the Spanish and who lives again each year in the dance of the conquest. The CUC was founded in Santa Cruz. The army considered it a "red zone" during the war. Attacks on the church were so extreme that Bishop Gerardi closed the entire diocese. Two of the CEH's four genocide cases are in El Quiché. While the popular movement was more than decimated (i.e., losing 10%)—probably closer to an "octadecimation," or 80%—there are survivors, like Domingo Hernández Ixcoy, drawing on those experiences and linking them to complex processes of "Mayanization" (Bastos and Cumes 2007). One expression is Waqib' Kej, an organization connecting Mayan cosmovision with labor and peasant struggles through research and outreach via radio, newspapers, and a *diplomado* (freestanding academic degree) that meets for two days twice a month for a year. "We have to keep things moving, get people together, help them think. And out here, away from the capital," Domingo said. "Many of the students are quite young and many are involved in the *consultas*. They come from all over and some travel overnight or even the whole day to get here, but they are really committed." While some of the coursework is very nuts and bolts—economic facts, accounting, radio and computer skills, leadership training—it's also philosophical and spiritual, studying indigenous epistemology, including Mayan glyphs. In 2012 the course was called "Returning to Mayan Being," "*Ser Mayab*," and, like number, it helps produce what it only seems to show.

Consultas "count" only after visitors show up with videos about Sipakapa, an economist explains a map, representatives from COPAE help organize, a class deciphers Mayan glyphs, *ser Mayab*, and accounting, people visit the mine and tell their neighbors about it, someone decides that something must be done. These are tendrils of projects, experiences, networks, and analyses, spreading over time and space, woven together to get people to the counting tables and to make those numbers count. These are Verran's "numbers as familiars" doing us as we do them, connecting people to each other and everyday experience to larger entities, concepts, becoming-cosmogonies.

Lolita said, "Territory is a concept that's hard to understand, even for lawyers! To get to it [she moved her hand as if plucking a grain of corn from a pile], you have to start small. We didn't talk about the *consulta* at first or politics. Here those ideas are scary. Instead, we started with water and connected it to health, crops. And then the protest over RENAP broke out" (see chapter 0).

Among the demands of the 15,000 who turned out were calls for a *consulta*. "When we took over the town hall we pretty much took the mayor hostage. He was for the mine, but when he saw 15,000 people he had to change his mind. We used the issue of water, too. He was thirsty, and we said we would all be thirsty if the mine came in. We pledged he would get no water until he signed on, but neither would any of us. K'iche' people are proud. We can bear it. He finally gave in and signed a pact, publicly declaring he would support us and provide logistics."

Over 20 community leaders came to the first meeting, including indigenous mayors, water committee members, *ajq'ij*, midwives, and doctors.

Then 30, then 70, until they had meetings with close to 800. "Buenísima!" said Lolita. "Then we had to find a name for trying to protect water, earth, and territory, so we decided on *Consejo de Pueblos K'iche' por la Defensa de la Vida, Madre Naturaleza, Tierra, y Territorio* (CPK), and we decided it couldn't be about just mining but monoculture, hydroelectrics, and transnational companies, too, so we decided to ask: "Are you in agreement with the exploration and exploitation of *bienes naturales* (natural goods)[6] like water, air, trees, forests, and land by transnational companies?"

That settled, they confronted other problems. Like power struggles with older peasant and indigenous organizations trying to take over (and take credit). "We were surprised at the people who came out in favor of the mine. They accused us of not conforming to the Mayan cosmovision, which is based on harmony!" The Opus Dei bishop also supported mining (although many parish priests were against it), saying communities had a right to development. Organizing with the spiritual guides, Lolita said most are "*solo velas*, only concerned with candles and ceremonies. They are supportive but not very political." The mayor promised government offices and businesses would close for the day, but when organizers met with the banks,

> They told us, "*Nosotros mandamos* [we're in charge]!" But we reminded them, *el pueblo manda*, and they had to give in. The academics were some of the hardest, "*Ay! Esos indios!*" was their reaction. But we used science, studies of cyanide, technical stuff. We showed them maps. And they came on board. Working with the mayor was also hard. He is FRG [Ríos Montt's party]. Like you say, he knows how to count, he knows a lot of people are for this. He made a radio ad seeming to support us, but behind the scenes he was saying it wasn't legally binding, so why waste your time? But we say it is not the enemy who decides what is binding. Our laws decide. Through *struggle*. Because we are the ones in charge.

It helped that the same things were happening in Cunén, Ixcán, and the Ixil region. "Although far away, they are El Quiché. A lot of stuff was happening around us."

They even outreached to *mareros*, the street kids and small-time gang members. "You can't just assume they're going to rob you. We treated them well and they got involved! They are the ones who told us a politician sent to the *barrio* known for cheap *sicarios*, hit men, to make a contract to 'scare us,' to do a quick kidnapping. But instead of taking the money the kids came and warned us. They are good kids. We were frightened, but we kept going."

The night before, pamphlets appeared warning that "blood will flow," but Santa Cruz held its *consulta*. "Since the war, this is the first time, the first time that we are *levantando*, rising up. In all that time!" The town hall provided computers to count the votes, the police were courteous, market women provided free food, and everything shut down so people could go vote. The army sent soldiers to guard the process. "We were in the town hall and they were all around, and at first they were pretty cold and suspicious. But we offered them food and that broke the ice, and they asked, 'What's all this about?' and we explained. They finally set down their guns and helped out. We ended up climbing over the weapons in all the back and forth, but we were so excited that we barely noticed. A famous Mayan ex-guerrilla came by and was furious the army was there, but we just laughed and said, they're *with* us!" In the hamlets there was a single show of hands, while in the city there were three voting times, morning, noon, and evening, and people signed. When I talked to people around town, there were definitely many who didn't have time to vote, who didn't really know about it, or who thought a mine would bring desperately needed jobs. Yet 27,000 men, women, and children said no. "We have to think of this like the short count and the long count [as in the Maya calendar rounds]," Lolita said. "This is only part of a greater process, one that helps us focus on the models of life we want, *utz kaslemal*, *buen vivir*, living well. We have to defend the *consultas* from the government's attempts to deny them. And get more. We are working in Chicamán, Chinique, organizing all of Quiché."

Lolita's story, told so generously after her initial dubiousness over an early morning breakfast that became a late lunch, reminds us of the flurrying divisions that make the simple addition of the *consulta*'s counting into complex algorithms, hard to calculate even when the town's computer is placed at your service. Yet treating the *maras* (delinquents) respectfully evoked a loyalty strong enough to forgo income from a "job"; inviting the young soldiers to eat tortillas, they were with us, not against us. The (local) state and the banks, in this case, and for a time, were brought to heel. "El *pueblo manda*." Blood did not flow. But it hovers close on the horizon of any action. Living with that and still doing something is part of the calculations of after-math.

What Counts?

> The extreme difficulty of making visible the health consequences of chemicals became the single most significant characteristic of "chemical exposures" as a scientific artifact.
> —Michelle Murphy (2006, 121)

The *consulta* movement builds on another realm of counting—what Lolita called "science, studies of cyanide, technical stuff"—*and* is necessary to make numbers, even ones produced by this seemingly all-powerful source, actually count. As with an algebra of genocide, where even injury as profound as death relies on politics and doing to be done, and despite the immensity of the mine's "thereness," it is difficult to count and thereby reveal the harm it does. As a woman said at the meeting with Vinicio, "When you hear there's a child with a rash, they pay so people won't say anything." Trying to document health issues, COPAE activists hear of a sick child, but literally from one day to the next, when they drive up to take testimony, they find people unwilling to say anything. There was the man who fell into the tailings lagoon and died soon after, but his widow, apparently promised help educating her children, would not talk. Kids have rashes and their hair is falling out, people have papers with numbers showing blood levels of heavy metal, but like the legal framework needed for the *consultas*, these data need context. What makes a quantity into a quality—a threshold or standard rather than just a number? How much is normal and when is it a danger? A health center run by the mine says one thing and other doctors contradict it. It's hard to know what is making people sick. It's hard to be precise about what causes misfortune.

Counting is an essential technology here, simultaneously powerful *and* weaker and more uncertain than we tend to assume. And some numbers are better funded than others. There is an enormous resource breach between Goldcorp's science—their well-stocked labs and well-paid experts, many with doctorates from the world's top research universities[7]—and the small-scale operation maintained by COPAE, staffed by a single biologist. With a master's from the national university, committed and smart, Teresa Fuentes makes the monthly rounds from San Marcos to San Miguel and Sipakapa to take water samples and analyzes them in a sturdy but bootstrap lab, relying on kids from the local university extension—whom she trains in microscopy—to help keep up. She said many people, even the nonscientists in COPAE, "think you just look in the microscope, but you need a lot of experience. We're working with very toxic stuff, it could even kill you. You need training, lab skills, and they just don't get that here." She is also training volunteers in the villages to take samples and what to look for with the naked eye. While unable to sample sources from the mine's full circumference, they have created an archive of over six years of monthly samples of three rivers and several wells. Their work has been complemented by quick-visit research by teams from Euro-America and by Guatemalan government ministries and is used in scientific reports tracking mining effects.

While these reports emphasize that Goldcorp scientists have been forthcoming with their material, the company also produces geographical and temporal limits that affect what can be measured. First, access to water sources is curtailed, and even the government has trouble sampling the tailings impoundment (and their findings are not public). Second, the company's environmental impact statement—which identified *no* potential negative effects of the mine—has been criticized on many fronts. This is the baseline for all subsequent measurements, but it included only two springs, no groundwater or aquifer tests, and no hydrological connections. This, and the fact that some of the baseline water sources have gone dry, makes changes over time difficult to prove. It also included essentially no geochemical information on acid-leaching potential. Also called filtration, this occurs when large-scale earth disturbances expose rock to air and water, allowing arsenic, mercury, and other toxic metals to drain into soil and water.[8] A study by the US nonprofit E-tech found that "in 2006 the tailings impoundment already exceeded guidelines for cyanide (3X), copper (10X), and mercury (20X) while arsenic and sulfate concentrations were growing in ground wells." They also noted, however, that the monitoring network was so sparse that neither source nor potential down gradient receptors were known (2010, 77).

Uncertainty, as Michelle Murphy (2006) suggests about toxic environments more generally, dogs every effort to count. Even guidelines, like so many apparently precise numbers, are not as clear-cut as they appear (see Dumit 2012). For example, there are no surface or groundwater quality standards at all in Guatemala. Until 2012 the World Health Organization's standards for arsenic in water were .05 milligrams per liter (mg/L; 50 parts per billion), although cancer-mortality risk at that concentration is 1 in 100 (Van de Wauw, Evens, and Machiels 2010, 2). WHO (2011) has lowered the suggested limit to .01 mg/L (the Canadian and US standard), but one study found a well downstream of the mine showing 2.61 mg/L levels (2010, 3). The National Academy of Science found that "arsenic in drinking water causes bladder, lung, and skin cancer, and may cause kidney and liver cancer . . . harms the central and peripheral nervous systems, as well as heart and blood vessels, and causes serious skin and hair problems. It also may cause birth defects and reproductive problems" (2010, 2). But WHO says, "although there is a substantial database on the association between both internal and skin cancers and the consumption of arsenic in drinking-water, there remains considerable uncertainty over the actual risks at low concentration" (WHO 2011, 10). Similarly, copper is associated with DNA mutations, nervous system damage, leukemia, nausea, headaches, skin rashes and loss of hair, but the word "uncertain" appears in 4 of the 5 concluding paragraphs in WHO's guidelines for copper in drinking water (2004, 17–18). (Of course, standards and thresholds, just like laws against murder, mean nothing without organized bodies empowered to punish infractions.)

These numbers come from the best practices of laboratory-based toxicology, which developed the threshold limit value (TLV) through both scientific observation and mathematical manipulation. (I spent a semester auditing a course on this, but Murphy explains it so well I rely on her here.) For each substance scientists use animal tests to develop the dose response curve, administering enough high concentrations of metals or chemicals to induce significant health effects. Then they mathematically extrapolate downward for lower concentrations to predict the concentration at which no health effects would be provoked. This concentration is then divided by 100 for an extra margin of safety, and (as it was done for US industry) guidelines are developed based on adult male workers' exposure, calculated at 8 hours a day, 5 days a week (Murphy 2006, 89–90). As I understand it, the number is taken to point to something real in the world, but it is a calculation, not an actual observation—which doesn't mean it's wrong. But as Murphy points out, it is meant to measure very particular things, wrought from highly controlled circumstances, and based on administering a single thing, say, arsenic, rather than a cocktail of arsenic, cadmium, chromium, lead, manganese, mercury, nickel, selenium, thallium, and zinc, with a pinch of cyanide (all found near the mine), administered in low doses from conception on.[9] At the mine, only water is being systematically sampled; air, soil, sediment, and food are not, so it's hard to measure their cumulative roles in human exposure. The WHO and EPA standards emerge from calculations based on men at work, assuming a particular adult, male, and adequately nutritioned body that for two-thirds of each day "escapes" exposure. In the hamlet of Agel, near the mine, bodies are chronically malnourished and may be old, young, and female. And lifeways are different. For peasants whose homes, milpa corn patches, pastures, and drinking supplies intimately border the mine, there's no "escape."

It's hard to actually see (or otherwise sense) arsenic and copper, and they are hard to measure in ways that clearly show significance.[10] It's also hard to see neural damage, gene mutations, or the seedlings of cancers that may not express for years. I have seen skin rashes, but even activists are careful to note causal uncertainty. Environmental NGO Madre Selva (not to be confused with the company's Sierra Madre) says "these effects might be related to contaminated water . . . as in Honduras and Peru. [More] scientific studies are needed" (Madre Selva, n.d.). Consulta participants note that children are the most affected, but the researchers who came to do just such a study in Agel didn't have IRB approval to test kids (they did find elevated blood levels of arsenic, copper, zinc, and urinary mercury in adults, although within US reference levels; Basu and Hu 2010). Even with lots of numbers, as Murphy says, ubiquitous "low-level and mixed exposures became de facto uncertain phenomen[a]" (2006, 92). Then (like the search for bones removed from clandestine cemeteries) there's the purposeful production of uncertainty, as people clam up when COPAE comes to investigate.

Nonhuman life is also affected. In 2011 Hermana Maudilia showed me cell phone pictures of dead cows next to a stream. "That's the baby," she said. "Poor thing, it died right there from drinking. Its mother made it part way up the hill before she died, too." But cause is hard to prove. Then there are the groves of avocado trees that have dried up and other crops that aren't producing like they used to. Some people are sure it's all the water the mine is stealthily pumping. "It's MOSCAMED," said a woman at the Sipakapa development meeting. "They are spraying poisons to destroy our crops so we have to sell our land to the mine." MOSCAMED, the Mediterranean fruit fly eradication system, which entails aerial spraying and scientists poking around on people's land to count flies, has increased in intensity as CAFTA goes into effect. But an elder gentleman told me, "It's a disease killing the trees. It has nothing to do with the mine!"

Rather than the uncertainties in measure itself, Goldcorp and the Guatemalan state pressed this uncertainty of cause (mine-created poisoning) and effect (skin rashes, illnesses, loss of productive resources and animal and plant companions) in their responses to the IAHRC ruling to close the mine. In December 2011 the court reversed itself, withdrawing its demand for mine closure as a precautionary measure. It simply encouraged the government to ensure access to safe water (although it is still examining the original complaint regarding proper prior consultation).

Balancing Accounts and Neocolonial Alchemy:
Gold into Scrap, Food into Poison, Addition into Division

> I am not a *moneda de oro*, a gold coin, so that everyone loves me.
> —Simón, San Miguel catechist

This was a blow. An activist at Madre Selva said, "It seems like people are just ready to give up on San Miguel, it's a sacrifice zone. It shows the enormous power the mine has, once it's installed. People there still want to have their *consulta*, but the national organizations decided it's too dangerous.[11] We don't think it could pass and that would be devastating to the larger movement. It's too bad. People there are feeling abandoned."

To explore why it couldn't pass, I turn to a third form of accounting: attempting to balance gains with loss, benefits (now) with risks ("how much later?"). Like El Millonario's victims, people in San Miguel are working to calculate, without particularly accurate information, quetzals to *cuerdas* of land, wages to labor, hopes for progress to war's devastation and the impossible existing relations of production. They are weighing "good faith consultations" and sustainable development against the political, economic, and legal powers of the mining concession, possible benefits (and dangers) of the mine with experiences like going to the coast to harvest and "leaving strong but coming back sick" or sending a "son to the US but there's no work. We borrowed 12,000 but with interest it became 60,000."

And even (like MLMs and Ponzi schemes) as the *consultas* become modular and transferable from Sipakapa to Concepción to Santa Cruz, the company (also infinitely better funded) has its tried-and-true countermeasures for leveraging such uncertainties. These are sometimes brutal, sometimes *suave* (subtle) efforts to penetrate and divide communities, luring people to count on its side.

In my notebook pages words twine around inexpert drawings of animals in several different hands. Sitting in my kitchen on a rainy October afternoon rereading them, I'm transported back to a hot afternoon in 2009, sitting on a stump half in the shade, with two children leaning on me, one half out of her mother's lap as we entertain each other and I listen to testimonials. Thirty international antimining activists are crowded on benches under an awning in San José Ixcaniché, one of the villages closest to the mine. Salomon is telling the story of the mine, which I will recount briefly, because it expresses some of the uncertainties of measure and the complexities of accounting for benefit versus cost, "human economy" versus extraction and exploitation (Graeber 2011).

"When the company first came in, it was easy. People came in *suave, sencillos* [soft, simple], with people just like us. We played *futból*, they killed animals and had a big cookout. They raffled bicycles and other gifts. People felt happy and fell in with the plans. There would be work, it would be an orchid farm, *así de suave*. They started buying land where the mountain was, gringos came, with machines. One day an engineer offered me work. He said bring 25 people. They taught me. Here will be work, gold and silver. That's when we discovered what it was.

"For two and a half years I worked with them. I walked all over these mountains for them, telling people this was development. But when I respected my neighbors, who wanted more money for the land they'd sold, they fired me. The neighbors blocked the roads and the company accused me of crimes I didn't commit. It was very expensive to get out of this. The communities gave lists of grievances to the company. They wanted a dialogue. People went in *tranquilos* and left the same way, but the company provoked them. They shot at people, hit people. And then they said that *we* hit *them*. They claimed we hit John Noyes on the head! How could that be? He is so tall! It was a public road, but he accused me, called in the district attorney. The authorities only care about people with money. In the countryside, you can just die."

For two years Salomon and six other people from the demonstration were under house arrest and consumed in expensive court cases for inciting violence, threats, and damage to property and person. COPAE supported them, and five were found not guilty, while two paid fines.

Salomon continued, "Now there are serious problems in the community. We are very divided. At a meeting yesterday a man tried to talk about the rashes and people turned on him. They want to make a rule that no one can say anything bad about the company. Now our lives are no longer *tranquilo*. Now I only trust my own family."

It was those "big cookouts," the apparently stringless gifts from the company that counted against the people of San José Ixcaniché. Although

Goldcorp is the third largest mining company in the world and profitable enough to pay its chairman over $20 million in salary, the World Bank gave them a $45 million loan (NISGUA 2008; Solano 2009). And the bank, under pressure for accountability, requires a *consulta* from the companies it funds. By 2003, when the company began touting the benefits of the mine, people were accustomed to NGOs providing food. Cookout attendees signed lists that were then presented as proof that people accepted the company. And now, as pressure from the *consultas* grows, mining companies offer "development," health care, computers in a school, a mother's day party with festive food like tamales, all playing skillfully on people's *estilo cooperativo*. Used to "*aportando*," giving and getting, as Hermana Maudilia said, "People are very respectful. How can they turn against someone when they have eaten their food?"

But Vinicio reminded us: "They are not a project. They didn't come here to bring you water and health. It's an industry. They took out 240,000 ounces of gold last year. That is worth about $125 million. One ounce of gold is worth more than Q8,000. If they want your land, they will take it. They are not here because you are poor and they want to help you." He did acknowledge that work in the mine pays well (and regularly), about Q1,500 a month ($180). But he also said that in Canada or the US salaries are much higher because the work is so dangerous. "That's the thing, they make a lot more money where workers are so cheap."[12] And that's the rub; as the song says, "Poor people are easy to buy." Over a third of Guatemala is under license for exploration, with 23 licenses in San Miguel alone. "Almost all the mines are where indigenous people are."

It's hard to measure causes and effects, but local people know for sure that the bonds of trust and community solidarity are breaking. Foreign activists tend to focus on environmental damage and human rights violations, but local denunciations always list community divisions among the first of mining's pernicious effects. Many are also pretty certain that people are being bought off. For the wages, some will talk well of the mine (as Saloman had before his disillusion). Like the mayor of Sipakapa, who had to be forced to sign off on the *consulta*. "He was bought by the mine," said one man. "How much did he cost?" I asked. "Maybe a million, mayors are expensive. But up in the villages, it's cheaper, 1,500 or even just 500. That's a lot for us, but not for them."

About three hours into the Sipakapa meeting with COPAE on alternative development, a rumor flew around the room that one of the antimining leaders was at a meeting with the mine to set up coffee production. People freaked out. Several denounced him as sold out, while others said he had just gone to check it out, as head of their own coffee cooperative. People got more and more agitated until suddenly the man appeared. He was relaxed and smiling and explained he had gone as a spy and was now happy because the company's project was pathetic. He'd been afraid, but now he knew what was going on. It took him, a long-term leader of the resistance, about half an hour to reassure people. Things have changed. They are not the friendly happy communities they once were. "There are lots of conflicts."

Of course, the company alone does not produce divisions. Pueblos chiquitos have never been the romantic closed corporate communities of urban nostalgia, especially in the aftermath of civil war. As with war reparations, the sudden eruption of lucre in a family or community, either through land or labor sales, can strain trust and provoke real and phantasmic inequalities. Divisions also emerge from within the very structures that are challenging the company's power. Many tendril out from power imbalances deeply embedded in the patriarchal hierarchies of the church and similar "traditions" that infrastructure Mayan and peasant communities. They may be compounded when well-intentioned outsiders side with particular people and channel resources in ways (often in the name of efficiency or of friendship) that discourage democratic decision making.

On the bumpy car ride to Sipakapa for the workshop, Maudilia and three catechists talked about the changes. Simón said, "I am not a moneda de oro (gold coin) so that everyone loves me. But it is sad. There are many divisions now. We used to all get along, to joke. We had really good times with people in city hall, with everyone. But not now. People won't respond when I greet them." Humberto said, "They'll come up and first say, 'Why are you against the mine? They help us. They say they're going to build a soccer field, with grass, stands, everything nice. So why are you against it?' But in the next breath they'll say 'You should be careful, you know there are threats against you.' If we try to talk about the contamination, people say there is none. They don't want to know." Then Simón told how he'd been eating in a restaurant in San Miguel with some COPAE people when a man came up to their table, a guy with the mine. "We know him, but that cabrón pulled out his wallet, all this money and he was hitting it on the table. Bang, bang! [he acted this out]. 'I have money and so I don't have to worry about anyone coming to get me.' Cabrón, amenazando, that asshole, trying to threaten us!" They laughed. But then Humberto said, "People stay quiet, they're very careful. They remember the war."

But as things got somber, Simón, smiling mischievously, pulled out a digital recorder and played a fake ad for Montana Explotadora (exploiter, not explorer) that communications students at the National University extension had made. Perfectly miming the announcer style, colloquial "person on the street" interviews and traditional marimba music, we hear a little girl say, "My daddy works in the mine and now, thanks to Montana Explotadora, I have two heads!" Then a woman's voice: "My husband works in the mine and now he has three penises; awwwwesoooome!" They doubted they could play it on the church's radio station where Simón DJs, but it was a hoot.

Counting does the special work of making visible what was "already there" and also produces what it seems to simply show. The efforts over years to organize a *consulta* and get the numbers on toxins, health, and environmental degradation help create the very resistance the *consulta* counts. It also challenges official equivalences with alternative calculations of worth—as in the song "A gram of blood is worth more than a thousand kilos of gold." Aniseto, in his speech, said a new Hilux and going around with two or three women may look sweet but less so when your health is in danger. In the workshop a man explains the mine offers false promises of progress: "They say there is work, but there's not enough for everyone, while *everyone* has problems with their crops, their children's health, miscarriages, poisoning. Maybe those with work can save or earn enough to get their Q80,000 little car, but they don't see it just requires more spending on tires, parts, gas; they are spending and spending. It will never stop." And more creepy, what happens to what really counts about people when they come to resemble commodities that can be bought and sold? When "authorities care only about people with money"? Progress does not equal respect. Adding some money does not balance out divisions in "my people," even if it means you don't have to worry about anyone coming to get you.

"Priceless!" and Other Mysteries of Value

I first went to San Miguel with Greg Grandin, a North American historian, and Federico Velásquez, a Maya-K'iche' teacher, researcher, and mountaineer, for the demonstration where Aniseto spoke. Passing one of Goldcorp's billboards Federico said, "Why was gold at $250 and now it's at $1,000?" Everyone in the car had read their Marx and knew that value is a tricky thing indeed. After a moment of silence we just burst out laughing.

But the laughter did not dispel the wonder/horror of the question. I feel a similar wonder/horror contemplating gold more generally, my ambivalence nicely condensed in a 2009 ad in the New York Times (there's also a TV version) showing a golden Egyptian sarcophagus being wheeled into a bank vault and headlined "Pharaohs believed gold could provide eternal wealth. You'll get no argument here." Like debates over the trillion dollar coin, it captures the rich tension between fetishism and market rationality, physics and metaphysics, reverence and the base desire for power and accumulation that surrounds this malleable metal, this pretty bauble, this useless, inedible anchor for the capitalist world system. "Ancient civilizations were a primitive and superstitious bunch. But their instincts about gold were second to none. Something about its physical beauty told them this was a natural resource with lasting value. That's why there's SPDR® Gold Shares, a precise way to access the gold market . . . It's simple, cost efficient and fully backed by the real thing. The advantages of gold are timeless. . . . Precise in a world that isn't."

Real, timeless, precise. People pulling out their gold teeth on the Cerro Kumatz. Hundreds of tons of it ritualistically reburied in the earth's heavily guarded sanctum, filling gigantic vaults under lower Manhattan (even as money officially floated free of it forty years ago). Teresa of COPAE saying how hard it was to stop wearing her jewelry, but it gradually came to feel ugly. Au, its chemical symbol from "glow of sunrise." "I'm not a moneda de oro so everyone loves me." "Gold" level in Omnilife. Gold medals. Gold records. The gleaming case in the National Museum of the American Indian where hundreds of pre-Columbian figures give way starkly to crosses, coins, and swords. Gold is the standard (even when it's not), the measure. Precious. "Precise." Yet its value is constantly changing. "Precise" comes from praecidere, "to cut off," yet turning and tossing an ounce it practically weighs ten. Gold seems inherently valuable. Yet, as with the pyramids in the last two chapters, we know it is its "fiduciarity"—or public trust and community confidence, its ability to circulate—that makes it so. Like electricity, it runs and flows, which is why it's called currency, even if, in your hand (or mouth), it just sits there.

Almost anything can be used as "money," the inert matter (and sometimes quite lively stuff) on which humans stamp or impress or simply project the idea of value, but gold has been at the dully glowing heart of the enigma of "something that could turn into everything" (Graeber 2011, 245). In the West it's because gold serves as a stand-in for the more general doubleness of coins. Both a piece of metal and something more, the material and the abstract, reality and concept: it brings us back to adequation. Maurer says, "It would be easy to dismiss the formula *adequatio intellectus et res* as a modern metanarrative . . . [yet] when faced with the question of money's being adequate to anything at all, people often stop in wonder." He argues that practitioners of Islamic banking and alternative currencies are "given to wonderment" yet resist an impasse between representation and reality with "a moral practical reason" (2005, xiv). This is what I think Verran means by both disconcertment and doing and being done. And I think something similar is going on as people formulate responses to the Marlin mine and to questions of value—that is, who and what counts?

After our (rather strained) laughter subsided, Federico told us about climbing a nearby volcano, where he came upon two young Mayan men who asked him if he knew how to find Juan Noj. Federico didn't. The men said, "We are very indebted. We are looking for the door into the volcano. We are trying to get some money.""Who is Juan Noj?" I asked. Greg snorted. "You anthropologists should know that!" Federico explained that he is a man or a spirit that lives in the mountain. Some say he is Satan, others that he makes life flourish in the hills, others that he lives beneath the stone in a palace of gold and silver and rewards the lazy and malicious with wealth but they must work off their debt in the afterlife or sacrifice a child as part of their contract (as in Aurora's stories of gain and terror). Noj is a Mayan name, but he is sometimes depicted as a ladino, the owner and overseer par excellence. Unsuccessful in their search, Federico helped them off the mountain, their souls intact.

June Nash (1993) tells of a similar figure in the mines of Bolivia, called El Tío, the earth owner, who controls what happens in the mines and is petitioned with coca leaves, cigarettes, 90-proof alcohol, and llama fetuses for there to be rich seams of mineral and no disasters. Whereas stories mix Juan Noj with bounty on the earth's surface, El Tío is kept distinct from the Pachamama, who rules the world of "natural" increase and reproduction. For her, none of that uncanny money-making-money or prices suddenly increasing fourfold for no apparent reason (and for something you can't even eat)!

Having encountered El Tío in the Cerro Rico of Potosí, Bolivia, a few weeks before, I asked Hermana Maudilia if there were similar ideas about the mine in San Miguel. She sighed. "You know they have taken away our culture. They forced us to become ladinos, by law! In the nineteenth cen-

tury. They made us work. That's why we don't even wear our own *traje* here."
Yet a few days later I heard her joking with a man "not to lose his head." I
asked what she meant and she laughed, "Oh, they say the mine demands
human heads and the company has to go out and find them."

Maudilia's brother, who works in the mine, showed me a video he'd made
on his cell phone of working one of the ginormous machines deep underground. Talking about dangers in the mine, the subject of heads came up.
"Oh yes," he said matter-of-factly. "Among the workers, we've all heard those
stories. We even asked the supervisor. We confronted him. And he admitted
they did that. But he said it was only during the construction phase, when
they first built the mine. He said they went to Guatemala City and got gang
members, drug addicts, prisoners. But we shouldn't worry. They didn't do
that anymore."[13]

Here was the dark equivalent for Goldcorp's publicity images of the
brightly lit mining installations, the reciprocation for "A mine with secure
technology for human health and the environment, strengthening the integral development of San Miguel." Such are the exacting demands of "millennial capitalism" (Comaroff and Comaroff 2001), the specters haunting
the speculation, the "primitive" and "precise" allure of mining and trading
gold.

Numbers seem to stand alone, transparently representing the world, but
everything depends on the systems of measurement and regimes of logic
that make them count. Gold, of course, has no "real" lasting value outside
of social relations. These relations *qualify* quantities—create "conditions that
must be met in order to exercise certain rights."

François Ewald traces two competing systems of accountability developed in Europe since the eighteenth century, both claiming totality and
operating via specific and mutually exclusive categories, regimes, and economies. "Risk" is characteristic of the insurance regime, which assumes that
all risk is calculable so that "even in misfortune one retains responsibility for
one's affairs" (1991, 207). Market decisions, like selling your land or granting
mining licenses, are supposed to work within this system of rationality in
which people try to maximize benefits. Similar to how double-entry bookkeeping made number seem "good," "insurance is a moral technology. . . .
To conduct one's life in the manner of an enterprise indeed begins in the
eighteenth century to be a definition of a morality whose cardinal virtue
is providence" (207). In this universe it is preposterous for someone who
got Q4,000 for a plot worth far less before the mining company arrived to

come back, once the mine is installed, and ask for more money. Really, it's immoral. But Ewald suggests that another system of measure has accompanied risk regimes: that of "fault," the legal or juridical understanding of responsibility that holds that damage is the result of an individual acting in a certain way. Thus "judicial decisions on accident compensation had to be linked to investigation of the cause of injury." Was it "due to natural causes, or to some person who should bear its cost" (Ewald 1991, 206)? In this system it is immoral *not* to defend oneself against those who injure you.

There is a similar tense simultaneity to the two regimes of perception that qualify the pollution numbers—both making them meaningful and limiting them. One, toxicology, is scientific and works (often quite effectively) by cutting off what is to be studied from its context, to trace "the effects of chemicals in stimuli-reduced experimental settings" (Murphy 2006, 106). The other, often called "popular," "lay," "creekside," or even "housewife" epidemiology, instead "maps human relationships in a muddy, unrestrained, lived place. This assemblage of tools, practices and subject positions makes perceptible, not specific causal pathways, but . . . evokes chemical exposure's proximate and diverse conditions to fashion an aggregate health problem out of an array of particularized experiences and to map a collectivity of health effects onto a concurring social inequality" (Murphy 2006, 106–7).[14] Phil Brown and Edwin Mikkelson say popular epidemiology emphasizes "social structural factors as part of the causative chain of disease" and involves "social movements and political and judicial remedies." It is "an extremely significant advance for both public health and popular democratic participation" (1990 126, 207).

In contrast to insurance and toxicology logics, fault and popular epidemiology measure the costs that hide "off-book." They focus on "externalities" like sick children, contaminated water, environmental degradation, lack of consultation, unfair distribution of profits and risks, and community divisions. The numbers assembled with *these* logics—and lashing together some tenacious lawyers, a UN convention, the Inter-American Court (for a while), and national and transnational activists who realize that *they* (we) are *also* the *pobrecitos*—have inspired another half a million Guatemalans to hold *consultas*, block roads, occupy installations, and in many other ways insist that they count. Leaching through the hemisphere, leading people from Canada and the United States to Chile to do the same.

Summing Up: Hidden Truths, Real Costs

These people are just poor peasants, same as we are!

—Humberto, San Miguel catechist

Humberto, one of the catechists we'd laughed with at the fake Montana ad two years before, seemed pretty nervous. He had traveled for two days to be in San Raphael las Flores, Santa Rosa, for a public forum, "Hidden Truths of Mining," and so was pretty tired. Plus he had to give a talk and the town's auditorium was beginning to fill up. But I think his nervousness was from being in the *Oriente*, Guatemala's ladino southeast, reputedly populated entirely by cowboys, assassins, and narcos. Humberto had spent time in the United States and so, unlike many from San Miguel, had experience in non-Mayan worlds. But there's something about the *Oriente*. We joked their *traje típico* was a machete on one side and pistol on the other. Most Maya fear it, tourists shun it, but army recruiters do well there.[15]

Humberto was called to the stage, joining ladino experts and Madre Selva activists. By now the hall was full and kids were running around as their parents chatted. Organizers had scared up a lot of chairs, but still some three hundred people were standing in the back. For over two hours on a sunny Sunday morning people listened to presentations on toxins, water use, and effects of acid leaching and saw photographs of tailing lagoons, water sources sporting psychedelic colors, and mountaintop removal. They seemed as moved as the women at Maudilia's meeting, especially by the children with rashes and houses with cracked walls. Lawyers explained the legal frameworks for a consulta and described the ones recently held just up the road in Santa Rosa. But it was when Humberto spoke that people squeezed in close, straining to catch his every word. He told how it felt to live in fear of drinking or touching the water, of how their once peaceful community was now riven with divisions and neighbor no longer talked to neighbor. How they couldn't sell their crops because buyers feared contamination. This sent waves of consternation through the crowd. Afterward people crowded around him, gleaning more details. Later, as we walked together to the local organizer's house for lunch, he said, laughing and surprised, "These people are just poor peasants, same as we are!"[16]

His realization, that indigenous and ladino might share interests, had been a turning point in the war. Armed revolution started in the *Oriente* in the early 1960s, as did Guatemala's modern counterinsurgency. The first death squads were organized there, as were the first scorched earth campaigns, assisted by US advisers brought directly from Vietnam. In the 1970s organizing moved into the western highlands. It was when the 1980 CUC strike joined indigenous and ladino workers that elites saw their carefully constructed divide-and-conquer strategies at risk and responded with the mix of mania and rationality that marked the early 1980s stage of the war. The enormous efforts of the genocide ruling to make the Maya count have somewhat discounted the mostly ladino losses from that earlier moment of the war. When I quoted CEH statistician Patrick Ball saying the scientifically defensible figure of 132,000 excluded (among other things) any deaths before 1979, it's because, for various technical and political reasons, they didn't count. This helps reproduce a postwar "race" divide between ladinos as perpetrators and Maya as (the only) victims (Oglesby and Ross 2009; González Ponciano 2013), reflected in Humberto's nervousness—and surprise. A similar divide had marked the *consultas*. As of August 2011 close to sixty communities had held one, but until Santa Rosa started organizing, these were only in Mayan areas.

In the early morning chill before driving to San Raphael, Johanna, a Madre Selva activist said, "The mining companies are throwing up their hands. Everywhere they turn there is a *consulta*. The whole province of Huehuetenango is effectively closed! Twenty-eight out of thirty *municipios* have voted no. A company spokesman even said 'We can't work with those Indians. Let's just go where people are easier to control!' You saw that, didn't you, Miguel?" "Yes," Miguel replied, still a bit sleepy. "It was up on their web page for awhile." But then he warmed to the topic. "They see the indigenous as rebellious, out of control. They've basically given up! We've won!" "But," Johanna said, "they've gotten a surprise with the ladinos in Santa Rosa! They're organizing, too!"

At the forum in San Raphael, activists like Humberto sought to show the "hidden truths" of mining. With the global recession, greatly diminished postwar foreign aid, and stepped-up deportation exacerbating Guatemala's staggering underemployment, mining and other megaprojects appear to offer hope of a job and what the Quiché bishop called "the right to development." But like *El Millonario*, it turns neighbor against neighbor. While equally invisible, these costs are even harder to quantify than cyanide in the water or percentages of royalties, yet are just as strongly felt. Insisting on other costs—plus toxins and illness, lack of water for people and crops, babies with rashes and long-term health consequences, reduced markets for produce—changes the equation to show profit is really loss. It sets up the different equivalence: "YES to Life = NO to Mining."

Maybe through similar tricky byways of making people count, this can alchemically transform other divisions into equivalences: ladino with indigenous, Oriente with Occidente, mining critics with ex-PAC, Maya bueno with indios bochincheros—pobrecitos just like us. This may also demand, to return to Robertson, insisting on how "the fact [just like money or number], the thing as it is without any relation to anything else, is a matter of no importance or concern whatever: its relation to what it evinces, the fact viewed as evidence, is alone important." By which I mean accounting for the larger structures and histories that produce these values, as well as such emerging categories as "territory," the ser Mayab,[17] and other "relations of one-to-many."

Mathematics (singular and plural), rooted in to "be alert; memory," make/s numbers part of a deeply human project—statistically holding on to each and every tragedy. And within a still very dangerous milieu, people struggle to count and for the accountability it brings: through exhumations of mass graves, through claims for reparations, through distributor redes and consultas, and through court cases, including genocide trials and rulings against huge, rich, international mining concerns. These are made possible by disembeddings of numbers—quantification—and the subsequent reembedding of them back into lived experience—qualification, in the sense of making fit for rights.

Standing Up

It was a dark, wet afternoon as Hermana Maudilia urged the Padre's big car up muddy hairpin turns for a village Sunday school class. On the way she chatted about learning to drive and how a gringa nun gave her a car so she didn't have to walk up and down the hills. "Of course, I gained a lot of weight!" Unfortunately, that car had been stolen at gunpoint in Guatemala City. Arriving, we walked through mud to a small chapel above the futból field. Men and women of various ages, most with kids, slowly filtered in. Several helped Maudilia arrange flowers and grasses in a circle where we started with the antimining song and prayers addressed to the four directions. Then she began her lesson: the differences between crawling and walking. Joking, getting people up and walking on all fours around the chapel, making good-humored comments about gender equality (leading one young man to mime breastfeeding his baby, to widespread giggles), having folks comment on a Bible story, she gracefully brought us to the mine, its effects, and the lesson.

Then she called on me to say a few words. "Me?" "Yes, tell them what you told me at dinner last night." So I rather awkwardly thanked them all for letting me be there and told them about how my hometown, nestled in the rolling hills of southern Ohio among small farms, had turned out to also house a nuclear facility, kept secret for many years. It was knowingly built over an important aquifer, and considered to be in the middle of nowhere, where "nobody" farmers were willing to sell their land. In the late 1970s, what had been individual tragedies of miscarriages or young people with strange diseases combined with the ecology movement and a public increasingly doubtful about its government. These networks revealed that the Fernald feed plant, complete with a Purina-style checkerboard water tower, had not been for animal feed but for uranium upgrade to "feed" bombs. Once people knew this (itself a long struggle), nearby families began to organize, look for allies, and confront the anger and fear about losing lucrative employment in a poor area during a deepening recession. Discovering contamination in wells and aquifers affecting nearby Cincinnati and undeniable cancer clusters galvanized organizing, and over several years the site was closed and the EPA and DOE began a Superfund-supported cleanup.[18] I ended my story, finally aware of Maudilia's plan, by saying that the whole project of taking on the US government and the nuclear establishment was started by one woman worried about her child's health.

Some of the women there had been at Vinicio's lecture and had heard how much better miners were protected and paid in North America. Everyone seemed genuinely shocked that the US government would treat its own people so badly. "You mean they lied about the pollution?" "They covered up the danger?" "They didn't want to clean up?" Then one man said, "That's why we had our *consulta* here. We know the dangers of the mine."

Maudilia ended the meeting with everyone searching for a symbol outside the chapel of what it meant to stand up. We made a circle in those high mountains, the clouds breaking up and the wind strong, the valleys stretching out around us, as people held flowers and stones and explained each of their symbols. And then we were treated to warm chicken soup in the glow of a fire as night fell and the rain began.

THIS IS A BOOK ABOUT LIGHT
It will tell you interesting facts about many simple, ordinary things, like a glass of water, mirrors, soap bubbles and hot pavements. —Irving Adler, The Secret of Light (1965) ###

7 Beyond Adequacy

This is a chapter about light and water. It will tell you interesting facts about many simple, ordinary things like rain, stars, presence, time, and electricity. And counting. It is structured like a cloud atlas.

A Postcard from Río Negro

Flood

The sky was bright with stars, luminescent, overwhelmingly populated. There was that great unfurling starry band, the Milky Way, the Mayan *Saq B'e*, white road, stretching back into stories of how time began and the world was created. A glyph meaning *och bih,* "he enters the road," is a euphemism for death, where the road is the Milky Way, the path of souls on their journey to Xilbaba, *inframundo,* land of the dead (Coe and van Stone 2005, 62). Freidel and Schele suggest the Western constellation Orion's belt was, for the Classic Maya, the three hearth stones laid to begin the cosmos on the back of a turtle—a frequent image of creation, as the maize god emerges from its cracked shell. The Milky Way, emerging from "Orion," was the mythic maize tree that raised the sky. Also called the foliated cross, with the double-headed serpent halfway up representing the ecliptic, it is both a story and a map, time and space (1993).

7.1 Disembarking in New Río Negro, July 2012. Author's photo.

A series of celestial events in 2012 had brought my eyes skyward, the startlingly beautiful sunset alignment of Venus, Jupiter, and Mercury in February; the annular eclipse in May; the transit of Venus on my birthday (the last in our lifetime); a day at an archaeoastronomy conference in Guatemala City; and, of course, all the inklings around 2012. Or as some Maya call it, *Oxlajuj B'aqtun*, or *Oxlajun Pik*, the beginning of the thirteenth period of 144,000 days since 13.0.0.0.0 (September 8, 3114 BC), when the current period of Mayan time began.

I was on the terrace of a guesthouse as my nephew Quinn picked out tunes on a guitar as that amazing night sky wheeled overhead and illuminated the steep drop to the dark lake below. Earlier in the day we skimmed across those waters in a small boat with Juan and his five-year-old daughter, Alma, to get to New Río Negro. After settling in, we began our Mayan "community tourism" experience with a steep hike to a cave where, before, offerings were made to telluric deities. During the war people hid there from the army. Alma, in her little sandals, ragged *corte*, and T-shirt, kept running ahead (straight up!), then running back to encourage us, then taking off again.

7.2 At the cave. Author's photo.

By the time we were done we were quite thankful for Isabela's delicious fried fish (Juan's wife, she'd attended a workshop on how to cook for foreigners) and a quiet afternoon exploring. The guesthouse walls are adorned with large posters about Maya-Achi culture, describing the language, children's games, corn cultivation and its sacred aura, and a famous local product: *petates*, or reed mats. These, along with the three stones of the hearth, were once the primary furnishings of indigenous dwellings. One was born on one's mother's *petate*, and a good death was to die on one's own several *katunes* (20-year cycles) later. Then you would be wrapped in it and consigned to the earth. To share a *petate* is to be married, and in the Classic Maya images, "taking the mat" is the ascension to the throne. On some stelae the glyphs are arranged in the same woven pattern (making them even harder to read!). In several Mayan languages the word for "mat" is *pop*, and people sit on them for meetings, thus the sacred text *Popol Vuh* means "book of council."[1] *Petates* carved into the stone walls of ancient buildings show they were council meeting places. Nikolai Grube, our teacher at the 2012 glyph workshop, explained that the *petate* is connected to time, to the idea of the calendar as a weaving, and that understanding it

7.3 Protest march of the Mutual Support Group for Families of the Disappeared (GAM), with names of their kinspeople written on *petates* (woven mats). January 1986. Patricia Goudvis. Used with kind permission.

requires similar calculations to women weaving clothing. In the mid-1980s, drawing on these layers of meaning linking relation, generation, the sacred, and death, members of GAM (the Mutual Support Group for Families of the Disappeared) painstakingly wrote the names of thousands of their kinspeople on *petates* for demonstrations. "They were really hard to write on!" Aura Elena Farfán said, laughing. "We had no idea when we started! It took forever!!"

Then we settled in with the family to watch a documentary about a little girl from Río Negro who had fled the violence and been adopted by a white family in Iowa. She came to realize only in her midtwenties, already married and with two children, that she was a survivor of one of the worst massacres of the war.[2] As was Juan.

And the next day he walked us straight up the mountain behind the town. On the way he explained how in 1982, one month after all the men had been called over the mountain to the pro-army village of Xococ for military training and had been summarily executed, the women and children of the town (he was nine) were rounded up by the army and civil patrollers

7.4 Walking up to Pak'oxom, where two mountains meet, where the sun appears, where the people of Río Negro were killed. Author's photo.

from Xococ and forced to climb to the top, along the very trail we were walking. At a place called Pak'oxom, which means "where two mountains meet,
where the sun appears," some women were raped and everyone was killed.
As he recounted the story, he lingered on the ages of the women and girls
who were raped, counting on his fingers: "12, 13, 14, 15, 16, and the young
mothers, 18, 19 years old," he said. Then he repeated the ages twice more.
Only eighteen children, Juan among them, were spared and taken over the
mountain to Xococ. There they were "adopted" by their families' assassins
(who even went to court to change their names) and forced to work in return for bitter rations. "They didn't think anyone survived, so they could do
what they wanted."

Río Negro was targeted for scorched earth counterinsurgency because
the residents had refused to be removed to make way for the Chixoy hydroelectric dam that had turned their Black River—where they fished and
swam, washed and drank—into the lake we had crossed. Survivors of Río
Negro held one of the first exhumations at the top of the mountain. It took
far longer to get permission to unearth the men's bodies outside Xococ and
even more time to get three of the patrollers—but not the army or their
backers—convicted on murder charges. By then, the man who had enslaved
Juan had died. But bodies from the massacre in nearby Los Encuentros were
dumped in the well and left deep underwater when the area was flooded.
Also often underwater now is a post-Classic Mayan site, Cauinal, which
some say was as important as Tikal. The stars were so awesome that night
because there is no electricity in Río Negro nor anywhere else in the area
surrounding the hydroelectric dam.[3]

Journal of a Hieroglyph Workshop

Water and Light

Chahk. There he is, swimming, dancing among the serpentine water-
bearing clouds, his knees delicately bent. His creamy thigh bears the curlicue
sign of water that, repeated over and over, densely layers moisture-related
references. The water mark itself, on thigh and arm, warns the viewer: do
not mistake this for an ordinary human.[4] One hand grasps his thunderbolt
hammer, the other his shield/*pakal*. *Pakal*! I know that word! Amid the show-
ers of unfamiliar Classic and Current Maya language, it was a relief to recognize something! *Pakal* was the name a friend chose in the early 1990s when

7.5 Chahk, altar O, Quiriguá. Matthew Looper. Used with kind permission.

he officially "came out" as Maya. "I thought," he told me later, "I will be a defense, a shield for my people."

Pakal and I, with about fifty Maya and some ten *kaxlan*,[5] were taking a weeklong glyph-reading workshop in Antigua, Guatemala, in July 2012, taught by German epigrapher Nikolai Grube.[6] Given the fraught year 2012, Nikolai had chosen to focus on Quiriguá, site of a stela referencing the beginning of time (or at least the last creation). Gathered around tables in the Lions Club salon, we gazed at Powerpoints® of drawings of Maya carvings from the 700s.

Zoomorph Altar O. Chahk, suspended, floating, sustained by a monumental "T," the glyph for *Ik'*, wind or air, also understood as life itself. *Ik'* is also one of the 20 days in the sacred round calendar I'd been trying to memorize (the "T" was, to my relief, at least recognizable). And the carving's multiple T glyphs contain other watery meanings; one is adorned with symbols for mountains which are crosscut by rivers and streams that feed its voluptuous vegetation, involuted by caves that breathe and offer access to the *inframundo* (Finamore and Houston 2010; Looper 2009).

And there he is again, smaller, now himself part of a glyph regarding the ascension of K'ahk Tiliw, ruler of Quiriguá. Nikolai told us, we know Chahk by the clouds / drops of water on his head. He carries his ax at the ready to throw and make thunder (I thought at first it was an earring). Having just seen *The Avengers* and being a bit taken with Chris Hemsworth, I wrote "Thor!" in the margin of my workbook. I'd recently visited Norway and learned my original patronym, Torkleson, was from, yes, Thor of thunder and lightning fame, and I felt this weird tug, a mini-interpellation you might say. It's a little embarrassing to tell you, the Joseph Campbellish cliché of an immigrant returning to a nonhome and finding she's named for a god. Seeking something like an authentic connection, something that extends back at least a little way in time? Please!

But then this does seem like some of the ways signifying is also happening for my workshop companions. That there are connections, the world is charged, things might not happen only by chance. Walter, twenty-two, Kaqchikel from the tourist mecca of Panajachel, studies art and graphic design and is shy but also resplendent with his long Maya-identifying hair (he was on his third workshop). He said, "In Pana everyone wants to be *de moda*, up to date, there's not much interest in traditions or the past." His parents are Catholic and his siblings mostly evangelicals. "No! Oh no!" he said, laughing, when I asked if they supported him in Maya pursuits. He studies on his own but has a group of friends who "support culture." His buddies are from more traditional towns and help him stay focused (they teased and horseplayed but were serious when we got down to work). "As I get more into it, I find so many things have meaning, there are so many subtleties. . . . I'm not sure why it's so important to me. Maybe it's the energy of my day but I feel like I've found my reason for being, my path. This is what I'm here for."

Chori, Walter's friend, is Kaqchikel from Sumpango, and is a Little Person and has to put up with a lot of (very un-PC) teasing (his nickname is from chorizo, making fun of his short, plump arms). But he said his life was transformed when he learned about the role of *enanos* in the Classic Maya court and saw something like his own image in the carvings and vase art. "There is an honored place for me." María Elena, in her forties,

Mam from San Marcos, is an elementary school teacher and wore a beautiful *guipil* she'd woven herself. She said, "This is ours but we did not know it. When we first started meeting [in local workshops in her home town], at first nothing! I understood nothing![7] But it's slowly starting to come clear. Now I'm *muuuuuy contenta*" (veeeery happy). Hector, Q'eq'chi from near Cobán, spends a lot of time away from his family giving such introductory workshops and said, "We are motivated to see the happiness and emotion that Mayan participants feel when they encounter references to the knowledges they practice or that they've heard from their parents or grandparents. This makes them feel that their roots are profoundly historical." Magdalena, in her midforties, a Poqomam from Palín, told me their area was not mentioned in the human rights reports, but "there was lots of war there, my uncle was murdered, disappeared, with no word of him since that time. People we worked with in bilingual education were killed. But we didn't count."[8] At the last lunch of the workshop, I sat with her and others from Palín to compose a thank-you speech for the organizers. We framed it with the Sacred Round calendar date, which everyone at the table (but me) seemed to know,[9] and Magdalena carefully wrote out our suggestions. But part way through reading it, she went off text saying, rather impassioned (and at far greater length), "We didn't recognize these things. Maybe we knew that they existed, but we didn't understand. We didn't see the connections. Now we do. This has made this a sacred time for us!"

Of course, some people feel the same way about the number 42, making my little romanti-sensor start to beep.[10] How different is such "contentment" from the facile *aha!* of horoscope reading? "Yes! That's me!" Or standard New Age grasping for meaning in a chaotic world? Is this any less problematic and ahistorical than the old anthropological fascination with "survivals"? Or the creepy embrace of apocalypse energizing the 2012 hoopla? I admit to being weirded out by a creeping raciology, as when people told me that they knew things, like the calendar, without study, because it was in their blood or their Mayan DNA. (At the workshop, however, most people—like María Elena—were very clear about how much effort it took. "*Quiere ganas!*" said one of my neighbors, seemingly every fifteen minutes.)[11] Nikolai said, "I think it's made not born [ethnic identity], but they should realize this belongs to them." The wise linguist Judie Maxwell told me, "You can feel the energy or you can't. It doesn't mean it's not there." And Iyaxel Cojtí, a young Mayan activist and coorganizer of the workshop, said:

"Many people now say they are Maya, but they don't know how to defend it. If someone says to them, 'How are you Maya? Prove it!' They can't say anything. That's what we want to change. Maybe it's not genealogical, but we share so much, the calendar systems, language roots, so many things that you can see every day!"

Which returns me to the larger questions of this book, thinking about the condensed significations of the workshop, people intermingling with *savoirs*, those lodestones of potential powers returning from the past like Chahk's flash of lightning, perhaps illuminating a different future in moments of danger.[12] What does it *mean* for a reviled people, poor, excluded, genocided, not counting, as Magdalena said, in every conceivable way, for a world-renowned authority like Nikolai to be there, frequently reminding us of the impressive counting abilities of their forebears? Learning glyphs by writing them, folding down fingers as one counts the days, Juan retelling his story of the massacre on that long hike up the mountain, are all labors to make count.

They may concatenate "past imperfect, present tense" with Sunder Rajan's "future perfect," as in this joke. A young Mayan man was attending a workshop on Guatemalan history in Quetzaltenango. After a morning devoted to the Spanish conquest he came out into the central square for a break. Some Spanish tourists were enjoying the sunshine, and he walked up to one and punched him in the face. When the tourist got up and demanded to know what that was for, the Mayan guy said, "That's for what you did to us during the conquest." "The conquetht??!?" said the Spaniard [it's good sport to make fun of Spanish accents]. "That wath 500 yearth ago!" "Yes, but I just found out about it today!"

The joke is charged with pain at the sorry state of Guatemalan education but also suggests that even if you're just now learning about the past, it can feel as material as a fist. And it can, maybe should, cause changes in the present. When folks were talking about how the workshop made them feel connected to history, I ventured to tell my little Thor story, and they asked, "Why don't you change your name back?"

Beautiful Liquid, Loops of Time

And here is Kawil, often associated with Chahk, on Stela H, perhaps (the deities are often multiple, overdetermined, at times quadripartite like the earth's four directions or working in pairs to represent productive "cosmic oppositions such as sky vs. earth, light vs. darkness"; Coe 109). The great stone, carved on every inch, monumentalizes K'ahk' Tiliw, a ruler who has overthrown his patrons and now represents himself, resplendent, as the young maize god, long hair/tassels flowing, emerging from the mountain. "You know this!" Nikolai says to his Maya audience, "It's in the *Popol Vuh*!"

K'ahk' Tiliw's head bears a mass of feathered plumage that even in stone seems to shift and sparkle. At his waist a deity head and streams of water flowing down. "Beautiful liquid," Nikolai says, "it is adorned with glyphs for flowers, *regando*," meaning flowing, irrigating, but also the word used for blood sacrifice, often taken from the genitals. On a nearby stela the same king is shown with a manta ray above his head whose spiny tail was used to extract the precious fluid. The flower glyphs in the water also represent seeds (past, present, and future collapsed) and zero (ending and beginning). On each of K'ahk' Tiliw's shoulders is Kawil again, armed with serpentine spear and shield, with which he opens the sky and opens the earth, cleaving the mountain, freeing water, allowing maize god to be born. Nikolai says the stela tells people that "the king protects. Through his ritual body sacrifice he ensures water and plant growth."

In *Kumix*, Julián López García (2010) discusses contemporary rituals of reciprocity and supplication for rain among the Maya-Chorti.[13] Summer 2012 was the Great Drought, as in parts of eastern Guatemala some 80% of the crops were lost. Drought in the US Midwest filled my mom's e-mails about her slowly dying garden *and* the Guatemalan newspapers. That's because in 2012 lack of rain in Iowa is big news in Guatemala, thanks to "free trade."[14] By forcing open local markets to US corn, local production is undermined, creating dependence on foreign grains, which cost three to four times more this year than last. Aniseto, the antimining activist in San Miguel, warned that these are the very rituals that will do no good once the mining companies come in—or as weird weather takes hold.

Ritual

Stela F, dedicated March 13, 761, where the long count dates are the lovely "head" numbers rather than bars and dots, has beautiful lunation records, which, Nikolai explained, are in every inscription that emplaces Maya in time. Lunar glyphs are part of all long counts and involve very complex calculations to figure out ecliptic nodes (the points in the trajectories of the

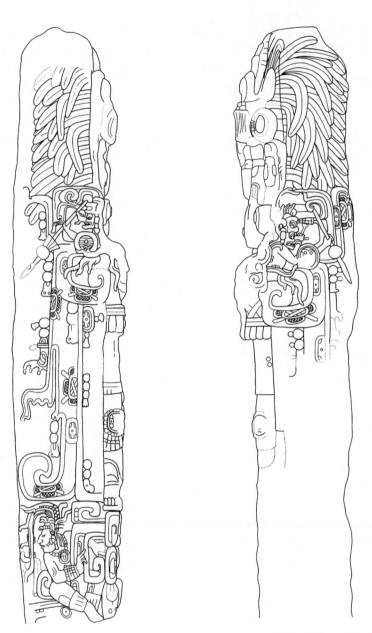

7.6 K'awil brandishing a shield and spear. He appears just under the feathered head-dress, on the shoulders of K'ahk' Tiliw, ruler of Quiriguá. Below him are glyphic representations of the sacred fluid of divine energy. Stela H. Matthew Looper. Used with kind permission.

sun and moon where they cross), which are important because the Maya knew that every five or six lunations an eclipse happens somewhere. The Dresden codex, which is basically an almanac, and the murals of Xultún, revealed in May 2012, are both lunar calculation devices based on multiples of 177 and 178 (and also for calculating Venusian cycles of 580 days and Martian of 780).[15] Nikolai reminded us that the Maya, unlike many highly regarded ancients (e.g., the Greeks), understood that Venus was a planet and not a star that did strange things (sometimes appearing at evening, then in the morning). Nikolai went on: "This shows there is astronomical justification for the sacred calendar of 260 days. There's enormous symmetry and we are just beginning to understand this, but the Maya knew!" On a tiny, exquisitely incised bone found at Tikal, there are counts in periods so large that one iteration takes us outside historic time, to March 13, 5661, and then December 14, 9897, "and they have calculated the day," Nikolai said. "Even today there are barely computers that are as intelligent as the *sacerdotes mayas*."

The stela itself recounts a ritual where drops were scattered. We don't know if they were blood or incense, but sacrifice was made. The dates and distance numbers on the stone connect what happened that day to an occurrence $19 \times 460,000,000$ cycles ago, which (I think I have the numbers right) is 875,520,000,000 years in the past and falls on the day 1 Ajaw in the month 13 Mol. Nikolai said, "K'ahk Tiliw is saying he is an eternal king, that the spirit of the predecessors is still with us.[16] It projects biographies into enormous time. The date is a very, very long time back. I did the calculations with a computer and it took a long time but *they* got actual dates, in a time period before the Big Bang. How did they do it?? We don't know. But you can do it, too, and I suggest you try, because then you will understand it better."

Then he asked, "Why is it important, this so far away date?" And a woman answered, "It's *memoria histórica*. These are their ancestors." "Yes," Nikolai said, "He is saying, 'Here where I am, on this Black Sea and on this same day, the gods celebrated and now I do, too.'"

Three days later we also stood in the Quiriguá plaza, the Black Sea,[17] in the very hot, very humid eastern lowlands, surrounded by a United Fruit Company banana plantation. And we did ceremonies, too. As he had at the beginning of the workshop, now in that bright hot plaza, Don Cristobal, Kaqchikel from Tecpán, wrapped his head in a red cloth (a glyph for ascension is a knot tied around the head, meaning "it is tied"—it being a

7.7 Nikolai Grube decrypting at Quiriguá with workshop participants. Author's photo.

7.8 Quiriguá stela and students. Author's photo.

headpiece, an item so important that, like kula shells or crown jewels, each had a name). Then he lit candles and incense and addressed the four directions, asking for energy to be focused on the task at hand and enjoining us, as did all the organizers, to work hard and remember. This learning is not just for us but is given in order to be shared.[18]

And there, in Quiriguá, we encountered Chahk again. Not at the arm's length of representation, safe on the screen in wan projected light or even, amazingly, in the original stones but in sky-filling masses of living, exuberant, terrifying light. We tried to huddle under the palm frond roofs protecting the stelae but were soon soaked through, awestruck by the crashes of noise, sluicing rainfall, overwhelmed and subjected, sutured by the punctum of the lightning's power. Not literally, thankfully, but the highland Maya with whom I'd descended that morning (leaving Antigua at 4 AM in a cramped Bluebird schoolbus) had never experienced anything like the storm. It continued through the night, rolling thunder and great startling flashes of light that held the sky on the same elongated timescale as earthquake seconds. It was the subject of every breakfast conversation. "Without being here, living through that storm, *Dios mio!!*" María Elena said, "I would never have understood! Now I see why Chahk! Why the king took his name! His hammer, his spear, the weapons. It would have stayed on paper, not in my body. I felt it in my blood, in my organs." Electrifying.

The Rabinal Mysteries

Presence

In 2008 I had the good fortune to accompany Maury Hutcheson to Rabinal, Baja Verapaz where he had worked for over ten years. We went for the June festival of San Pedro and he introduced me to people preparing for the dances, holding a velada (vigil) for the saints' images, and for the masks to be worn, with people eating good food and drinking strong liquor (the wooden masks imbibe as well), and with music accompanying them through the night. Maury explained that each mask carries within it the *nawal*, or spiritual co-essence, of all the performers who have worn the mask and performed in its role. The *antepasados*, who are the dead, "the ones who have gone before," will arrive, if properly greeted with candles and incense, to inhabit the masks and perform once more.

Maury also took me to the nearby hamlet of Xococ (yes, that Xococ) to visit the musicians and dance master for one of the traditional dances performed at the feast of San Pedro, a "twin" to the feast of San Pablo in January (twins are central to the Popol Vuh, and in both festivals the images of Peter and Paul accompany one another). Like Manuel and Francisco with the Dance of the Conquest in Joyabaj, the patron or dance master is responsible for organizing rehearsals and performances, and paying for drinks, food, candles, costume rental, travel, etc. These duties bring respect and authority, but are very expensive and considered heavy burdens, a sacrifice. Like ritual specialists everywhere, he negotiates the liminal spaces between the everyday world and that of the spirits/ancestors. It is believed in Xococ, as it was in Quiriguá, that the past isn't over, that the dead remain with us, intervening in our affairs.

The first musicians' practice each year is important so that the *antepasados* will know people are initiating the activities. The two musicians began to play variations on a haunting tune, one each for each mask's character, as day fell slowly into evening. And then our host seemed to go into a trance; without costume or mask, he began to dance in the courtyard. Later he told us, that was when he felt their presence. He lit incense and prayed at his altar and at the doors and windows. Months later, watching Maury's video, I feel anew the charge that seemed to fill the space. At one point he took off the musician's hats, to show respect to the gathering. After the practice we caught a late bus back to Rabinal. Maury said that his friendship and respect for this man had kept him from ever inquiring about the war.

Time Out

Nodes

Before turning to other sites concerned with light, water, presence, loops of time and *memoria histórica*, I'd like to provisionally pull out some of the strands I've been weaving here. One is what Michelle Murphy (2013) calls latency, the sense that there are potential dangers (like toxins) but also powers in places, things, and people. There are also technologies, like ritual processes or workshops, that usually include sacrifice (if only burning a candle, carrying a burden, or putting in the energy or *ganas*), necessary to activate or unleash them. In other words there's a charge—a price—for their use.

7.9 Full body numbers and time periods. Stela D, Quiriguá. Matthew Looper. Used with kind permission.

And quantity is qualified: the Quiriguá stelae show time measured in numbers expressed as heads and even entire bodies embracing (playing with? wrestling?) mythic birds, perhaps the ones from the originary tree that separated the waters from the sky, and here also signifying great expanses of time, like multiple b'aqtun, each 440 of our years.

"Maybe it's the energy of my day," Walter said. Counting the days, as the folks at Magdalena's table do, means keeping track of their passing, their energies, perhaps also their relation to stars and planets, equinox and solstice, times to plant and reap, via calculations that move forward and backward in time and draw on practices buried deep in the past that, even so, challenge today's high-tech (and energy-sucking) computers to keep up. And perhaps, just as the glyphs ascribe qualities, or personality, to number, these are ways to qualify, or charge with value, people who have traditionally not counted.

And now, for a bit of physics:

What Is the Function of a Resistor?
Answer: Electrical resistance describes how an electrical conductor (a wire) opposes the flow of an electrical current (flow of electrons). To overcome this opposition a voltage (an energy) must be dropped (used) across the conductor (wire). Resistance can be described by Ohm's law:

$R = V/I$ (resistance = voltage/current) (resistance measured in ohms) where
voltage [V] = energy lost across a component (measured in volts)
current [I] = the charge (electrons) flowing through a component (measured in amps)

Electrical resistance can be thought of as sticking your hand out a car window. The faster [current] you drive, the harder the wind presses [resistance] against your hand and therefore it takes more energy [voltage] to hold your hand steady. When trying to overcome electrical resistance, the electrical energy lost is turned into heat. This is how the elements of a household stove, toaster, and fan heater work. Because of the vacuum in a lightbulb, the electrical energy is instead turned into light. It can be seen that the electrical resistance plays a large role in modern life. Wiki-Answers.[19]

Report from the People's Tribunal

> The settlers' town . . . is a brightly lit town . . . a well-fed town, an easygoing
> town; its belly is always full of good things.
> —Frantz Fanon

> To conceive beyond reality, to desire beyond adequacy, to create beyond need.
> —Maya Deren

It seemed my harried, stressed (and expensive) attempt to fight Guatemala City morning traffic and get to the hallowed USAC National University campus on time was useless. While much of the campus had been turned over to the Third Social Forum of the Americas, with Guatemala and USAC chosen for their historic commitments to social and economic justice (and correspondingly long lists of martyrs), apparently some right-wingers had infiltrated the university hierarchy enough to keep the building where the people's tribunal was supposed to be held tightly locked up.

This was my first social forum, a regional submeeting of the World Social Forum, founded in 2001 to counter its great capitalist rival, the World Economic Forum of Davos, Switzerland. It was a boisterous, serious, artistic, intense convergence of activists, NGO-ists, and alter-globalizers of many colors, stripes, and tendencies. This is the great in-gathering for optimists of the will, and its creed is "Another World Is Possible." The 2008 meeting bridged October 8, Day of the Heroic Guerrillero, commemorating Che Guevara's capture and assassination, and October 12, formerly known as Columbus Day and now (at least here) a celebration of indigenous resistance (Becker 2008). At the entrance was an enormous altar, and the forum was inaugurated with indigenous spiritual practices drawn from across the continent.

The schedule was overwhelming, with speakers, panels, performances, workshops, films, shopping, installations, presentations, and roundtables addressing human rights, revolution, sexual diversity, youth, feminism, impunity, mining, food sovereignty, *buen vivir*, racism, education, alternative media, militarization, and the criminalization of peaceful protest—a real smorgasbord! This is where I first realized the depth and breadth of the *consulta* movements. An entire building was dedicated to *memoria histórica*, a huge tent accommodated Via Campesina, and a large auditorium was dedicated to transhemispheric indigenous issues.

But today I'd ducked out of translating so I could hear the testimonies of the Permanent People's Tribunal. Created in 1979 as the successor to the Russell Tribunals on Vietnam (1966–67), the January 1983 Madrid Tribunal on Guatemala was a watershed event, culminating in charges of war crimes handed down by highly regarded jurists (though not legally binding; Jonas et al. 1984). It was thrilling to be present at a second one on (and in!) Guatemala. Yet here we were, stuck outside, missing all the other cool stuff, while the frustrated and embarrassed student hosts tried to go over the head of the recalcitrant dean. Of course, this increased my anticipation. If all the other radicalness was given free rein, this must be really intense. We finally got inside, through the tech setup and florid introductions, and I settled in for the unveiling of truths. To my utter surprise people were complaining about their electric bills.

I sat through it, kind of disbelieving, waiting for the "real politics" to emerge. The bills were surely high, especially for poor indigenous peasants, but given the disappearance, torture, forced displacement, and violent suppression of antimining and other cultural-ecological movements being addressed elsewhere, it seemed, I admit, a bit ridiculous. These folks had only recently been electrified. Was it really a "human right?" Getting bored and a bit nasty, I reflected on the Forum's emphasis on indigenous issues and how many of the talks I'd translated deployed discourses of the sustainable, Mother Earth–centered, alter-imaginings of originary peoples. So how did Mayan denunciations of bureaucratic malfeasance, overcharging, and anger that their radios and refrigerators were frizzling from power surges mesh with these "Other Worldly" discussions? Even economist Luis Solano's careful diagramming of connections among Guatemalan elites, transnational capital, and the enormous profits made from privatizing the National Electrification Institute (INDE) just didn't seem as galvanizing as what I'd heard elsewhere. The pain and anger were clearly sincere, especially at the state's violent responses to attempts to negotiate with Unión Fenosa, the Spanish company that now owned most of the grid (now part of Gas Natural). But in terms of first and second orders of human rights, I was not sure where listening to *rancheras* on your radio, or even—lectorphile that I am—reading at night without a candle fit.

It's taken me a couple years to realize that fundamental rights are indeed at stake. That's partly because infrastructure is so radical (in the sense of root). Electricity—its generation, transmission, and adequate delivery— like the waterworks (and now the Internet), is a "public utility." Its usefulness is unquestionable, it is public because everyone needs it, and being expensive to set up, everyone contributes. Pondering my disgruntlement forced me to acknowledge how stupid privilege makes me. A magical disappearing act is performed by infrastructuring something so world-transforming as electricity, the lifeblood of the Second Industrial Revolution. Franklin, Edison, Ohm, Maxwell, Faraday, Tesla, the 1892 Colombian Exhibition, AC/DC, the TVA, Hetch Hetchy, server farms, all discreetly hidden away in the absolutely banal everydayness (at least in the global north) of flicking the switch.

In 1851 Charles Babbage dreamed of "a small motive power—ranging perhaps from the force of half a man to that of two horses." Now compare the "conversion efficiency" of food to human or animal labor versus coal, water, or wind to electricity so that now this other actant, harnessing formerly impossible quantities of body powers, projects the Powerpoint®, shoulders the burdens, computes the calendar calculations. Electricity transformed these forms of "equivalence." Now it is the precious fluid, beautiful liquid, flowing in currents, and dependent in turn on another flow: money/currency.

Amazed by its possibilities, Lenin said, "Communism is the soviets plus electrification of the country." Yet shock doctrines (electricity again!) have mostly impossibilitized such communal governance, and we are left with the world of the Google night map revealing in sharp dark and light how the distribution of electricity isomorphs with the geographies of planetary inequality. In Guatemala, rural indigenous areas have the least coverage yet are, like Río Negro, the most affected by hydroelectric projects.

Shockingly, given that it's one of the poorest countries in the hemisphere, Guatemalans pay the highest electricity costs in Central America and the third highest on the continent. And the service is generally terrible. It's rare that a week goes by without a blackout.[20] Joined with random power surges, they ruin people's *electrodomésticos* (home appliances), turning the sweet allure of light, warmth, and connection into the crushing loss of hard-earned apparatuses, most especially those (expensive) technologies whose phylogeny condenses an entire ontogeny of the arduous steps toward the modern and cosmopolitan: the radios, televisions, cell phones, and computers, with their invisible tendrils reaching out into the ether. In a hamlet like Patzulá, electrified only in the past two years, they mark a collapsed temporality and emerging class distinctions, as some households boast only a radio and one lightbulb, others sport cell phones, and now Encarnación and Juan's family has a full-spectrum entertainment center.

Such losses enrage people and galvanize increasingly militant activism against the energy companies and complicit governments, including street protests, payment strikes, and legal cases, in addition to the complaints taken to the Tribunal. On three occasions (Vienna 2006, Lima 2008, and Madrid 2010) Tribunals found that restrictions on access to electric energy service *do* violate human rights through unapproved and frequent rate hikes (in Guatemala totaling over 340% over ten years); charges for services never provided; fees for nonexistent infractions; bills arriving too late to be paid (which must be done in person, often requiring expensive and time-consuming travel); electrocution caused by substandard parts; and abuses connected to electricity meters, including faulty readings and charges based on computer calculations that frequently calibrate 20% or more over actual consumption. Finally, there is no indemnification for human or commercial losses due to faulty service (Tribunal 2008, 31–52). I draw your attention to the role of the electricity meters (*contadores*), betraying numbers' great promises of exact calculations, objective assessment, and trustworthiness. Claimants reveal such allures as cloaking devices for those little high-tech parasites tightly attached to each person's house, silently sapping the family's tenuous stock of quetzals.

People's resistance to these abuses is met with violence, both overt and structural. The Tribunal found that "European Union transnational corporations can proceed undisturbed thanks to the complicity and cooperation of local and national governments. All this can occur in spite of popular dissent since those same governments do not hesitate to . . . crack down on environmental, social and labour movements. All of these violations combined with the erratic behaviour of financial markets and the unbearable burden of the foreign debt result in a major attack on economic and social rights to development" (Tribunal 2008). At a shareholder's meeting in 2008 Unión Fenosa announced profits of five billion quetzals, 91% of which went to the company, 9% to a coterie of wealthy Guatemalan investors.

The Tribunal's resolutions emphasize that privatized property is theft. Public utilities are directly paid for by taxpayers, who see none of the profit from the intensely corrupt selloffs.[21] But in many areas of Guatemala it was not a "generalized" public that developed the "utility" but residents themselves who raised money and provided free labor to build local hydroelectric generators. For example, the people of San Pablo Tacaná, San Marcos, began to organize for electrification in 1979. Interrupted by the war, they succeeded twenty years later, with Q700,000.00 invested by the community. But the generator was connected to INDE's network and therefore (apparently unbeknownst to the community) part of the 1998 privatization deal. To their shock, company workers suddenly showed up accusing the inhabitants of stealing electricity and demanded Q180,000 or they would be cut off. "This is when the community realized their right to property had been violated," and they sued—an expensive thing to do (Tribunal 2008, 71). They won, but the company appealed (similar to Goldcorp fighting the Sipakapa consulta). The community won again, and it was appealed, until the case reached the (notoriously corrupt) Supreme Court, where, people suspect, payoffs led to a ruling favorable to the company.[22]

Despite the high rates, electricity service for small usuarios is not Unión Fenosa's priority. The Tribunal clearly shows that current plans for damming almost every major Guatemalan river are to serve elite and transnational capital invested in maquila production and resource extraction—which suck up both electricity and water—and for export. Antimining activist Crisanta Perez of Agel confronted exactly this when Goldcorp summarily seized a chunk of her already tiny corn plot to erect a large post supporting high-tension wires. She provoked a short circuit, cutting power to the mine. But she was responsible for property damage (not the mine) and for the great heresy: being "against development." As Aniseto mentioned in his speech, she spent months in hiding to avoid arrest.[23] Guatemalan people will be displaced, tiny landholdings further constricted, and ecosystems increasingly fragmented and degraded, but the electricity generated is not for them.

Now, this is a rather banal story of how neoliberalism and subpriming work—somehow, amazingly, extracting surplus out of people and places where there would seem to be none. What seems almost as miraculous, though, is the light these resisters/resistors are throwing on the magical disappearing act of flicking the switch. They (smarter than the disgruntled gringa) understand this as a collective dispossession and insist they, too, are entitled to a dignified life, including access to energy and water, no more separable now than when Chahk was first carved in stone.

To circle back to the beginning of this book, light, illumination, warmth, power—like Dr. Frankenstein's electrical capacities to bring back the dead— are metaphors for human rights struggles: opening archives, exhuming bodies, revealing responsibilities, "charging" evildoers with their crimes, demanding repair. But they are also material experiences, emotionally and electrically charged: no longer a property belonging only to the sun or those higher up in Maslow's hierarchy. These resistors insist that the thrill of thwarting darkness, as our feeble human hands grasp such power for our own, pertains to us all. The poetic and the pragmatic intertwine, coming out of darkness, backwardness, into the light of progress, children enlightened, a nation moving toward the future and prosperity. The folks I was rolling my eyes at are rejecting futilitarianism and are not content with "expectations of modernity." They demand full citizenship in the world promise of electricity's flow and boundlessness. The well-lit town and the full belly are for settlers and natives (Fanon 1968, 39). We all have the right "to desire beyond adequacy" (Deren 1958, 138; also Martínez 2010).

The Mirror at the Center, Lightning's Serpentine Spear

It can be seen the electrical resistance plays a large role in modern life.

In Chapter 6, I told you about Lolita Chávez and the Santa Cruz del Quiché *consulta* against megaprojects like mining and hydroelectric dams. They won, handily, but suffered a setback in late 2011, when the right-wing military Patriotic Party won the mayor's office and the national election. Public officials began to denounce Chávez and the K'iche' People's Council (CPK), even organizing an astroturf demonstration in the town square saying that terrible electric service and ruined *electrodomésticos* were Lolita's fault, for rejecting "development." On June 12, 2012, José Tavico Tzunun, a member of CPK, was shot and killed outside his home after receiving a number of death threats (no one has been arrested), and on July 4 a lynch mob waylaid a bus carrying Lolita and women members of the CPK shouting "Mayor Castro is in charge here and we're here to do the mayor's justice." Several people were injured, but the quick-thinking bus driver got them away. The attackers then filed a suit against Lolita claiming she victimized them.

Yet on July 19, in one of those serendipitous acts of justice carried out by a nonhuman actant, Mayor Castro accidently touched a live wire that electrocuted him, throwing him off a roof to his death. Lolita said his followers tried to blame her for his death, as proof she is a witch. She laughed, "You know, it was K'an, the day of the snake!"

K'ahk' Tiliw's stelae (in which he holds a double-headed serpent bar) proclaim a temporally looping connection to Chahk, who forced open the sky and earth to release water, power, maize. We don't know how the Maya who quarried and carried (without wheels or beasts of burden, remember) those stones understood that relation, expressed, at least by the king's lapidary PR, as reciprocal. He literally bled "for" them. The Guatemalans who are carrying the burden of privatized electricity and export-oriented hydroelectric projects—that will fuck them as surely as they did the people of Río Negro—are quite clear that sacrifice is involved, but it is not reciprocal. Some can be calculated, metered, credited, debited. Yet some calculations are more complicated, almost as difficult as counting back to a date before the Big Bang.

The Rabinal Mysteries

Calculations

When Juan and Alma dropped us off at the dam for our ride back to Cobán, my nephew Quinn, almost shaking, said about the people of Xococ, the ones who helped carry out the massacre, "I hate them! I hate them!" And I did, too. But going back to read the CEH report, I found that Xococ was also subjected to military repression, with the army assassinating eighteen people in fall 1981. "In February 1982 a group of armed men, possibly guerrillas, burned the market of Xococ, killing five persons. As a result of the fact that the Army identified the peasants of Río Negro with the guerrillas, residents of Xococ broke trade relations with Río Negro and declared them their enemies." People from Río Negro protested that the market was as important to them as for Xococ, so why would they burn it? But an inhabitant of Xococ said: "When the war began, friendship was lost." Rabinal's Catholic priest said, "There was a pact so that the people of Xococ were to cooperate fully, in exchange for not being killed" (CEH Annex 1, Ch. 10, 7; Rodriguez 2007). Fear and hatred, instead of trade goods and friendship, now ran back and forth across that mountain as the Chixoy dam polarized what were once cordial relations. It now produces about 15% of the electricity used in Guatemala. The highest electricity prices in the hemisphere should include these costs (and the fifty years the Xococ patrollers are serving for their crimes "in exchange for not being killed"), even if they are not itemized on the bill. Xococ, at least, has electricity.

Lodestone: Magnetite possessing polarity, something that strongly attracts.

I think I had some inkling of the allure of "the Maya" from getting hooked early on *National Geographic*, but it really hit me when I walked into the Antigua Camino Real Hotel in June 2012 and noticed the Grupo Golan Security Guards along the drive, clustered at the door, stationed on the staircase down to the conference center, and even positioned four along each wall for "Mayan Prophecies? 13 B'aktun: The Last Days of the Mayan Long Count®, Sixth World Maya Archaeological Conference 2012." (This was in addition to the transport police and a special forces combined police/military patrol stationed outside the hotel.) I don't know who, but somebodies important were in attendance.[24]

Costing Q100 a day for the general public, the three-day conference was sponsored by Pacunam, the Foundation for Maya Culture and Natural Heritage, a "corporate partner" with Progreso Cements, Walmart Central America, Citibank, Blue Oil, the sugar refineries Pantaleón and Madre Tierra, and DISAGRO (fertilizers and agrochemicals). This lineup is pretty much a perp walk of the Guatemalan elite's family-capital nexus, many of whose members are currently locked in ferocious battles over land and labor rights and contaminating extractive industries with the popular movement (Solano 2009, 2013). Many consider them the "intellectual authors" of the war crimes of the 1980s. Such issues went unmentioned in their glossy publication detailing how they were saving the "awe-inspiring temples of the Maya world" and "the heart of one of the last and best preserved rainforests in the Americas." Lush photos of archaeological sites, charismatic megafauna like jaguars, Classic Maya artwork and glyphs, and hardworking archaeologists illustrate what is in danger. The threat comes from looting, poaching, and "encroachment through high-profile human activity," including wildcat loggers, squatters, and drug traffickers. Oil drilling and the mass deforestation and human displacement caused by sugarcane and African palm plantations—surely the greatest threats to the Petén area and objects of intensive investment for many of these families—are not mentioned (ISLA 2012).[25] (To be clear, I'm not condemning anyone who takes their money. My own funding is equally impure.) It's shored up by a celebrity endorsement from Mel Gibson and that historically heavy hand on Guatemala's political scales, USAID. It's a brilliant combination of green- and red-washing, simultaneously saving the forest, the ruins (once painted red), and indigenous people.

Presenters discussed 2012, emphasizing it was not the end of time itself! (You get by now that a b'aqtun is a cycle of 20 k'atunes—some 144,000 days, right?) It is a new period following the Maya long count, but it's just turning the page of a calendar. They described some very cool stuff:[26] pollen samples showing maize domesticated by 2000 BC; the first evidence of the long count calendar from 36 BC; and why Mayan time is counted by tuun, or stone, also a period of 360 days. Sometimes called flowers from the center (or earth), stones are powerful, eternal. People build homes from them, mimicking caves, which are related to Chahk (who opened the earth, remember) and thereby to rains and corn. The stones condense the beginning of time, when/re deities set the three stones for the world hearth and lit the fire that brings life to creation. Glowing in Orion's belt, base for the great tree of the Milky Way, when earthly beings put up a stela made of stone, it loops time, re-creating creation.[27] Stone is also the site of sacrifice and, far more quotidian, where corn (which is people in Mayan cosmology) is ground by women to make tortillas.

Several weeks later, at the little museum in New Río Negro, surrounded by photographs of the dead mounted on a petate, I saw grinding stones, some from the pre-Columbian site of Cauinal and others left from the 1982 massacre. They looked exactly alike.

Still

A member of the Arbenz government of the early 1950s, Alfonso Bauer Paiz, reputedly said "I care more about living Indians than dead ones" to justify building affordable housing over the ruins of Kaminaljuyú in Guatemala City. This seems like a dig at just the sorts of fascinated Golan-protected, Pacunam-supporting elites attracted, as I was, to the conference's lodestone but who may not care much about actually existing Maya. While presenters insisted that much of what they described was "still" living knowledge (though, as I have been gently reminded by Mayan activists, the word assumes an unavoidable demise), it took Alejandro Garay, USAC student and member of Sak Chuwen, to put it bluntly, "the Maya are not reliquaries of the past. Many here today call ourselves Maya. We still count."

Out of an audience of over a hundred, however, I saw only two women in traje and a few men who seemed to identify as Maya. One of them, Victor

Chitay, kindly offered me a ride. He gave me his card and told me to look up his website, called "awakening of consciousness/conscience, school of the tiger." As we walked to his car he said, "When they spoke of the Wayab, we do that, fast, give penance on certain days," and he told me about his herbal medicine store in Guatemala City. His website offers weekly Mayan ceremonies (held at 10 AM every Sunday), training to become a Mayan priest, and Mayan weddings and baptisms. When we got to his car, it was a Beemer.

It's also where I met Julio Cochoy, who became interested in Mayan things through his work on the DIY truth commission report in his town, Santa Lucía, which "hadn't counted" in the REMHI or CEH. He'd especially liked the talk by Dr. Ruud van Akkeren on a guardian of the *inframundo*, described in the *Popol Vuh* as having an undefined body consisting of thirteen sticks tied in a bundle. Made from the wood of the *tz'ite* tree, whose seeds are used for divining, it fuels the fire into which the Hero Twins of the epic throw themselves, giving birth to the sun. Van Akkeren said, "This guardian is fire, that is his substance, and he must be greeted with cigars and candles. And he is still with us, as Maximón." Julio, who grew up near a town with a strong cult for this fallen saint, sometimes identified with Judas (and who actually smokes the cigars brought in offering!), said, "My father used to call him *Mam abuelo atado* (tied up respected grandfather),[28] just like the talk! It made me realize that maybe it is degenerated, but the knowledge is still there!"

He told me his cousin was killed in 1979, then his uncle ("he was left cut open, like a butchered pig, his guts all hanging out"), and then his mother's entire family was massacred in 1981. He managed to complete a degree from USAC in economics but felt he hadn't really escaped what had happened. "My healing (*saneamiento*) was talking, talking, telling the stories," and that's when he decided, in the mid-2000s, to help gather testimonies. At first people closed the door. "*Odio, temor, temor, odio*, there was so much fear and so much hatred. It was POISON. But little by little people opened up, beginning with my family, then others, until we had thirty-six testimonials, all taped, mostly of widows." He was the one who told me about the woman who had also found healing through her stories and through the reparations check she placed on her altar. Julio said that it was through her that he became interested in Mayan spirituality. His dad, an alcoholic, had converted to Protestantism. "He cut our family off entirely from the Maya." But Julio began studying, going to ceremonies, attending workshops. He said, "I've even seen Rigoberta Menchú at the Wayab ceremonies. I was surprised, but it was good to see her there. She has suffered so much! I don't think her family was Maya either, they were Catholic Action, church purifiers." He laughed again, "Just like the Protestants, they see us as Satan, as demons, but it's part of our *saneamiento*. It's important for us. Slowly, I'm coming back."

So I'm also trying to think about "the Maya" via the weird looping of Classic and Current, as a *source* of power. Like an electric current (and currency, which isn't always "money") they charge the elites (and other folks) sitting in those conferences, where men and women of science prove, beyond a shadow of a doubt, that those people counted. Some may, as Iyaxel Cojtí said, deny connections to living Maya, who are themselves, of course, sources of power via superadequation: both their bodily efforts (even as their calorie conversion power is threatened by drought) and their money, extracted through Omnilife, Mayan pyramid schemes, electric bills, and other charges. But when people learn to defend themselves—say, through the Glyph workshops—they can contest that, too. Knowledge and practice, archaeology and spirituality, also charge people like Victor and Julio, helping one accrue wealth and helping the other to *sanear*. Like electricity, visible mostly through its effects, these are not easy to differentiate from the "material."

In telling you these stories, I'm not saying that the people in Río Negro or Xococ or in the glyph and archaeology courses or those petitioning the Tribunal and running the *consultas* are all the same people (although some of them are). In bundling these stories, linking these nodes, I want to suggest crosscutting currents, energetic transfers, and looping timescales among sets of activities, including knowledge production, that in turn relate to light and water. These, in turn, raise questions about sacrifice and understandings of what "belongs" to whom. In some ways I'm making an extremely simple point, that even if they are treated as such, these lodestones, these sources of power—water, light, "decodings," people—are not "resources" in any easily controllable way. (They are not simply resistant, either.) And, again, very simply, that in addition to ritual, ordinary and extraordinary violences are deployed to release those energies.

A Postcard from Río Negro

Loss, Repair?

> They finger death at their gloves' end as they piece and repiece the living wires.
> —Rudyard Kipling, "Sons of Martha" (1907)

What I remember most about New Río Negro—more powerful even than sitting at Pak'oxom on the top of the mountain, just near the massacre site, and having Juan's words as he described that awe-full day move through my body as I translated them for Quinn—was how Juan touched the plants. The careful way he brushed them aside as we walked or, explaining their properties, how he would cradle them in his palm, firmly, but almost a caress, saying which ones were used as food or medicine when people lived in the mountains, escaping the soldiers. There is a glyph on the stela at Quiriguá of a hand holding a fish, gently, almost stroking it. It means "to conjure."

Juan lost almost everything that day. Home, mother, clothes, his town. His father was already dead, killed in Xococ the month before with 54 other men and 19 women. Seventy women, 1 elderly man, and 107 children were killed in Río Negro, and those who fled to nearby Agua Fria were also killed, along with their hosts, 97 in all. Ten communities in the river basin were destroyed by massacre, with over 5,000 people killed in the Rabinal area. For several years Juan was enslaved by the man who legally adopted him, until an aunt, forcibly resettled in Pacux, a militarized hamlet on the edge of Rabinal, realized he was still alive. With the war still on and with no resources, I don't know how she took on the army allies in Xococ, but she did and—though they fought her, saying the children were now legally theirs— she won. But it was a harsh victory, as she and her husband could barely feed their own children. There was no land for farming or even for gathering firewood. In a town full of refugees everyone was struggling to survive. Starving, only twelve years old, Juan began to migrate to the coast. At sixteen he was forcibly recruited into the army. He was terrified they would kill him when they learned where he was from, but mostly they were incredulous: "But we finished everyone off there!" he said they said. "They were all guerrillas!" He was sent to the Ixcán—like Rabinal, a place where terrible things happened.

With similar tenacity to Juan's aunt, survivors and their allies carried out one of the first exhumations at Pak'oxom, even before the war was over (EAFG 1995). As Julio said, Rabinal and Río Negro were some of the first

u–TZAK–AW
s/he conjured

7.10 To conjure. Mark Van Stone. Used with kind permission.

to receive reparations from the National Program. They have also presented their case to the Inter-American Court for Human Rights and continue to pressure for more adequate restitution from the state and INDE, as well as the banks who funded the dam. In 2005 they commissioned the *Chixoy Dam Legacy Issues Study*, as an accounting for use in their negotiations. It came to five volumes. In addition to counting the dead it echoes Rosalina Tuyuc as it recounts:

> hydroelectric energy development occurred at the cost of land, lives, and livelihood . . . and considerable profits were achieved. Inter-American Development Bank (IADB) reports revalued interest income of US$139,628,376.29 from Chixoy Project loans. . . . No one can . . . undo the violence . . . dam-displaced communities cannot go home. No amount of money can move these communities back in time to a "before-dam" river valley and the associated way of life. Governments and financing institutions can, however . . . take action to restore the dignity, identity, and integrity of previously self-sufficient communities. (Johnston 2005, 6–7)

7.11 Chixoy hydroelectric dam. Author's photo.

In 2010 the government formally accepted the reparation plan to provide additional compensation of $154 million, but the Patriotic Party has so far refused to disburse the funds. Ongoing pressure won a major victory, however, when the US appropriations bill for 2014 restricted the State Department from disbursing military aid until steps were taken to implement the plan. It also instructed US directors of the World Bank and IADB to pressure for implementation.[29]

At the massacre site on Pak'oxom, Juan spoke of how waves of loss extended from that place through so many years. "If I had my father, my mother, I could have studied. I would have learned to read and write. I would have a real job. This is what they took from me. No money can repair that." And later he said again, "My eyes are blind. I can't read or write. I can't get a real job, in an office. I could earn 3,000 a month. But all that is lost." This metaphor of light (not blindness) describes a painful if phantasmic loss of a "modern" life. A life of ease, of salaried labor, the kind of life promised by vitamins, by finance, and by electrification.

In the back of the pickup truck, crossing the dam after we left Juan and Alma at the boat, Quinn said, "I hope he knows how unhappy people are who work in offices." And a bit later he added, "And he'd never see Alma!" Quinn has seen his kinsmen labor themselves into deep depressions and life-threatening illnesses employed in law, insurance, and accountancy. Raised by a hardworking single dad, he also knows what it means to not see much of a parent. Literally separated in that moment by the terribly material and simultaneously wafer-thin metaphoric divide of the hydroelectric apparatus, I felt I watched these two men contemplate each other's lives across it, calculating happiness and loss, reality, adequacy, and need.

In Río Negro we didn't hear the ambivalence Julio expressed about reparation as money. When asked, Juan and Isabel agreed that it divided some families. "And yes, some people thought it was bad money. But most of us used it to get on our feet again." They used the Q40,000 they received for the loss of his parents to pay for school and buy a cow, which they breed and whose milk we enjoyed with our morning coffee. Yet what would *saneamiento* entail in the Chixoy River basin? Even as sixteen families have remade a different Río Negro, "no one can go back in time" to an integral self-sufficient community. And that's in part because they're in that same terrifying lag time of compound interest. Just as debt grows even when you make your payments, the sacrifice and struggle to force recognition and reparation are always already behind. In part because what counted as self-sufficiency and adequacy in the 1970s has been transformed. School fees, taxes, fertilizer, pesticides, gasoline, all require currency.

Costumbre

Juan has told his story many, many times, to testimony takers from the church, to the UN and the forensic anthropology teams, to solidarity visitors and anthropologists, to judges and reparations program workers—and now he partly makes a living from it. Yet he still cried, with us, at the massacre site. The bodies have all been exhumed and are buried together in the Rabinal cemetery under large, impressive monuments detailing the history of violence. A Catholic altar was placed at Pak'oxom for anniversary commemorations and, more recently, a Mayan one. Bits of bone and clothing still surface when the ground is opened. Juan told us that an elder, Don Andrés, who used to do the cave ceremonies, was bundled up like a ball and thrown off the mountain by the soldiers that day. He was very old, in his nineties, but they said he did witchcraft: he could prophesy army movements. The soldiers said, "You are humans during the day but animals at night. You are all *brujos* here (witches)." Unlike in Xococ, which was *puro costumbre* (all traditional religion), most people in Río Negro were heavily involved with Catholic Action, and Don Andrés had not trained a replacement. Now Mayan ceremonies are conducted for the anniversaries but by someone brought in from Rabinal. "The church is not so against it anymore," Juan said as we followed him up the mountain, "so we are starting to do it again, a little." (But when I asked if he knew the calendar, he responded a bit sharply. "No! Oh no. We don't know anything about that!")

The land in New Río Negro is not as fertile as the now inundated river bottoms, but Juan's family grows corn, beans, squash, and some fruit. There are fish and, although the hills are heavily deforested, firewood. He relearned how to weave roofing from *petate* material. Though not modern (and therefore disdained by some neighbors), it's cheaper than tin, more comfortable, and "It's important we don't lose the knowledge." The men and boys have started up intervillage *futból* matches and have even won some trophies, proudly displayed in the guesthouse. (They learned to play in the army.)

Pacux, the refugee village they left, has electricity, but trauma, inadequate resources, and overcrowding make social relations quite tense.[30] In New Río Negro people work together on the tourism project, "even Protestants and Catholics," Juan said proudly. "They tried to destroy us and our culture, but we are passing it on. We are working hard so our children know the language. And we tell them what happened here. So they know the stories." They would like more serious excavations in the surrounding post-Classic sites and imagine their little museum replete with treasures to join the "Maya bones," the remains of the ancestors turned up by their hoes, which are already there.

Walking up to the cave on our first day, he spoke of mountain plants and wild animals, like the coral snake, bright red. Then he indicated the little red necklace Alma wore. "That's why some of the Protestants say we should not wear those, it's poison, like a snake. But our *abuelos* did it, it is our *costumbre*. It protects us." On our walks he also spoke about "natural food, what we eat here, it is much better. It is our ancestral food. That's why we are strong. I see the changes in my children, people living in town. *No aguantan*, they can't bear things. The food is not so good. They have to buy everything, things in cans. It's not what we ate before."

As far as I know they aren't eating mountain-grown pansies (*pensée sauvage*), but there is some wild thinking here, a looping of time with *memoria* histórica, a bricollaging presence that endures, a current running alongside the lack of "a real job." A conjuring.

Adequation

> You should know we have told our stories to other people who did not live this. So they can also be guides and tell these stories. But I am Original! I am not a copy. I saw this. For some reason God saved me so I could tell you this story. So you can also tell this story. That is why, I guess.
> —Juan

Knowledge about the Classic Maya is a lodestone that attracts and also gives off enough power to implode time. But even as indigenous people are important players in decoding and, increasingly, transmitting, much of "it" has been activated by outsiders. The same might be said for the electricity that the petitioners to the Tribunal and people in New Río Negro so desire. This is not, of course, an argument for colonialism but a complexification of calculations, a linking of scales, and equi-valuing. When people in Río Negro and throughout Guatemala organized in the 1970s, perhaps it was not explicitly for "communism" in Lenin's sense (although it certainly was for some), but it *was* for the larger promises of electrification to be commonly available. To desire beyond adequacy. But how might we adjust our Comrade's equation for today, when we need to add Gaia and every romantic attitude toward Mother Earth if we are to get the numbers right?

"Adequation"—from the Latin phrase *adequatio intellectus et res*, meaning "the bringing-into-relation of words and things"—has been harder than I expected when I set out to tell you some interesting facts about simple ordinary things like light and water, presence and electricity. About numbers and money, bones, vitamins, pyramids, and mines. And counting. I've found Chahk's wild lightning and "community tourism," parastatal justice systems and glyph workshops, the mysteries of presence and causation and the subpriming state-capital nexus, whose meters somehow always overcharge. All are unsteady but necessary sources of illumination. Felt in our bodies, our blood, our organs. They serve as aletheiometers, drawing on the sense of truth (*aletheia*) as "unconcealment," which is grounded for Heidegger in the moment of bringing out the dead. Entering the *och-bih*, the Milky Way road. In early October 2012, 8 Mayan men were killed and 35 people wounded when the army opened fire on demonstrators protesting increasing electricity rates.

I close this genocide trilogy of books spanning 1985 to now, joining body politics, reckoning, and after-math, knowing that such violences tend to loop through time, less overcome than going latent for spells. They infra-structure global divides between the *dichosa* and survivors but also, through all the numbers and counting, weave patterns we all inhabit, through which we conjure and come to matter. As I finish this book, I will have spent over half my life trying to understand what it means to be a gringa, a white North American, in relation to Guatemala. I have tried to conjure that experience for you, dear reader, and I hope my hands have been as gentle and firm around the lives I have encountered as those glyphs, as Juan's on the plants, as yours, as I pass on this charged story.

Notes

-1. Chapter Minus One

1. The verdict was suspended on a technicality, not on its merits, and the trial is set to reopen in 2015. His sentence, eighty years in prison, points to larger issues around number explored here. It is precise and backed by law but, given his age, also impossible, symbolic, a quantity with qualities that exceed the empirical.

0. Bookkeeping

1. A hedge is what it sounds like, a shrubbery, often used as a boundary, a barrier, or defense—it is supposed to protect you. Like many things exposed to the alchemy of financialization, it has slipped its mooring in the bustling prickly world and become abstract and commodifiable so that "hedge funds" traffic in instruments that are meant to lessen risk, but the more they get dissociated and traded, the more risk they create.

2. The Persian poet Ferdowsi (ca. 997 CE) tells this story about exponential growth. A king wants to reward the inventor of chess, who asks that for the first square of the board he receive one grain of rice, two for the second one, four for the third, and so on. The ruler, mathematically unaware, accepts and is even offended at the low price. But the treasurer takes more than a week to calculate and finally tells the king that all the kingdom's assets are insufficient to fulfill the promise of 18,446,744,073,709,551,615 grains; http://en.wikipedia.org/wiki/Wheat_and _chessboard_problem (accessed Jan. 26, 2014). As Carl Sagan said, "Exponentials can't go on forever, because they will gobble up everything."

3. I contemplated footnoting every person quoted with their story of surviving "common crime" (they *all* have one). I hope that foregoing that tactic in the interest of space and focus does not suggest that such survivals don't count.

4. And "be" better—more frugal, more moral, more, well, white and Protestant.

5. Lochlann Jain (2013) searingly denaturalizes the experiences of "living in prognosis" and the devastating "marginal losses" of inhabiting the disjuncture between the specific and the aggregate of cancer worlds.

6. When Roger Bacon promoted Hindu-Arabic mathematics in the thirteenth century he was condemned to life in prison for dabbling in magic. Venetian merchants, influenced by Fibonacci, did take them up, but it took four hundred years for René Descartes to introduce them to "high society." Luca Pacioli lost his mathematical models when French invaders burned them as satanic. His book *De Viribus quantitates*, "On the Power of Numbers," a compendium of magic and recreational mathematics (think Sudoku), was never published (Gleeson-White 2011, 40, 83). In the mid-sixteenth century the mathematician John Dees vacillated between respected scientist and imprisoned "magician." Based on his interest in indigenous America, Ron Eglash speculates that Dees connected Descartes to the two-axis, fourfold symmetry of Tenochtitlán (2009b).

7. Brian Rotman (1987) elucidates zero's transformative effects, making thinkable new forms of number, vision (as in the vanishing point), money (as paper and futures trading), and subjectivity.

8. Think of the imperial space/time anchoring performed by the institution of Greenwich Mean Time. Which is why, in Joseph Conrad's *Secret Agent*, the "anarchists" target the Greenwich Observatory as the next best thing to "throw[ing] a bomb into pure mathematics" (2010). Guyer says, "African monetary systems were never continuously governed by *any* of the principles that were institutionally established in capitalist Europe and treated as systemic and invariant in economic theory: that is, the value of money, the irreducible purity of number, and the stability of state legal frameworks for property, contract and credit" (2004, 16).

9. Bookkeeping thus helped consolidate a particular *version* of "masculinity."

10. "Race" might be considered another scale or hierarchy of value that is "troped" here, as anti-Semitism undergirds these arduous productions of virtuous profit and disinterested selves so that "good Christians" can safely enter the unsavory realms of "usury."

11. The English word "individual" is a mathematical proposition—the not dividable.

12. Paula Worby reminded me this is fundamentally weird, even if it happens every day through insurance payouts or, in Guatemala's terrifyingly widespread kidnapping market, through ransom.

13. Linking to chapter 7, plans are under way to flood the entire Xingu reserve behind the Belo Monte hydroelectric dam.

14. The story of "a tribe somewhere" that can only count to 3 still has legs, as coverage of the 2004 tsunami in the Andaman Islands used exactly this criterion (only having words for 1 and 2) to index "primitiveness." Linguistic traces of a similar primacy

of 1 and 2 infuse many European languages with words for 3 (and 9) related to "new," "over," or "beyond" (Latin *trans* and *novus*, French *très*). Most of them also only conjugate for 1 (I, Yo), 2 (You, Tu/Ud) and many (Us, Nosotro/as, They, Uds). At the programming level, our most intimate prosthetic the computer, also can't count higher than 2. And BTW, this damaging quote from Dr. Chomsky does not diminish his enormously brave decades-long struggles for justice.

15. Ron Eglash reminds me of heroic "counter counters" (those counting against the grain of quantification as dehumanization): "Ida B. Wells' use of statistics to expose lynching and the invention of the polar coordinate diagram by Florence Nightingale to show deaths due to lack of hospital facilities, and her fight against Galton's (a founder of probability) biological determinism" (personal communication).

16. Two films that draw on this uncanny luminous sequence are Walt Disney's Academy Award nominee *Donald Duck in Mathmagic Land* (1959) and *The Da Vinci Code* (2006).

17. In the film *Infinity* (1996), about physicist Richard Feynman, this "advance" gets an explicit racial marking as the budding genius, showing off for his girlfriend, challenges an abacus-wielding Chinese-American shopkeeper to a calculating duel, which he easily wins using only his head.

18. And as I've been suggesting through the footnotes, the apparent divide between statistics and superstition is no more an anchor than the balance, which depends on imaginary numbers and has to stop time to function.

19. The debates about the ontological primacy of space and time are beyond my scope here, but the staying power of forms for measuring them is impressive. Current Euro-American base-60 timekeeping (minutes to an hour) dates from Sumer and Babylonia, and despite concerted efforts from the state (beginning in 1866!) to bring the United States in line with the "metric system" used by the rest of the world (except for Liberia and Myanmar), most people hold steadfast to their miles, quarts, pounds, and gallons. The powers-of-10 International System of Units (meters and kilograms) is a powerful example of the way a historically and geographically specific system (French) came to seem universal. Many of my non-US friends marvel that the United States remains so "behind" rather than question this "mono-ontological occupation of the planet by the One-World world" (Escobar, n.d.). Until decimalization in 2001, stock trades in the United States were made in increments of one-eighth of a dollar, or 12.5 cents, based on the Spanish real (pieces of eight) which in turn was based in a finger-counting system that didn't count the thumb as a finger. The French language retains traces of base-20 and base-60 counting with 70, *soixante-dix*, 80, *quatre-vingts*, 90, *quatre-vingt-dix*.

20. Studying the history of math (Devlin 2000, Ifrah 1986, Rotman 1987) shows this is not as obvious as it seems!

21. People confirm the presence of herd animals by running through their names (Urton 1997, 53). The rainbow's colors, always appearing in the same order, establish and display the proper order of relations of contiguity, hierarchy, and succession and are considered an inseparable continuum, with the darkest colors understood as "mama," the origin and generation of color, and of the universe in the dark clouds that

intersperse the Milky Way (Urton 1997, 93). Like double entry, such accountings both take for granted and help *produce* ideas about gender.

22. There are many examples of people who can count but decide, really, what's the point? Closs (1986) tells an Inuit folktale of two hunters arguing about whether a wolf or caribou hide has more hairs. To settle it, they decide to count them and become so engrossed they die of hunger.

23. And underfunding—why the 2012 Guatemalan census was canceled (thanks Ted Fischer).

24. Perhaps pointing to a discomfort, similar to the Quechua, with counting and individualizing reproductive units.

25. http://quoteinvestigator.com/2012/11/15/arc-of-universe/ (accessed Feb. 22, 2013).

1. Before and After-Math

From this point on, all definitions are taken from *Webster's Dictionary, Second Edition*.

1. The other three were 1. Maya-Q'anjob'al and Maya-Chuj in Barillas, Nentón, and in San Mateo Ixtatán in the department of Huehuetenango; 2. Maya-Ixil in Nebaj, Cotzal, and Chajul (plaintiffs in the 2013 Ríos Montt case), and 3. Maya-Achi in Rabinal, Baja Verapaz (see chapter 7; CEH, vol. 5, 48–49).

2. While not exactly a census, the Guatemalan government is trying to "modernize" the state-identity document through RENAP (National Registry of Persons). People are suspicious about the information it carries (in a bar code, so unavailable to the carrier) and furious at the process: agonizingly slow and dogged by denunciations of racism (ladinos served first, not accepting Mayan names, problems for people—especially indigenous women—whose original papers were not in order) and worries that it will deny voting rights. Controversial for privatizing a state function, high costs, and risk of putting sensitive information in the hands of a for-profit foreign enterprise, there have been protests and even riots, as when the "F.B.I." descended on Santa Cruz del Quiché.

3. For example, the 1872 British census reports in India that helped consolidate Muslim and Hindu identifications.

4. The quetzal is the Guatemalan currency, named after the lustrous bird; on average, Q7.5 equal US$1.

5. I realize this is highly gendered, which doesn't mean I can just stop feeling it! It's precisely the gendered and raced affect and the not so subtle temporal hierarchy (a backward and a forward embedded in the term "still") that I contest throughout this book. And I'm not a complete arithmophobe (one who fears numbers), considering the range of terrors and fascinations surrounding it: tetraphobia, fear of 4; triskaidekaphobia, fear of 13; the "23 enigma"; and hexakosioihexekontahexaphobia, fear of 666.

6. On number and wonder: Pacioli, the merchant-monk on whose door so much desacralizing is laid, also saw mathematics involved in "almost every human activity,

from astrology, cosmography, and theology, architecture, painting, sculpture, and music, to business, law, and military strategy . . . 'weapons of war are nothing else but geometry and proportion . . . [examining] each one of the other sciences. . . . [T]here is not one which does not use in some way harmony, measure, and proportion' [without which] . . . everything ceases to exist'" (Gleeson-White 73). Beautiful and ingenious instruments developed in the seventeenth century made mathematics, via astronomy, navigation, horology, and mensuration, more accessible. They "enraptured" monarchs and inspired "delight" and "'love'" (Poovey 1998, 139–41). In my "Anthropology of Numbers" class several students said they experience number as colors, what is called number-form synesthesia, and they said it is very beautiful—perhaps like Third's yarrow.

7. I borrow the tech term "2.0," a bit tongue in cheek, to refer to a new version with cumulative changes that attempt to fix earlier glitches. Joe Dumit reminds me that adopting such a version is always a risk, usually undertaken by intrepid tinkerers.

8. A Santiago Atitlán *ajq'ij* was recently killed by a shadowy "civilian patrol" for suspected witchcraft.

9. Western temporalities retain similar embedded histories and sacred traces: days from Norse deities (Thors-day, Wotans/Wednesday); our chaotic months (leap years? really?) from Roman gods and emperors (Janus/January, Julius/July); our base-7 Judeo-Christian Sabbath cycles embedded in everything from antibiotic treatments to the tenure clock. When I describe "traces" in "Western" thoughts and practices, I don't mean to suggest a linear progression in which "they" still retain "our" past but more a multiverse of concurrent space/time understandings and possibilities.

10. Every fifty-two years the two calendars begin again on the same day, which only ever happens on four days, which are the *Mam*, or "year bearers." Intriguingly, Kondratiev cycles of boom and bust also tend to be about fifty-two years.

11. Megan Ybarra reminds me that while *ajq'ij* is a widely used term, it is a K'iche' word (so, like Awakateko for the Chalchitekos, kind of colonial).

12. This displaced coca from a beloved plant companion that shared people's days to an alienated and now highly policed mode of exchange. In the opposite direction, the great, rich Cerro Rico, that sublime deadly place, became representable as a great pyramidal Virgin. Mathematical and dynamic sublime combined, as it/she is prayed to as monstrous provider and withholder of all that is precious and simultaneously addressed in the most intimate ways as mother and lover.

2. The Algebra of Genocide

1. Edelberto Torres-Rivas says the clear ideological filiation of the author does not disqualify him, but it's useful to know that Sabino is a member of the Mont Pelerin Society, as once were Milton Friedman, Karl Popper, Ludwig von Mises, and Friedrich von Hayek, and which has connections to the World Economic Forum. Torres-Rivas accepts that the cardinal numbers may be open to question but not that "95% of the dead were civilians, most killed in the most disgraceful ways" (2009, unpaged).

2. This section's title is borrowed from Houston, Stuart, and Taube (2006).

3. Dr. Temperance Brennan, a character in the television series *Bones*, is a forensic anthropologist, and in the pilot episode she is returning from an exhumation in Guatemala.

4. This essay, written before the exhumations started, is an extraordinary display of what statistical analysis and infraknowledges of state terrorism can do with just a list and brief descriptions. It also illuminates bureaucratic heroism as, amidst such barbarity, the cemetery attendants kept trying to do their job.

5. Although no one mentioned it, low salaries make this a labor of love and political conviction.

6. With techniques developed for victim identification after 9/11, this is "the complete solution for . . . Missing Persons casework . . . uniquely able to make sense of huge quantities of data. . . . [Enabling] *one-to-many* and *many-to-many* searches based on user-defined thresholds for statistics or allele counts . . . 'complex pedigrees' and to integrate non-DNA data." www.genecodesforensics.com (accessed March 4, 2013).

7. To get a sense of the labor of *producing* exactitude, DNA profiling via PCR and STRs uses highly polymorphic regions that have short repeated sequences of DNA, because unrelated people almost certainly have different numbers of repeat units. The STR locations on a chromosome are targeted and amplified, and the resulting fragments separated and detected using electrophoresis, which runs an electric current through to exploit the mobilities with which different-sized molecules pass through the gel. Each STR is polymorphic, but the number of alleles is very small, typically shared by around 5 to 20% of individuals. When multiple STR loci are looked at simultaneously, allele patterns can identify an individual quite accurately. The true power of STR analysis is in its statistical power of discrimination, generating match probabilities of 1 in a quintillion (1×10^{18}) or more. Condensed from Wikipedia DNA profiling (accessed March 4, 2013).

8. I draw on the Quechua for suggestive parallels, not to suggest indigenous knowledges are the same everywhere.

9. "Hundreds" or "thousands," are, of course, numbers and appear factish-y, but for base-10 peoples they are a way to guesstimate while still sounding credible. Closs says "to form the largest units in a given count notions of the superlative or the indefinite are sometimes employed . . . in English 'thousand' is derived from Gothic *pus-hundi*, 'strong hundred,' and 'million' is derived from Italian *milli-one*, 'great thousand'" (1986a, 12). Incredibly, the word *billion* can mean both a thousand million (France, United States) and a million million (Germany, England), while *trillion* in the United States is the fourth power of a thousand (one thousand billion, or 1 followed by twelve os), while in Great Britain it's the third power of a million (1 followed by eighteen os). So maybe getting confused by a brazillion isn't so odd! http://www.etymonline.com/index.php?search=billion (accessed April 1, 2013).

10. I translate "Castilian" directly to acknowledge Spain's linguistic diversity.

11. A time before the global surge in human rights NGOs and in a place, eastern Guatemala, with few journalists or survivor organizations.

12. Given the Guatemalan army's counterinsurgency metaphor of "draining the water from the fish," with the civilian, primarily indigenous population as the water and the guerrilla the fish, there's a certain poetry to this method.

13. Although this was also a response to their inflationary logic, as the United States found in Vietnam.

14. Or even older gendered debts, as Manuel Mayorga told me the original police station was built from fines on sex workers.

15. Similar to the forenses, are the difficult working conditions. The young, dedicated staff must wear masks and special clothes for protection (and warmth), earn almost nothing, and endure a high psychic toll. Primarily ladinos, many are children or grandchildren of the disappeared people they seek.

16. Alberto joked that the bats had "historic memory," returning despite their best eradication efforts (including hanging garlic!). I told him I'd just learned that the bat in Classic Maya glyphs references scribes.

17. The very (hard-fought-for) human rights formulations that differentiate "acts" from "crimes" of war also create a divide between subversive deserving of death and innocent civilian (Ross 2008). They both make count and can make counting more difficult by silencing those actively engaged in political struggle.

18. "It is the first time that a former head of state is being tried for genocide in a credible national court, by the national authorities, in a country where the alleged crimes took place," and under a government in total sympathy with the accused (Mersky 2013). Imagine bringing George W. Bush to trial in the United States for war crimes.

19. Findings from reports I helped write in 1985 and 1986 were included as evidence.

20. Sofia references the army campaign detailed in 359 pages of internal documents acquired by the National Security Archives and entered as evidence (Doyle 2009).

3. Reunion of Broken Parts

1. Ron Eglash warns, "by exalting the empires of the ancient Egyptians, Maya, Chinese, Hindus, and Muslims, we risk further considering the tribal and band societies that surrounded them as primitives" (2001, 15).

2. TV's *Multiplication Rock* has titles like "My Hero, Zero," "Three Is a Magic Number," "Naughty Number Nine," and "The Good Eleven."

3. Compare to the bonesetting of algebra, to double-entry's balance, and to cybernetics, "the sine qua non theory for the cold war era, emphasizing . . . equilibrium and stasis" (Collins 2008, 31).

4. Maxwell says "the counting systems in Mayan languages manifested in the early colonial period, before heavy Spanish influence, counted jun rukak'al for 21. Literally, one its-second-twenty, the //ru-// is the third person singular ergative marker, the possessor, cf. rutz'i' A Xwan, his-dog Mr. John. I usually explain the jun rukak'al, ka'i' rukak'al as "one in the second twenty" "two in the second twenty," but this doesn't gloss the possessor //ru-// the owner of the second twenty is not the one or two, though,

the possessor is unnamed, but might be thought of as the entities/quantities being counted" (personal communication).

5. At Quirigua and Palenque it was associated with the dark of night just before the new moon (Looper 2003 143).

6. In some variants of tarot card reading, 1 and 2 are understood to be straining toward or yearning for the completion of 3; 4 and 5 toward 6; and all single digits toward the triple completion of 3 in 9.

7. Insurance companies in Guatemala, however, consider judges too bad a bet and won't insure them.

8. Gang violence and femicide are also understood as "the consequence of all the blood of people without guilt" (2010b, 305).

9. Yet the state is two faced—it and us—in the sense that the moneys disbursed come from taxes or from bonds and loans for which citizens are responsible.

10. The smart, committed staff and advisers of the PNR, at least from 2005 to 2012, were painfully aware of this (see PNR 2007, 2008, 2009).

11. Megan Ybarra reminded me that this is why using the PNR database to rectify the CEH numbers will still never count them all.

12. Or as the comedian Dave Chappelle says, "Our money looks like baseball cards with slave owners on it."

13. Similarly astonishing, when asked to compare the homicide rates from 1982–83 to the present day, Ball stated that the rate for nonindigenous people was ten times less but for the indigenous population the rate was a hundred times higher than the present day.

4. 100% Omnilife

1. While both are scales of value, sexism within indigenous communities is not exactly equivalent to racism in society at large, although courageous Mayan women have explored both intimate and structural gender violence (Alvarez 1996; Chirix 2003; Velasquez Nimatuj 2013; also Worby 2013).

2. Although it's mostly using K'iche' to teach Castilian rather than science, literature, or history.

3. The online article was accompanied by an ad for Centrum vitamins. It includes photos of two sets of Mayan children, one raised in Guatemala, the other in Florida. The height difference is striking.

4. The call can be quite insistent, including debilitating illnesses that defy medical nosology (Tedlock 1982).

5. The website shows gleaming machinery, clean-room-suited employees, and lists of accomplishments, including:

    1. Certification as Clean Industry
    2. Certainty proof for exportation pursuant to Good Sanitary Practices
    3. Gender Equity Model certification

It's Sergio González Rodríguez's "transparent factory," projecting "cleanliness and an environmental equilibrium among a population that enjoys a high quality of life" (2012, 30) contrasted with the opaque Ciudad Juárez *maquila* he calls the "femicide machine."

6. Peter Cahn's excellent book (2011) about Omnilife in Mexico describes Vergara's complex relation to Herbalife, the US parent firm, including regulatory issues surrounding the supplements and the form of their distribution and how he retroengineered, then patented, the commodity chemicals more attuned to Mexican tastes for powders. See also Wilson 2004 on similar "intimate economies" in Thailand.

7. Cahn says Vergara's purchase of the famous Guadalajara Chivas *futból* team "helped toughen the company's feminine tinge, framing the drinks not so much as maternal home remedies but as Gatorade-like performance enhancers" (2011, 34).

8. Surely true at the individual level, but structural racism and urban-centrism starve rural clinics, so doctors and nurses are harried and face lack at every turn. An exception was the Cuban doctors based in Joyabaj since Hurricane Mitch in 1998. One evening in Patzulá, José's wife and daughter were bitten by a dog. Somehow word got down to town and to everyone's shock the Cubanos showed up early the next morning to check for rabies. No one had ever received a house call before.

9. Years later she still recalls, with gales of laughter, how we had shared a *tuj* (traditional steam bath) and I was so huge I hardly fit. "So big!" she repeated, giggling. "You're gigantic!"

10. David Stoll (2013) chronicles the financial crash these algorithms caused in the Ixil area.

11. Cahn concurs, you don't need a bank loan, previous work experience, a business plan, or a credit rating (an incredibly powerful number-human matrix; see Poon 2009).

12. The modular qualities of MLM (standardized pieces ready to travel) are extraordinary. Tales from inside Amway and other "cults of free enterprise" (often aggrieved; see Butterfield 1999; Fitzpatrick 1997; Scheibeler 2004) tell surprisingly similar stories— to each other, to Cahn's findings, and to Santos's experience—of mass ecstatic states, and willingness to endure taxing hours and other sacrificial labor.

13. Felipe has one indigenous parent. Death threats sent him into a twenty-year internal exile.

14. Vergara also produces films, including Alfonso Cuarón's *Y tu mamá tambien* (he cameos) and Guillermo del Toro's *Devil's Backbone*.

15. In the United States former Yippie Jerry Rubin and Black Panther Bobby Seale were distributors in the first version of Omnilife, called Omnitrition. Rubin claimed "it's almost socialistic capitalism" (Cahn 2011, 26–27).

5. Mayan Pyramid (Scheme)

1. Moral hazard is the fear that in sharing risk, say, through insurance, people will behave more recklessly. An example is copayment in US medical insurance, meant to keep people from "misusing" "free" care.

2. In 2008 a stash estimated at Q1 million worth of cocaine and marijuana was seized in Joyabaj.

3. Analyzing Albanian pyramid schemes, Smoki Musaraj emphasizes people's corporeal and tactile relations to "stacks of cash" in undergirding the "euphoria" (2011).

4. This resonates with lore of people invited to enter mountains by the dueños and sometimes rewarded with costales of riches or the souls of the suffering.

5. It is said only sorcerers sacrifice turkeys (Saler 1960), but there are images of just such offerings in the Dresden codex.

6. A muscular expression of outrage even Elie Wiesel, among Bernard Madoff's other victims, might relish. Wiesel said, " 'Psychopath'—it's too nice a word for him. . . . Asked how Madoff should be punished, he said: 'I would like him to be in a solitary cell with only a screen, and . . . every day and every night, there should be pictures of his victims . . . all the time a voice saying, "Look what you have done to this old lady, look what you have done to that child"' (Strom 2009, A1, A4). At "Madoff: A Jewish Reckoning," audience suggestions of appropriate punishment included "an eye for an eye?" "Stoning?" (Widdicombe 2009, 23).

7. Also amazing (to me) is that he is openly gay.

8. The "PIGS" supposedly responsible for Europe's financial woes are Portugal, Italy (and Ireland), Greece, and Spain.

9. Some anguished responses to Madoff's scam in Jewish communities suggest the same fear that he reinforces racist stereotypes, although Elyse Crystal reminded me that no one called for Protestant soul-searching when Ken Lay defrauded millions at Enron.

10. The aggregation of a flock of sheep captured by Christian metaphors of pastoring is both a dream of state power and a terror when, as with liberation theology, it turns against the state. Liz Oglesby reminds me that a strong case could be made for a Genocide of Catholics, and Luis Solano shared with me the propaganda supporting Ríos Montt from the "Foundation against Terrorism" (former death squad members). It claims Indians and/as Catholics were "hegemonized" (yes, they cite Gramsci) by left-wing priests so they "all" were guilty of subversion, meaning it was not a crime to kill them "all" (FCT 2013).

11. As the joke goes, "Marxists have predicted all ten of the last three crises."

12. As Guyer argues, margins (along race, color, and gender divides) and border zones, whether temporal (moments of technological innovation), spatial (between countries, like Ponzi's currency differentials), or both (between communism and capitalism, as in Eastern Europe, or on the nineteenth-century US frontier, when swindlers fleeced newly "pacified" indigenous people) are often prime sites for the gains of subprime extraction.

13. Also tried and jailed, after confessing to family members who went to the FBI (a son later suicided), he resides up the road from me at the federal penitentiary in Butner, NC.

14. Carol Jones, a nurse, helped me notice this fundamental transformation in the mid-1990s. Attending a demonstration of a new diagnostic device with other health

care workers, she was surprised when the first question asked was not about function or medical benefits but if the company were publicly traded. This was around the time my recently divorced mother joined a "Beardstown Ladies" investment club (1996).

15. Yes, I often feel like Dorothy Gale.

16. Though I'd been tracking the burgeoning indebting options available in the highlands, I was surprised at how many financial institutions saw Fidelia's family as a source of marginal gains.

17. I've been told this is unlikely, but it's what she said.

18. These are, of course, the animal rhythms, the live-stock of $1+1 \neq 2$, but more, the family and barnyard agricultural grounding for getting something for nothing, now run amok in the "stock" market calculations of half a million quetzals, trillions of dollars lost.

19. Lolita has pushed her to learn to read so she can get paid as an organizer, but she said, "Now I'm too old, it's too hard."

6. A Life's Worth

1. A bit like a billion, a measurement of different size, depending on location. Based in medieval Spanish land grants to cavalry officers, it's 33 acres in Cuba, about 111 in Guatemala.

2. Rainforest Action Network executive director Michael Brune said, "I've seen oil spills in the Amazon, walked in clear-cuts so large they can be seen from outer space and have toured some of the nastiest toxic waste dumps imaginable. But when it comes to complete and hopeless environmental devastation, nothing compares to a mountaintop removal site" (Biggers 2009, 18).

3. The company claims $1 million has been set aside for this purpose, while independent studies suggest reclamation and monitoring will demand a minimum of $49 million. As with reparations, "restoration" does not mean the mountain is ever coming back.

4. One day in the capital I came across just such a delegation, about 200 people waiting for an audience at the National Palace. A young man came up to me speaking fluent English. He'd been deported about a year ago and had been very depressed, but then a friend told him about the dangers of mining and he'd gotten involved with their consulta. "I think God had me deported because I was supposed to work in this."

5. Famous for the miners' spectacular 1977 march to the capital for labor rights.

6. Using the word "goods," not "resources" evokes a moral valence and things useful for the general welfare.

7. Although due to significant errors Goldcorp has switched labs several times (E-tech 2010, 39).

8. Bacteria and archaea, aka extremophiles, are encouraged by the access to water and oxygen provided by mountaintop removal and the cyanide-leaching process, releasing toxins and transforming the pH of water, disrupting stream ecosystems. E-tech says, "Testing should have included whole rock chemistry, acid-base accounting,

short-term leach testing, long-term kinetic testing, and mineralogic analysis" (2010, 73). "Filtration" echoes Carolyn Merchant's description of the dangers of ignoring "Renaissance" ideas: "As long as the earth was conceptualized as alive and sensitive, it [was] a breach of ethical behavior to carry out destructive acts against it" (1991, 43). Stripping her literally unleashes destructive powers.

9. WHO lists only about 900 chemicals tested for carcinogenicity, "a tiny proportion of over 100,000 substances released by industry since 1940, at a rate of several million tons a year . . . [of which] *only one* has been recognized as *non*-carcinogenic" (Servan-Schreiber 2009, 83).

10. Remember how long and well tobacco companies kept the relation between errant molecule "A (nicotine) released at moment B causing symptom x, y, and z" from counting? How they threw "the very reality of exposures into question" (Murphy 2006, 92)?

11. A number of hamlets have counted themselves and the no votes have won, but the municipality as a whole has not voted. Joyabaj has not held a *consulta*, but Patzulá did and No won.

12. In 2012, pressured by the *consultas*, Goldcorp increased royalty payments from 1% to 4%, 50% of which is supposed to go to the municipal governments of San Miguel and Sipakapa. Goldcorp has also been censured for not paying import taxes.

13. I have no idea if the manager actually said this, but it was more the tone of absolute normalcy that struck me. It also gestures toward the new "genos" of lives that don't count, those young so-called gangbangers "sacrificed" as the death tolls reach similar levels to the early 1980s war years, sending thousands of children northward, desperate to avoid this fate (an on-going exodus that reached crisis proportions in summer 2014).

14. Murphy genealogizes this to W. E. B. Du Bois's *The Philadelphia Negro*, which documented "a social condition and environment . . . rather than discrete causes" (2006, 97).

15. Matilde González-Izás says Guatemalan *criollo* elites divided the country into the indigenous western highlands, providing *mozos*, and the ladino *Oriente*, providing the soldiers to control them (2014).

16. Race and class are scales of value, and although many well-intentioned Guatemalan Marxists held the latter could anchor the former, the performances and institutions of radical *and* decolonizing Mayan Organizing 2.0 link them without settling.

17. Humberto was participating in the Waqib K'ej course with Domingo Hernández.

18. Where my mother and sister both worked.

7. Beyond Adequacy

1. The Mayan development organization Cooperation for Rural Development of the Occidente (CDRO) has reworked the *pop* to represent both method and cosmology (De-Hart 2010).

2. I teach with this film, called *Discovering Dominga* (2003), but it was something else again to see it where the events occurred, to walk the same sere hills. A similar kinetics

occurs in the film. Denese (her gringa name) really is a small-town Iowa girl. She has forgotten Achi' and doesn't know Castilian. Her relatives in Guatemala recognize the family resemblance, but nutritionally and cosmetically she looks quite different. Yet the moment she wraps a *corte* around herself you see the sense memory take hold. She starts to become Dominga (her original name).

3. We watched the film off a generator. Gas is bought in town and trucked across the dam (requiring army permission and about Q20) and then by boat (also requiring gasoline). The town of Rabinal is about a nine-hour hard walk, and as Juan and Isabela's older children undertake the endurance sitting of school, they find it harder and harder.

4. Deities "have 'god markings' along the outer borders of their limbs and torsos," symbolizing mirrors (Coe 2005, 109), as do glyphs using body parts, like a disembodied hand. Studying glyphs deeply affected my perception, as I came to see meaning everywhere—perhaps appropriately, as many glyphs work as puzzles. Mary Jo McConahay said she didn't get it until Linda Schele explained: it's like *ghoti* spells "fish" (think *gh* from enough, *ti* from action, etc.).

5. Because it's so easy for anthropologists to dichotomize and hierarchize indigenous and non, I note that these folks were extremely dedicated to understanding Classic Maya knowledge and came well prepared, with books, computer programs, syllabaries, and the like, which they generously shared. One of them, Giovanni, said, "Among most nonindigenous there is very little interest. Because of the low level of education. But I've been fascinated since high school. It's like alcohol for a drunk. I call it *glifoterápia*."

6. He took over the workshops, based on the idea that Mayan knowledge should be available to Mayan people, in the mid-1990s, when founder Linda Schele passed away.

7. We were attending an "advanced workshop," organized by the Proyecto Lingüístico Francisco Marroquin (PLFM). Founded in 1972, it's really Mayan Organizing ground zero. With its daughter OKMA (Oxlajuuj Keej Maya Atziib), PLFM organizes small, local introductions and large, centralized workshops. When OKMA disbanded, members—and some of their students who formed Sak Chuwen—continued. With their own time and resources (although recipients help cover costs, and NGOs like FAMSI, the Foundation for the Advancement of Mesoamerican Studies, kick in), they go where they're invited, to schools and study groups across the highlands.

8. A number of participants had been affected by the war, losing family members, living through displacement. Some were members of CUC and there were even several Omnilife distributors.

9. Organizers encourage thanking Nikolai using glyphs, helping us deploy them for current purposes (it is cool to see your name spelled out syllabically!), and because they are really grateful for his energy and time. Iyaxel Cojtí said, "We are the third generation and we have to thank Linda Schele and Nikolai for that, for what we know. Not many who understand all this are so involved in helping us. In fact some [here she named some names] deny this has anything to do with the Maya of today. We really want to thank Nikolai so he doesn't abandon us. We have to make sure there is a fourth and fifth generation." She counted her father, Demetrio Cojtí, and his cohort as the first

generation; Lolmay, Hector, Ajpu, and others of OKMA as the second; and their small organization, Sak Chuwen (perhaps not incidentally run by women), as the third.

10. Douglas Adams's *Hitchhiker's Guide* (1979) reveals 42 as the meaning of the universe.

11. See Blaser (2010), de la Cadena (2010), and Escobar (2012) on this fraught space of honoring indigenous epistemologies without ignoring the impacts of history.

12. Even as they are, ambivalently, detoured through the colonial-inflected knowledge apparatus, as Mayan anthropologist Dorotea Gómez angrily reminded me after my glowing report-back on the workshop. "What does a damn German know about us? Who does he think he is to tell us about ourselves?" She has, of course, more nuanced readings, but the intense frustration is justified: it's not only about control of knowledge but access to the educational infrastructure that allows me to live off the Maya, while for many Guatemalans the enormous efforts to finish a degree still don't mean you can get a job in your field—or a job at all.

13. Most ethnographies of the Current Maya discuss such rituals. Classic Maya blood and its letting are controversial among archaeologists and Mayan intellectuals (and, so far as I know, not a major component in revitalization). Linda Schele is renowned as a popularizer, in part due to *Blood of Kings*, a late 1980s museum exhibit and book that emphasized *bloodline* in pre-Columbian ruling families and blood *sacrifice* as legitimation strategy. She was criticized for focusing on cruelty and gore at the very time the Maya were being genocided (Klein 1988; Montejo 1993; see Mel Gibson's *Apocalypto* for an exuberant version). Yet many images clearly show bloodletting (and tools bearing human blood are found in funerary offerings). One shows a woman ruler of Yaxchilán drawing an enthorned string through her tongue, conjuring a vision serpent, perhaps her *way* (meaning "animal companion soul," as well as "sleeping" and "dreaming"). The glyphs across the top are backward, suggesting she is in another dimension.

14. In 2004 CAFTA was passed by just one vote in the US Congress. Before 1985 not a grain of corn was imported to Guatemala, but it's close to 40% now, including increasing amounts of transgenetic grain (Maldonado and Barrientos 2008; *Countercurrents* 2012).

15. There are some pretty funny responses to the 2012 hoopla (thanks, Paula!), but a comment on the *USA Today* story on the Xultún discovery is my favorite: "All of these Mayan calendars found, and not one of them has puppies or kittens, or a hot Mayan babe in a bikini. Mayan calendars suck."

16. Marvin Cohodas says this emphasizes "the cyclicity even of the long count and is fully in character with current *Costumbrista* Maya concern with following the practices laid down and thus sanctified by their ancestors" (personal communication). Cook and Offit, however, suggest that new, universalizing orthodoxies of Mayan Organizing 2.0 can clash with more local practices (2013).

17. When the nearby Motagua River floods, the plaza became a lake, dark like the obsidian mirror. This is the same Motagua where Ulmil's uncle rests uneasily, as they can't afford to exhume him.

18. Mary Jo McConahay attended a "modern" Mayan ceremony at Tikal in 1994, describing her *ajq'ij* friends sneaking in incense and sugar, nervous at challenging the status

quo (2011, 233–37). The AIDPI (peace accord on indigenous rights) led *ajq'ij* to struggle for sanctioned access to sacred spaces, and now there are permanent altars at Tikal, Quiriguá, and most major sites and state-issued photo IDs granting registered specialists free entrance and permission to stay past closing. While bringing spiritual practice under governmental surveillance and creating (via what criteria, I'm not sure) a gatekeeping mechanism, it's also nice, as Judie Maxwell reminded me, to get state backing, especially given scary continuing charges of witchcraft and the violence those can bring.

19. "What Is the Function of a Resistor?," Answers.com, accessed Feb. 5, 2015, www .answers.com/Q/What_is_the_function_of_a_resistor. I realize this is not a standard way to visualize Ohm's law, but I could not resist the Answers.com comment on "modern life."

20. Although blackouts in Joyabaj have left me with happy memories of lying out on the old army airstrip in a jumble with Aurora's four kids and drinking in the stars.

21. Twenty years ago the government controlled 100% of the electricity market, and INDE was self-sustaining and growing. But in 1996 privatization was imposed in order to obtain credit from multilateral banks. Now INDE controls less than 30% and is under pressure to privatize the rest.

22. The same court that vacated Ríos Montt's genocide conviction on a technicality.

23. When the police caught her in 2010, a crowd blocked the road and liberated her.

24. My friend Vicky, not indigenous or from an elite family, said her brother's school required him to attend a lecture about Mayan archaeology and he'd kvetched, "Who cares?! It's all stupid," but was shocked and amazed at the number of attendees and how many were *fresa* (upper class). "Who knew *those* people thought this was important!?" he said.

25. Nothing prepared me for my first trip to the Petén since the early 1990s, going overland with Quinn from Cobán. The dense forest was really gone, an oil pipeline accompanied us much of the way, and in some areas the African palm plantations stretched to all four horizons, mile after mile after mile (see also Solano 2011).

26. I draw from the talks by Dr. Tomás Barrientos, Licda. Matilde Ivic de Monterrosa and Lic. José Crasborn Chavarría.

27. And on December 20, 2012, new stelae, carved in glyphs and detailing both long and recent history, including the 1980s genocide, were planted at Iximché and other highland sites, "the first Maya inscribed stelae to go up in over a millennium" (Maxwell 2012; thanks also to Tim Smith). Cached below it is Dr. Cojtí's most recent book.

28. Mam is one of the twenty-two Mayan languages and also, as here, means "sacred one." It's also the acronym for the NGO Mayas for Ancient Maya, which supports the PFLM and Sak Chuwen.

29. While not quite what activists hope for—like the banks themselves paying survivors out of profits from the loans—it pressures them to attend to human rights when funding infrastructure, hopefully making an imperfect present tense into a different future (Russell 2014; Tran 2014).

30. INDE provided free electricity to compensate for removal, but with privatization people now have to pay.

References

AAAS (American Association for the Advancement of Science). 2013. "Assistance to the Guatemalan Commission for Historical Clarification: AAAS Scientific Responsibility, Human Rights and Law Program." Accessed March 3, 2015. http://shr.aaas.org/guatemala/ceh/ceh.htm.

Adams, Douglas. 1979. *A Hitchhiker's Guide to the Galaxy*. New York: Pocket Books.

ADISMI (San Miguel Association for Integral Development). 2007. "Los impactos negativos de la mina Marlin en territorialidad Mam y Sipakapense." Report. Guatemala City: ADISMI.

Adler, Irving. 1965. *The Secret of Light*. New York: International Publishers.

Adorno, Theodor, and Max Horkheimer. 2007. *Dialectic of Enlightenment: Cultural Memory in the Present*, edited by Gunzelin Schmid Noerr. Stanford, CA: Stanford University Press.

Ahmad, Attiya. 2010. "Explanation Is Not the Point: Domestic Work, Islamic Dawa and Becoming Muslim in Kuwait." *Asian Pacific Journal of Anthropology* 11 (3–4): 293–310.

AHPN (National Police Archive). 2011. *Del silencio a la memoria: Revelaciones del Archivo Histórico de la Policía Nacional*. Vol. 1. Guatemala City: AHPN.

Alianza contra la Impunidad (Alliance against Impunity). 2004. *Reconciliación*. Guatemala City: Alianza.

ALMG (Guatemalan Mayan Language Academy), Comunidad Lingüistica Awakateka. 2003. *Xe'tzb'il xtxolb'il ajla'n le qayool: Introducción al sistema de numeración Maya Awakateko*. Guatemala City: ALMG.

Alvarez, Francisca. 1996. "Las mujeres mayas etnocidas." *elPeriódico Domingo*, Nov. 24.

America's Watch. 1985. *Guatemala: The Group for Mutual Support 1984–1985*. Washington, DC: America's Watch.

Andrés, Asier. 2012. "El estado ha pagado Q162 millones en condenas de la CIDH." *elPeriódico*, July 10, 4–5.

Apocalypto. 2006. Mel Gibson, dir. Touchstone Pictures. Burbank, CA.

Asher, Jana. 2008. Introduction to *Statistical Methods for Human Rights*, edited by Jana Asher, David Banks, and Fritz J. Scheuren. New York: Springer.

ASINDI (Association for Research and Integral Development Rex We). 2009. *Vigencia y aplicación de la cosmovisión Maya: Nimaqtaq ajmayab' ixim ulew; Grandes descendientes mayas*. San Cristóbal Verapaz, Guatemala: ASINDI.

Auden, W. H. 2007. *Collected Poems*. New York: Random House.

Barkan, Elazar. 2001. *The Guilt of Nations: Restitution and Negotiating Historical Injustices*. Baltimore: Johns Hopkins University Press.

Bastos, Santiago, and Manuela Camus. 1993. *Quebrando el silencio: Organizaciones del pueblo maya y sus demandas (1986–1992)*. Guatemala City: FLACSO.

———. 1995. *Abriendo caminos: Las organizaciones mayas desde el Nobel hasta el acuerdo de derechos indigenas*. Guatemala City: FLACSO.

———. 2003. *Entre el mecapal y el cielo: Desarrollo del movimiento maya en Guatemala*. Guatemala City: FLACSO and Cholsamaj.

———. 2013. "Difficult Complementarity: Relations between the Mayan and Revolutionary Movements." In *War by Other Means: Aftermath in Post-Genocide Guatemala*, edited by Carlota McAllister and Diane M. Nelson. Durham, NC: Duke University Press.

Bastos, Santiago, and Aura Cumes. 2007. *Mayanización y vida cotidiana: La ideología multicultural en la sociedad guatemalteca*. Guatemala City: Cholsamaj.

Basu, Niladri, and Howard Hu. 2010. *Toxic Metals and Indigenous Peoples near the Marlin Mine in Western Guatemala: Potential Exposures and Impacts on Health*. April. New York: PHR (Physicians for Human Rights).

Batz, José Mucía. 1996. *"Nik": Filosofía de los Números Mayas; Un aporte al rescate de la cultura Maya*. Chimaltenango, Guatemala: Editorial Rutzijol.

Beardstown Ladies' Investment Club. 1996. *The Beardstown Ladies' Common-Sense Investment Guide: How We Beat the Stock Market—and How You Can Too*. New York: Hyperion.

Becker, Marc. 2008. "Guatemala: America's Social Forum Rejects Neoliberalism, Celebrates Resistance." Blog, Oct. 14. Accessed Oct. 18, 2012. http://upsidedownworld .org/main/content/view/1524/1/.

Beidler, Philip D. 2001. "Solatium." *Michigan Quarterly Review* 40 (4). Accessed April 24, 2013. http://hdl.handle.net/2027/spo.act2080.0040.418.

Bennett, Jane. 2001. "Commodity Fetishism and Commodity Enchantment." *Theory and Event* 5 (1). Accessed June 8, 2014. https://jscholarship.library.jhu.edu/bitstream /handle/1774.2/32811/5.1bennett.html.

Berlant, Lauren. 2011. *Cruel Optimism*. Durham, NC: Duke University Press.

Biggers, Jeff. 2009. "The Coalfield Uprising." *The Nation* 289 (12): 16–21.

Bishop, Alan. 1990. "Western Mathematics: The Secret Weapon of Cultural Imperialism." *Race and Class* 32 (51): 51–65.

Blaser, Mario. 2010. *Storytelling Globalization from the Chaco and Beyond*. Durham, NC: Duke University Press.

Bloch, Ernst. 1995. *The Principle of Hope*. Vol. 2. Translated by Neville Plaice, Stephen Plaice, and Paul Knight. Cambridge, MA: MIT Press.

Blue, Victor J. 2011. "The Lost: Can Guatemala's Disappeared Be Found?" *Background: Visual Narratives on Issues of Policy* 1, no. 3 (summer): 4–27.

Borges, Jorge Luis. 1999. "On Exactitude in Science." *Collected Fictions*. Translated by Andrew Hurley. New York: Penguin.

Brett, Roddy. 2007. *Una guerra sin batallas: Del odio, la violencia y el miedo en el Ixcán y el Ixil 1972–1983*. Guatemala City: F&G.

Brown, Phil, and Edwin Mikkelsen. 1990. *No Safe Place: Toxic Waste, Leukemia, and Community Action*. Berkeley: University of California Press.

Butterfield, Stephen. 1999. *Amway: The Cult of Free Enterprise*. Boston: South End Press.

Cahn, Peter S. 2011. *Direct Sales and Direct Faith in Latin America*. New York: Palgrave Macmillan.

CALDH (Human Rights Legal Action Center). 2011. *Un paso más para hacer visibles a las miles de víctimas que ya no están: Primera sentencia por desaparición forzada en Guatemala; Análisis de su impacto jurídico, social, y cultural*. Guatemala City: CALDH.

Casaus Arzú, Marta. 1992. *Guatemala: Linaje y Racismo*. San José Costa Rica: FLACSO.

CECEP (Pokomchi Community Education Center). 2012. *¿Qué fue lo que pasó? Chajari xc'uluri? Recuperación de la memoria histórica de San Cristóbal Verapaz*. San Cristóbal Verapaz, Guatemala: CECEP.

CEH (UN Historical Clarification Commission). 1999. *Guatemala Memory of Silence, Tz'inil Na'tab'al*. Vols. 1–12. Guatemala City: United Nations.

Chirix García, Emma Delfina. 2003. *Alas y Raíces: Afectividad de las mujeres mayas / Rik'in ruxik' y ruxe'il: ronojel kajowab'al ri mayab'taq izoqi'*. Guatemala City: Grupo de Mujeres Mayas Kaqla.

Closs, Michael P. 1986a. "Native American Number Systems." In *Native American Mathematics*, edited by Michael P. Closs. Austin: University of Texas Press.

———. 1986b. "Mathematical Notation of the Maya." In *Native American Mathematics*, edited by Michael P. Closs. Austin: University of Texas Press.

———. 2001. "Mesoamerican Mathematics." In *Mathematics across Cultures: The History of Non-Western Mathematics*, edited by Helaine Selin. Dordrecht: Kluwer.

Coe, Michael D., and Mark van Stone. 2005. *Reading the Maya Glyphs*. London: Thames and Hudson.

Cojtí Cuxil, Demetrio. 1991. "Los censos nacionales de población: ¿Medios de oppression del Pueblo Indio?" *Revista A Saber*. Guatemala City: Alianza Francesa de Guatemala.

Colby, Benjamin N., and Lore M. Colby. 1981. *The Daykeeper: The Life and Discourse of an Ixil Diviner*. Cambridge, MA: Harvard University Press.

Collins, Samuel Gerald. 2008. *All Tomorrow's Cultures: Anthropological Engagements with the Future*. New York: Berghahn.

Comaroff, Jean, and John L. Comaroff. 2001. *Millennial Capitalism and the Culture of Neoliberalism*. Durham, NC: Duke University Press.

———. 2009. *Ethnicity, Inc*. Chicago: University of Chicago Press.

Conrad, Joseph. 2010. *The Secret Agent: A Simple Tale*. Project Gutenberg E-book, unpaginated. Accessed June 13, 2014. www.gutenberg.org/files/974/974-h/974-h.htm.

Consorcio Actoras de Cambio. 2006. *Rompiendo el silencio: Justicia para las mujeres víctimas de violencia sexual durante el conflict armado en Guatemala*. Guatemala City: Instituto de Estudios Comparados en Ciencias Penales de Guatemala.

Contact. 1997. Robert Zemeckis, dir. Warner Brothers.

Cook, Garrett W. 2000. *Renewing the Maya World: Expressive Culture in a Highland Town*. Austin: University of Texas Press.

Cook, Garrett W., and Thomas A. Offit. 2013. *Indigenous Religion and Cultural Performance in the New Maya World*. Albuquerque: University of New Mexico Press.

Countercurrents. 2012. "US Biofuel Is Consuming Corn While the World Is Facing Food Crisis." Countercurrents.org. Accessed Oct. 29, 2012. www.countercurrents.org/cc 111012A.htm.

Creswell, Julie, and Landon Thomas Jr. 2009. "The Talented Mr. Madoff." *New York Times*, Sunday Business section, 1, 8. Jan. 25.

Crosby, Alison, M. Brinton Lykes, and Brisna Caxaj. 2016. "Moving beyond Suffering: Mayan Women's Struggles for Reparation in Postconflict Guatemala." *Journal for Genocide Research*.

Cuevas Molina, Rafael. 2011. 300. San José, Costa Rica: Euna.

Currier, Cora. 2013. "Hearts, Minds and Dollars: Condolence Payments in the Drone Strike Age." *Propublica*, April 5. Accessed March 28, 2015. http://www.propublica .org/article/hearts-minds-and-dollars-condolence-payments-in-the-drone -strike-age.

de Genova, Nicholas, and Nathalie Peutz. 2010. *The Deportation Regime: Sovereignty, Space, and the Freedom of Movement*. Durham, NC: Duke University Press.

de Grieff, Pablo. 2008. *The Handbook of Reparations*. Oxford: Oxford University Press.

DeHart, Monica. 2010. *Ethnic Entrepreneurs: Identity and Development Politics in Latin America*. Stanford, CA: Stanford University Press.

de la Cadena, Marisol. 2010. "Indigenous Cosmopolitics in the Andes: Conceptual Reflections beyond Politics." *Cultural Anthropology* 25 (2): 334–70.

Deren, Maya. 1953. *Divine Horsemen: The Voodoo Gods of Haiti*. New York: Vanguard.

Devlin, Keith. 2000. *The Language of Mathematics: Making the Invisible Visible*. New York: Holt Publishers.

Discovering Dominga. 2003. Patricia Flynn and Mary Jo McConahay. Jaguar House Films.

Doyle, Kate. 2009. "Operation Sofia: Documenting Genocide in Guatemala." NSA (NATIONAL SECURITY ARCHIVES). Accessed March 31, 2013. http://www2.gwu.edu /~nsarchiv/NSAEBB/NSAEBB297/.

———. 2010. "'I wanted him back alive.' An Account of Edgar Fernando García's Case from inside the 'Tribunals Tower.'" NSA (National Security Archives). Accessed March 31, 2013. http://nsarchive.wordpress.com/2010/10/26/i-wanted-him-back -alive-%E2%80%9D-an-account-of-edgar-fernando-garcias-case-from-inside -tribunals-tower/.

Doyle, Kate, and Emily Willard. 2011. "27 Years Later, Justice for Fernando García." National Security Archive Electronic Briefing Book no. 337. NSA. Accessed March 29, 2013. www.gwu.edu/~nsarchiv/NSAEBB/NSAEBB337/.

Dumit, Joseph. 2012. *Drugs for Life: How Pharmaceutical Companies Define Our Health*. Durham, NC: Duke University Press.

EAFG (Guatemalan Forensic Anthropology Team). 1995. *Las Masacres en Rabinal: Estudio histórico antropológico de las massacres de Plan de Sánchez, Chichupac y Río Negro*. Guatemala City: EAFG.

ECAP (Community Studies and Psychosocial Action Team). 2009. *Tejidos que lleva el alma: Memoria de las mujeres maya sobrevivientes de violación sexual durante el conflict armado*. Guatemala City: F&G.

Eglash, Ron. 1999. *African Fractals: Modern Computing and Indigenous Design*. New Brunswick, NJ: Rutgers University Press.

———. 2001. "Anthropological Perspectives on Ethnomathematics." In *Mathematics across Cultures: The History of Non-Western Mathematics*, edited by Helaine Selin. Dordrecht: Kluwer.

———. 2009a. "Oppositional Technophilia." *Social Epistemology* 23 (1): 79–86.

———. 2009b. "Native American Analogues to the Cartesian Coordinate System." In *Culturally Responsive Mathematics Education*, edited by Brian Greer, Swapna Mukhopadhyay, Arthur B. Powell, and Sharon Nelson-Barber. New York: Routledge.

Ehrenreich, Barbara. 2009. *Bright-Sided: How Positive Thinking Is Undermining America*. New York: Metropolitan.

Eng, David. 2011. "Reparations and the Human." *Columbia Journal of Gender and Law* 21 (2).

England, Nora. 1996. *Introducción a la lingüística: Idiomas mayas*. Guatemala City: Cholsamaj.

Escobar, Arturo. 2012. *Notes on the Ontology of Design*. Unpublished MS, University of North Carolina, Chapel Hill.

ESEDIR. 2001. *Ciencia y tecnología maya*. Chimaltenango, Guatemala: Saqil Tzij.

E-Tech International. 2010. "Evaluation of Predicted and Actual Water Quality Conditions at the Marlin Mine, Guatemala." August. Accessed Jan. 9, 2013. www.etechinternational.org/082010guatemala/final/MarlinReport_Final_English_0811.pdf.

Ewald, François. 1991. "Insurance and Risk." In *The Foucault Effect: Studies in Governmentality*, edited by Graham Burchell, Colin Gordon, and Peter Miller. Chicago: University of Chicago Press.

FAFG (Guatemalan Forensic Anthropology Foundation). N.d. "Casos del conflict armado interno, El Quiché." Accessed March 31, 2013. www.fafg.org/paginasCasos/Quiche.htm.

———. 2009. "Mi nombre no es XX." www.fafg.org/pagTemas/2009Mayo.html. Accessed Feb. 26, 2013.

———. 2010a. "Acreditación del laboratorio de genética forense." Accessed Feb. 26, 2013. www.fafg.org/pagTemas/2010/AcreditacionLaboratorioDeGeneticaForense.html.

———. 2010b. "Las dos erres." Part 2. Accessed March 23, 2013. www.fafg.org/pagTemas /2010/Junio2010.html.

———. 2011a. "Exhumación Osario Dos La Verbena." Accessed Feb. 28, 2013. www .fafg.org/pagTemas/2011/Febrero/ExhumacionOsarioDosLaVerbena.html.

———. 2011b. "Investigaciones antropológico forenses." Accessed Feb. 26, 2013. www .fafg.org/pagTemas/2011/Septiembre/Investigaciones_Antropologico_Forenses _FAFG.html.

Falla, Ricardo. 2011. *Negreaba de zopilotes . . . Masacre y sobrevivencia: Finca San Francisco Nentón, Guatemala (1871 a 2010)*. Guatemala City: AVANCSO.

Fanon, Frantz. 1968. *The Wretched of the Earth*. New York: Grove Press.

FCT (Foundation Against Terrorism). 2013. "La farsa del genocidio: Conspiración marxista desde la iglesia católica." March. Pamphlet.

Ferguson, James. 2006. *Global Shadows: Africa in the Neoliberal World Order*. Durham, NC: Duke University Press.

———. 2009. "The Uses of Neoliberalism." Antipode 41 (S1): 166–84.

Finamore, Daniel, and Stephen D. Houston. 2010. *Fiery Pool: The Maya and the Mythic Sea*. New Haven, CT: Yale University Press.

Fink, Leon. 2003. *The Maya of Morganton: Work and Community in the Nuevo New South*. Chapel Hill: University of North Carolina Press.

Fischer, Edward. 2002. *Cultural Logics and Global Economies: Maya Identity in Thought and Practice*. Austin: University of Texas Press.

Fitzpatrick, Robert. 1997. *False Profits: Seeking Financial and Spiritual Deliverance in Multi-level Marketing and Pyramid Schemes*. Harrisonburg, VA: Herald Press.

Flores, Carlos. 2001. *Bajo la Cruz*. Coban, Guatemala: Centro Ak'kutan.

Foucault, Michel. 1973. *The Order of Things: An Archaeology of the Human Sciences*. New York: Vintage.

———. 1979. *Discipline and Punish: The Birth of the Prison*. New York: Vintage.

Freidel, David, Linda Schele, and Joy Parker. 1993. *Maya Cosmos: Three Thousand Years on the Shaman's Path*. New York: Perennial.

Fultz, Katherine. 2009. "Explotando la quebrada: Género y sociedad en las publici-dades corporativas." Paper presented at the Eighth Congreso de Estudios Mayas.

Fundación Guillermo Toriello. 2006. *Memoria de los caídos en la lucha revolucionaria de Gua-temala*. Guatemala City: Piedra de Rayo.

Galeano, Eduardo. 1979. *The Open Veins of Latin America: Five Centuries of the Pillage of a Continent*. New York: Monthly Review Press.

Gans, Eric. 2002. "The Kantian Sublime." Oct. 5. Accessed Feb. 22, 2013. www .anthropoetics.ucla.edu/views/vw271.htm.

Garrard-Burnett, Virginia. 2011. *Terror in the Land of the Holy Spirit: Guatemala under General Efrain Rios Montt 1982–1983*. Oxford: Oxford University Press.

Ginsborg, Hannah. 2013. "Kant's Aesthetics and Teleology." In *The Stanford Encyclopedia of Philosophy*, edited by Edward N. Zalta. Accessed Feb. 22, 2013. http://plato.stanford .edu/archives/spr2013/entries/kant-aesthetics/.

Gleeson-White, Jane. 2011. *Double Entry: How the Merchants of Venice Created Modern Finance.* New York: Norton.

Globe and Mail. 2014. "Goldcorp Profit, Revenue Fall." May 1. Accessed July 21, 2014. www.theglobeandmail.com/report-on-business/industry-news/energy-and -resources/goldcorp-profit-revenue-fall/article18360189/.

Goldin, Liliana R. 2009. *Global Maya: Work and Ideology in Rural Guatemala.* Tucson: University of Arizona Press.

González, Patricia. 2005. "Piden permiso a la tierra para explorar mina de niquel." *elPeriódico.* Jan. 8.

González-Izás, Matilde. 2002. *Se cambió el tiempo: Conflicto y poder en territorio K'iche' 1880–1996.* Guatemala City: AVANCSO.

————. 2014. *Territorio, actores armados y formación del Estado.* Guatemala City: Universidad Rafael Landívar.

González Ponciano, Jorge Ramón. 2013. "The Shumo Challenge: White Class Privilege and the Post-Race, Post-Genocide Alliances of Cosmopolitanism from Below." In *War by Other Means: Aftermath in Post-Genocide Guatemala,* edited by Carlota McAllister and Diane M. Nelson. Durham, NC: Duke University Press.

González Rodríguez, Sergio. 2012. *The Femicide Machine.* Translated by Michael Parker-Stainback. Cambridge, MA: MIT Press / Semiotext(e).

Gowan, Gwen, and Joan Martelli. 2010. "Severe Stunting, Twelve Years Going on Five." *ABC 20/20,* Dec. 14. Accessed June 7, 2012. http://abcnews.go.com/Health/malnutrition -severe-stunting-guatemalan-children/story?id=12381731#.UbHRS_aMGEN.

Graeber, David. 2011. *Debt: The First 5,000 Years.* Brooklyn: Melville House.

Grave, Carlos. 2012. "PNR resarce a víctimas de conflicto." *Prensa Libre,* July 26.

Gray, Mary W., and Sharon Marek. 2008. "The Statistics of Genocide." In *Statistical Methods for Human Rights,* edited by Jana Asher, David Banks, and Fritz J. Scheuren. New York: Springer.

Greenaway, Peter. 1996. *Fear of Drowning by Numbers.* London: Dis Voir.

Grondland, Melissa. 2011. "Inventory/A Pedantry of Nouns." *Cabinet* 41: 7–11.

Grose, Jessica. 2008. "Life in the Time of Oprah." *New York Times,* C1, C4, Aug. 17.

Grupo Hace 25 Años (Anne Arévalo, Ruth del Valle, Renée de Flores, Ada Melgar, and Myra Muralles). 2006. *Voces que cuentan, memoria nuestra: Hace 25 años, ¿vos dónde estabas?* Guatemala City: Grupo Hace 25 Años.

Gutiérrez, Marta Estela, and Paul Hans Kobrak. 2001. *Los linchamientos pos conflicto y violencia colectiva en Huehuetenango, Guatemala.* Guatemala City: CEDFOG (Center for Research and Documentation of Guatemala's Western Border).

Guyer, Jane. 2004. *Marginal Gains: Monetary Transactions in Atlantic Africa.* Chicago: University of Chicago Press.

Hale, Charles R. 2006. *Más que un Indio / More Than an Indian: Racial Ambivalence and Neoliberal Multiculturalism in Guatemala.* Santa Fe: School of American Research.

Harney, Stefano, and Fred Moten. 2013. *Undercommons: Fugitive Planning and Black Study.* Wivenhoe, UK: Minor Compositions.

Harper, Richard. 2000. "The Social Organization of the IMF's Mission Work: An Examination of International Auditing." In *Audit Cultures: Anthropological Studies in Accountability, Ethics, and the Academy*, edited by Marilyn Strathern. London: Routledge.

Harvey, T. S. 2006. "Humbling, Frightening, and Exalting: An Experiential Acquaintance with Maya Healing." *Anthropology and Humanism* 31 (1): 1–10.

Hayden, Cori. 2007. "A Generic Solution? Pharmaceuticals and the Politics of the Similar in Mexico." *Current Anthropology* 48 (4): 475–95.

Hendrickson, Carol. 1995. *Weaving Identities: Construction of Dress and Self in a Highland Guatemala Town*. Austin: University of Texas Press.

Henriques, Diana. 2011. *The Wizard of Lies*. New York: Times Books.

Herbert, Victor (music), and Glen MacDonough (lyrics). 1903. "I Can't Do the Sum." From *Babes in Toyland*, 1st production.

Holzer, Jenny. 1977–79. "Truisms." Text in public space. New York, NY.

———. 1983–85. "Survival." Text in public space. New York, NY.

Houston, Stephen, David Stuart, and Karl Taube. 2006. *The Memory of Bones: Body, Being, and Experience among the Classic Maya*. Austin: University of Texas Press.

Huet, Alfonso. 2008. *Nos salvó la sagrada selva: La memoria de veinte comunidades Q'eqchi'es que sobrevivieron al genocidio*. Cobán, Guatemala: ADICI Wakliiqo.

ICC (International Criminal Court). 2002. "Rome Statute of the International Criminal Court." The Hague: ICC.

Ifrah, Georges. 1985. *From One to Zero: A Universal History of Numbers*. Translated by Lowell Bair. New York: Viking.

Impunity Watch ("Women and Men of Santa Lucía"). 2011. *Porque queríamos salir de tanta pobreza: La memorable historia de Santa Lucía Cotzumalguapa contada por sus protagonistas*. N.p.: Impunity Watch.

ISLA. 2012. "Grupos de poder en Petén: Territorio, política y negocios." Accessed March 3, 2015. http://isla.igc.org/GuatemlElctns/the-peten-report.pdf.

Jain, Sarah S. Lochlann. 2006. *Injury: The Politics of Product Design and Safety Law in the United States*. Princeton, NJ: Princeton University Press.

———. 2013. *Malignant: How Cancer Becomes Us*. Berkeley: University of California Press.

Jameson, Fredric. 2005. *Archaeologies of the Future: The Desire Called Utopia and Other Science Fictions*. New York: Verso.

Johnston, Barbara Rose. 2005. *Chixoy Dam Legacy Issues Study*. Santa Cruz, CA: Center for Political Ecology.

Jonas, Susanne, Ed McCaughan, and Elizabeth Sutherland Martínez, eds. 1984. *Guatemala: Tyranny on Trial; Testimony of the Permanent People's Tribunal*. San Francisco: Synthesis.

Jones, Chris. 2013. "Tekun Uman and Tata Mon Fistfight in Heaven: Indigenous Imaginaries and Decolonization in Highland Guatemala." PhD diss., Anthropology Department, Tulane University.

Klein, Cecelia. 1988. "Mayamania: 'The Blood of Kings' in Retrospect." *Art Journal* 47 (1): 42–46.

Klein, Naomi. 2008. *The Shock Doctrine: The Rise of Disaster Capitalism*. New York: Picador.

Kipling, Rudyard. 1907. "Sons of Martha." Accessed March 3, 2015. http://www.online -literature.com/kipling/920/.

Koerth-Baker, Maggie. 2013. "Death and the Mainframe: How Data Analysis can help Document Human Rights Atrocities." *Boing-Boing*, June 25. Accessed July 1, 2013. http://boingboing.net/2013/06/25/death-and-the-mainframe-how-d.html.

Konefal, Betsy. 2010. *For Every Indio Who Falls: A History of Mayan Activism in Guatemala, 1960–1990*. Albuquerque: University of New Mexico Press.

Krugman, Paul. 2013. "The Antisocial Network." *New York Times*, A19, April 15.

La Isla: Archives of a Tragedy. 2009. Stelzner, Uli, dir. Guatemala City: ISKA Films.

Lara Figueroa, Celso. 2002. *Leyendas populares de aparecidos y animas en pena en Guatemala*. Guatemala City: Artemis Edinter.

Latour, Bruno. 1987. *Science in Action: How to Follow Scientists and Engineers Through Society*. Cambridge, MA: Harvard University Press.

Lave, Jean. 1988. *Cognition in Practice: Mind, Mathematics, and Culture in Everyday Life*. Cambridge: Cambridge University Press.

Leal Ferreira, Mariana Kawall. 1997. "When $1 = 1 \neq 2$: Making Mathematics in Central Brazil." *American Ethnologist* 21 (1): 132–47.

LeBor, Adam. 2010. *The Believers: How America Fell for Bernard Madoff's $50 Billion Investment Scam*. New York: Orion.

Lévi-Strauss, Claude. 1968. *The Savage Mind*. Chicago: University of Chicago Press.

Lincoln, Abraham. 1865. Second Inaugural Address, Washington, DC, March 4. Accessed March 17, 2015. http://www.bartleby.com/124/pres32.html.

Looper, Matthew G. 2009. *Lightning Warrior: Maya Art and Kingship at Quiriguá*. Austin: University of Texas Press.

López García, Julian. 2010. *Kumix*. Guatemala City: Cholsamaj Press.

Lowrey, Annie. 2013. "A Trillion-Dollar Coin as a Way to Handle the Debt Hits a Jackpot of Jests." *New York Times*, B2, Jan. 10.

Lubiano, Wahneema. 2014. "Falling Into and Out of Despair: Thinking as Romance," paper presented at the SEWSA (South East Women's Studies Association) Conference, 17 April.

Luxemburg, Rosa. 1951 (1913). *The Accumulation of Capital: A Contribution to an Economic Explanation of Imperialism*. New York: Monthly Review Press.

MacKenzie, Donald. 1993. *Inventing Accuracy: A Historical Sociology of Nuclear Missile Guidance*. Cambridge, MA: MIT Press.

———. 2006. *An Engine Not a Camera: How Financial Models Shape Markets*. Cambridge, MA: MIT Press.

Madden, Marguerite, and Amy Ross. 2009. "Genocide and GIScience: Integrating Personal Narratives and Geographic Information Science to Study Human Rights." *Professional Geographer* 61 (4): 508–28.

Madre Selva. N.d. "Minería y efectos a la salud." Guatemala. Photocopied handout.

Maldonado, Norma, and Beatriz Barrientos. 2008. "Maiz, mucho más que tortillas." Unpaged pamphlet.

Malkin, Elisabeth. 2013. "In Effort to Try Dictator, Guatemala Shows New Judicial Might." *New York Times*, A6, March 16.

Manz, Beatriz. 1988. *Refugees of a Hidden War: Aftermath of Counterinsurgency in Guatemala.* Albany, NY: SUNY.

Martin, Emily. 2009. *Bipolar Expeditions: Mania and Depression in American Culture.* Princeton, NJ: Princeton University Press.

Martin, Randy. 2002. *Financialization of Daily Life.* Philadelphia: Temple University Press.

Martínez, Samuel. 2010. "Excess: The Struggle for Expenditure on a Caribbean Sugar Plantation." *Current Anthropology* 51 (5): 609–28.

Marx, Karl. 1911. *A Contribution to the Critique of Political Economy.* Berkeley: University of California Press.

Maurer, Bill M. 2002. "Anthropological and Accounting Knowledge in Islamic Banking and Finance: Rethinking Critical Accounts." *Journal of the Royal Anthropological Institute (formerly Man)*, 8 (4): 645–67.

———. 2005. *Mutual Life Limited: Islamic Banking, Alternative Currencies, Lateral Reason.* Princeton, NJ: Princeton University Press.

Maxwell, Judith. 2012. "Oxlajuj B'aqtun / Oxlajun Pik: The Dawning of the New Maya Era Ixq'anil." Author's blog, Tulane University. Accessed June 12, 2014. http://tulane.edu/liberal-arts/blogs/maxwell/new-maya-era.cfm.

McAllister, Carlota. 2003. "Good People: Revolution, Community and *Conciencia* in a Maya-K'iche' Village in Guatemala." PhD diss., Department of Anthropology, Johns Hopkins University.

———. 2013. "Testimonial Truths and Revolutionary Mysteries." In *War by Other Means: Aftermath in Post-Genocide Guatemala*, edited by Carlota McAllister and Diane M. Nelson. Durham, NC: Duke University Press.

McConahay, Mary Jo. 2011. *Maya Roads: One Woman's Journey Among the People of the Rainforest.* Chicago: Chicago Review Press.

McLeish, John. 1991. *Number.* New York: Fawcett Columbine.

Merchant, Carolyn. 1992. *Radical Ecology: The Search for a Livable World.* New York: Routledge.

Mersky, Marcie. 2013. "The Ríos Montt Trial Looks at the Past, but Shapes the Future of Guatemala." *Al Jazeera*, March 23. Accessed July 14, 2014. http://m.aljazeera.com/story/2013323164622824769.

Minow, Martha. 1998. *Between Vengeance and Forgiveness: Facing History After Genocide and Mass Violence.* Boston: Beacon Press.

Montejo, Victor D. 1993. "In the Name of the Pot, the Sun, the Broken Spear, the Rock, the Stick, the Idol, Ad Infinitum and Ad Nauseum: An Exposé of Anglo Anthropologists' Obsessions with and Invention of Mayan Gods." *Wicazo Sa Review* 9: 12–16.

Muehlmann, Shaylih. 2012. "The Malaise of Enumeration in Mexico's Colorado River Delta." *American Ethnologist* 38 (2): 339–53.

Murphy, Michelle. 2006. *Sick Building Syndrome and the Problem of Uncertainty.* Durham, NC: Duke University Press.

———. 2013. "Chemical Infrastructures of the St. Clair River." In *Toxicants, Health and Regulation since 1945*, edited by Soraya Boudia and Nathalie Jas. London: Pickering and Chatto.

Museo Comunitario Rabinal Achi. 2003. *Oj K'aslik Estamos vivos: Recuperación de la memoria histórica de Rabinal (1944–1996)*. Rabinal, Guatemala: Museo Comunitario.

Nash, June. 1993. *We Eat the Mines and the Mines Eat Us: Dependency and Exploitation in Bolivian Tin Mines*. New York: Columbia University Press.

Naveda, Enrique. 2008. "La gran estafa." *elPeriódico, Revista Dominical*, Feb. 17.

Nelson, Diane M. 2009. *Reckoning: The Ends of War in Guatemala*. Durham, NC: Duke University Press.

NISGUA (Network in Solidarity with the People of Guatemala). 2008. "Mining Expansion and the Communities That Say NO." Newsletter.

Nojib'sa. 2003. *Matemática maya: Guia para el aprendizaje de la escritura de los numeros maya de 0 a 1000*. Guatemala City: Nojib'sa.

Oglesby, Elizabeth. 2003. "Machos, machetes y migrantes: Masculinidades y dialécticas del control laboral en Guatemala." *Estudios Migratorios Latinoamericanos* 17 (52): 651–80.

———. 2013. "We're No Longer Dealing with Fools": Violence, Labor, and Governance on the South Coast." In *War by Other Means: Aftermath in Post-Genocide Guatemala*, edited by Carlota McAllister and Diane M. Nelson. Durham, NC: Duke University Press.

Oglesby, Elizabeth, and Amy Ross. 2009. Guatemala's Genocide Determination and the Spatial Politics of Justice. *Space and Polity* 13 (1): 21–39.

O'Neill, Kevin Lewis. 2009. *City of God: Christian Citizenship in Postwar Guatemala*. Berkeley: University of California Press.

———. 2012. "The Soul of Security: Christianity, Corporatism, and Control in Postwar Guatemala." *Social Text* 30 (2–111): 21–42.

Onion, The. 2007. "Proposed Bill Would Bring 4,000 Troops Back to Life." Nov. 21, Issue 47.52.

Piot, Charles. Forthcoming. "Hedging the Future." In *African Futures: Essays on Crisis, Emergence, and Possibility*, edited by Brian Goldstone and Juan Obarrio. Chicago: University of Chicago Press.

Pitarch, Pedro. 2010. *The Jaguar and the Priest: An Ethnography of Tzetal Souls*. Austin: University of Texas Press.

PNR (National Reparations Program). 2007. *La vida no tiene precio: Acciones y omisiones de resarcimiento en Guatemala*. First Thematic Report 2006–2007. Guatemala City: PNR.

———. 2008. *Memoria de Labores*. Guatemala City: PNR.

———. 2009. *Memoria de Labores*. Guatemala City: PNR.

PNUD (UN Development Program). 2011. Human Development Report. Guatemala City: PNUD.

———. 2012. *Guatemala: Un país de oportunidades para la juventud? Informe nacional de desarrollo humano 2011/2012*. Guatemala City: PNUD.

Poon, Martha. 2009. "From New Deal Institutions to Capital Markets: Commercial Consumer Risk Scores and the Making of Subprime Mortgage Finance." *Accounting Organization and Society* 35 (5): 654–74.

Poovey, Mary. 1998. *A History of the Modern Fact: Problems of Knowledge in the Sciences of Wealth and Society.* Chicago: University of Chicago Press.

Porras Castejón, Gustavo. 2007. "Introducción al programa nacional de resarcimiento: Cómo se quiso, cómo es y cómo debe ser." *La vida no tiene precio: Acciones y omisiones de resarcimiento en Guatemala.* First Thematic Report 2006–2007. Guatemala City: PNR.

Porter, Eduardo. 2008. "Ponzi Schemes: The Haul Gets Bigger, but the Fraud Never Changes." *New York Times*, A24, Dec. 27.

Porter, Theodore M. 1995. *Trust in Numbers: The Pursuit of Objectivity in Science and Public Life.* Princeton NJ: Princeton University Press.

Pullman, Philip. 1995. *The Golden Compass.* New York: Ballantine.

Raxché (Demetrio Rodríguez Guaján) and Obdulio Son Chonay. 1995. *Ajilanïk: La numeración kaqchikel.* Guatemala City: Cholsamaj.

Redress. 2013. "What Is Reparation?" Accessed April 13, 2013. www.redress.org/what -is-reparation.

Rees, David. 2004. *My New Filing Technique Is Unstoppable.* New York: Riverhead.

REMHI (Recuperation of Historic Memory Project). 1998. *Guatemala: Nunca más.* Vols. 1–4. Guatemala City: ODHA (Human Rights Office of the Archbishop of Guatemala).

Remijnse, Simone. 2001. "Remembering Civil Patrols in Joyabaj, Guatemala." *Bulletin of Latin American Research* 20 (4): 454–69.

———. 2002. *Memories of Violence: Civil Patrols and the Legacy of Conflict in Joyabaj, Guatemala.* Amsterdam: Rozenberg.

Rich, Frank. 2009. "Some Things Don't Change in Grover's Corners." *New York Times*, CII, March 8.

Rodríguez, James. 2007. "The Chixoy Hydroelectric Dam and Genocide in Rio Negro." Aug. 30. Accessed July 22, 2014. www.mimundo-photoessays.org/2007/08/chixoy -hydro-electrical-dam-and.html MiMundo.org.

Rosenberg, Tina. 2012. "The Body Counter: Meet Patrick Ball, a Statistician Who Has Spent His Life Lifting the Fog of War." *Foreign Policy*, March/April. Accessed July 2, 2013. www.foreignpolicy.com/articles/2012/02/27/the_body_counter?page=0,5.

Ross, Amy. 2005. "The Iraq War: U.S. Deaths Not Only Ones That Matter." *Atlanta Journal-Constitution*, April 26.

———. 2006. "The Creation and Conduct of the Guatemalan Commission for Historical Clarification." *Geoforum* 37 (1): 69–81.

———. 2008. "The Body Counts: Civilian Casualties and the Crisis of Human Rights." In *Human Rights in Crisis*, edited by Alice Bullard. Burlington, VT: Ashgate.

Rotella, Sebastian, and Ana Arana. 2011. "Finding Oscar: Massacre, Memory and Justice in Guatemala." *ProPublica.* Accessed March 3, 2015. http://www.propublica.org /article/finding-oscar-massacre-memory-and-justice-in-guatemala.

Rotman, Brian. 1987. *Signifying Nothing: The Semiotics of Zero*. Stanford, CA: Stanford University Press.

Russell, Grahame. 2014. "US Government Holding World Bank and IADB Accountable to Ensure Reparations for Chixoy Dam Victims in Guatemala." *Upside Down World*, Jan. 21. Accessed March 3, 2015. http://upsidedownworld.org/main/guatemala-archives-33/4654-us-government-holding-world-bank-and-iadb-accountable-to-ensure-reparations-for-chixoy-dam-victims-in-guatemala.

Ryman, Geoff. 1987. *The Unconquered Country*. Toronto: Bantam.

Sabino, Carlos. 2008. *Guatemala: La historia silenciada 1944–1989*. Vol. 2, *El dominó que no cayó*. Mexico City: Fondo de Cultura Económica.

Sáenz de Tejada, Ricardo. 2004. *¿Victimas o vencedores? Una aproximación al movimiento de los ex-PAC*. Guatemala City: FLACSO, Editorial de Ciencias Sociales.

Salvado, Camilo. "Democracia, minería y luchas por el agua en territorio mam: Consulta comunitaria en San Marcos." AVANCSO working paper.

Sanford, Victoria. 2003. *Buried Secrets: Truth and Human Rights in Guatemala*. New York: Palgrave Macmillan.

Scheibeler, Eric. 2004. *Merchants of Deception*. Lexington, KY: Keystone Solutions Group.

Sedgwick, Eve Kosofsky. 2007. "Melanie Klein and the Difference Affect Makes." *South Atlantic Quarterly* 106 (3): 625–42.

Servan-Schreiber, David. 2009. *Anticancer: A New Way of Life*. New York: Viking.

Shakespeare, William. 2003 (1610). *The Tempest*. New York: Norton.

Sicko. 2007. Michael Moore, dir. Dog Eat Dog Films. New York, NY.

Sipakapa NO se vende: Resistencia del pueblo Maya ante la minería de oro. 2005. Guatemala: Caracol Productions.

Smith, Carol A. 1990. *Guatemalan Indians and the State: 1540 to 1988*. Austin: University of Texas Press.

Snow, Clyde Collins, Fredy Armando Peccerelli, José Samuel Susanávar, Alan G. Robinson, and José Maria Nájera Ochoa. 2008. "Hidden in Plain Sight: XX Burials and Desparecidos in the Department of Guatemala, 1977–1986." In *Statistical Methods for Human Rights*, edited by Jana Asher, David Banks, and Fritz J. Scheuren. New York: Springer.

Solano, Luis. 2009. "La transnacionalización de la industria extractiva: La captura de los recursos minerales e hidrocarburos." *El Observador* 4, no. 19 (June–July): 3–36.

———. 2011. "La Palma Africana: agronegocio que se expande." *El Observador* 6, nos. 28–29 (Dec.–March): 18–38.

———. 2013. "Development and/as Dispossession: Elite Networks and Extractive Industry in the Franja Transversal del Norte." In *War by Other Means: Aftermath in Post-Genocide Guatemala*, edited by Carlota McAllister and Diane M. Nelson. Durham, NC: Duke University Press.

Spirer, Herbert F., and William Seltzer. 2008. "Obtaining Evidence for the International Criminal Court Using Data and Quantitative Analysis." In *Statistical Methods for Human Rights*, edited by Jana Asher, David Banks, and Fritz J. Scheuren. New York: Springer.

Spivak, Gayatri Chakravorty. 1987. "Scattered Speculations on the Question of Value." In *In Other Worlds: Essays in Cultural Politics*. London: Routledge, 212–43.

———. 1999. *A Critique of Postcolonial Reason: Toward a History of the Vanishing Present*. Cambridge, MA: Harvard University Press.

Squier, Susan Merrill. 2012. *Poultry Science, Chicken Culture: A Partial Alphabet*. New Brunswick, NJ: Rutgers University Press.

Stand and Deliver. 1988. Ramón Menéndez, dir. Warner Brothers.

Starn, Orin. 1991. "Missing the Revolution: Anthropologists and the War in Peru." *Cultural Anthropology* 6, no. 1 (Feb.): 63–91.

Stewart, Kathleen. 1999. "Conspiracy Theory's Worlds." In *Paranoia within Reason: A Casebook on Conspiracy as Explanation*, edited by George E. Marcus. Chicago: University of Chicago Press, 13–20.

Stiglitz, Joseph E. 2003. *The Roaring Nineties: A New History of the World's Most Prosperous Decade*. New York: Norton.

Stoll, David. 2013. *El Norte or Bust! How Migration Fever and Microcredit Produced a Financial Crash in a Latin American Town*. Lanham, MD: Rowman and Littlefield.

Stone Allucquére, Roseanne. 1996. *The War of Desire and Technology at the Close of the Mechanical Age*. Cambridge MA: MIT Press.

Strathern, Marilyn. 2000. "Introduction: New Accountabilities; Anthropological Studies in Audit, Ethics and the Academy." In *Audit Cultures: Anthropological Studies in Accountability, Ethics, and the Academy*, edited by Marilyn Strathern. London: Routledge.

Strom, Stephanie. 2009. "Elie Wiesel Levels Scorn at Madoff." *New York Times*, A1, A4, Feb. 27.

Sunder Rajan, Kaushik. 2006. *Biocapitalism: The Constitution of Postgenomic Life*. Durham, NC: Duke University Press.

Suskind, Ron. 2004. "Faith, Certainty and the Presidency of George W. Bush." *New York Times Magazine*, Oct. 17.

Sznaider, Natan. 2002. "Money and Justice: Toward a Social Analysis of Reparations." *Human Rights Review* 3, no. 2 (Jan.–March): 104–10.

Taibbi, Matt. 2009. "The Great American Bubble Machine." *Rolling Stone*, July 9. Accessed March 3, 2015. http://www.rollingstone.com/politics/news/the-great-american-bubble-machine-20100405?page=8.

Tate, Winifred. 2007. *Counting the Dead: The Culture and Politics of Human Rights Activism in Colombia*. Berkeley: University of California Press.

Taussig, Michael. 1980. *The Devil and Commodity Fetishism in South America*. Chapel Hill: University of North Carolina Press.

———. 1987. *Shamanism, Colonialism, and the Wild Man: A Study in Terror and Healing*. Chicago: University of Chicago Press.

Tedlock, Barbara. 1992. *Time and the Highland Maya*. Albuquerque: University of New Mexico Press.

Theidon, Kimberly. 2010. "Histories of Innocence: Post-War Stories in Peru." In *Localizing Transitional Justice*, edited by Rosalind Shaw, Pierre Hazan, and Lars Waldorf. Stanford, CA: Stanford University Press.

Tilly, Charles. 1985. "War Making and State Making as Organized Crime." In *Bringing the State Back In*, edited by Peter Evans, Dietrich Rueschemeyer, and Theda Skocpol. Cambridge: Cambridge University Press, 169–91.

Torpey, John. 2008. *Making Whole What Has Been Smashed: On Reparations Politics.* Cambridge, MA: Harvard University Press.

Torres-Rivas, Edelberto. 2009. "*Guatemala: La historia silenciada de Carlos Sabino: Análisis.*" El Diario del Gallo blog. Accessed March 3, 2015. http://diariodelgallo .wordpress.com/2009/10/20/guatemala-la-historia-silenciada-de-carlos-sabino -analisis/.

Tran, Mark. 2014. "Guatemala's Indigenous Communities Boosted by Landmark Reparations Bill." *The Guardian*, Jan. 17. Accessed March 17, 2015 http://www .theguardian.com/global-development/2014/jan/17/guatemala-chixoy-dam -reparations-bill.

Transnational Institute. Permanent People's Tribunal. Accessed March 3, 2015. www .tni.org/taxonomy/term/460/all.

Tribunal Permanente de los Pueblos. 2008. "Informe de Caso: Unión Fenosa en América Latina." Lima, Peru. Accessed Oct. 17, 2012. www.stopcorporateimpunity .org/?p=1435.

"Trillion Dollar Coin." 2013. *The Daily Show with Jon Stewart*, Jan. 10.

Tuyuc, Rosalina. 2007. "El programa nacional de resarcimiento al servicio de las víctimas y familiares de las víctimas del conflicto armado interno." In *La vida no tiene precio: Acciones y omisiones de resarcimiento en Guatemala*. First Thematic Report 2006– 2007. Guatemala City: PNR.

Tzian, Leopoldo. 2009. *Kajlab'alil Maya'ib' xuq mu'sib': Mayas y Ladinos en cifras; El caso de Guatemala*. Guatemala City: Cholsamaj.

Uk'u'x B'e, Asociación Mayab'. 2008 (5123 era Maya). *Reconstitución del ser Mayab, Jik b'ey pa ri qa K'aslem*. Chimaltenango, Guatemala: Uk'u'x B'e.

Urla, Jacqueline. 2012. *Reclaiming Basque: Language, Nation, and Cultural Activism*. Reno: University of Nevada Press.

Urton, Gary, with Primitivo Nina Llanos. 1997. *The Social Life of Numbers: A Quechua Ontology of Numbers and Philosophy of Arithmetic*. Austin: University of Texas Press.

Van Der Maaten, Maria. N.d. "Changing Development Strategies in Rural El Salvador as a Result of Proposed Gold Mining." Master's thesis, University of Colorado.

Van de Wauw, Johan, Roel Evens, and Lieven Machiels. 2010. "Are Groundwater Over-extraction and Reduced Infiltration Contributing to Arsenic-Related Health Problems near the Marlin Mine (Guatemala)?" CATAPA, Oct. 14. Accessed March 10, 2013. www.catapa.be/files/marlin.pdf.

Vela Castañeda, Manolo. 2013. "Perpetradores de genocidio: Aproximaciones históricas y sociológicas desde el caso Guatemala." *Nueva Sociedad* 246: 159–69.

Velasquez Nimatuj, Irmalicia. 2013. "'A Dignified Community Where We Can Live': Violence, Law, and Debt in Nueva Cajolá's Struggle for Land." In *War by Other Means: Aftermath in Post-Genocide Guatemala*, edited by Carlota McAllister and Diane M. Nelson. Durham, NC: Duke University Press.

Verran, Helen. 2000a. "Accounting Mathematics in West Africa: Some Stories of Yoruba Number." In *Mathematics across Cultures: The History of Non-Western Mathematics*, edited by Helaine Selin. Dordrecht: Kluwer, 345–71.

———. 2000b. "Aboriginal Australian Mathematics: Disparate Mathematics of Land Ownership." In *Mathematics across Cultures: The History of Non-Western Mathematics*, edited by Helaine Selin. Dordrecht: Kluwer, 289–311.

———. 2001. *Science and an African Logic*. Chicago: University of Chicago Press.

Viaene, Lieselotte. 2010a. "Life Is Priceless: Maya Q'eqchi' Voices on the Guatemalan National Reparations Program." *International Journal of Transitional Justice* 4: 4–25.

———. 2010b. "The Internal Logic of the Cosmos as 'Justice' and 'Reconciliation': Micro- level Perceptions in Post-Conflict Guatemala." *Critique of Anthropology* 30 (3): 287–312.

Vrana, Heather. 2013. "'Do Not Tempt Us!' Guatemalan University Students and the State 1944–1996." Diss. Department of History, Indiana University.

Wald, Priscilla. 2008. *Contagious: Cultures, Carriers, and the Outbreak of Narrative*. Durham, NC: Duke University Press.

Way, J. T. 2012. *The Mayan in the Mall: Globalization, Development, and the Making of Modern Guatemala*. Durham, NC: Duke University Press.

Wayne, Leslie. 2009. "The Mini-Madoffs: Troubled Times Are Bringing More Ponzi Inquiries to Light." *New York Times*, B1, B4, Jan. 28.

Weld, Kirsten. 2014. *Paper Cadavers: The Archives of Dictatorship in Guatemala*. Durham, NC: Duke University Press.

WHO (World Health Organization). 2004. "Copper in Drinking-Water: Background Document for Development of WHO *Guidelines for Drinking-Water Quality*." Geneva: WHO Press.

———. 2011. "Arsenic in Drinking Water: Background Document for Development of WHO *Guidelines for Drinking-Water Quality*." Geneva: WHO Press.

Widdicombe, Lizzie. 2009. "Thief or Crook?" *New Yorker*, Jan. 26, 22–23.

Wilson, Ara. 2004. *Intimate Economies: Tomboys, Tycoons, and Avon Ladies in the Global City*. Berkeley: University of California Press.

Wilson, Richard. 1995. *Maya Resurgence in Guatemala: Q'eqchi' Experience*. Norman: University of Oklahoma Press.

Worby, Paula. 2013. "A Generation after the Refugees' Return: Are We There Yet?" In *War by Other Means: Aftermath in Post-Genocide Guatemala*, edited by Carlota McAllister and Diane M. Nelson. Durham, NC: Duke University Press.

Zarsky, Lyuba, and Leonardo Stanley. 2011. "Searching for Gold in the Highlands of Guatemala: Economic Benefits and Environmental Risks of the Marlin Mine." Medford, MA: GDEI (Global Development and Environment Institute), Tufts University.

Žižek, Slavoj. 1992. *Enjoy Your Symptom! Jacques Lacan in Hollywood and Out*. New York: Routledge.

Index

accounting: difficulties in, 9, 86, 123, 260; as favorite class, 79; and financial crash, 167; history of, 12–15; human rights and, 182–83, 268n21, 275n8; as modern fact, 4, 20, 59, 152, 185, 207; multiple forms of, 37, 40, 56, 126, and Omnilife, 140, 142, and Ponzi schemes, 170–71. *See also* double entry bookkeeping; Poovey, Mary

adequacy, 17, 43, 46, 58; beyond, 227, 246

adequation: as *adequatio intellectus et res,* 45, 73, 117, 220, 262; and gold, 220; and race, 122–23

AHPN (National Police Historical Archives), 86, 88–90, 116

aletheia: and aletheiometer (Golden Compass) 46, 80, 82, 145, 262; and Martin Heidegger, 46, 73, 262; as unconcealing, 46, 73, 125, 262

algebra: algebra of genocide, 64, 210, 269n1; and *al Jabr,* 18, 63; as bone-setting, 69, 85, 109, 113, 271n3; and human rights, 69, 74, 100; and reparations, 69, 85, 113; of subversion, 92

ALMG (Guatemalan Mayan Language Academy), 43, 50, 94, 123

Amway, 144, 273n12. *See also* multilevel marketing

apocalypse: 2012 and, 22, 235; Maya and, 4, 22

archaeology, 256, 279n24, forensic, 66, 252–53. *See also* FAFG

arsenic, 211–13

Auden, W. H., 25

audit: culture, 13, 79, 110, 146, 201–2

Awakateko: concept of zero, 98, 116; identity, 43, 269n11. *See also* Chalchiteko

AVANCSO (Association for the Advancement of the Social Sciences in Guatemala), 30, 106

Babes in Toyland, vii, 46

Babylonians, 3

balance, 15, 40, 63, 64, 74, 90, 98, 101, 105, 106, 110, 218, 267n18; as golden rule, 13, 34; gain and loss, 2, 8, 12, 14, 15, 47, 85, 100, 102, 108, 116, 214. *See also* double entry; zero

gangs, 21, and *El Millonario*, 163–64, 167, 173, 184; members as sacrifice 221, 276; outreach to, 208–9; and violence, 9, 10, 183, 272n8. *See also* drugs

García, Edgar Fernando, 88, 116. *See also* GAM

gender, 16, 44, 58, 205, 225, 271n14, 272n1, 273n6; and bookkeeping, 59, 86, 184, 267–68n21; changing it, 123, 126, 154; and counting for the state, 44, 203, 174n12; and math (me being bad at it), 22, 45, 167, 265, 268n5; Mayan women and weaving, 56, 96, 230; and Omnilife Basic Course, 1, 149, 152, 181, 272n5; and power, 3, 14–15, 38, 149; Quechua women, 97, 98, 268n24; and wages 191;

genocide, 27–28, 43, 56, 105, 117, 126, 138, 166, 210, 274n10; and CEH, 38, 39, 44, 76, 91, 107, 171, 206; and Mayan identity, 3, 27, 40, 49, 51, 58, 113, 118, 123, 153, 278n13; and number, 7, 13, 21, 40, 42, 44–45, 100, 198, 224–25, 236; and rape, 114; and reparations, 80, 103, 279n27; and Ríos Montt denial, 3, 72, 81, 90–91, 111, 271n18, 279n22

Genocide Trilogy, 9, 263

Gerardi, Bishop Juan, 81, 206. *See also* Catholic Church, REMHI

Gibson, Mel, 253, 278n13

glyphs: 8, 44, 53–54, 229, 232–42, 253, 258, 263, 271n16; as beautiful 20; and Mayan organizing, 207, 277n4n9, 278n13, 279n27; and number, 97, 99, 245

gold: and cyanide, 193, 203; mining, 9, 38, 39, 57, 191, 192–93, 196, 214, 215–17; as useless, inedible anchor for the capitalist world system, 219; and value 39, 58–59, 109, 115, 117, 141, 155, 190, 193, 218–19, 221. *See also* finance; money

Goldcorp, 192, 195–96, 202, 204–5, 210, 211, 213, 216, 218, 221, 250, 275n7, 276n12

González, Matilde, 30, 114, 116, 276n15, 279n26

Graeber, David, 25, 145, 182, 215, 219

Gramajo, General Alejandro Hector, 105

great vampire squid, 39, 185

Grube, Nikolai, 32, 99, 229, 233, 234–36, 237, 239, 240, 277n9

Guatemala: Memory of Silence. See CEH

Guatemalan Workers Party. *See* PGT

guerrillas: and counterinsurgency, 84, 148, 162, 178, 266, 271n12; former, 54, 57, 110, 153, 209; and Maya, 19, 64, 80, 92, 103, 105, 166, 252, 257; why people joined, 147

Guyer, Jane, 12, 13, 15, 21, 27, 33, 96–97, 110, 182, 266n8, 274n12

Harvey, T.S., 133

health: care and service, 99, 121, 132, 136, 153, 170, 274–75n14; collective healing, 39, 133, 146, 226; and mining, 189, 193, 197, 203, 207, 210, 212, 216, 218, 221, 224; and Omnilife, 127, 129, 131–34, 137, 139–40; as profiling device, 132–33, 185, 222; and stunting, 125–26. *See also* economy; poverty

Heidegger, Martin. *See* aletheia

Hernández Ixcoy, Domingo, 21, 30, 33, 124, 206

Hernández-Salazar, Daniel, 30, 35, 48 (photo credit), 89 (photo credit)

housewife epidemiology, 222. *See also* toxicology

human rights: algebra of, 69, 74; and counting, 13, 38, 63, 71, 73, 79, 90, 101, 182, 235; and Mayan rights, 79, 100, 109, 247, 279n29; organizations, 40, 64, 88, 170–71, 270n1; and qualification, 64, 81, 83, 109; violation, 3, 12, 44, 87, 103, 106, 216, 249–50, 271n17.

206, 220, 239; calendar, 20, 22, 51, 56, 58, 94, 96–98, 132–33, 209, 228, 278, 239, 253–54, 278n16; classic, 20, 40, 51, 58, 227, 229, 233, 253, 256, 262, 271n1, 277n5, 278n13, 279n28; and "community tourism" 228, 262; "culture" 101, 105, 133, 153, 205, 223, 229, 237; current, 1, 26, 46, 128, 154, 180, 204, 233, 254–56, 278; and genocide, 3, 4, 27, 32, 74, 91–92, 100, 110, 113–14, 116, 118, 123, 153, 278n13; glyphs, 8, 93, 233–35, 239, 271n16, 277–78n9, 279n27; mob of, 21–22, as movement, 21, 41, 51, 103, 107–8, 224; as *mozos* (workers), 251–52; number of, 9, 43–44, 94; number of languages, 43, 98; 100% (in Plan Sofia), 92; Organizing 1.0, 41, 49; Organizing 2.0, 50, 58, 278n16; pyramids, 154, 165–67, 169, 171, 184, 253; and *ser Mayab*, 58, 207, 225; and zero, 3, 20, 53, 95, 116. *See also* ALMG

McAllister, Carlota, 10, 33, 51, 71, 77, 111, 118, 145, 166

McKenzie, Donald, 29, 42

measure: of land 191; and gold, 211, 213, 215, 216, 219, 221; as insurance and as fault, 9, 221–22, 275n1; by 20, 93–94, 95, 99, 101; uncertainties in, 10, 25, 191, 213, 216

Menchú, Rigoberta, 21, 202, 256

metal: gold and silver as actants, 59; heavy (toxins); 189, 210–12; and money, 115, 219–20. *See also* mining

Merchant, Caroline 16, 275–76n8

migration 39, 47, 121, 123, 135, 137, 154, 157, 166, 189, 205, 214, 216, 276; and banks, 136; and remittances, 136, 164, 176. *See also* debt; deportation; El Millonario; slaughterhouse

Milky Way 227–28, 254, 262, 267–68n21

mining, 2, 9, 193, 216; and disasters, 11, 59; effects on water 196–97, 207, 211–14; open sky, 57, 189, 192–93; resis-

tance to, 57, 189, 185, 186, 191, 195–96, 198–204, 206, 208, 215 217–18, 223–25, 246, 251, 275n4; and statistics, 38, 39, 59, 221, 225; and tailings lagoon, 197; toxicity, 205, 208, 211; and world history, 11, 25, 59, 73, 190, 210, 220–21, 226. *See also* filtration; gold; Goldcorp; metal

Mó, Romelia, 32, 99, 103

modernity, 38, 55, 122–23, 152, 279n19; and bookkeeping, 7, 19–20, 56, 59, 84; and Maya, 58, 128, 153, 167, 181, 184, 248, 251, 261; and zero, 3, 23. *See also* Ferguson, James

money, 1, 4, 8, 9–11, 14, 16, 25, 26, 37, 40, 43, 59, 88, 135–37, 158–59, 175, 180, 208, 215, 217, 220, 256, 266n7, 266n8; ambivalence towards, 98, 217–18; as checks, 108–9, 130, 132, 145, 159–63, 166–68; direct deposit of, 47; as enchanting, 47, 165, 171–73, 180–81, 183; as extortion, 10; as fiction, 109, 113, 115, 163, 168–69, 171–178; and gods, 15; as reparations, 17, 41, 56, 105–14, 179, 222, 260; and slave owners 272n12; slime and sublime, 46, 114, 168; transformation, 38, 46, 78, 114, 154, 184–85, 218–19, 248; two sides, 110, 272n9. *See also* finance; Krugman, Paul; metal; Stewart, Jon

Montana Company, 207, 209–12, 216, 232, 237 as Montana Explotadora 232. *See also* Goldcorp

multilevel marketing (MLM), 144, 169, 173, 214, 273n12; as pyramid, 173–74. *See also* Amway; Omnilife

Murphy, Michelle, 33, 34, 210–13, 222, 243, 276n10, 276n14

Narcotrafficking. *See* drugs

National Police Archive. *See* AHPN

New Río Negro, 110, 228, 254, 261, 262. *See also* Río Negro number: abstract, 12, 14, 17, 18, 20, 23, 25–27, 37, 38, 46, 55–56, 83, 97, 99–100, 109, 123, 185, 204, 221, 225, 266n7, 270n9; with armies, 20, 22, 25, 45; as dangerous, 4, 201, 268n5, 268–69n6; of dead, 2, 9, 12, 18, 25, 26, 39, 40, 63–64, 68, 73, 75, 78–83, 84–87, 90–92, 110, 113, 117, 167, 174, 182, 269n1, 272n11; of disappeared, 45, 84, 91; as fact, 3, 4, 8, 30, 40, 41, 45, 47, 49, 69, 84, 134, 136, 138, 141–44, 198, 199, 202, 204, 205, 207, 210–213, 218; as familiars, 181–82, 207; as friend, xi–xii, 4; history of, 2, 4, 13, 15–20, 24, 37, 44, 51, 53, 152, 154, 157, 165, 266n6, 266n8, 267n18; materiality of, 33, 47, 51, 59–60, 79, 84, 109, 249, 262–63, 265n1; of Maya, 21, 40–42; of Mayan ethno-linguistic groups, 42–43; Mayan, 92–100, 103, 116, 239, 244–45; as sacred, 45, 53–54, 80, 235; struggles over, 12, 13–16, 21, 22–23, 29, 52. *See also* accounting, ethnomathematics, glyphs, mathematics, zero

NGO (nongovernmental organization), 32, 39, 54, 57, 64, 125, 127, 128, 135, 148, 158, 193, 201, 206, 213, 216, 246, 270n11, 277n7, 279n28

Oglesby, Elizabeth, 30, 40, 47, 122–23, 136, 137–39, 142, 224, 274n10

OKMA (Oxlajuuj Keej Maya Atziib) 32, 277n7, 277–78n9

Omnilife, 57; accounting, 131, 134, 142–43, 145; and Atlantis resort, 128, 130, 145, 154; Basic Course, 1, 147, 149; point system, 1, 59, 131, 140–41; prizes, 2, 129, 134, 151; cruise, 2, 139, displace product, 140, 153; factory 272–73; and gender, 2, 135, 149, 273; health and economy, 37, 127, 129, 131–34, 139, 151–53; and multilevel marketing, 57. *See also* multilevel marketing; red; Vergara, Jorge

100%: electricity market, 279n21; guerrilla support, 19, 166, 172; indigenous, 125, 202; Omnilife, 57, 121, 128, 145; say no, 203, 206, 207

O'Neill, Kevin, 142–43

Oxlajuj B'aqtun, 228, 277n7. *See also* apocalypse; 2012

PAC. *See* civil patrols

Pacioli, Luca, 7, 13–14, 68, 266n6, 268n6. *See also* accounting; double-entry bookkeeping

PACUNAM, 253, 254

Paz y Paz, Claudia, 34, 90

peace accords, 43, 57, 58, 103, 279n18

Peccerelli, Fredy, 66, 91. *See also* FAFG

Permanent People's Tribunal, 247

Petty, William, 25–26, 39

PGT Guatemalan Workers Party, 88, 116

Pitarch, Pedro, 132–33, 185

Plan Sofia, 92, 166, as Operation Sofia, 271

PNR (National Reparations Program), and accounting, 109, 272n10; and genocide, 104, 107–8, 272n11; and rape of Mayan women, 114, 137. *See also* reparations; Rosalina Tuyuc,

Ponzi scheme, 57, 59, 165, 168–69, 171, 173, 181–83, 274n12

Poovey, Mary, 11–12, 14–15, 23–25, 26, 27, 33, 81, 84, 87, 108, 182, 268–69n6

postcolonial, 38, 44, 205

poverty, 9, 21, 26, 40, 104, 189, 197, 203. *See also* debt; economy

Projecto Lingüístico Francisco Marroquin (PLFM), 277n7

Protestantism, 15, 51, 54, 71, 143, 160, 183, 195, 255–56, 261n4, 275n9

precision, 20, 138, 145, 154; as achievement, 73, 75, 81, 91, 113, 117, 126, 142, 199, 210–11; of counting dead, 64, 69; and gold, 219, 221; and reparations,

uncertainty, 9, 182, 199, 202, 211; and
risk, 14, 212–13. *See also* precision
Unión Fenosa, 247, 249–50
United Fruit Company, 239
United Nations, 2, 3, 26, 45, 222. *See also*
CEH
United States, 29, 39, 64, 102, 122, 151,
158, 168, 171, 174, 222, 267n19, 270n12,
271n13, 273n15; AID, 111, 253; and
CAFTA, 203, 213, 278N14; CIA, 10; eco-
nomic policies, 174, 171; and migra-
tion, 3, 78, 136, 137, 139, 158, 174–75,
223; relations with Guatemala, 9; and
reparations, 102, 111, 271n18. *See also*
CAFTA; CIA; genocide; United Fruit
Company
URNG (Guatemalan National Revolution-
ary Unity), 103, 170
Urton, Gary, 3, 24, 73, 74, 94, 96–99,
267–68n21

Vergara, Jorge, 129–32, 137, 140, 153, 185,
273n14. *See also* Omnilife
Verran, Helen, 18, Aboriginal number,
20; counting as journey, 107, 126; dealing with number 13, 79, 81, 100; doing
number, 7, 83, 118, 207, 220; and ledger
books, 174, 199; politics, logic, and
mathematics, 1, 12; Yoruba number
181–82
Viaene, Liselotte, 72, 104–5, 108–9, 112,
117
violence, 29, 90, 123, 135, 167, 201, 215,
249, 272n8, 278–79n18; counting it,
3, 24, 25, 40, 84, 114; dealing with, 3,
49, 65, 82, 112, 116, 146, 153, 173, 260,
272n1; disappearance, 64, 82, 91; mas-

sacre, 4, 68, 82, 90, 230; reparations
for, 110, 112, 258. *See also* civil war
vitamin, 1, 2, 134, 137, 138, 143, 153

Waqib' Kej, 206, 276n17
Way, JT, 116, 135
Weld, Kristen, 86–88, 116
WHO (World Health Organization), 138,
211, 276n9
winaq, 20, 95–96, 116
women 26, 86, 102, 113, 123, 124, 136,
146–47, 159, 161, 177, 225, 232, 251, 254,
257; counting, 14, 38, 42, 91, 92, 98,
114, 134, 203, 256, 268n2, 277–78n9;
and mining, 190–93, 196–97, 209,
218, 223; and Omnilife, 1, 2, 149–50,
183, 272n1; wages, 48–49, 85, 99, 226;
weaving, 94–95, 230. *See also* gender
World Bank, 111, 216, 259
World Economic Forum, 246, 269n1

XX ("John Doe," unidentified remains),
65, 66, 68–70; solving for, 73, 100.
See also DNA

yearning, to look white, 121–24; and numbers, 100, 272n6; for reparation, 105

Zacualpa, 2, 136, 147, as finca de mozo,
123; as genocide case 3, 38, 76; and El
Millonario 57, 158–60, 163, 169–70,
173, 180
zero, 13, 29, 164, 183, 271n2; ex nihilo, 29,
98, 126; and genocide, 9, 13, 118, 126;
ground zero, 3, 13, 29, 277n7; Mayan,
3, 20, 53, 93–95, 98–99, 102, 116, 237;
zero balance, 8, 15, 34, 49